Human Resource Management

Also available from Continuum:

Principles of Hospitality Law (2nd Edition): Boella and Pannett
The Tourism Development Handbook: Godfrey and Clarke
The Fundamentals of Hospitality Marketing: Mawson
Using Computers in Hospitality (2nd Edition): O'Connor
The Tourist Experience: Ryan (ed.)

HUMAN RESOURCE MANAGEMENT

International Perspectives in
Hospitality and Tourism

Edited by
NORMA D'ANNUNZIO-GREEN,
GILLIAN A. MAXWELL
AND SANDRA WATSON

continuum
LONDON • NEW YORK

Continuum

The Tower Building	370 Lexington Avenue
11 York Road	New York
London SE1 7NX	NY 10017–6503

www.continuumbooks.com

First published 2002

British Library Cataloguing-in-Publication Data
A catalogue record for this book is available from the British Library.

ISBN 0-8264-5765-7

Typeset by YHT Ltd, London
Printed and bound in Great Britain by Bookcraft (Bath) Ltd, Midsomer Norton

Contents

Editors and Contributors

Norma D'Annunzio-Green is a Lecturer in Human Resource Management at Napier University Business School, Edinburgh, UK. Her current research interests include international human resource management in the hotel sector, with particular focus on resourcing and development issues for international managers. Current research projects include a study of international managers' attitudes towards human resource management in Russia and a cross-unit comparison of organizational cultures which exist in Russian hotels. Before joining education, Norma worked for a large multinational hotel company in a senior human resource management position.

Gillian A. Maxwell is a Senior Lecturer in Human Resource Management in the Caledonian Business School at Glasgow Caledonian University in Scotland, UK. Her main research interests are in the context of service industries and on issues related to strategic HRM. Publications include a chapter contribution to, and the co-editing of, *Hospitality, Tourism and Leisure Management: Issues in Strategy and Culture* (1997). Current research interests and publications include managing diversity and service quality. In her research activities, Gillian draws from her experience in line and human resource management in the hospitality and retail sectors.

Sandra Watson is Head of Human Resource Management at Napier University Business School, Edinburgh, UK. Prior to entering academia she had over ten years' experience in hotel human resources. Sandra has taught in the area of human resource management for over fifteen years. Her research interests are in human resource development issues in hospitality and tourism, with a focus on management development. She has co-edited *Understanding Human Resource Development: A Research Perspective*. Other projects include an analysis of managerial skill requirements in the Scottish visitor attractions sector of tourism, a case study on management development in the licensed house industry and an evaluation of training initiatives during downsizing in the hospitality sector.

Debra F. Cannon, PhD, is an Associate Professor in the Cecil B. Day School of Hospitality Administration, Georgia State University, Atlanta, Georgia, USA. In addition to over ten years in the academic field, Dr Cannon has over twelve years' experience in hotel human resources. She worked for Hyatt Hotel Company as a director of human resources and the Ritz-Carlton Hotel Company as a director of human resources for two properties and corporate director of professional development. Her doctorate degree, from Georgia State University, is in human resource development.

Shirley Chappel is Senior Lecturer in Tourism and Hospitality at the University of South Australia. Her interest in tourism as an academic study began in the late 1970s when she conducted tours of Asia for tertiary Asian Studies students. During the 1980s and early 1990s she was involved in training vocational educators, including hospitality practitioners with considerable experience in the international tourism and hospitality industries. Her current research interests are emotional labour, methodologies for teaching tourism and hospitality, and gastronomic tourism.

Julia M. Christensen Hughes, PhD, is an Associate Professor in the School of Hotel and Food Administration at the University of Guelph, Ontario, Canada. Her research interests include human resource management issues within the North American hotel and restaurant industries. Julia has spent time in the internationally acclaimed resort community of Whistler, British Columbia, Canada, where she studied the strategies businesses used to recruit, select, train and retain a highly qualified and motivated workforce. Her other research interests include empowerment, the management of change and workforce diversity.

Michael Davidson is a former general manager of a five-star hotel and the foundation head of Griffith University's School of Tourism and Hotel Management in Australia. He is currently completing a PhD on Organizational Climate and its Influence on Performance of Australian Hotels. Michael teaches in the area of organizational behaviour, operations and management. He is currently Director of Griffith University's Centre for Business Education and Development.

Margaret Deery, PhD, is the Associate Director of the Centre for Hospitality and Tourism Research and Course Director of the Master of Business in Event Management at Victoria University, Melbourne, Australia. She has ten years' experience as a hospitality and tourism researcher, specializing in the field of human resource management issues. Dr Deery's doctoral dissertation investigated the impact of turnover culture and internal labour markets on labour turnover in the hotel industry. Her prior work experience includes managing several small businesses in the hospitality industry and managing an educational consultancy.

Ria Duddy has a background in education in the UK and New Zealand, with an emphasis on language and communication. Now based in Queensland, Australia, she is a freelance researcher and writer whose interest in services marketing and management has resulted in the presentation and publication of various international papers. She is a recipient of the Highly Commended and Citation of Excellence Award (1999) for her journal work.

Kathy Elvin is a personnel advisor at the Universal College of Learning in Palmerston North, New Zealand. She was named Massey Scholar due to the high standard she attained during her BBS. She was also the winner of the New Zealand Tourist Board Prize for 1998 for a report on the way forward for tourism in New Zealand.

Steven Goss-Turner is Principal Lecturer (HRM) and Deputy Head of School in the

School of Service Management of the University of Brighton, UK. He spent fifteen years with the then Trusthouse Forte plc, mainly in the human resource management function, leaving the company in 1991 as Training Director for the London and International division. His research work includes the publication of two editions of the book, *Managing People in the Hospitality Industry*, and contributing to a number of other books, journals and trade-oriented publications. In the last three years his research interests have centred upon the subject of multi-unit management within the hospitality industry and in other service sectors.

Barrie Humphreys is a Senior Lecturer in Human Resource Management at Massey University School of Business Palmerston North, New Zealand, where he teaches undergraduates, postgraduates and Master's students Human Resource Management and Employee Relations. Prior to emigrating to New Zealand Barrie worked as a senior lecturer in Human Resource Management at Oxford Brookes University.

Jay Kandampully, PhD, is an Associate Professor and Head of Services Management and Hospitality at the School of Tourism and Leisure Management, University of Queensland, Australia. With over 50 published articles to his credit in service quality management, and services management and marketing, he was awarded the Literati Award in 1997 and the Citation of Excellence Award in 1999 for his work on the concept of service loyalty. He is co-editor of *Service Quality Management in Hospitality, Tourism and Leisure* (with C. Mok and B. Sparks) and the author of *Hotels as Integrated Services*. He is also the editor of the journal *Managing Service Quality*.

Conrad Lashley is the Professor of Hospitality Retailing in the School of Tourism and Hospitality Management at Leeds Metropolitan University, UK. His commercial research has largely been concerned with a range of employee management issues relating to the licensed retail sector and his publications cover human resource and service quality issues with a particular focus on empowerment. He has research interests and publications in hospitality management education with particular reference to student learning styles. His books include *Empowering Service Excellence: Beyond the Quick Fix* and *Hospitality Retail Management*, and he has co-edited *Franchising Hospitality Services* and *In Search of Hospitality: Theoretical Perspectives and Debates*.

J. John Lennon is the Director of the Moffat Centre for Travel and Tourism Business Development at Glasgow Caledonian University in Scotland. The centre was established in 1998, employs eleven full-time staff and focuses mainly on contract research and data provision for the travel and tourism industry, and business development consultancy for a range of hospitality, tourism and travel businesses. The Moffat Centre (www.moffatcentre.com) is the largest provider of such services in Europe. Professor Lennon is the author of a wide range of journal and industry-focused articles. He has also contributed to and edited six texts, which include *Dark Tourism* (2000) (with M. Foley), *Current Trends in International Tourism Statistics* (2001) and *Museums and Galleries: Alternative Approaches to Funding and Revenue Generation* (2001) (with M. Grahm and I. Baxter).

Bruce Millett, PhD, is currently Head of the Human Resource Management and Employment Relations department, Faculty of Business, at the University of Southern Queensland, Australia. He earned his PhD, in the management of organizational change, at Griffith University. He is co-author of two textbooks on organizational behaviour and has published articles and book chapters on managing organizational change, human resource management and organizational learning. His current research interests include the learning organization, strategies for large-system change, performance management across different organizational contexts, and the work of consultants.

Connie Mok, PhD, is an Associate Professor in the Conrad N. Hilton College of Hotel and Restaurant Management at the University of Houston, USA. She is the author, or co-author, of over 70 published articles in academic journals, conference proceedings, books, and trade/professional journals. Her research articles have been published in the United States, the United Kingdom, India, Hong Kong, China, Thailand, Australia and New Zealand. She is co-editor of *Service Quality Management in Hospitality, Tourism, and Leisure.* She serves on the editorial broads of seven refereed academic journals and guest edited a special issue of the *Journal of Hospitality and Tourism Research* on advances in consumer behaviour research in hospitality and tourism. Dr Mok received her PhD in Marketing from Murdoch University.

Samantha Quail is an HR consultant with an American company specializing in the outsourcing of human resourcing for Global 500 Companies, Exult. She has extensive experience in line and human resource management in the hospitality sector, particularly in luxury hotels and resorts. This includes working as a human resource manager with Hilton. To recognize her contribution to the hospitality industry, Samantha was, in 2000, awarded a UK national prize, an Acorn Award.

Nils Timo, PhD, is a former industrial advocate for the Australian Workers Union in the area of tourism and hospitality. He has negotiated over 100 workplace agreements in the hotel and related industries and continues to act as an industry consultant. Recently Nils worked on enterprise bargaining for Accor Australia in North Queensland. His PhD, from the University of Southern Queensland, was on Employment Relations and Hotel Management. He lectures in industrial relations and workplace change. His current research is focused on examining comparative management practices and employee relations in the hotel industry.

Megan Tranter is the Australian National Workplace Safety Manager for a multinational, quick-service restaurant. Prior to this, she was employed as a lecturer in occupational health and safety at various Australian universities including her most recent position at the University of Western Sydney. She has been involved in teaching undergraduate and postgraduate programmes in occupational health and safety, and human resource management in Australia and Hong Kong. She is currently researching her PhD in the area of occupational health and safety experiences of young, casually employed workers in the hospitality industry.

Foreword

I have great pleasure in welcoming this latest addition to a growing reflective literature on human resource issues in the international hospitality and tourism industry. At the time when I assembled a similarly titled book,[1] some eight years ago, there was little available to the student, researcher or practitioner that provided a comparative international framework for consideration of human resources in our sector. Texts available were prescriptive, mono-cultural and inclined to steer clear of the controversial debates that exist in most countries regarding this area. Subsequent work by, among others, Wood,[2] Lashley [3] and Hofmann et al. [4] have all contributed to a broadening of discussion and the reflective illustration of key facets of human resource management (HRM) in hospitality and tourism.

Reflective comparison, questioning and lesson-drawing [5] are essential to the student seeking to integrate learning about HRM with his/her understanding of the international hospitality and tourism sector. They are also vital to the professional grappling with the complex and often contradictory tensions that are generated by HRM in practice. Living with contradiction and accepting that there are few certain answers are important but difficult lessons to learn. It is also important to recognize that possible answers may be in found in local best practice or in the experience of international colleagues operating in a very difficult environment.

This book provides a wonderful opportunity to learn from the research and applied experience of others in addressing key human resource issues in international hospitality and tourism. Geographically, the book locates discussion in Australasia, North America, Europe and South Africa and takes a largely developed world perspective. Functionally, this volume covers three key themes of employee resourcing, employee development and employee relations.

There is little doubt that issues and conclusions in this book will spark debate and, probably, disagreement. If this is the case, and this debate takes place in the classroom and the staffroom, then the collective efforts of the editors and contributors will have been vindicated. I am certainly looking forward to making productive use of this work.

Professor Tom Baum
The Scottish Hotel School
Strathclyde University
Glasgow, UK
June 2001

NOTES

1. Baum, T. (1993) *Human Resource Issues in International Tourism*. Oxford: Butterworth-Heinemann.
2. Wood, R. (1997) *Working in Hotels and Catering*. (2nd edn). London: International Thomson Business Press.
3. Lashley, C. (1997) *Empowering Service Excellence*. London: Cassell.
4. Hofmann, S., Johnson, C. and Lefever, M. (2000) *International Human Resource Management in the Hospitality Industry*. Lansung: Educational Institute of the AHMA.
5. Rose, R. (1993) *Lesson Drawing in Public Policy: A Guide to Learning Across Time and Space*. Chatham, NJ: Chatham House Publishers Inc.

1

Human Resource Management Issues in Hospitality and Tourism: Identifying the Priorities

Sandra Watson, Norma D'Annunzio-Green and Gillian A. Maxwell

ABSTRACT

Delivering hospitality and tourism products and services across international frontiers to discerning customers in highly competitive and dynamic market conditions presents a range of organizational challenges. Human resource management (HRM) represents a valuable tool for meeting many of these challenges and adding value in organizations. This chapter provides an insight into key HRM issues in international hospitality and tourism organizations. Examination focuses on a review of international HRM and discussion of strategic HRM. The chapter draws from the authors' worldwide survey of current and prospective human resource issues preoccupying international hospitality and tourism organizations.

INTRODUCTION

The purpose of this chapter is, first, to outline the literature on international and strategic HRM. Secondly, the results of an international survey, conducted by the authors, provide an analysis of current and future HRM issues facing hospitality and tourism multinationals. The survey also exposes which HRM issues are perceived as being strategic. This allows the authors to draw parallels between the theoretical and empirical issues facing the international hospitality and tourism industry. This chapter also provides the context for the other chapters in this text, by highlighting the rationale for the selection of specific topics covered by the authors. Internationality is defined, straightforwardly, in this text as hospitality and tourism organizations which operate in more than one country.

THE FRONTIERS OF INTERNATIONAL HUMAN RESOURCE MANAGEMENT

Interest in international human resource management (IHRM) has seen a rapid growth 'especially in the last five years' (Kamoche, 1997, p. 213). The correlation between global organizations' human resource practices and the success of their global business strategy is a well-argued and recurring theme in much of the IHRM literature (Wellins and Rioux, 2000; Ulrich and Black, 1999; Schuler *et al.*, 1993). Effective HRM strategies are seen to be essential because international expansion and operation places additional stress on all resources, but particularly on people (Joynt and Morton, 1999).

For many hospitality and tourism operators, expansion opportunities in local, domestic markets have recently been limited by intense competition. At the same time there are attractive and often lucrative opportunities for business growth in foreign markets (Go and Pine, 1996). Expanding international travel, technological advances and the emergence of seamless organizations have further fuelled the rapid expansion of hospitality and tourism organizations (Kriegl, 2000). 'The global economy is now a reality' (Luthans *et al.*, 1997, p. 183) and globalization has become a fundamental part – even a priority – of business operations for many hospitality and tourism organizations, irrespective of their size. The challenges for organizations operating in international markets present something of a new frontier for human resource management, as Wellins and Rioux (2000, p. 79) point out: 'although operations, sales and marketing functions have generally made great strides in adapting to the global reality, most human resource functions are still breaking new ground in developing policies, structures and services that support globalization'. Luthans *et al.* (1997, p. 183) go further in expressing the essential challenge in IHRM: 'the challenge facing international human resource management is not whether to use widely recognized human resource concepts and techniques but how to effectively adapt and fit them across cultures'.

Defining International Human Resource Management

Morgan's (1986) definition of IHRM, which is adopted for this chapter, reflects the challenge and scope of IHRM; it also differentiates IHRM from the more domestic focus that is the thrust of much of the general HRM literature. As defined by Morgan (1986) IHRM is the interplay between:

- basic human resource functions (e.g. human resource planning, recruitment and selection, performance management, training and development, employee relations);
- the different types of employees (e.g. expatriates, local and host country nationals); and
- the different countries of operation within which subsidiaries operate.

Thus, in broad terms, IHRM involves many of the same functional areas as domestic HRM but has the added complexity of working across different national boundaries and with more groups of employees. The role of IHRM in international hospitality and tourism companies is important, even central, according to Napier and Vu (1998, p. 43) who see it as the 'glue' that holds together a business's global activities relating to acquiring, developing, appraising and rewarding all employees – local and non-local – alike. To ensure business success, it is important to ensure IHRM practices are 'consistent across units within the firm while being adjusted to local conditions' (*ibid.*). Insight into cultural and political awareness and dimensions in different countries is arguably an 'overwhelming challenge' (Schneider and Barsoux, 1997, p. 150) for IHR managers. The difficulty of the challenge does not, however, detract from the importance of developing vertically and horizontally aligned human resource policies and practices in the key areas of employee resourcing, employee development and employee relations. With this in mind, the text has been divided into three discrete, but interrelated areas of human resource management: employee resourcing, employee development and employee relations. The Chartered Institute of Personnel Development in the UK recognizes these three as key human resource activity areas. The next section will briefly provide an overview of these key areas.

Central Issues in International Human Resource Management

Resourcing – particularly the recruitment and selection of international staff – is high on the agenda. Baum (1995) argues for better utilization of human resources in terms of productivity and short-term, bottom-line profitability, within the context of a longer-term HR strategy. Go and Pine (1995) and Powell (1999) stress international labour supply issues at both an operational and managerial level, to ensure that a lack of suitable staff and competent managers will not impede the ability of international hospitality and tourism operators to continue their expansion. Labour markets are tight in many parts of the world and the shortage of skills coupled with the high-level resource requirements of many companies result in stiff competition for the best talent. Selection and recruitment (Baum, 1993) and managing labour turnover (Deery and Iverson, 1996) are issues addressed in much of the literature. The problem is exacerbated and complicated in the international arena when global companies need to find staff who are willing to be geographically mobile and who possess the requisite skills and competencies to equip them to work internationally, as opposed to just having the technical or operational experience for the job. As a response to these challenges, companies are reviewing their global recruitment and selection processes by, for example, reassessing the required global management competencies, using new and innovative recruitment methods, such as the World Wide Web and company intranets, and developing assessment centres to identify the best talent from both external and internal staff supply.

Within the area of employee development, there is a particular focus on training and development as a key challenge facing multinational operators in both the generic literature (Bartlett and Ghoshal, 1992; Evans, 1992) and the applied literature (Baum, 1993; D'Annunzio-Green, 1997; Gliatis and Guerrier, 1993; Jayawardena, 2000). Many multinational corporations have been under immense pressure to develop managerial talent that will enable them to grow in the future (Watson and Litteljohn, 1992). This is further magnified because of the need for strong leadership capabilities and competencies and the ability to lead in different cultural contexts and in different corporate cultures.

Closely associated with this is managing the performance of international managers (Wellins and Rioux, 2000). As global corporations struggle to balance critical global HR strategies and local initiatives, a good performance management system is essential to enable the company to set broad corporate strategies and cascade them down to local business subsidiaries. Responses to these challenges are varied and include, on the one hand, cross-border harmonization of management development policy to raise the profile and internal supply of future managers, and more investment in localization policies on the other hand. There is a trend towards formalization of the management development policy, and more attempt at centralization or regionalization to ensure consistency, control and quality. Another response is clearer marketing and communication coupled with more differentiation of the international development opportunities available to staff, both internally and externally. The importance of developing skills for managing service quality is highlighted by many researchers, including Heskett *et al. (*1994) and LaLopa (1997). Issues which are seen to be changing the role of HRM in organizations include the need for HRM managers to be aware of the wider business needs (Keenoy, 1990) and to encompass new initiatives such as organizational learning and knowledge management (Harrison, 2000).

Finally, the area of employee relations, an area which has received relatively little attention in the UK hospitality literature apart from work by Lucas (1995), Lashley (1997) and Hoque (1999). The manner in which organizational dialogue takes place has undergone dramatic change. This change has resulted in an increased focus on the individual at work and the need to connect and communicate directly with employees to enable a mutual understanding of the needs of both parties in the employment relationship. Consequently, the following challenges, outlined by Parkinson (1999), are presented. First, to manage the internal communication process within organizations and ensure that diversity within the employee group is accounted for. Secondly, to ensure that messages and communication from managers and various managerial practices directed at employees are consistent with those the organization wants to send to an increasingly diverse workforce, particularly when developing more modern communication methods such as attitude or climate surveys, or managerial practices such as team working or empowerment. Empowerment has received much attention by academics in the field of hospitality and tourism, as it seen as particularly pertinent to improving service quality; for example, Lashley and Watson (1999) and D'Annunzio-Green and MacAndrew (1999).

Another area which is becoming prevalent is the area of emotional labour (Casey, 1995 and Fineman, 1993). Solutions to these challenges mainly centre on an awareness of the barriers to communication such as language, culture, and varying legislative and institutional contexts in which employee relations are conducted. This is influenced by the readiness of global organizations to invest time and resources in sending consistent messages both across subsidiaries and within them. The importance of employee commitment is an area that has been given much attention by social science researchers (Meyer and Allen, 1997). The importance of having committed employees to provide quality of service in the hospitality industry has been addressed by many researchers, as indicated earlier.

THE BOUNDARIES OF STRATEGIC HUMAN RESOURCE MANAGEMENT

It is clear from the above discussion that there is a range of HRM issues facing international hospitality and tourism organizations. These issues are, theoretically, viewed as being important. The development of vertically and horizontally aligned HR policies then become essential to achieve integration of employee resourcing, development and relations with organizational strategy. In practice, however, there is evidence to suggest that HRM is not typically embraced at strategic levels in organizations (Legge, 1995). The general failure of US and UK organizations in adopting strategic HRM is recorded, for example, by Singh (1992), Storey (1992), Armstrong and Long (1994) and Martell and Carroll (1995). Arguably, this is due in part to difficulties in defining strategy. Business and corporate strategy can be defined in a number of ways, for example by process, level and type, and in options, implementations, trends and developments (Knowles, 1999). The definition used here is that offered by the widely acclaimed Johnson and Scholes (1999, p. 10) as it captures the key elements: 'strategy is the *direction* and *scope* of an organization over the *long-term*: which achieves *advantage* for the organization through its configuration of resources within a changing environment, to meets the needs of *markets* and fulfil *stakeholder* expectations'.

On this basis, what defines strategic HRM in this chapter can be reduced to two central characteristics: inclusion in business strategy and in long-term planning horizons. Strategic HRM, in theory at least, has acute relevance in the context of international hospitality and tourism organizations because of the intrinsic nature of organizational reliance on service quality. Practically, though, there is scant evidence that HRM approaches have been adopted in these sectors, particularly in the UK, where Price (1994) and Goldsmith *et al.* (1999), for example, testify to the general marginalization of the HR function. Overall there is a relative lack of research activity currently centred on strategic HRM in these sectors, as signalled by Lashley and Watson (1999), despite the growing interest in IHRM and the: 'increasing global competition and globalization of [tourism and hospitality industries'] products and consumer expectations and ... the increased centrality of the human factor, in the ability to deliver quality products and services within all areas of tourism and hospitality' (Baum, 1997, p. 221).

In summary, human resource management is presented, within the critical and prescriptive literature, as an important function which should be substantiated with a strategic presence in hospitality organizations. However, for this text the authors wished to explore if the issues proposed by secondary sources are seen as being imperative by practising human resource directors/managers. To this end, the authors undertook primary research.

RESEARCH METHODS

The empirical work on which this chapter is based aims to inform insights into the current nature of international and strategic HRM. It centres on two areas of questioning: first, what issues do HRM specialists consider to be a priority at the time of the primary work (1999/2000) and important for the future (2001–6), and secondly, which of these issues are included in organizational strategic planning.

The survey instrument – a self-administered questionnaire (in English) – invited the most senior human resource specialist in each organization to prioritize current and future (defined as the period 2001–6) human resource issues. Inclusion of prospective issues is considered important as their identification offers some insight into the extent of forward planning for human resource issues. Questionnaires are often used in

Table 1.1 Human resource issues in international hospitality and tourism

Category	Issue areas
Employee resourcing	Recruitment/selection/ technology/ international operations and management
Employee development	Training/development/reward management/ /service quality/ learning organizations
Employee relations	Employee relations/diversity/flexibility/ commitment/ law/line managers/mergers etc.

tourism research (Veal, 1997) and lend themselves to simple data capture (Robson, 1999). Using the three areas of resourcing, development and relations as a framework to examine a range of issues, a questionnaire was constructed encompassing theoretical issues identified as potentially important. This is summarized in Table 1.1.

The secondary literature review yielded 39 potential issues for inclusion in the questionnaire. In constructing the questionnaire the main objective was to address the two research questions indicated above. In doing so, a deductive or positivist stance was adopted where attempts were made to see if the issues presented in the literature were relevant in international hospitality and tourism organizations. Respondents were asked to rate current and future importance on a Likert scale, with 'not an issue' being rated lowest (1) and 'very high priority' (5) the highest in terms of importance. In each category, respondents were asked to identify any other current/future human resource issues. (The respondents identified no further items.) Lastly, respondents were asked to indicate which issues are included in their organization's strategic plans. Following piloting, the questionnaire was administered in 1999 to HR directors/managers in the head offices of international hospitality and tourism organizations. The questionnaire database comprised a comprehensive list of 472 international hospitality and tourism organizations (defined as operating in two or more countries) across every continent, compiled by trawling a range of industry-specific databases. The initial response was rather predictably low so reminder letters were distributed. Sixty-seven questionnaires have been returned (14.5%). Though the response rate does not allow any claims of generalizability, it is possibly indicative, and certainly interesting with its span across 32 countries and coverage of over 300,000 employees.

Results

The intention of the survey was to reach the top HR representative within international organizations. The survey was predominantly completed by human resource managers/ directors (63% of respondents) and training and development managers (15%). Ten per cent were returned by partners/directors, with the remaining 12 per cent comprising operations/general managers. The majority of the returns (66%) were received from hotel companies, 16 per cent from travel companies, 12 per cent tourism and the remaining 6 per cent from restaurant organizations. The majority of the organizations (57%) were found to be operating in less than five countries, with 24 per cent operating in over fifteen countries. Sixty-three per cent of the returns were received from the main company. Fifty-four per cent of the organizations employ over 2000 staff, with 48 per cent operating over twenty units. Thirty-three per cent operate less than ten units. The spread of locations was worldwide, with all continents except Antarctica being represented in the returns. Forty-eight per cent of the sample owned all their units, 20 per cent had franchised units, while 32 per cent used management contracts. The sample provides a good range of size, ownership and geographical spread, which can be used as an appropriate basis for discussing the findings from the survey.

In analysing the current issues, the Likert ratings of 1–5 were allocated to the importance ratings, which allowed a numerical value to be used to assess relative importance. Those items with a mean value over 4.50 would be rated as very high priority; when a mean rating was between 3.50 and 4.49 it would be deemed to be of high priority, between 2.50 and 3.49 was deemed low priority, and when the mean rating was between 1.50 and 2.49 the issue would be rated as very low priority. Table 1.2 presents the ranking of the current items, with associated means. It also includes the per centage of organizations that included the item in strategic planning.

What is evident, from Table 1.2, is that all the items were rated as having some priority across the sample. However, none of the items were rated as very high priority. This is a telling result as it immediately locates *all* the HR issues as less than very high priority. Fifteen per cent of the items were rated as being of very low priority. In examining these, 50 per cent fall within cross-cultural issues. Issues with means of less than 3.00 in the low priority section can be seen to be relating to cross-cultural issues. This suggests that priority HR issues may not focus on international HRM as per the definition discussed earlier.

Another interesting finding is that just over 50 per cent of items have been rated as having a high priority. Three of the highest priority items can be seen to be similar to issues which are as pertinent to domestically oriented hospitality and tourism organizations. Service quality, training and development, and staff recruitment and selection, are all HRM issues which are reported as being important across much of the industry (Baum, 1997; Go and Pine, 1995; Kelliher and Johnson, 1997). These are all stated as being included in 60 per cent or more of the organizations' strategic planning. Although having slightly lower means, management development and employee commitment were also included in strategic plans in 60 per cent or more of organizations. Low priority was given to such issues as skills shortages, career management, cross-cultural awareness of staff, learning organization, knowledge management and information technology in human resource management. With the exception of career planning, these issues were reported as being included in strategic plans by less than 50 per cent of organizations.

When analysis of the strategic presence is conducted it can be seen that there is a predominance of development issues in strategic planning. Resourcing issues, including staff recruitment and selection, managing labour turnover and succession planning, are also seen to be included in strategic plans in over 50 per cent of cases, with less evidence of strategies to deal with workforce flexibility and skills shortages. Employee relations issues, including commitment and legislative considerations, were found in strategic planning for over 50 per cent of organizations. Less evidence was found for cross-cultural issues being included in the strategic plans.

Two distinct findings emerge from analysis of current issues. First, a wide range of HR issues are priority (but not rated as very high priority) and most of these are included in strategic planning. Whether or not the treatment of these issues is in keeping with international HRM is not clear, though the explicit exclusion of cross-cultural dimensions from the higher priority and strategic planning does make it doubtful.

In addressing future issues, a three-point scale was used. This was to ease completion of the survey instrument, although the authors realized the potential impact of this on central tendency. In analysing the data, mean values of 3.00–2.50 were seen to be very important; 2.49–1.50 important; and 1.49–1.00 were considered unimportant. All the

Table 1.2 Current HRM issues and strategic planning presence

	N	Mean	Category	Strategic plan (%)
Service quality	67	4.31	Development	60
Training and development of staff	67	4.21	Development	78
Financial/business awareness and control	67	4.12	Development	67
Staff recruitment and selection	67	4.07	Resourcing	69
Team-building	67	3.94	Relations	44
Professionalism of managers	67	3.93	Development	55
Management Development	67	3.93	Development	63
Gaining employee attitudinal commitment	67	3.91	Relations	60
Legislation	66	3.82	Relations	54
Personal effectiveness of managers	67	3.79	Development	49
Leadership	66	3.79	Development	51
Line managers responsibility for decision-making	66	3.76	Development	54
Development of local management talent	67	3.72	Development	39
Employee relations	66	3.71	Relations	51
Managing labour turnover	67	3.70	Resourcing	55
Workforce flexibility	67	3.57	Resourcing	39
Performance appraisal	67	3.54	Development	52
Managing diversity	66	3.53	Relations	37
Succession planning	67	3.51	Resourcing	57
Reward management	67	3.51	Resourcing	56
Skill shortages	67	3.49	Resourcing	37
Career planning	67	3.46	Resourcing	52
Knowledge management	67	3.45	Development	43
Cross-cultural awareness in operational staff	67	3.40	Relations	31
Computerized training/ICT	67	3.40	Development	52
Learning organizations	67	3.19	Development	39
Technology in HR	67	3.10	Resourcing	43
HR implications of acquisitions	63	3.05	Relations	31
The management of multi-cultural teams	66	2.95	Relations	22
Management competencies for international projects	65	2.94	Resourcing	27
Succession planning for international managers	63	2.79	Resourcing	28
Compensation and employment issues for staff operating in countries other than the home country	65	2.69	Resourcing	25
Transfer of HR management policies and practices in culturally diverse counties	64	2.66	Relations	25
HR implications of strategic alliances	64	2.47	Relations	30
Transfer of HR management policies and practices in developing countries	62	2.45	Relations	25
HR implications of international joint ventures	63	2.43	Relations	33
HR implications of mergers	63	2.38	Relations	27
Role of HR consultants in aiding IHRM specialists	63	2.35	Relations	18
HR systems for staff operating in a variety of disparate global locations	63	2.30	Relations	18

items can be seen to be of importance to the respondents, but only six fall into the very important grouping, namely gaining employee commitment, training and development, service quality, staff recruitment and selection, team-building and management development. With the exception of team-building, all the issues were included in strategic planning in 60 per cent or more of organizations. Although team-building is reported as being very important, it is included in only 44 per cent of respondents' strategic plans.

Again there is the predominance of cross-cultural issues being located at the lower end of the table, indicating that these are not seen as being of significant importance to the respondents. These issues aside, it appears that a wide range of HR issues will remain on the organizational agenda, with most included in strategic planning.

DISCUSSION

The above analysis reveals a number of interesting findings which highlight some contradictions when comparing theory with practice and which are worthy of further discussion. The sample provides a mixed cross-section of organizational types, size and geographical spread.

The low importance given to cross-cultural issues by organizations (both now and in the future) could be interpreted in a number of different ways. First, it may be a reflection on the strategic approach taken to HRM. This finding would be appropriate in organizations taking either an ethnocentric or polycentric perspective (Perlmutter, 1969), i.e. not an international perspective as defined earlier. A second interpretation could be that the cross-cultural issues are so embedded within these organizations that they are not seen as being a priority. A third explanation could be that these are not seen as being of importance, which is supported by the low reported inclusion of these issues in strategic plans. Further, this interpretation is contrary to the views on the importance of cross-cultural issues espoused in the literature review (Luthans *et al.*, 1997; Napier and Vu, 1998). However, it would appear to be consistent with Wellins and Rioux's (2000) thesis that organizations are still breaking new ground in developing policies, practices and procedures to support globalization.

In relation to issues identified as being of high priority, only one – development of local management talent – was seen to be within the cross-cultural category. The majority can be seen to be within labour market and performance management categories. Many of these are HR issues which have been identified as critical in hospitality research across the world, for example training and development of staff, management development, selection and recruitment, managing labour turnover and employee commitment. Service quality and team-building are also issues that have been given much attention in hospitality research. Interestingly, the need for human resource managers to have financial/business awareness, and the impact of devolving human resources to line managers, have also been seen as high-priority areas. These have been highlighted in generic HRM literature, but afforded less attention in hospitality literature.

It is worth noting that the very important future issues are similar to current high-priority areas, with employee commitment taking over pole position from service quality. The importance of having committed employees to provide quality of service in the hospitality industry has been addressed by many researchers, as indicated earlier.

Finally, the strategic presence of human resource management issues is evidently less

Table 1.3 Future HRM issues

	N	Mean	Category
Gaining employee attitudinal commitment	66	2.76	Relations
Training and development	65	2.63	Development
Service quality	64	2.61	Development
Staff recruitment and selection	67	2.58	Resourcing
Team-building	64	2.53	Relations
Management development	67	2.52	Development
Professionalism of managers	67	2.46	Development
Financial/business awareness and control	66	2.45	Development
Career planning	66	2.41	Resourcing
Workforce flexibility	66	2.38	Resourcing
Personal effectiveness of managers	67	2.37	Development
Performance appraisal	66	2.36	Development
Employment law	66	2.36	Relations
Line managers responsibility for decision-making	64	2.34	Development
Managing labour turnover	67	2.34	Resourcing
Employee relations	67	2.34	Relations
Leadership	65	2.29	Development
Skill shortages	66	2.29	Resourcing
Development of local management talent	62	2.27	Development
Reward management	66	2.27	Resourcing
Computerized training/ICT	67	2.27	Development
Succession planning	67	2.27	Resourcing
Managing diversity	65	2.26	Relations
Knowledge management	66	2.21	Development
Cross-cultural awareness in operational staff	64	2.16	Relations
Technology in HR	65	2.14	Resourcing
Learning organizations	64	2.11	Development
HR implications of Acquisitions	62	2.10	Relations
Management competencies for international projects	61	2.05	Resourcing
The management of multi-cultural teams	63	2.02	Relations
Succession planning for international managers	59	1.88	Resourcing
Transfer of HR management policies and practices in culturally diverse countries	58	1.83	Relations
Transfer of HR management policies and practices in developing countries	55	1.80	Relations
HR implications of international joint ventures	62	1.79	Relations
Compensation and employment issues for staff operating in countries other than the home	60	1.78	Resourcing
HR implications of strategic alliances	63	1.78	Relations
HR systems for staff operating in a variety of disparate global locations	58	1.71	Relations
HR implications of mergers	61	1.70	Relations
Role of HR consultants in aiding IHRM specialists	58	1.64	Relations

than the mainstream literature might advocate, but also more than the hospitality and tourism-specific literature might predict. The status of HRM in hospitality is often cited as being low, for example by Price (1994), Wood (1992) and Kelliher and Johnston (1997). The survey indicates that in total some seventeen current issues are included in the strategic planning of the respondent organizations.

It appears, overall, that the hospitality and tourism organizations in this sample are failing to address the complexities of IHRM highlighted in the literature. The responding organizations are evidently only at the edge of the frontiers of international human resource management. This may result in the 'glue' (Napier and Vu, 1998) not being strong enough to ensure that these organizations are able to exploit fully the challenges of the international market-place. Although the majority of respondents appeared to be operating at a strategic level, as evidenced by their titles, HRM issues may not be considered as important as other organizational functions.

STRUCTURE OF TEXT

In compiling this text, the editors utilizd the information gleaned from the literature review and their survey to assist them in selecting the chapter topics. In addition, the editors wished to include authors from a wide geographical spread. The contributors are located in North America, UK, Australia and New Zealand. However, these contributions provide examples and cases from Russia, South Africa and Australasia. This reflects the dominance and research focus of academics in these locations. It could also be seen as an indicator of the importance of hospitality in these economies. The chapters reflect a broad range of pertinent issues worthy of further scrutiny. Each chapter provides an overview of the topic as well as presenting a case study to illustrate good practice.

The first section of the book, 'Employee Resourcing', commences with two chapters addressing recruitment and selection from Canadian and Australasian perspectives. Issues surrounding workforce availability, flexibility, human resource planning and reward management are highlighted within the domain of selection and recruitment. Selection and recruitment was identified as being of key importance in the survey and was found to be included in strategic planning by over two-thirds of the respondents. This is followed by a chapter on labour turnover, which was rated as being of high importance. Within this chapter issues surrounding flexibility, succession planning and development are also explored. The problem of skills shortages is addressed by the last two chapters in this section, through addressing the role of information technology and the identification of managerial competencies. A central argument of these chapters is the need to address the development of new and different skills, which involves addressing career/succession planning and reward management.

Employee development issues have been given much prominence in both the literature and the survey. The second section of the book, 'Employee Development', commences with a chapter on service quality. It examines how one international organization has linked service quality to human resource management and development at a strategic level. The second chapter focuses on training and development of staff, reflecting on the importance of training and development, prior to exploring how benefits can be measured. This enables exploration of the link between training and organizational performance. The third chapter locates the issue of management development within the context of multi-site management. Here, there is an exploration of issues around the importance of financial, business awareness, control and professional development. The next chapter exposes performance management as a critical strategic tool in international hospitality organizations. Within performance management, concepts of reward management, development and succession planning are discussed. The final chapter examines the national context and approaches to training in the economies of Fiji and South Africa.

The third section of the book covers aspects of 'Employee Relations'. Within this section the issue of employee commitment is scrutinized. Commitment has been identified as an important issue, both now and in the future. The chapter examines the concept of organizational commitment within the context of international organizations, highlighting the complexities of cultural diversity. The second chapter examines the importance of legislation, through presenting an analysis of issues which managers used to address in relation to occupational health and safety, and proposes a systematic approach to minimizing risks. The third chapter contemplates approaches to employee relations within the context of cost-cutting and service quality strategies. Issues surrounding flexibility of labour models are also exposed. The next chapter examines the issue of employee relations through the lens of empowerment. It explores ways in which the employment relationship shifts, depending on the empowerment approach adopted, and highlights issues of motivation teamwork and decision-making. The fifth chapter addresses the issue of managing diversity. Although this did not appear high on the agenda of the surveyed organizations, it is a concept receiving much attention by the academic community. The chapter presents a range of approaches to managing diversity in the international hospitality industry. The final chapter covers the contemporary topic of emotional labour. This explores the emotional utilization of labour by international hospitality organizations, highlighting the possible conflicts which may emerge in different cultures. It presents the challenge of effectively managing the employment relationship within this context.

Although it has not been possible to address all the issues associated with managing human resources in the international hospitality and tourism industry, it can be seen that the chapters encompass the majority of the issues which appear to be dominant in the industry.

REFERENCES

Armstrong, M. (1992) *Human Resource Management: Strategy and Action*. London: Kogan Page.

Armstrong, M. and Long, P. (1994) *The Reality of Strategic HRM*. London: Institute of Personnel and Development.

Bartlett, C. A. and Ghoshal, S. (1992) 'What is a global manager'. *Harvard Business Review*, **92**, 124–32.

Baum, T. (1993) *Human Resource Issues in International Tourism*. Oxford: Butterworth-Heinemann Ltd.

Baum, T. (1995) *Managing Human Resources in the European Tourism and Hospitality Industry*. International Thomson Business Press.

Baum, T. (1997) 'Policy dimensions of human resource management in the tourism and hospitality industries'. *International Journal of Contemporary Hospitality Management*, 9/5/6, 221–9.

Casey, C. (1995) *Work, Self and Society after Industrialism*. London: Routledge.

D'Annunzio-Green, N. (1997) 'Developing international managers in the hospitality industry'. *International Journal of Contemporary Hospitality Management*. 4 & 5/6, 199–208.

D'Annunzio-Green, N. and MacAndrew, J. (1999) 'Re-empowering the empowered – the ultimate challenge?' *Personnel Review*, **28**(3), 258–78.

Deery, M. A. and Iverson, R. (1996) 'Enhancing productivity: interventions strategies for employee turnover', in N. Johns (ed.), *Productivity Management in Hospitality and Tourism*. London: Cassell.

Evans, P. (1992) 'Management development as glue technology'. *Human Resource Planning*, **25**, 185–206.

Fineman, S. (1993) *Emotions in the Organizations*. London: Sage.

Go, F. and Pine, R. (1995) 'Globalization in the hotel industry', in Kotas *et al.* (eds) *The International Hospitality Business*. New York: Cassell.

Goldsmith A., Nickson D., Sloan D. and Wood R. C. (1999) *Human Resource Management for Hospitality Services*. London: International Thomson Business Press.

Gliatis, N. and Guerrier, Y. (1993) 'Managing international career moves in international hotel companies.' *Progress in Tourism, Recreation and Hospitality Management*, **5**, 229–41.

Harrison, R. (2000) *Employee Development*. IPD.

Heskett, J. L., Jones, T. O., Loveman, G. W., Sasser, W. E. and Shlesinger, L. A. (1994) 'Putting the service profit chain to work'. *Harvard Business Review*, March–April, 164–74.

Hoque, K. (1999) 'Human resource management and performance in the UK hotel industry'. *British Journal of Industrial Relations*, **37**(3), September, 419–43.

Jayawardwena, C. (2000) 'International hotel manager'. *International Journal of Hospitality Management*, **12**(1), 67–9.

Johnson, G. and Scholes, K. (1999) *Exploring Corporate Strategy: Text and Cases*. Prentice-Hall Europe.

Joynt, P. and Morton, B. (1999) *The Global HR Manager*. London: IPD.

Kamoche, K. (1997) 'Knowledge creation and learning in international HRM'. *The International Journal of Human Resource Management*, **8**, April, 213–25.

Keenoy, T. (1990) 'HRM: a case of the wolf in sheep's clothing?' *Personnel Review*, **19**(2), 3–9.

Kelliher, C. and Johnson, K. (1997) 'Personnel Management in hotels – an update: a move to human resource management?' *Progress in Tourism and Hospitality Research*, **3**, 321–31.

Knowles, T. (1999) *Corporate Strategy for Hospitality*. Harlow: Addison Wesley Longman Ltd.

Kriegl, U. (2000) 'International hospitality management'. *Cornell Hotel and Restaurant Administration Quarterly*, **41**(2), April, 64–71.

LaLopa, J. (1997) 'Commitment and turnover in resort jobs'. *Journal of Hospitality and Tourism Research*, **21**(2), 11–26.

Lashley, C. (1997) *Empowering Service Excellence*. London: Cassell.

Lashley, C. and Watson, S. (1999) 'Researching human resource management in the hospitality industry: the need for a new agenda?' *International Journal of Tourism and Hospitality Research*, **1**(1), 19–40.

Legge, K. (1995) *Human Resource Management: Rhetoric and Realities*. London: Macmillan Press.

Lucas, R. (1995) *Managing Employee Relations in the Hotel and Catering Industry*. London: Cassell.

Luthans, F., Marsnik, P. and Luthans, K. (1997) 'A contingency matrix approach to IHRM'. *Human Resource Management*, **36**(2), 183–99.

Martell, K. and Carroll, S. J. (1995) 'How strategic is HRM?' *Human Resource Management*, **34**(2), summer, 253–67.

Meyer, J. P. and Allen, N. J. (1997) *Commitment in the Workplace*. Thousand Oaks, CA: Sage Publications.

Morgan, P. V. (1986) 'International human resource management: fact or fiction'. *Personnel Administrator*, **31**(9), 43–7.

Napier, N. and Vu, V. T. (1998) 'International human resource management in developing and transitional economy countries: a breed apart?' *Human Resource Management Review*, **8**(1), 39–77.

Parkinson, A. (1999) 'Sustaining constructive relationships across cultural boundaries, in Joynt, P. and Morton, B. *The Global HR Manager*. London: IPD.

Permutter, H. (1969) 'The tortuous evolution of the multinational corporation'. *Columbia Journal of World Business*, January/February, 12.

Powell, S. (1999) 'Is recruitment the millennium timebomb for the industry world-wide?' *International Journal of Contemporary Hospitality Management*, **11**(4), 138–9.

Price, L. (1994) 'Poor personnel practice in the hotel and catering industry: Does it really matter?' *Human Resource Management Journal*, **4**(4), 44–62.

Robson, C. (1999) *Real World Research: A Resource for Social Scientists and Practitioner Researchers* (2nd edn) Oxford: Blackwell.

Schneider, S. and Barsoux, J. L. (1997) *Managing Across Cultures*. Hemel Hempstead: Prentice-Hall.

Schuler, R. S., Dowling, P. J. and DeCieri, H. (1993) 'An integrative framework of strategic international human resource management'. *International Journal of Human Resource Management*, **1**, 717–64.

Singh, R. (1992) 'Human resource management: a sceptical look', in B. Towers (ed.) *The Handbook of Human Resource Management*. Oxford: Blackwell, pp. 127–43, cited in Goldsmith A., Nickson D., Sloan, D. and Wood R. C., *Human Resource Management for Hospitality Services* (1997) London: International Thomson Business Press.

Storey, J. (1992) 'HRM in action: the truth is out at last'. *Personnel Management*, April, 28–31.

Ulrich, D. and Black, J. S. (1999) 'Worldly wise'. *People Management*, 28 October 1999.

Veal, A. J. (1997) *Research Methods for Leisure and Tourism: A Practical Guide* (2nd edn) London: Pitman Publishing.

Watson, S. and Litteljohn, D. (1992) 'Multi- and transnational firms: the impact of expansion on corporate structures', in R. Teare and M. Olsen (eds) *International Hospitality Management Corporate Strategy in Practice*. London: Pitman.

Wellins, R. and Rioux, S. (2000) 'The growing pains of globalising HR'. *Training and Development*, May, 79–85.

Wood, R. C. (1992) *Working in Hotels and Catering*. London: Routledge.

Part I Employee Resourcing

2

Recruitment and Selection Issues and Strategies
within International Resort Communities

Julia M. Christensen Hughes

ABSTRACT

The recruitment and selection of employees is a critical human resource function; one
that has been described as a 'millennium time bomb' for the tourism industry.
Customer service expectations are increasing, while it is becoming increasingly harder
for employers, particularly in remote seasonal locations, to staff their operations
effectively. This chapter provides an overview of the recruitment and selection function
in the tourism industry. It also presents six contextual issues that can dramatically
impact the availability of labour to the industry. These are: the image and nature of
work in the industry; management philosophy and practice – turnover, pay and
benefits, and training and development; issues of seasonality; the local labour market –
population size, unemployment rates, demographics; local cultures – attitudes towards
tourism; and government policies and priorities. Recruitment and selection strategies,
and their interrelationship with these six issues are explored by drawing on the
experiences of associations and employers in a remote tourist destination – Whistler
Village in British Columbia, Canada.

INTRODUCTION

According to a recent study by D'Annunzio-Green, Maxwell, and Watson (2000),
employee recruitment and selection is one of the top three human resource issues within
international hospitality and tourism organizations today. This finding is supported by
David Wood, Chief Executive of the Hotel & Catering International Management
Association, which represents 23,800 professional managers in 106 countries. Wood has

suggested that the mismatch between labour supply and demand in hospitality is a 'millennium time bomb'. According to Wood:

> Economic growth, greater affluence, increased leisure time, and earlier retirement for many have led hospitality to be the biggest growth industry in the UK and many other economies. Worldwide, the industry already employs one in ten of the global population while in the UK it creates one in five new jobs. Perhaps the most significant problem we face is in recruitment. The millennium time bomb of the industry worldwide is staffing! (Powell and Wood 1999, p. 138)

In addition to this staffing challenge, customer expectations for quality are increasing, presenting the industry with a double-edged sword; at the same time that qualified labour is becoming harder to find and keep, customers are demanding increasingly higher levels of service excellence. Linking this issue with seasonality, a common characteristic of tourism enterprise, Baum and Hagen (1999, p. 310) wrote, 'The lack of sustained employment, which is characteristic of seasonal operations, undermines the ability of operators to deliver quality, which the marketplace, increasingly, expects.'

Many in the industry have advocated paying more attention to this critical issue. Timo and Davidson (1999, p. 25) suggest that tourism operations need to 'expend greater energy on choosing the "right" person and adopt more widespread compensation and benefits packages in order to retain the right staff'. However, the challenges associated with effectively recruiting and selecting employees often extend beyond the purview of individual operators, requiring creative and collective responses to factors embedded within the industry itself. For example, one of the reasons staffing can be so challenging is that when resorts are developed, much more attention tends to be paid to capital projects (e.g. the building of roads, hotels and airports) and marketing campaigns than to human resource issues (Baum, 1993). As a result, resorts can be constructed in areas with little in the way of available human resources, and with little thought as to how to acquire them. In addition, industry contextual factors and associated human resource practices have done little to improve the attractiveness of the industry: 'industry-wide issues of seasonality, fluctuating demand and product perishability often result in low pay, limited career progression, inadequate rostering and long, often unsocial working hours' (Timo and Davidson, 1999, p. 25).

For tourism operations to be successful, it is imperative that ample consideration is given to human resource issues, in particular the recruitment and selection of qualified staff. This chapter is dedicated to the exploration of these issues. To begin, standard approaches to recruitment and selection within the tourism industry are reviewed. Next, six contextual issues that contribute to labour supply, or the number of people pursuing and maintaining employment in the tourism industry, are discussed. Following, a case study of the recruitment and selection challenges and strategies found within a Canadian tourist community – Whistler Village in British Columbia, Canada – is presented. The data for this case were collected by the author through in-depth, semi-structured interviews and a review of archival data (e.g. strategic plans, recruitment material, employee handbooks) during 1998 and 1999. The chapter concludes with suggestions as to how employers can develop sound recruitment and selection strategies. The aims and objectives of this chapter are as follows:

1. To provide an overview of the recruitment and selection function.
2. To identify contextual issues related to the supply of potential employees in the tourism industry.

3. To present strategies for ensuring an adequate supply of potential employees, achieving a satisfactory fit in selection decisions and retaining quality employees.
4. To present, in case-study format, community and business-specific strategies that have been found to be effective for dealing with recruitment and selection challenges in Whistler, BC, Canada.

RECRUITMENT AND SELECTION

Recruitment is the process of attracting a pool of qualified job candidates from which the organization may select appropriate individuals to meet its job requirements. Effective recruitment strategies flow from the careful consideration of several factors including the number 'of people required at each level of each category of skill, providing for expansion, attrition and internal development needs' (Mahesh, 1993, p. 30). Candidates may be recruited using either internal or external strategies. Internal recruitment strategies (e.g. promotion from within, lateral transfers) are often supported by career planning, skills inventories and internal job-posting systems. Many international organizations use sophisticated HRIS (human resource information systems) to aid in the matching of employee skills with job vacancies on a worldwide basis. Internal recruitment can be effective for retaining top performers and demonstrating commitment to employee development. However, companies moving into new international markets must also be sensitive to the conflicts that can develop between locals and expatriates. Companies must carefully balance the advantages of promotion from within, with the developmental needs of the local workforce and community (D'Annunzio-Green, 1997). External recruitment strategies (e.g. employee referrals, walk/write-ins, advertisements in newspapers and professional journals, private and public employment agencies, websites, job fairs, educational institutions and professional associations) can be effective when many new employees are required (i.e. as with the opening of a new business, or where there are extreme seasonal fluctuations), and for introducing new skill sets and ideas to the organization.

Both internal and external recruitment approaches are often undertaken with the explicit recognition that considerable training and development will be required, particularly when skilled labour is in short supply. 'Some hoteliers have changed their attitude in the hiring of staff: instead of hiring experienced supervisory staff, which is rather difficult, they have tended to hire junior staff with the right attitude, personality and, above all, potential for development, and to provide them with the necessary opportunity for training' (Heung, 1993, p. 169).

Selection is the process of narrowing down the pool of potential job candidates and choosing the one person (or people) that best meets the requirements of the job. The process should also allow prospective candidates to determine for themselves how compatible they are with the job and the company. Selection processes typically involve several stages, with applicants being removed from the applicant pool once they are deemed (or have deemed themselves) unsuitable for the position. The first stage can sometimes occur without the applicant knowing they are being assessed; applicants can be weeded out because of their telephone manner when inquiring about the job or their personal manner when they drop off their resumé. Most often, however, the process begins with the review of application forms or resumés. This is called *pre-screening*. Those who claim to have the requisite characteristics and experience (job and/or educational), move on to the second stage, which typically involves an *interview*.

Interviews may take place over the telephone, via video-conference, or in person – any approach that allows for a two-way exchange of information. While management theory advocates the use of formalized interviews and delaying the decision until after the interview is over (i.e. to avoid bias and snap decisions), in practice, interviews vary substantially (Dessler and Turner, 1992, p. 182). In some organizations, one casual interview in which the manager tries to get an intuitive 'feel' for the candidate may be the norm. In other organizations, a much more formal process may be used. In formal situations, interview questions are often scripted and asked in identical order (i.e. this aids in the comparison of responses among candidates). Other techniques include:

- fact-based questions (i.e. to clarify details on the resumé);
- opinion-based questions (i.e. candidates may be asked about their strengths and weaknesses, or what they think they would do in a particular situation);
- open-ended questions (i.e. which allow the candidate to elaborate on points not previously covered);
- problem-solving questions (i.e. candidates are presented with problems that they are asked to analyse and describe how they would solve them); and
- behaviour-based questions (i.e. candidates are asked to describe previous behaviours).

With respect to the latter, behaviour-based questions are becoming increasingly popular as they provide information that goes beyond the opinions of the candidate, and therefore tend to be less biased (Janz *et al.*, 1986). This type of questioning is based on the belief that the best predictor of future performance is past performance. With behaviour-based interviewing techniques the interviewer typically begins by asking about a particular type of incident (good or bad), and then asks a series of probing questions to find out exactly what the person did, given the circumstances. Examples of behaviour-based questions include:

- Describe a work situation in which you were very disappointed/pleased by the level of customer service you delivered.
- What contributed to the situation?
- What did you do about it?
- What was the outcome?

In addition to the style of questions asked, the format of the formal interview can vary. Examples of common formats include:

- team-based/panel interviews (i.e. interviewers take it in turn to ask questions and record responses);
- multiple-candidate interviews (i.e. the interpersonal skills of the candidates are assessed *vis-à-vis* one another);
- staggered or serial interviews (i.e. the candidate proceeds through a series of interviews, often involving various management representatives and potential co-workers); and
- videotaped/tape-recorded interviews (i.e. allows for review of both the candidate and the interviewer).

Sometimes *testing* is also used as part of the selection process. Testing can pertain to psychological disposition (e.g. attitude towards customer service), aptitude (e.g. the candidate demonstrates his or her potential to perform a task), achievement (e.g. a pen-and-paper test to demonstrate knowledge), and medical tests (e.g. to demonstrate fitness to work). Lastly, *reference checks* should be conducted for those candidates who succeed during the testing and interview stages, before an offer of employment is made.

Contextual Factors Impacting the Supply of Human Resources Available to the Tourism Industry

In developing a comprehensive and effective recruitment and selection strategy (i.e. deciding on the best alternatives identified in the preceding section), many factors need to be taken into consideration. As previously stated, this includes *labour demand* factors such as the number and types of employees required as well the amount of lead time (i.e. the urgency in filling the position(s)). However, issues of *labour supply* are also very important. For example, when labour demand is high and supply is not, a much more aggressive or creative recruitment approach is required. The potential labour supply is affected by the number of qualified employees seeking work in the industry, as well as the retention rate of existing employees. Contextual issues which affect the labour supply include (adapted from Baum 1993):

1. the image and nature of work in the industry;
2. management philosophy and practice (e.g. turnover, pay and benefits, training and development);
3. issues of seasonality;
4. the local labour market (i.e. population, unemployment rates, demographic trends);
5. local cultures; and
6. government policy and priorities (including education).

Each of these factors is now briefly considered in turn.

The Image and Nature of Work in the Industry

In general, the tourism industry has a negative image that affects its ability to attract potential employees. This image is not entirely undeserved and, consequently, many tourism-related businesses are also challenged to retain the quality employees that they do manage to hire. This is true even among students of tourism and hospitality management programmes. Fuelled by the dichotomy between their expectations and the reality of work within the industry, many stay for only a short time before moving on to other careers (Barron and Maxwell, 1993). The industry's image (and hence, supply) problem is related to several factors (Baum *et al.*, 1997, Chol *et al.*, 2000):

* its roots (e.g. links with domestic service and colonial legacy);
* the perception that tourism jobs are unskilled (e.g. the hospitality industry is the largest employer of unskilled labour in many countries);
* poor wages;
* long, erratic, and/or unsociable working hours;

- acceptance by managers of high rates of turnover (i.e. leading to assumptions of impermanence by managers and the lack of job security for employees);
- unpleasant working conditions (i.e. dirty jobs, unattractive uniforms, customer harassment);
- the perception in developing countries of limited opportunities for advancement (i.e. fueled by the widespread use of expatriate labour in senior positions);
- exposure to the industry through first-job (and often naïve) experience; and
- general lack of respect from the public.

While there are sectors, job positions and geographic locations within the tourism industry for which these conditions do not hold true, they are, in fact, common.

> The perceptions are a mirror of reality... The effect of these perceptions is to impose a barrier to employment and employment choice among school and college leavers, parents and career guidance teachers which has been very difficult to counter (Baum *et al.*, 1997, p. 223).

Management Philosophy and Practice (e.g. turnover, pay and benefits, training and development)

Several aspects of common management practice in the tourism industry deserve particular attention with respect to their impact on labour supply. These include attitudes towards turnover, pay and benefits policies, and training and development opportunities. Organizations wishing to increase their labour supply are increasingly paying attention to these issues.

Turnover in the tourism industry can range from a low of 3 to 4 per cent in developing countries to a high of 300 per cent in developed locations (Mahesh 1993, Pizam and Ellis, 1999). The costs of this turnover are staggering. A recent study by the National Restaurant Association found that turnover costs approximately $5000 for hourly employees and $50,000 or more for management (Worcester, 1999). It should go without saying that a high and steady rate of turnover places enormous pressure on the recruitment function. Further, high turnover is often accompanied by a poor reputation as an employer, making it difficult to attract additional quality recruits.

Organizations interested in achieving improved success with staffing are wise to focus on reducing their turnover rates. According to Timo and Davidson (1999, p. 23), addressing turnover 'includes better recruitment and selection practices, higher wages, more training, career advancement, multi-skilling and worker participation'. For example, unrealistic job previews (i.e. when jobs are unrealistically portrayed during the recruitment stage) can lead to high rates of absenteeism and turnover (Pizam and Ellis, 1999). Pizam and Ellis also advocate that turnover can be reduced through the provision of job security (i.e. long-term contracts); effective induction or orientation programmes with an emphasis on long-term employment; appropriate benefits (e.g. retirement plans, group vision, group dental, group life); a focus on internal labour markets or 'promotion from within'; and availability of supervisory and management career-path programmes. Lastly, Baum *et al.* (1997, p. 223) argue 'the rewards and benefits structure of the tourism and hospitality industries can act as a barrier to the recruitment and retention of quality employees' and, further, that skills shortages are linked to the 'reluctance, within some industry sectors and businesses, to invest in the skills development of their key personnel' (p. 223).

Heeding these observations, some hospitality organizations are experimenting with their pay and benefits and training and development policies. For example:

> In 1989, Mandarin Oriental Hotel Group ... launched a $10M profit-sharing scheme for 1700 of its 1900 employees. The incentive package includes offering the employees free shares in the group, increased annual bonuses and home mortgage subsidies. The Hong Kong Hilton spent $20M on four-month bonuses, overseas training programmes and incentives such as helicopter rides for model employees. The Peninsula substantially increased salaries and wages for the group employees. These measures were geared up for increased competition for labour, especially the need to retain staff at a time when the unemployment rate is below 2% and more new hotels are in the development stage. (Heung, 1993, p. 168)

Issues of Seasonality

While the aforementioned strategies can be beneficial for organizations with a relatively constant level of consumer demand, many tourism destinations experience extreme seasonal fluctuations. This results in the challenge of having to ramp up employee numbers during the peak(s) and drop them back during the valley(s). These fluctuations make it difficult for operations to 'attract and keep trained tourism personnel and compete with year-round ... resorts' (Twining-Ward and Baum, 1998, p. 137). It can also make it particularly difficult to offer a consistently high level of service quality. In order to address staffing issues in seasonal locations, some tourism businesses have partnered with others with opposite demand cycles. For example, a number of seasonal Irish hotels have collaborated with operations in Switzerland (Baum and Hagen, 1999, p. 310). Twining-Ward and Baum found the same solution being used in the Baltic islands: 'the only feasible way around this problem seems to be to develop reciprocal personnel schemes with winter resorts elsewhere in the region' (p. 139). Another solution has been to recruit migrant workers during peak seasons. In such circumstances, however, the cost of living and lack of affordable housing can serve as major deterrents. In some locations, employers have supported this strategy (either independently or as a community), with food subsidies and ensuring the availability of decent, affordable accommodation (Baum and Hagen, 1999, p. 311).

Lastly, the use of automated human resource information systems (HRIS) have been found to be useful in keeping track of past employees who enjoy seasonal work, and in re-hiring them each year for the peak season. For example, during the Calgary Stampede, a major annual tourism event in Alberta, Canada, the number of employees swells from 230 full-time, permanent employees to over 3000 during the event itself. Their HRIS automatically generates nearly 2000 letters with an invitation to re-apply, which are sent to successful past employees each year (Farber Canziani, 1999, p. 97).

The Local Labour Market (i.e. population, unemployment rates, demographic trends)

The smaller the labour market from which an organization has to generate a pool of potential employees, the more challenging the staffing function. The size of the labour market is affected by several factors. Most obvious is the size of the population within which the business is located. Tourism enterprises located in remote or peripheral areas can be particularly challenged to attract a quality workforce. The unemployment rate can also dramatically affect the availability of labour. Within developed countries, expanding economies have resulted in a significant reduction in the number of people seeking jobs in the tourism industry.

Demographic trends are also important, particularly given the industry's reliance on younger workers. 'Typically, young people (under 24) dominate the hotel workforce, choosing this type of work for reasons of ease of entry, travel opportunities, variety and friendliness' (Timo and Davidson, 1999, p. 22). Organizations wishing to attract and retain younger workers need to be aware of these reasons and direct resources accordingly. Social events, a fun working atmosphere and approachable management are important elements of such a strategy. When numbers of younger workers are in decline, the industry increases its focus on immigrants and older workers. Doing so effectively requires managers to become much more sensitive to issues of culture and age. Describing those attracted to the industry, Baum *et al.* (1997, p. 223) noted, 'many entrants to the sector do so with assumptions of impermanence – this is work to be undertaken on the way to somewhere else, a first exposure to the demands of the workforce but one to be shed when better opportunities arise elsewhere in the economy'.

Local Cultures and Tradition

Culture and tradition can dramatically influence the willingness of people to seek jobs in the tourism industry. Religion and local custom can explicitly restrict some kinds of work and working conditions (i.e. particularly when alcohol or revealing dress is involved). Culture can also affect the level of prestige and awareness that is associated with tourism jobs. During China's Cultural Revolution, for example, people were taught that service work was demeaning (Huyton and Sutton, 1996). Due to travel and economic restrictions, they also had little exposure to first-class service. Further, Communist ideology taught unquestioning obedience. In order to counter these cultural influences (i.e. develop a large, empowered, service-oriented workforce within China), tourism enterprises such as Holiday Inn Corporation (Asia/Pacific) have established training schools within the country. Large-scale recruitment campaigns and job fairs are also held to help give 'potential recruits first-hand knowledge about hotel work' and the chance to 'inquire about job and career opportunities directly from the hotel's existing staff and executives' (Heung, 1993, p. 170).

Government Policy and Priorities (including education)

With growing recognition of the importance and complexity of the human factor in supporting the tourism industry, the need for government involvement has also been acknowledged. For example, according to Inskeep (1991, p. 431) 'there needs to be a co-ordination among national, regional, metropolitan and local levels of government on policy and planning and in developing infrastructure ... and between the public and private sectors at each level'.

Government policies related to the supply of labour for the tourism industry include employment standards (e.g. hours of work, minimum wage), tax incentives (e.g. to encourage hiring or training programmes), immigration laws (e.g. numbers and types of immigrants), educational policy (e.g. the availability of hospitality and tourism programmes, the length of the school year), transportation issues (e.g. ease of access to the recruitment and/or employment site, the availability of public transit), housing policy (e.g. the availability of affordable housing), and unemployment support. Tourism investors should be aware of relevant national and regional policies and, where necessary, should collectively lobby to ensure that they are supportive of the tourism context.

In summary, staffing is a critical human resource activity. The ability of the tourism industry to provide an appropriately high level of service is dependent upon it. Effective recruitment and selection strategies are developed with consideration of many factors, including those that relate to the demand for labour (e.g. numbers, skills, timing) and those that relate to the supply (e.g. industry image, management philosophy and practice, seasonality, local labour market, local cultures, government policy).

THE CASE: WHISTLER, CANADA

Located in the Coast Mountains of British Columbia, 75 miles from Vancouver, Whistler Village attracts more than 1.9 million visitors annually. In 1969, Whistler Mountain was a virtually unknown, low-capacity ski destination with minimal amenities. Today, Whistler is home to approximately 8600 permanent residents, 115 accommodation businesses (hotels/condos/bed&breakfasts), 93 restaurants, lounges and bars, and 207 retail shops (Whistler Resort Fact Sheet, 1998/1999). Demand is spread fairly evenly over both the winter and summer months; however, swings in the shoulder seasons are dramatic. The average number of visitors ranges from a low of approximately 5000/day in October and November to over 15,000/day in February and August (Whistler Quick Stats, 1997/98). Accommodating these fluctuations effectively, while maintaining a high level of customer service, is an ongoing challenge for the many businesses that are located in the Village – a challenge that is taken very seriously.

For the past seven years, Whistler has been voted the 'best ski resort in North America' by *Mountain Sports & Living* magazine (Whistler Resort Association). While its skiing facilities and scenery typically receive top scores, Whistler has also been recognized for the high level of service and value that guests receive. In 1999, Canadian Pacific's Chateau Whistler Resort was also rated the 'number one ski resort hotel in North America'.

This success can be attributed in large measure to the priorities of several of Whistler's most influential community organizations (i.e. the Whistler Resort Association – now known as Tourism Whistler, the Whistler Chamber of Commerce and the Whistler Housing Authority) as well as to the human resource practices of Whistler's major tourism businesses (e.g. Whistler & Blackcomb Mountains, Chateau Whistler). To begin, each of these community organizations and their link to employee recruitment and retention are described briefly.

Whistler Resort Association

The Whistler Resort Association (WRA) is a not-for-profit organization that is charged with 'marketing Whistler to the world'. Its efforts not only attract tourists, but potential employees also. The WRA operates a central reservation booking service, information centres, the Whistler Conference Centre and the Whistler Golf Club. A priority of the association is customer service. According to Kim Forbes, past Director, 'we want excellent customer service from the moment you get into town'. The WRA employs about 110 employees in its peak season, the summer.

Finding qualified hourly employees is not a problem for the Association and is handled by advertising in the local paper. Employees are also cross-trained to allow for skill transfer between summer and winter jobs. To retain these employees, the Association endeavours to create a family atmosphere. Employee benefits include ski passes, monthly events organized by a social committee and pizza parties.

Finding good middle and senior management is much more difficult, as is keeping them. In 1997 all of the senior management positions in the Association 'turned'. This was attributed in part to the salary differential between management jobs in Whistler and Vancouver and the higher local cost of living. To fill these positions, advertisements are placed in Vancouver and national newspapers. Recruitment firms are also used for hard-to-fill sales and marketing positions. Shortlisted candidates are interviewed and given a tour of the surrounding area as an enticement. The Association also claims to offer the best benefits package in the Village (including dental, medical, life insurance and a retirement savings plan).

Whistler Chamber of Commerce

Given that the WRA markets the town, Whistler's Chamber of Commerce is able to focus on supporting other needs of area businesses. One of their earliest initiatives was the establishment of an Employment Centre which co-ordinates job postings and interview schedules. In the early 1990s they also began to address training issues, recognizing that if local businesses had training support the number and quality of potential employees would increase dramatically. Ultimately, the Chamber partnered with the Canadian Federal Government to launch a comprehensive training programme, and generated enough money to build a $200,000 training centre. Most recently, they surveyed employers and held a roundtable forum to discuss training needs. Current plans include hiring a training co-ordinator for the Village. This individual will plan and offer centralized training, as well as co-ordinate the sharing of training information and opportunities between local businesses.

Whistler Housing Authority

The Whistler Housing Authority's (WHA) mandate is to regulate the development of housing. Of primary concern is the availability of affordable housing, particularly for those who want to live and work in the community. With average prices of $600,000–$800,000 for a typical three- to four-bedroom suburban home, home ownership is not an option for many. The answer to the problem, according to Tim Wake of the Whistler Housing Authority, is to work closely with employers and to implement a solution which results in a fully integrated community (i.e. as opposed to developing an 'employee district' or having few employees actually living in the Village). Strategies implemented in Whistler to help accomplish this goal include:

- encouraging the development of suites/basement apartments in single family homes (there are now approximately 1000);
- having the Municipality build employee-only rental accommodation (i.e. by leasing crown land);

- facilitating the development of employee-only housing by private developers;
- arranging the lease of WHA properties and private homes to employers, who in turn sublet them to their staff (i.e. homeowners are guaranteed rent and the return of the home in good condition);
- implementing a development surcharge (e.g. developers must build one employee bed or contribute $5000 for every hotel room or 50 square metres of commercial space built). By 1996 this fund had generated approximately $7 million to fund the development of rental accommodation;
- building one-, two- and three-bedroom homes for purchase at 0.5 to 0.75 market value, with restricted resale and rental conditions (a waiting-list system was used to prioritize buyers).

Taken together, these organizations provide an extremely positive context within which Whistler's tourism enterprises recruit and select their staff. Two of these enterprises, and their respective recruitment and selection issues and strategies, are profiled next.

Whistler & Blackcomb Mountains: Intrawest Corporation

Whistler & Blackcomb Mountains (the Mountain) is owned by Intrawest, a publicly traded mountain resort and recreational real-estate development firm. Intrawest's interests are primarily North American although it also has an alliance with Compagnie des Alpes (CDA) with operations throughout France.

The Mountain is the largest employer in Whistler and its products and services include ski-lifts, retail outlets, food and beverage, and ski schools. The number of employees ranges from just under 1000 in the summer to almost 5000 during the winter peak season. Of these, approximately 400 are permanent full-time staff. For the winter season, the remaining staff are comprised of approximately 1400 returning employees, 1400 new employees, 1400 volunteers (new and returning) and 50 exchange positions arranged with ski resorts in Australia and New Zealand. In-season, turnover at the Mountain is very low (about 14 per cent) and their goal is to bring this down even further (to about 10 per cent).

Informing the Mountain's human resource practices are a number of guiding principles. Intrawest's stated values include a focus on teamwork, a passion for excellence, spontaneous celebration, and 'creating a culture and environment in which the human spirit will soar' (Employee Handbook, 1998/1999). The human resource department's (known as the Employee Experience Department's) mission is 'to promote the best mountain experience for our past, present and potential employees'. Recognizing the impact of word-of-mouth advertising on their ability to recruit, the Mountain endeavours to ensure the satisfaction of their employees; 'happy current employees = longer retention in the company'; 'happy past employees = great word-of-mouth, and plentiful supply of future employees' (Division Direction, 1998/1999). The department also has what they refer to as 'a big, hairy, audacious goal', which is to be recognized as an 'employer of choice' by the year 2003. Linked to this goal is a recruitment strategy that emphasizes attitude (e.g. 'we hire for attitude and train for skill') and an attractive benefits programme (Ahrens, 1998).

Full-time employees and volunteers (who work at least one day a week) receive a free ski pass, a 50 per cent discount on food and beverage, 50 per cent off lessons, a 10 per cent retail discount and a uniform. Unlike many organizations, the Mountain's ns are considered a benefit. Helping their employees feel proud and comfortable (warm and dry) while at work is an explicit objective, one on which the company recently spent approximately $500,000 (i.e. in uniform upgrades). First-time employees are also eligible for guaranteed staff accommodation for which they pay $8 to $15 a day. This benefit is regarded as 'absolutely key' to the Mountain's success: 'employees need a place to sleep and it's where your culture lives – it is everything' (Ahrens, 1998). Other benefits include a comprehensive medical, insurance and stock-purchase plan, participation in international exchange programmes, skiing privileges at other Intrawest properties, participation in health and wellness programmes, an equipment allowance of $700 per year and regular staff celebrations. With all these benefits the Mountain is a popular place to work. Their biggest recruitment challenge is effectively processing thousands of applicants, while projecting an image consistent with their values – caring and fun. Recruitment activities include sending letters and an occasional newsletter to all previous employees and volunteers, holding employee reunions, advertising in the local Whistler paper (as a courtesy), word-of-mouth, and sending posters to colleges and universities across Canada. The posters profile the mountain, covered in snow, with slogans such as 'WORK HARD. PLAY HARDER.' and 'THIS COULD BE YOUR OFFICE. THE BEST PART IS THE RIDE HOME.' Another approach involves free advertising. The need to hire thousands is considered newsworthy and so the Mountain is profiled each fall on BC television and radio news programmes.

Selection occurs over a six-week interview period from mid-September to the end of October. During this time, previous successful employees and volunteers are encouraged to arrange their re-employment over the phone. Also, through an arrangement with the WRA, many employees who work at the Whistler Golf Course in the summer, switch to the Mountain in the winter: 'we share the workforce – they work the slopes in the winter and the golf courses in the summer – we both win' (Ahrens, 1998). New employees, however, must go through a detailed selection process which begins with an innovative pre-screening interview.

Applicants are asked to phone to make an appointment for an interview (many are arranged the same day), and to bring a current resumé and social insurance number or working visa with them. A well-advertised job hotline provides details of the available positions. Upon arriving at the interview site, applicants first encounter an enthusiastic 'greeter'. This person welcomes them and asks them to wait in the reception area – videos, popcorn and pictures of staff having fun help create a relaxed and fun atmosphere. The greeter then enters each applicant's name into a computer file and the selection process begins. As the person waits, the greeter observes him or her unobtrusively and enters comments into the file. These comments may pertain to demeanour as well as to interactions with others. Sometimes a Mountain employee may be 'planted' in the waiting-room to engage the applicants in conversation, asking what job they're hoping to get and why they are interested in applying. Another technique is to have a game out in the middle of the waiting-room – such as Twister – to see who decides to play. If they don't do so automatically, the greeter or the 'plant' might start the game and encourage others to join in. People who don't participate are often considered not outgoing enough for the job.

The purpose of the first interview is to weed out any applicants who obviously don't fit the desired profile and to determine in which area of the operation each suitable candidate is most interested in working. Those who are successful go on to at least one further interview with the management in their chosen areas. Each successive interviewer has access to the comments made by the previous ones (via computer file), including the greeter. Interviewers post their reactions, suggest questions that might be asked at the next stage, and issues to double-check. Group interviews may also be used as an additional check of interpersonal skills. At the end of the final interview candidates are given a card with a phone number and a date and time when they are to call back. This is done because many applicants don't have accommodation in Whistler and can be difficult to locate. The final step involves reference checks – no employee is hired without one, even those who come from outside Canada. When the applicants call back, those who are successful are told when to come for their orientation.

Chateau Whistler Resort: Candian Pacific Hotels and Resorts

Canadian Pacific Hotels and Resorts Inc. (CPH) recently entered into an agreement with Fairmont Hotel Management to create a new management company, Fairmont Hotels & Resorts Inc. The new entity has landmark hotels across Canada and the US, as well as Princess Resort properties in the US, Bermuda, Barbados and Acapulco. CPH places tremendous value on its people. During a 1997 conference of its human resource managers, it was repeatedly stressed that by focusing on employee morale, commitment and retention, customer and investor value would be maximized. Key 'strategic thrusts' were also identified, including 'becoming an employer of choice' and 'focusing on management succession'.

The Chateau, Whistler's flagship hotel, has 558 guest rooms, 28,000 square feet of meeting space, a health club and spa, and a golf course. Staffing levels fluctuate between approximately 250 employees, during the fall, to 640 employees during the winter months. Turnover at the Chateau has been considered problematic (i.e. in-season turnover ranges from 80 to 90 per cent for staff and is also high for managers. In 1997 the entire human resources department turned.) Factors contributing to this turnover were identified by the previous human resource director, Carole Gosse, as including:

- Whistler's high cost of living and lack of affordable housing;
- lack of work satisfaction where physical requirements are high (e.g. housekeeping, stewarding);
- boredom during the 'valleys';
- burn-out during the 'peaks';
- difficulty balancing career and lifestyle; and
- unrealistic corporate expectations.

Elaborating on this last point the director suggested that 'On a corporate level, I don't think resorts are well understood.' She explained that their monthly financial targets, as a percentage of sales, were the same across the chain, regardless of location (i.e. city centre or resort). Consequently, these targets failed to take into account issues unique to a resort location. For example, Carole was frustrated by pressure to reduce labour costs during the fall shoulder season. While sales were slower during this time, this was also when staff used up their accumulated holidays, and when recruitment and training costs were at their peak. The director also described a turnover cycle (i.e. a negative spiral with an ever-increasing rate of turnover) that they were in the process of addressing. This cycle began with a high rate of turnover, which in turn resulted in many operational challenges:

- departments find it challenging to maintain adequate staffing levels;
- existing staff are overworked;
- service problems arise and 'fire-fighting' ensues;
- managers are unable to delegate as much as they'd like;
- the constant influx of newly hired staff require attention and training;
- management turnover goes up;
- new managers make changes in departmental priorities;
- employee stress increases; and
- staff turnover increases.

Contributing to this negative spiral was the Chateau's past approach to recruitment and selection. The director explained that, traditionally, the Chateau would hold a job fair each November and hire 'the best available of those looking for work'. However, the applicants tended to be skiers and boarders and were not reliable; 'absenteeism would skyrocket whenever there was fresh powder [snow]'; 'If you asked [in an interview] why they were here it was always for the skiing – nothing about a career with the company or in the hospitality industry.' Recognizing the link between their own recruitment and selection practices and their high levels of absenteeism and turnover, the Chateau changed its approach.

One tactic was a reduction in the number of types of positions (e.g. all food and beverage positions were combined into one, all guest service agents were cross-trained in reservations, front desk and switchboard). Not only did this reduce the number of 'types' of people that needed to be hired and employed at any one time, but it also created much more scheduling flexibility. Other elements of the Chateau's new approach included:

- tracking turnover and departmental forecasts on a monthly basis;
- developing customized recruitment strategies for each department or position;
- offering $50.00 to employees who 'refer a friend' and another $50 if the friend stays for six months;
- hiring volunteers for the golf course (volunteers are provided with free golf);
- holding two annual job fairs (Whistler in October and Vancouver in May);
- hiring the best of the locals;
- conducting two annual recruitment trips to Canadian colleges and universities with hospitality management programmes (25 programmes);
- marketing the Chateau as a 'training centre';
- cultivating relationships with internationally renowned hotel management schools;
- increasing participation in university co-op programmes;
- cultivating a partnership with the local high school for help during peak months;
- advertising in ethnic newspapers in Vancouver and the surrounding area;
- encouraging and maintaining internal succession planning;
- encouraging and co-ordinating employee transfers from sister properties with opposite peak seasons;
- exploring overseas recruiting (i.e. to increase pool of candidates with well-developed culinary and language skills – German and Japanese);
- developing an internet job board;
- developing a competitive benefits programme (e.g. discounted ski and golf passes, housing allowances, transportation subsidies, education allowances, day care subsidies, clothing allowances);

- establishing an 'Activities and Communications Co-ordinator' (i.e. to organize staff parties and meetings, publish an employee newsletter, co-ordinate employee award programmes and recognition events, provide information on housing and shopping, and organize social events – movie nights, bowling etc.); and
- advertising employment opportunities in economically depressed areas of Canada.

With respect to the latter, the director was very pleased with their success recruiting in Canada's Eastern provinces where she found an 'excellent work ethic and spirit' as well as a relatively high rate of unemployment. The recruitment approach included advertising in local newspapers, getting free press from regional television news programmes, holding a job fair over two or three days (approximately 150 potential candidates were identified), holding follow-up structured telephone interviews (once back in Whistler), reference checks and mailed contracts (to be signed and returned). Using this approach, twenty people were hired from a 1998 job fair in St. John's, all of whom were still with the company a year later. In order to support their retention and improve similar recruitment efforts, focus groups were also convened with the new hires shortly after their arrival. The biggest concerns identified pertained to the lack of information they had received about the high cost of living and the difficulty associated with finding affordable housing. Although in its early stages, the human resources director was very pleased with the impact these strategies were having on their staffing and retention challenge.

Discussion and Conclusions

In this section the strategies and contextual factors that were identified in the literature review are brought together with those that were evident in the associations and businesses profiled within the Whistler case study. The chapter concludes with generic recommendations for recruitment and selection in the tourism industry.

Recruitment

The businesses profiled used both internal and external recruitment strategies. One common internal strategy was the use of transfers from internal sources (i.e. sister properties with opposite demand cycles, internal succession planning). In addition, the Mountain was able to cover off approximately 50 per cent of its annual hiring by attracting back past employees and volunteers. This approach was supported through a sophisticated human resource information system as well as a management philosophy that fostered employee satisfaction and the development of long-term relationships with seasonal employees (e.g. a positive working experience, newsletters, reunions). Through their internal recruitment strategies, the Mountain and the Chateau minimized the number of external recruits required, as well as associated orientation and training costs. This practice can also contribute to a culture in which employees feel valued.

Common external strategies included advertising in newspapers, local job fairs, visits to educational institutions, co-op placements, employee referrals, and unsolicited resumés. Innovative strategies included a phone 'hot line' with job listings, targeting recruits in areas of high unemployment, taking advantage of free news coverage, partnering with other employers (both within Whistler and elsewhere) with opposite demand cycles for employee exchanges, holding job fairs in major cities, advertising in ethnic newspapers in neighbouring communities, and focusing on people with a long-term commitment to the industry. Another interesting strategy used by both companies was to recruit volunteers.

Selection

The predominant selection strategies used included pre-screening, interviews and reference/visa checks. Both employers favoured serial interviews with some structured elements. Innovations in selection included using 'greeters' and 'plants' as a pre-screening device, the use of a computer system to track each employee through the process, the use of games as part of the pre-screening process (e.g. Twister), holding follow-up interviews over the phone and providing applicants with a 'call-back'card to facilitate making offers of employment. Both employers also stressed the importance of focusing on attitude and commitment (with an expectation that job training would follow).

The Image and Nature of Work in the Industry

Within Whistler there was a strong sense of co-operation and community in addressing staffing issues. There also appeared to be an understanding that Whistler's success depended on the ability of all staff, from the entire Village, to exceed customer expectations. As a result, local associations and businesses worked hand-in-hand in promoting the Village, developing pride in the workforce and providing quality employment and developmental opportunities. In addition, both the Mountain and the Chateau had identified becoming an 'employer of choice' as a significant goal. This approach likely increased the size of the labour pool from which they could make their selection decisions.

Management Practice (e.g. turnover, pay and benefits, training and development)

Staff turnover was considered an extremely important issue by the Mountain and the Chateau; both had targeted achieving reductions in their turnover rates. Low rates of staff turnover were associated by these employers with well-developed recruitment and selection processes, generous benefits, opportunities for development and a focus on hiring employees with a long-term commitment to the industry. The Chateau, in particular, had recognized the need to confront its negative turnover spiral and had implemented substantial changes in its selection and recruitment processes in order to do so.

Issues of Seasonality

Both the Mountain and the Chateau experienced significant seasonal swings in demand. Strategies for dealing with these swings included aggressive recruitment campaigns in the fall, hiring seasonal employees and volunteers during peak months, cross-training employees for multiple roles, co-operating with local and international businesses with opposite demand cycles and using the shoulder seasons for staff holidays and training.

The Local Labour Market (i.e. population, unemployment rates, demographic trends)

The local permanent population within Whistler was small (8600). As a result, seasonal employees had to be attracted to the resort (which was achieved in part through the WRA as well as individual recruitment efforts). In addition, potential employees from neighbouring communities (i.e. a 45-minute drive) were targeted through local ethnic newspapers. Unfortunately, this sometimes resulted in the unavailability of key staff (i.e. when either of the two roads coming in or out of the resort were blocked – through mud or snow slide). Benefits such as transportation subsidies were used to reduce the cost of commuting. Considerable attention was also paid to the availability of affordable housing.

In terms of demographics, many of Whistler's potential labour pool were young. The Mountain specifically targeted younger employees with the right attitude, and used its recruitment processes to identify those with an appetite for creativity and fun. Both the Mountain and the Chateau considered their benefits programmes and social events as being particularly important in attracting and retaining young employees.

Local Cultures

The local culture appeared to be very supportive of tourism and those who worked in the industry. This can probably be attributed in part to the area's international reputation and prestige, the fact that Whistler was created as a tourist destination and the strength of the local associations (e.g. the WRA, Chamber of Commerce and the WHA). Policies that restricted development beyond a certain level, and the work of the WHA in integrating those employed in the tourism industry with the rest of the population, contributed greatly to this culture. In addition, the widespread practice of hiring volunteers, in return for golfing and skiing privileges, resulted in the hiring of many from the local community, who essentially became ambassadors for the area.

Government Policy and Priorities (including education)

The case study offers an excellent example of collaboration between various levels of government and tourism enterprises, in the interests of supporting tourism. Most significant was Whistler's well-co-ordinated efforts at marketing, recruitment, training and the provision of affordable housing. Whistler was also fortunate to be located in a province with many colleges and universities which offered programmes in hospitality, tourism and recreation management. Both the Mountain and the Chateau specifically targeted students from these programmes, as well as elsewhere in Canada and internationally. The Chateau also established a programme, with the local high school, for hiring students into simplified jobs during the peak months.

CONCLUSION

The effective recruitment and selection of employees is a critical issue for tourism enterprises. In developing an effective strategy, organizations must clearly identify their labour needs (e.g. numbers, types and timing) as well as deciding upon appropriate recruitment sources and approaches (i.e. internal, external, or a combination) and the right selection approach (e.g. pre-screening, interview questions and format). Further, organizations should develop their strategies with careful consideration of contextual factors which can have a dramatic impact upon potential labour supply. These contextual factors include: the image and nature of work in the industry; management philosophy and practice, including attitudes towards turnover, pay and benefits, training and development; seasonality; the size and nature of the local labour market; local cultures and the degree of support for the tourism industry; and government policies and priorities with respect to employment, transportation, housing and education. When supply is short, the development of an effective recruitment and selection strategy becomes significantly more challenging.

Organizations can affect the size and the quality of the labour supply in several ways. They can contribute to improving the image and nature of work in the tourism industry by becoming 'employers of choice'. This goal will be furthered through forward thinking management practices that emphasize the creation of positive employee experiences, long-term employment commitments (even for employees who are hired on a seasonal basis), generous and creative benefits packages, and training and development opportunities. Employers can also target potential employees who themselves have a long-term commitment to the industry (e.g. students within hospitality programmes). The impact of seasonality can be reduced by hiring back previous employees, developing co-operative arrangements with employers in areas with opposite demand cycles, and using the off-season for accumulated staff holidays. When the size of the local labour market is small, employers must recruit more broadly. Targeting the closest sizeable population, or communities with low employment rates, are strategies that may prove successful. Employers must also be sensitive to the needs of the targeted demographic group. Younger employees are often looking for a sociable and fun working environment which employers can help foster. With respect to the local culture, employers can help by being sensitive to local concerns, which can be achieved by being well-connected with local associations and by involving locals in the business (e.g. through volunteer positions). Lastly, by collaborating with other employers, industry associations and government agencies, employers can help influence policies related to employment, housing, transportation and education. Following these suggestions should go a long way in helping the industry mitigate the impact of the millennium time-bomb.

ACKNOWLEDGEMENTS

I am grateful for the generous support I received from Whistler's associations and businesses in the completion of this study: Gord Ahrens (Intrawest), Kim Forbes (formerly with Whistler Resort Association (now known as Tourism Whistler)), Carole Gosse (formerly with Chateau Whistler), Thelma Johnstone (Whistler Chamber of Commerce) and Tim Wake (Whistler Housing Authority).

SELF-ASSESSMENT QUESTIONS

1. Identify what you believe to be the three most challenging recruitment and selection issues facing tourism businesses in resort communities today. Provide supporting arguments.
2. What specific recruitment or selection strategies would you advise a resort operator to implement in response to each of these challenges?
3. Outline the major steps involved in recruitment and selection. For each step, provide an innovative example. Draw your examples from the chapter and/or your own experience.
4. Critique the recruitment and selection approach used at Whistler & Blackcomb Mountains. What are its strengths? What, if anything, would you change?

5. Describe the turnover cycle experienced at the Chateau Whistler and critique their response. Which of the Chateau's identified strategies do you think will be most successful? What, if anything, would you change?

REFERENCES

Ahrens, G. (1998) Interview transcripts. Whistler, BC.
Barron, P. and Maxwell, G. (1993) 'Hospitality management students' image of the hospitality industry'. *International Journal of Contemporary Hospitality Management*, **5**(5), v–viii.
Baum, T. (1993) *Human Resource Issues in International Tourism* (ed. T. Baum). Oxford: Butterworth-Heinemann.
Baum, T., Amoah, V. and Spivack, S. (1997) 'Policy dimensions of human resource management in the tourism and hospitality industries'. *International Journal of Contemporary Hospitality Management*, **9**(5/6), 221–9.
Baum, T. and Hagen, L. (1999) 'Responses to seasonality: the experiences of peripheral destinations'. *International Journal of Tourism Research*, **1**, 299–312.
Chol, J., Woods, R. and Murrmann, S. (2000) 'International labor markets and the migration of labor forces as an alternative solution for labor shortages in the hospitality industry'. *International Journal of Contemporary Hospitality Management*, **12**(1), 61–6.
D'Annunzio-Green, N. (1997) 'Developing international managers in the hospitality industry'. *International Journal of Contemporary Hospitality Management*, **9**(5/6), 199–208.
D'Annunzio-Green, N., Maxwell, G. and Watson, S. (2000) 'Human resource issues in international hospitality, travel and tourism: a snapshot'. *International Journal of Contemporary Hospitality Management*, **12**(3), 215–16.
Dessler, G. and Turner, A. (1992) *Human Resource Management in Canada*. Scarborough Ontario: Prentice-Hall.
Division Direction (1998/1999) Whistler and Blackcomb Mountains, Employee Experience Department, Whistler, BC.
Employee Handbook (1998/1999) Whistler and Blackcomb Mountains, Employee Experience Department, Whistler, BC.
Farber Canziani, B. (1999) 'Information technology for human resources', in Darren Lee-Ross (ed.) *HRM in Tourism and Hospitality*. London: Cassell, pp. 92–108.
Heung, V. (1993) 'Hong Kong', in T. Baum (ed.) *Human Resource Issues in International Tourism*. Oxford: Butterworth-Heinemann, pp. 161–76.
Huyton, J. and Sutton, J. (1996) 'Employee perceptions of the hotel sector in the People's Republic of China'. *International Journal of Contemporary Hospitality Management*, **8**(1), 22–8.
Inskeep, E. (1991) *Tourism Planning*. New York: Van Nostrand Reinhold.
Janz, T., Hellervik, L. and Gilmore, D. (1986) *Behaviour Description Interviewing*. Boston: Allyn and Bacon.
Mahesh, V. (1993) 'Human resource planning and development: micro and macro models for effective growth in tourism', in T. Baum (ed.) *Human Resource Issues in International Tourism*. Oxford: Butterworth-Heinemann, pp. 30–46.
Pizam, A. and Ellis, T. (1999) 'Absenteeism and turnover in the hospitality industry', in Darren Lee-Ross (ed.) *HRM in Tourism and Hospitality*. London: Cassell, pp. 109–131.
Powell, S. and Wood, D. (1999) 'Is recruitment the millennium time bomb for the industry worldwide?' *International Journal of Contemporary Hospitality Management*, **11**(4), 138–9.
Timo, N. and Davidson, M. (1999) 'Flexible labour and human resource management practices in small to medium-sized enterprises: the case of the hotel and tourism industry in Australia', in Darren Lee-Ross (ed.) *HRM in Tourism and Hospitality*. London: Cassell, pp. 17–36.
Twining-Ward, L. and Baum, T. (1998) 'Dilemmas facing mature island destinations: cases from the Baltic', *Progress in Tourism and Hospitality Research*, **4**, 131–40.

Whistler Resort Association, (1997/1998) *Whistler Quick Stats*, Whistler Resort Business Performance Statistics, Department of Research, Whistler, BC, Canada.

Whistler Resort Association, (1998/1999) *Whistler Resort Fact Sheet*. Whistler, BC, Canada.

Worcester, B. (1999) 'The people problem'. *Hotel and Motel Management*, **214**(4), 38-42.

3

A Critique of the Systematic Approach to Recruitment and Selection in an International Hospitality Business

Barrie Humphreys and Kathy Elvin

ABSTRACT

This chapter gives an overview of the areas of recruitment and selection. It is not intended to be a statement of the only way to operate, but rather it suggests types of approaches and processes that have been found to be effective and efficient in practice, both in mainstream human resource management and in the hospitality industry specifically. This overview is followed by a case study looking at how one hotel that is a part of an international chain throughout Australasia operates in the areas of recruitment and selection, followed by a critique of these practices and some suggestions for improvement.

INTRODUCTION

Recruitment and selection is important for any organization, but as Roberts (1999) suggests, more so for the hospitality industry in that 'recruitment and selection of staff appropriate to the present and future needs of the organization is a critical success factor, as often the staff can and do make or break the organization' (1999, p. 66). The overall aim of recruitment and selection should be to obtain, at minimum cost, the number and quality of employees required to satisfy the human resource needs of the organization (Armstrong, 1996; Roberts, 1999). Armstrong (1996) argues that the source and methods chosen for recruitment should encourage only the best applicants to apply, rather than attracting a large number of unsuitable applicants. However, many other authors recommend attracting a large pool of applicants from which the organization can choose the best applicant (Stone, 1998; Torrington and Hall, 1998; Rudman, 1999).

A deciding factor in choosing whether to attract few or many applicants can be the cost. Good recruitment is expensive. Costs are direct, for advertising or travel expenses, or indirect such as staff time. However, bad recruitment is even more costly. Bad recruitment processes are those that are too long, use excessive resources, select poor applicants or result in no applicant being selected. The costs are related to high staff turnover, lower productivity, higher wastage, compromised service quality, increased training and supervision and disruption of employees (Eade, 2000; Rudman, 1999).

Despite the many reasons for getting recruitment right, in many organizations recruitment is just something to be done when a vacancy occurs, either as a result of someone leaving or due to expansion. Recruiting may be the most obvious tactic, but according to Torrington and Hall (1998) it is not necessarily the most appropriate. The need for recruitment should always be assessed and the alternatives to recruitment considered. Some alternatives include making the job part-time, redistributing the work, using a contractor or agency worker or using overtime. That recruitment should not be automatic is the first of three assumptions made by Rudman (1999) about effective recruitment. The second is that recruitment should be job-centred, and, thirdly, he argues that recruitment and selection procedures should be consistently monitored. Decisions about whether to recruit rather than cover the position in some other way can only be taken once the organization is clear about its human resource needs both now and in the future. Roberts (1999) suggests that in order to recruit and select effectively, the organization must first have a sensible human resource plan.

Who is responsible for recruitment? Eade (2000) and Rudman (1999) recommend that the operation is shared between managers and human resource departments, but the responsibility for effective operation should be placed with one person. That person may be from the human resource department or may be a line manager. The important thing is that whoever is responsible should have sufficient authority to enforce standards. This means that they need to be relatively high in the hierarchy. According to Compton and Nankervis (1991) 'in companies of 100 to 200 employees where no personnel specialist may be employed, but the load is too large for one person to handle, the operation could be split up' (p. 62). For example, in the hospitality industry the general manager could recruit all management level staff, the food and beverage manager recruits food and beverage staff and the rooms division manager can recruit reception and housekeeping staff. The immediate supervisor has the advantage in recruiting of knowing the job and therefore is able to assess the applicants' technical ability; they know the work team and should be able to choose a compatible team member (Compton and Nankervis, 1991). In these cases, though, the recruiters may need help with advertising and complying with the law. In light of legislative requirements the organization should have prepared a policy on recruitment. This would be co-ordinated with overall organizational policies, it would be influenced by legislation, union agreements and labour market conditions and it should include a promotion and hiring guideline (Stone, 1998).

An organizational policy on recruitment would also outline the recruitment process, which begins when a vacancy arises. From here the recruitment process would review the job design, the need for replacement and the human resource plan, following this job analysis is conducted, and then terms of appointment and selection criteria methods should be agreed upon (Rudman, 1999). Each of these steps will be discussed as an effective recruitment process is outlined.

The aim of this chapter is to provide an overview of the component parts of a systematic approach to recruitment and selection and outline the essential policies and processes that will enable an organization to choose the right candidates with the right skills at the right time in order to have a positive impact on the organization's profitability and productivity. The chapter will also examine and provide a critique of a case study set in an international context, of an actual recruitment and selection process with a view to suggesting areas for improvement based on recent research in the hospitality area. Areas for improvement will be highlighted with reference to the literature and suggestions made as to the way forward for the organization.

PREPARING TO RECRUIT

Job Analysis

Job analysis is the process by which job descriptions and person specifications are produced. Eade (2000) suggests that in order to operate efficiently the organization needs to be completely aware of the efforts of each of its employees. Job analysis is therefore a vital part of the recruitment and selection process because it provides benchmarks and standards for the protection of both parties: 'job analysis asks what a position is about and why it exists' as well as 'the attributes desired in a person to fill it' (p. 253). The information collected from job analysis has many uses including human resource planning, performance appraisal, training and development and compensation (Stone, 1998). Additionally, the job description and person specification should form the basis of the recruitment and selection process. Rudman (1999) recommends that recruiters consider job descriptions and person specifications as fixed pictures of the job and person and as well as thinking of present organizational requirements recruiters need to consider future possibilities. This inflexibility and closed definition is cited as a reason why less than half of personnel departments use job analysis and its products for recruitment and selection (Torrington and Hall, 1998).

In using the job description and person specification as the basis of the recruitment and selection process, the documents should outline essential and desirable characteristics required of applicants. This is deemed essential to set baseline standards and criteria early in the recruitment process. The job description and person specification should therefore define in specific and measurable terms areas such as skills, knowledge, experience and personal characteristics. Increasingly, competency profiles are also being used by organizations. These define the 'underlying characteristics of a person which results in effective or superior performance' (Torrington and Hall 1998, p. 225).

Sources of Recruits

'The final stage of preparation is to identify possible sources of candidates for this should influence the organization and scope of the recruitment exercise' (Rudman 1999, p. 279). According to Millar *et al.* (1998) the first place from which to source staff is inside the organization. When a vacancy arises current employees should be considered first because internal recruitment is not only a cost-effective option but beneficial in other ways. These benefits include increased employee morale and motivation, a more thorough knowledge of the applicant, an applicant who knows the organization and the fact that an organization would ultimately only need to hire entry-level candidates if a series of successful promotions is possible. There are disadvantages, however, and these include the following: competition for promotion can affect morale; in-breeding can stifle creativity; and innovation and excellent training and development programmes are necessary to enable the promotion potential suggested above.

Some organizations, however, prefer to recruit externally as well as internally, the arguments for external recruitment being: a larger pool of applicants are possible; new blood is introduced; and external applicants have not experienced the internal socialization process. Despite this, it is more difficult to attract and select an unknown applicant. There will be a definite need for training and orientation, and there is a risk of poor selection (Stone, 1998). Internal recruitment methods include advertising internally on notice boards, in newsletters or personal letters. It is important to ensure that the information on all positions should be made available to all interested employees. Additionally, managerial nominations or skill databases can be used to identify suitable employees.

Using employee referrals can be an effective, low-cost method of recruitment because current employees know the job and what the organization requires and are likely to sell the good points of the job to the applicant. However, equal opportunities policies and legislation requirements need to be considered as do possible effects on the person making the referral if the recruit fails to perform or if the referral is rejected. Approaching tertiary institutions or schools to recruit and increase organizational awareness is another popular approach. Methods include making visits, contacting the career adviser or placing advertisements on notice boards. In addition to these, Rudman (1999) identifies work-experience schemes as advantageous to the organization and the student, the work samples contributing to better recruitment decisions. Work and Income New Zealand and Student Job Search are examples of public employment agencies which form a network covering most towns/cities and which act as agents for potential employees/employers. They are particularly concerned with manual and junior positions in administration, clerical and retail areas (Breaugh, 1992, cited in Rotta-Graydon, 1999). Private agencies act upon a detailed briefing from the employer, they produce and arrange advertisements, receive applications and shortlist qualified applicants. From here the organization makes the final selection (Rudman, 1999). These agencies can also be 'useful for organizations which do not themselves have recruitment expertise' (p. 280). In addition, executive search consultants or 'head-hunters' undertake assignments to locate suitable candidates on behalf of the organization. They seldom advertise, preferring to approach people directly. The consultants' fees tend to be high and their activities restricted to senior positions or specialist roles for which there is high demand (Rudman, 1999).

Finally an organization may take advantage of unsolicited applicants. These are often called 'walk-ins', and are people who inquire about employment opportunities which have not been advertised by the organization. They can be a valuable source of recruits as confirmed by Stone (1998) who found that 'walk-ins' performed better than applicants recruited from agencies or newspaper advertisements.

Attracting Applicants

The first stages of the recruitment process are vital because the best person for the job cannot be appointed if they do not apply for it. Moreover, having the best person apply for the job is vital in achieving a successful appointment and the goal of a competent, productive and committed workforce. Advertising is the most obvious methods of attracting recruits, but it may not always be necessary, as other sources of recruits, as mentioned above, are available. In deciding what method to use in finding or attracting applicants, Armstrong (1996) refers to the three criteria of cost, speed and the likelihood of providing good candidates. He proceeds to list the objectives of an advertisement as needing to attract attention, create and maintain interest, and stimulate action. When deciding upon the media for recruitment advertising the advertiser should have carefully considered the target audience (Millar *et al.*, 1998). Boella (1996) suggests that specialist catering and hospitality journals are very effective in targeting the appropriate audience. Readership and circulation information provided by the advertising agent will also assist in assessing the media's effectiveness. Newspaper advertising has large coverage and readership, and another advantage cited in Beardwell and Holden (1994) is that some national and high-profile local papers are an accepted medium for those seeking particular posts. However, the main disadvantages are the cost and wastage, in that many inappropriate applicants are reached. Radio and television are not often used for recruitment due to the expense, especially if only one position needs to be filled. Radio is, however, more effective than television in reaching a specific audience. Alternative advertising media include posters, career exhibitions, conferences or open days. These methods can be useful if the cost is justified or if a larger number of positions were to be filled.

A method which has become more popular recently is using the internet as a source of recruits. Caggiano (1998) estimated that the internet was used by 9.7 per cent of employers for recruiting, which illustrates that it is not yet utilized to its full potential but is certainly recognized as a new and innovative development. Comments made by employers using the internet for recruitment include that it is effective, cheaper, faster and the creative possibilities are endless. Third-party sites, such as www.starchefs.com for restaurant workers, can even do the recruitment on the employers behalf (Caggiano, 1998).

The internet's true recruitment value lies in its immediacy and ability to interact with potential employees. However, there are still limitations. The internet is still evolving, and it would be unwise for organizations to rely on it solely as a method for attracting applicants (Sunoo, 1998). Sunoo also argues that 'it cannot replace background checks, skills tests, face to face interviews and other steps to assess attitudes and behaviour, that are vital to finding qualified employees' (p. 17).

Torrington and Hall (1998) describe the recruitment process as being an 'expensive, time-consuming process with legal pitfalls, so you need some process to monitor the effectiveness of the process' (p. 217). Millar *et al.* (1998) agree, and suggest that evaluation of the recruitment process is necessary to ensure the organization is meeting its strategic business objectives, containing costs, satisfying equal opportunity objectives and improving recruitment efficiency and effectiveness. There are many measures for the effectiveness of the process including the number and quality of applicants generated by a particular source or method, and the quality of those actually employed. A measure of the efficiency of the process includes the acceptance to offer ratio (the number of acceptances measured against the number of offers made) and the cost per applicant (Stone, 1998).

SELECTION

Rudman (1999) defines recruitment as 'attracting a pool of qualified candidates' (1999, p. 284) suggesting that the recruitment process ends as soon as the applications start arriving. However, the vacancy is not yet filled at that point and the decision of who will fill it is yet to be made; this is where the selection process begins. The selection process involves collecting and assessing information about applicants to decide who has the knowledge, skills and attributes required for successful performance on the job (Rudman, 1999).

Traditionally, selection has been viewed as a one-way process, with managers choosing their subordinates. But increasingly, given the high level of competition for good employees, the two-way nature of the process is being accepted, whereby applicants are also choosing their potential employers. As a result, both parties require information, and to facilitate this 'organizations must find ways to put applicants on a more equal footing during the information-gathering and decision-making phases of the selection process' (Rudman, 1999, p. 284). Organizations, now and in the future, must also accept the importance of the applicant in the selection process, realizing that the applicant can also withdraw from the process at any time.

Another point, which organizations should consider, is being able to predict whether, and how well, an applicant will perform on the job and in the organization. This is referred to as predictive validity. Stone explains this as the 'extent to which a predictor (such as level of education and scores on an aptitude test) correlates with criteria identified as measuring job performance (such as measures of productivity)' (1998, p. 214). Reliability, or the consistency of results, of selection methods is also important. For example, the unstructured interview does not often give consistent results because interactions between the interviewer and the applicant vary from interview to interview (Stone, 1998, p. 216).

The chapter will now progress to an examination of the selection process which includes the steps of: receiving applications; shortlisting; job interviews; job previews; occupational tests; references; making the selection decisions; making the appointment; and informing unsuccessful applicants.

Applications for Employment

Many organizations ask applicants to complete an application form that is available on request; others require written applications in which the applicants have more choice regarding the information they provide. Application forms can be tailored specifically to the requirements of the job or the organization and in this way a detailed application form can play a significant part in the selection process. Another advantage is that application forms organize the various applicants' information in a way which enables comparison between applicants and against the job requirements (Boella, 1996; Roberts, 1999).

Rudman (1999) suggests application forms should at least contain key personal data, training and employment history. Moreover, information of any kind that indicates an intention to discriminate should not be collected. Therefore, information such as age, gender, marital status or nationality is not often relevant or job-related and should therefore be avoided.

The curriculum vitae, or resumé, is another source of information about applicants.

They can be requested at the application stage, although it is recommended that an application form be completed also. Rudman (1999) provides a critique of the CV *vis-à-vis* the application form, in that an application form that meets the organization's needs and relates closely to the job will be more useful and easier to handle by the recruiter than a CV containing general and unspecific information.

In addition to the applications received in response to advertising, organizations can receive unsolicited applications. As mentioned, all applicants are possible customers, employees or stakeholders and should therefore be treated courteously. In this case the jobseeker should be asked to complete an application form, should be informed whether or not their CV will be held and whether or not there are future employment possibilities. Additionally, they should be informed if there is no real prospect of future employment. The shortlisting process involves sorting through the application forms and CVs and assessing them against the requirements of the job description and person specification. Following this, the most suitable applicants would be informed that they will be involved in the next stage of the selection process. Shortlisting can be approached in two ways: applications can be checked against basic criteria, such as experience or educational requirements, and applicants that do not meet the criteria may be ruled out; or applicants can be assessed in terms of who should be included rather than excluded, and thus a list can be drawn up of all those who meet the essential criteria determined by the job description and person specification (Torrington and Hall, 1998). Torrington and Hall assert that taking care with shortlisting 'increases the chances of being fair to all applicants and lessens the likelihood of calling inappropriate people for interviews' (p. 219).

Job Interviews

The interview provides the organization with information about the applicant. It predicts how they would perform in the job and it also provides the applicant with information about the organization and job in order to facilitate their decision-making (Torrington and Hall, 1998). The interview, although it is criticized for being unreliable, invalid and subjective, is still the most widely used selection technique (Torrington and Hall, 1998; Stone, 1998). Some of the many criticisms arising from the literature include the fact that interviewers are often unprepared, the same standards are not often applied to each applicant and interviews are therefore inconsistent. Other problems cited by Rudman (1999) include that interviewers can also be biased because they form first impressions, use stereotypes, judge applicants by their appearance, are influenced by applicants with similar biographical data to their own, give more weight to negative information and may fail to appreciate cultural differences.

Lopez (1975) points out that all of the criticisms argue that it is the interviewer, not the interview itself, that is problematic. Riley (1996) supports this view and states that if the interviewer is well trained and conscientious the interview is a useful selection method. Riley also suggests that the opposite is true; a poor interviewer will produce a poor interview. Focusing on this, there are some basic recommendations that can improve an interview's effectiveness. First, the human resource specialists or line managers who conduct interviews should be trained in interview-planning and in assessing applicants in job-related terms (Millar *et al.*, 1998), in order to avoid, or at least reduce, the impact of their own subjective reactions and judgements. Secondly, an interview should be structured. Interviews should follow a predetermined outline with some questions prepared in advance. This will ensure all relevant information is covered systematically and the results will be more consistent and accurate than with an unstructured interview.

Unstructured interviews have been favoured because they are less restrictive, but they are also less consistent. In fact, the structured approach is supported by most research, reasons for this are: an applicant's expectation for the interview to be controlled by the interviewer; it ensures all relevant areas are covered and irrelevant ones are not; it looks professional; and it ensures time is used in the most effective way (Rudman, 1999). Furthermore, structured interviews ensure all applicants are treated equally and so reduce the possibility of discrimination.

There are two types of structured interview – behavioural or situational. Accepting that past behaviour is the best predictor of performance, the behavioural interview asks applicants to describe what they *did* in a particular situation. Situational interviews ask hypothetical questions, such as asking an applicant to describe what they think they *would do* in a specific situation. The applicant's responses are noted and scored against model answers or preferred behaviours. Rudman (1999) notes an increased use of behavioural techniques as organizations turn to more sophisticated selection methods in an attempt to increase predictive validity.

Another type of interview that is increasingly used is the panel interview. These have advantages, including increased reliability and consistency, they can guard against the possibility of bias and discrimination, and several interviewers tend to recall information more accurately than a solitary interviewer. Therefore the improved quality of the selection decision would outweigh the increased financial costs and the additional time and effort it takes to co-ordinate, and review the interview.

Job Previews

Job previews aim to inform the applicants realistically of all aspects of the job, favourable or unfavourable. This could include characteristics of the work to be done, training and development possibilities or even a tour of the work area. By providing applicants with realistic expectations it is shown that job satisfaction improves, early turnover reduces and communication is enhanced (Rudman, 1999).

In addition, applicants can be asked to demonstrate their ability to perform the job, as a 'preview'. The job preview is not a trial period of employment. Therefore, there are fewer legal implications. The applicant simply must be informed that the one- or two-hour preview is a selection method and that their performance in it will assist in making a selection decision. The preview should be paid and the applicant should be asked to display the skills they would need to display on the job. For example, a chef should be asked to cook, thus demonstrating his/her ability and food knowledge. The disadvantage is that an applicant will modify his/her behaviour because he/she is being observed. However, it will quickly become clear if the applicant is not suitable and, alternatively, if he/she performs well the organization will know and expect the applicant to perform at this higher level in the subsequent job role.

Occupational Tests

Torrington and Hall (1998) assert that the use of employment tests for selection is increasing. Reasons for this could be the increased availability of tests or a realization of the importance of accurate prediction of job performance or organizational fit to organizational success (Rudman, 1999). The tests used for selection are called psychometric tests and they provide an objective means of measuring individual skills, knowledge, abilities or characteristics. The main types of tests are *general mental ability*, which measures, for example, an ability to think critically; *specific ability*, which measures, for example, numeracy or manual dexterity; and *personality questionnaires*, which tests for personality traits such as values or learning styles (Rudman, 1999).

There are a number of issues surrounding the use of tests in the selection process, including how valid they are as predictors of future performance, whether they are fair or whether tests disadvantage certain applicants, and finally, that the tests need to be relevant to the assessment of the job skill or personal attribute requirements. Rudman acknowledges these criticisms and recommends that 'tests should be only one of part of the information-gathering and decision-making process' (1999, p. 306). Finally, the appropriateness of tests in the selection process will depend on the size of the organization, the acceptable cost of the selection exercise and the importance of the position being recruited for.

References

Three types of references are available: personal; documentary evidence of educational or profession qualification; and descriptions of work experience by former employers. It is the latter type of reference that is of most use to employers and, if handled properly, references can be a valuable source of information. However, it is important to acknowledge that applicants will not usually suggest a referee unless they know they will volunteer only positive comments. Compton and Nankervis (1991) suggest contacting several referees, such as immediate supervisors, customers or clients, because, as with the panel interview, multiple perspectives are more likely to be accurate. Rudman (1999) suggests preparing questions to ask of the referee to ensure, again, that all applicants are treated equally and that all the information needing to be checked is covered. Additionally, specific information about applicants' skills, abilities or characteristics should be collected and the applicant's permission sought before approaching referees. Recruiters need to consider how much information they need about the applicants, especially considering the limitations and bias that may mislead them into making an incorrect decision. Many organizations choose to conduct reference checks on a very small number of applicants at the final stages of the selection process. This, as well as protecting the privacy of applicants, reduces time and effort spent checking references and reduces the possibility of being mislead into accepting inadequate applicants or rejecting suitable ones (Rudman, 1999).

The Selection Decision

The final step of the selection process is when a decision has to be made between the final few applicants. The purpose of the selection process until now has been to provide information to enable and justify this decision.

Stone (1998) identifies two ways to approach the selection decision; the compensatory and the 'successive hurdles' approach. The compensatory approach is when all of the selection information is considered together, favourable or unfavourable, to gain an overall impression. The argument here is that because not one selection technique is relied upon, the decision should be more accurate. This is however, a time-consuming and expensive approach. The successive hurdles approach is better if there are minimum criteria that the applicants should meet. For this, the applicants progress through the selection techniques, from the most effective technique to the least effective, and applicants who fail to meet the minimum criteria for any hurdle are rejected. By making selection decisions throughout the process the final decision is less complicated. This approach is also very economical if there are many applicants as the best candidate can be identified early (Stone, 1998).

Rudman (1999) reminds managers that despite a systematic and professional approach to selection it is possible that there may be no applicants with the attributes for the job, and the decision may be not to hire anyone. But 'selecting the best person available – which many people seem to use as their recruitment standard – may not provide you with someone who can do the job!' (Rudman, 1999, p. 319). This quote illustrates the complexities and frustrations inherent in the recruitment and selection process.

THE COACHMAN HOTELS RECRUITMENT AND SELECTION PROCESS

The case study examines the processes adopted by a hotel to recruit and select staff. The information was gathered through semi-structured interviews and observation over a three-month period. The Coachman Hotel is part of the International Circle Hotel Group that operates throughout Australasia. Each hotel has autonomy in the operation of its human resource procedures. The Coachman Hotel employs 90 staff and is characteristic of the hospitality industry in that a high level of turnover is experienced. The person responsible for the recruitment and selection process at the Coachman Hotel is the assistant manager who performs the role in conjunction with that of Rooms Division Manager. The general manager and the food and beverage manager have also been involved in the recruitment and selection process.

Compton and Nankervis (1991) state that in organizations without personnel specialists or where the load is too large the function could be split up. At the Coachman the process is not split up, instead, all three managers are involved in interviewing the applicants consecutively. All three have an input into selection decisions and are consulted in designing job descriptions and person specifications when necessary. The aim of the Coachman recruitment and selection process is to employ the right type of person for the job. This person should be able to perform the requirements of the job to the required standards as well as fit in well with the organization's culture, and, ideally, would be committed to, and able to, demonstrate excellence in providing hospitality service.

The recruitment process that currently operates at the Coachman is as follows: when a vacancy occurs, an 'ideal person' is outlined, verbally, to those who will be interviewing, and the job description is reviewed (if it is a senior position). The position is advertised or an employment agency is used. Unsolicited applications, previous applicants and management or employee recommendations are also considered at this stage. It is at this point, when applications are received, that the recruitment process ends and selection begins.

The process outlined above is a guide only, and many situational factors, such as manager availability, may influence it. In particular, the general manager has been increasingly involved and often this has resulted in a digression from normally accepted procedures as specified by the assistant manager. An example of this is that job advertisements have been placed before other sources are explored, and this can increase costs and affect the perception of the organization both by internal and external applicants. Additionally, this has led to a lack of structure in the selection process; the multiple interviews currently used encourage repetition and therefore do not assess the applicants in as much depth or with as much continuity as could be achieved if one person conducted the interviews or if only one interview was conducted by a panel of managers.

The assistant manager acknowledges the benefits of the job-analysis process and its products and, therefore, makes a point of reviewing job descriptions, but this occurs only when a senior position is being filled. At the Coachman, the person specification is not kept in writing. Instead, it is outlined verbally with those who will be interviewing.

An important stage in preparing to recruit is determining possible sources of recruits. This depends on the positions being recruited for and the suitability of internal sources, and, in turn, the sources chosen will determine the scope of the exercise and how it will be organized. The Coachman currently recruits both internally and externally to attract a large pool of applicants from which they attempt to choose the best. Internal sources are usually considered alongside external sources in an attempt to gain a good pool of staff from which to select. Internal applicants are either self-applicants or recommended by management. Their suitability is not assessed prior to external applications being sought. Instead they are often made to follow the same process as external applicants. Moving on to external sources, employee referrals have been used at the Coachman. However, disadvantages, such as employees feeling let down when an applicant they recommended is not successful on the job, has affected the perceived suitability of using employee referrals. Due to this, the managers now ask referrals to follow formal channels and referrals as a recruitment source are not relied upon.

The Coachman has used various employment agencies. More recently, Action Personnel has been used to recruit for senior positions with successful people recruited at a reasonable cost. This method is easily justified when recruiting to management or senior positions. Student Job Search has also been used in the past, usually as a source of employees for the busy Christmas period when the number of applicants responding to advertisements drops off significantly. The type of applicants from this source are not of the quality usually desired at the Coachman, as they tend to lack the desired experience, skills and commitment.

Palmerston North's large student population means that hundreds of unsolicited applications are received at the beginning of each year and there is a large student base to attract to positions during the year. Applicants are informed that their application will be held for three months and that it is their responsibility to collect their CV if they want it back. Suitable applicants are approached before advertising any position that becomes available, thus avoiding the expense of placing advertisements.

The primary medium for recruitment advertising at the Coachman is local newspapers. However, for senior positions, the *Auckland Herald* and the *Wellington Dominion* would be used, in addition to the *Palmerston North Evening Standard*. For housekeeping positions using the *Lintonian Mag* (a publication circulated around households on the Linton Army Base) has produced high numbers of suitable applicants and is a very suitable method of recruitment. The Coachman uses adverts that contain the minimum information and, consequently, unqualified or under-qualified people are able to apply. The effectiveness of the recruitment process at the Coachman is usually only called into question when the process fails, when either an unsuccessful applicant is hired or few applications are received.

Selection

The selection process currently undertaken by the Coachman Hotel is as follows: the applications are assessed and shortlisted, with the 'yes' pile invited for an interview. Interviews with either two or three of the managers take place consecutively. The successful applicant is notified and given a contract and an orientation on their first day. All applications received as a result of an advertisement are then advised that the position is filled and the remaining 'yes' applicants are asked if their CVs can be held in case another position becomes available. Applications for employment at the Coachman are either unsolicited or are in response to a recruitment effort. Unsolicited applicants are required to complete an application form to include with their CV, whereas applicants responding to an advertisement are asked to apply in writing, in which case a letter and a CV are usually received, and these applicants will complete an application form if they are invited to an interview.

The Coachman's application form is reasonably comprehensive and detailed. The information collected includes personal information, contact details for two referees and the person's current employer, health status, any criminal convictions, and availability. The assistant manager approaches shortlisting by sorting through applications for employment and any accompanying CVs, determining whether the applicants are a 'yes' (we will consider these people for employment) or a 'no' (we will not consider these people for employment). Criteria used to determine the applicants' suitability includes whether they meet any age requirements, and consideration is given to any previous experience or training that is relevant and sets them apart from other applicants. However, decisions are based mainly on a 'gut feeling'. The Coachman uses interviews as the main method for assessing and rating applicants, despite the many criticisms of interviews. The selection interview itself at the Coachman is unstructured or semi-structured and is not specifically job-related. Areas such as experience, abilities, availability and goals are addressed, as well as more general information. Additionally, as previously noted, the Coachman favours using multiple interviews. The Coachman has avoided trial employment periods in which an applicant is selected but employed on the condition that they must perform satisfactorily.

Rudman (1999) details a steady increase in the use of occupational tests in recruitment and selection in recent years. The Coachman has not yet ventured into this area. Considering that the majority of positions in the organization do not require specialized training or experience, this decision is valid.

The organization's application form asks the applicant for contact details for two referees as well as collecting the applicant's current employer's details. In fact, these are the only sources on the application form that could inform the Coachman of the applicant's relevant skills and experience. References are used, but their limitations are recognized and considered. The Coachman uses a type of successive hurdles approach to making a selection decision, i.e. an applicant is asked for an interview, they progress through the interviews and the reference checks but if they are found to be unsuitable at any of the stages of selection they do not continue to the next stage.

Finally, the Coachman recognizes that recruitment is not foolproof, but with planning and careful evaluation the success rate can be increased. However, if a recruitment effort results in numerous unsuitable applicants, the Coachman's policy is to 'never employ the pick of a poor bunch'.

Critique of the Coachman's Approach

The recruitment and selection process at the Coachman needs to be approached in a more organized and systematic manner. Rather than the assistant manager suggesting loose recruitment and selection guidelines, there needs to be standard operating procedures which any manager must follow and adhere to in order to ensure consistency throughout the organization. This would reduce any inconsistencies and non-standard approaches noted in the previous section. The multiple interviews currently used encourage repetition and, therefore, do not assess the applicants in as much depth or with the continuity that could be achieved if one person conducted the interviews or if only one interview were conducted. Split managerial responsibility for an area such as this can lead to a situation where no one actually takes the responsibility. There is nothing wrong with creating a team to drive the process and enlist the help of other people, but one person needs to have overall responsibility and authority.

The reasons for not carrying out thorough job analysis for non-managerial positions are that managers often lack the time to conduct a job analysis, job descriptions have to be updated and they reduce flexibility. However, even with positions such as cleaner, receptionist and waitering staff, having a job description and person specification can only be advantageous. By providing a definite description of what the job entails the applicants can form realistic expectations, the interviewers can make the interview job-focused and they will know specifically what skills to ask the applicant to demonstrate.

The verbal nature of job descriptions and person specifications also creates problems for the interviewer. Having criteria such as skills, knowledge, experience and personal characteristics defined ensures that the suitability of applicants can be measured and they can then be rated in terms of suitability. In addition, the need for a job description and person specification is emphasized by Torrington and Hall (1998) who assert that without defined selection criteria it will be impossible to make credible selection decisions, it will be difficult to select appropriate selection procedures and even more difficult to validate the process, for example, against accusations of discrimination. Hinkin and Tracey (2000) suggest that most labour turnover occurs in the first three months of employment. If this is accurate, then part of the reason must be that the wrong candidate was selected. One of the reasons for the wrong selection decision being made is that the organization did not define clear enough criteria and, as a result, gave inaccurate information to the interviewer and the interviewee. Having a thorough and written set of documents would remove that possibility. Smith *et al.* (1996) recommend a systematic and disciplined approach to recruitment and selection. This includes producing high-quality job descriptions and person specifications that are then used to guide the whole process.

Armstrong (1996) recognizes that selection decisions are difficult at the best of times and, therefore, recommends a recruitment method that encourages only the best applicants to apply. This is different to theorists who prefer a high recruitment/selection ratio to get the best field of applicants. However, this relies upon the organization's ability to determine which applicants are suitable or unsuitable. To encourage self-selection by applicants, applicants are given large amounts of information about the organization, the job and its requirements. For example, applicants must have a high level of experience, must have demonstrated ability, must have a desire to have a career in hospitality, and should be told what pay rate can be expected.

The Coachman relies on students throughout the year and in terms of student job search. They find that the type of applicants from this source are not of the quality usually recruited at the Coachman, as they tend to lack the experience, skills and commitment to the job. Reliance upon this method, considering the unsuitability of most applicants, could be reduced by planning for the need for staff in advance, for example by approaching suitable applicants during the year to ask if they would consider working over busy times or by running advertisements in other areas targeting tertiary students who may be returning to Palmerston North during holidays and who want to earn money.

Evaluation of all recruitment and selection systems is essential and must be conducted regularly. Simply responding to failures results in a reactive as oppose to a proactive approach, and this is unlikely to improve the hotel's systems in the long term. Each stage of the process should be monitored every time it is used and changes made in areas that were not effective. Apart from basic information regarding the candidates' current positions or referees' comments, the application form used by the hotel does not request any information regarding training or experience relevant to the position, or why the applicants believe they are suitable for the position. To sort through numerous CVs to find this additional information will be time-consuming and expensive, and for this reason questions regarding the additional information should be included on the form.

To make shortlisting fairer for applicants and to reduce the likelihood of calling inappropriate persons for interviews, the application form should be structured more in terms of the criteria against which the applicants will be assessed.

As suggested earlier, the Coachman uses interviews as the main method for assessing and rating applicants despite the many criticisms of interviews. Mostly, however, it is the interviewer, not the interview, which is the problem. Interviewers are subject to bias, and to avoid this, interviews should be planned and structured, and applicants should be assessed in job-related terms. Law and Wong (1997) have shown that the interviewers influence the effectiveness of the interview in three major ways: (a) how they conduct the interview; (b) their level of skill in interviewing; and (c) how objectively and accurately they evaluate the interviewees. Implicit in these findings is the need for consistency in each interview and over all interviews. The process at the Coachman, at best, reduces this consistency and, at worst, removes it altogether. Considering the expense of the interviewers and the applicant's time, better use could be made of the interview. More detailed information needs to be collected regarding whether the person has the skills, knowledge and ability to do the job well. The interview should be structured around open-ended and behavioural questions.

The reason for the use of multiple interviews is that two heads are better than one. But when recruiting for less-senior positions, such as waitering staff, is this extra cost justified? Currently, the interviews lack structure and the need for multiple interviews is not justified.

A job preview is an opportunity for the applicant to demonstrate skills, knowledge and ability. This type of assessment would be of value for positions in which abilities are difficult to verbalize; for example cooking, waitering, communicating or up-selling. Job previews are recommended because they will illustrate instantly the applicant's ability to do the job, they will increase the accuracy of selection decisions and they have relatively low cost implications. The issue for the Coachman here is that prospective new employees must be informed of their performance during trial employment and given the opportunity to correct this performance. The previews should be paid, the applicants need to be reminded that this is still part of their assessment and that selection decisions are still to be made.

CONCLUSION

The recruitment and selection process at the Coachman operates effectively to the extent that it produces sufficient people to keep the hotel operating. The managers who operate the system are reliable and conscientious. There are, however, areas of weakness and areas where improvement could be achieved relatively easily: the area of job analysis; the process of interviewing; the application form; and evaluation of the systems in use all require a more proactive approach. The job-analysis process is not sufficiently accurate and, as a result, the whole of the recruitment and selection process is based on rocky foundations. Thorough job analysis and written job descriptions and person specifications would enable the managers to operate a much more targeted and, therefore, more effective process.

The interview process lacks consistency and the managers lack training in the skills of interviewing. As a result the interview process is not necessarily producing the 'best candidate'. With proper training the interviews could be much more effective. By giving responsibility for interviews to one person and one person alone the inconsistency could be eliminated.

At present no formal evaluation of processes takes place. The advertising process and the predictive validity of selection methods are methods which could be regularly evaluated and subsequently modified according to identified strengths and weaknesses.

Finally, the Coachman Hotel may need to assign overall responsibility for recruitment and selection to one person who is trained and who has time to devote to managing and monitoring the processes. This person will need to convince other managers to invest time and money in the policies and stress the potential cost of poor selection decisions to the company. Often, gaining commitment to investment in areas such as these is made easier if arguments are based on the potential savings and improvements to the company as a result of the changes.

SELF-ASSESSMENT QUESTIONS

1. Outline and explain the main decisions to be made during a recruitment exercise.
2. Discuss the advantages and disadvantages of internal versus external recruitment.
3. What is a realistic job preview? How can it be used to reduce labour turnover?
4. What is the purpose of job analysis, the job description and person specification in recruitment?
5. If interviews are so problematic, why do most organizations continue to use them?
6. Would you recommend that employers use an application form or ask for CVs? Why?
7. Why are structured interviews more likely to have greater validity than unstructured interviews?
8. How would you evaluate the success of your present approach to recruitment and selection?

REFERENCES

Armstrong, M. (1996) *A Handbook of Personnel Management Practice*. London: Kogan Page.
Beardwell, I. and Holden, L. (1994) *Human Resource Management: A Contemporary Perspective*. London: Pitman Publishing.

Boella, M. (1996) *Human Resource Management in the Hospitality Industry*. Cheltenham: Stanley Thornes.

Caggiano, C. (1998) 'How to hire: part two – picking up the new tools'. *Inc.*, **20**(14), 39–40.

Compton, R. L. and Nankervis, A. L. (1991) *Effective Recruitment and Selection Practices*. Sydney: CCH Australia Limited.

Eade, V. H. (2000) *Human Resource Management in the Hospitality Industry*. Scotsdale, Arizona: Holcomb Hathaway.

Hinkin, T. and Tracey, J. (2000) 'The cost of turnover: putting a price on the learning curve'. *Cornell Hotel and Restaurant Administration Quarterly*, **41**(3), 14–21.

Law, R. and Wong, M. (1997) 'Evaluating the effectiveness of interviews as a selection method'. *Australian Journal of Hospitality Management*, **4**, 27–35.

Lopez, F. M. (1975) *Personnel Interviewing, 2nd Edition*. Maidenhead: McGraw-Hill. Cited in Torrington and Hall (1998).

Millar, J. E., Porter, M. and Drummond, K. E. (1998) *Supervision in the Hospitality Industry*. Toronto: John Wiley and Sons.

Riley, M. (1996) *Human Resource Management in the Hospitality and Tourism Industry*. Oxford: Butterworth Heinemann.

Roberts, J. (1999) *Human Resource Practice in the Hospitality Industry*. London: Hodder and Stroughton.

Rotta-Graydon, L. (1999) 'Recruitment'. Unpublished special topic report, Massey University, Palmerston North, New Zealand.

Rudman, R. (1994) *Human Resources Management in New Zealand: Contexts and Processes*. Auckland: Longman-Paul.

Rudman, R. (1999) *Human Resources Management in New Zealand: Contexts and Processes*. Auckland: Longman.

Smith. K., Gregory, S. R. and Cannon, D. (1996) 'Becoming an employer of choice: assessing commitment in the hospitality workforce'. *International Journal of Contemporary Hospitality Management*, **8**, 3–9.

Stone, R. J. (1998) *Human Resource Management*. Brisbane: John Wiley & Sons.

Sunoo, B. P. (1998) 'Internet recruiting has its pros & cons'. *Workforce*, **77**, 17–18.

Torrington, D. and Hall, L. (1998) *Human Resource Management*. London: Prentice-Hall Europe.

4

Labour Turnover in International Hospitality and Tourism

Margaret Deery

ABSTRACT

This chapter addresses the key issues related to labour turnover. In particular it aims to analyse the current debate in relation to labour turnover within the hospitality and tourism industries. It explores the current theories from a variety of perspectives: economic, sociological and psychological. In examining these perspectives, the causes of, and solutions to, dysfunctional labour turnover will be investigated. The chapter also provides examples from an international hospitality company. The case study will be devoted to examining the employment issues and labour turnover of two hotels within an international company. This section will examine the ways this company attempts to overcome issues related to promotional opportunities and employee development within its national boundaries. In concluding, the chapter will provide recommendations for best practice in managing and maintaining staff to reduce dysfunctional turnover.

INTRODUCTION

Managing organizations and the people who work in those organizations has been an area of research and debate since Frederick Winslow Taylor wrote his treatise, *The Principle of Scientific Management* in 1911. The key focus for today's debate on managing the people within organizations is not so different from Taylor's concerns: how to maximize employees' performance while at the same time developing staff and gaining their loyalty. Organizations spend time, energy and money in the quest for greater productivity and a stable, efficient workforce.

This concern, perhaps obsession, with the organization's need to create an efficient and loyal workforce, has implications for the hospitality and tourism industries. The decline of manufacturing industries and the upsurge in service-oriented industries has meant a change in the type of workforce required for successful businesses. A key area of development has been in the growth area of hospitality and tourism, and researchers in this area have focused, to an extent, on the development of an appropriate workforce. However, the issues of retaining staff differ in each of the three sectors mentioned above. Turnover rates in the travel and tourism sectors tend to be lower, particularly in Australia (Industry Commission, 1996), than those of the hospitality sector. As a consequence, this study focuses on the retention of staff in the hospitality sector where the rates of employee turnover are higher.

The retention of tourism accommodation employees is the core issue for this study. In particular, the focus is on the influences within an organization which encourage employees to either stay with that organization or leave. With the burgeoning of the accommodation sector, Porter's (1990) competitive advantage has become an imperative for survival. A loyal, efficient and stable staff is argued to be one of the keys to competitive success. However, it is not just the retention of staff that is of most interest here; it is the examination of those elements over which the organization has some control. For example, in examining the components of organizational commitment and job satisfaction, issues such as the repetitiveness and the stresses of hospitality industry work will be investigated. To that end, it is anticipated that the study of organizational influences on employee mobility would be of practical assistance to managers within the industry.

While research into the problems and prevention of high turnover rates is almost as abundant as the statistics and research examining the tourism industry *per se,* the results of inquiry into the causes of the high turnover rates within the hospitality industry are only beginning to emerge. Some studies have looked at the cost of hotel employee turnover (Deery and Iverson, 1996) while others have investigated the potential reasons for the high turnover rates in the industry (Timo, 1996). The following discussion provides an overview of the key issues pertaining to employee turnover in the hospitality industry.

LABOUR TURNOVER IN THE HOSPITALITY INDUSTRY

Wood (1992) argues that there are two distinct views on the issue of employee turnover within the hotel industry and suggests that the industry perceives advantages and disadvantages with high turnover rates. Not only is employee turnover problematic, but it is also always topical. For example, Manley (1996) debates the positive and negative effects of the industry's high turnover rate, arguing that it is necessary to develop the right organizational environment if the industry is to control the level of turnover. Part of this environment is to create a sense of belonging, or what might be characterized as a culture, which emphasizes the value of long-term employment. However, if turnover is not viewed as a problem for the industry, then the 'culture of belonging' may not be nurtured. Regardless of whether a high level of turnover is perceived as positive or negative, if high turnover is either to be encouraged or discouraged, it is important to understand its precursors. This enables the identification of all the relevant variables and the relationships between them, so that the system may be managed more effectively, according to management's view.

The key argument presented by those who do not view employee turnover as dysfunctional revolves around the value of mobility for staff (Bowey, 1976). Bowey argues that this mobility facilitates skill acquisition for employees. Riley (1980) argues that labour mobility is an important factor in the development of skills and that turnover is encouraged by the presence of external labour and product markets. Riley argues also that a lack of internal labour markets drives employees to seek employment elsewhere. In particular, limitations of training within one organization push many employees to seek skills in another organization. The arguments which both Bowey and Riley make are taken from the viewpoint of the employee, rather than that of management. Wood (1992) similarly argues that high labour turnover among hotel staff should not necessarily be seen as dysfunctional to hotels.

In examining the opposing view – that employee turnover is an obstacle to increased productivity and efficiency in the hotel industry – Johnson (1981) argues that high employee turnover rates affect the quality of services and goods and incur large replacement and recruitment costs and, therefore, decreased profitability. Costings of the employee turnover phenomenon confirm the loss of revenue in high turnover rates (Deery and Iverson, 1996). Manley (1996, p. 10) discusses some so-called 'subliminal' effects of high turnover: regular guests who are not given recognition from new staff, and the guests who follow favourite staff to another organization. It is also argued that excessive rates of employee turnover contribute to employee morale problems (Deery and Iverson, 1996).

Research into the causes of employee turnover in the hotel industry has been conducted at varying levels of intensity, but there has been a constant interest in the phenomenon. Recent research by Riley *et al.* (1998) has concentrated on the impact of job satisfaction and organizational commitment on the intention to leave. They found that job satisfaction and organizational commitment relates negatively to the intention to leave. These findings are informative in that while this particular study displayed only a mild relationship between these two variables – satisfaction and commitment – the sample of employees from UK hotels exhibited high levels of job satisfaction. Riley *et al.* also found a fairly strong level of intention to stay, and this propensity increased with age. What is particularly interesting from this study is the very strong dissatisfaction with pay and the lack of a statistically significant relationship to employee turnover.

The finding of Riley *et al.* on the importance of pay to the overall satisfaction of hotel work confirms research by Deery and Iverson (1996), studying the determinants of employee turnover in the hotel industry. Deery and Iverson found that pay dissatisfaction was not a determinant of turnover. Another study, by Mok and Finley (1986), examined the impact of job satisfaction and demographics on the turnover behaviour of hotel food-service workers in Hong Kong. The findings from this study, which used the Job Descriptive Index (JDI), show that while satisfaction with pay was low there was not a significant relationship between pay and turnover. As Riley *et al.* (1998) suggest, the meaning of pay in the hotel industry is used as a recruiting agent and has little bearing on performance. Contrary to these findings, however, are those by Sparrowe (1994). This study found that pay was related significantly and negatively to the intention to leave. A key difference between Sparrowe's study and that by Riley *et al.* was the sample. Sparrowe's sample contained employees from a range of hospitality organizations such as restaurants, hotels, motels, and institutional food-service organizations. The findings, therefore, cannot be generalized to the hotel industry. Similarly, in a study by Boles *et al.* (1995) of restaurant employees, pay was not found to be related to turnover intentions. This finding supports the results of a study by

Cotton and Tuttle (1986) who argue that pay is not as consistently related to turnover in service organizations as it is in other organizations, but there must be caution in generalizing from these results.

Other research into the causes of the high turnover rates in the hospitality industry revolve around demographic variables. For example, Boles *et al.* (1995) examined information from pre-employment application forms to test the relationship between the demographic information and the intention to leave. Education was found to be positively related to the intention to leave, while income potential (in this case tips) and work experience were found to be negatively related to the intention to leave. Again, however, the sample of restaurant employees may have provided different responses to employees in the hotel industry.

Research into employee turnover in the hotel industry acknowledges that turnover is a problem in the industry. Turnover rates can vary in the industry from 20 per cent in CBD hotels to over 300 per cent in remote resort hotels. However, some of the research in this area addresses the issue of how to combat the symptoms rather than investigate the causes. For example, Bonn and Forbringer (1992) argue that improved recruitment and selection procedures, together with retention programmes which include monetary incentives, educational incentives and childcare centres, assist in reducing turnover. Similarly, Denvir and McMahon (1992), in their study of London hotels, which experience annual turnover rates of between 58 per cent and 112 per cent, investigated the cost-effectiveness of turnover preventative measures. Their findings are mixed, but they do conclude that some hotels spend considerable money on attempting to address the symptoms of high turnover without examining the causes. The authors conclude that some hotels are spending more money than can be justified. Another study, by Ohlin and West (1994), examines the effect of fringe-benefit offerings on the turnover of hourly housekeeping workers in the hotel industry. The findings suggest that:

> contrary to the generally accepted assumption that an abundance of benefit offerings is valuable in terms of motivating workers to stay with the firm, in fact, many benefit offerings seem to have no statistically significant impact on reduced turnover. (p. 331)

These authors find four benefits which were associated with lower turnover rates and suggest that these offerings seemed to be 'related to fostering and enhancing a long term relationship between the property and the employee' (p. 331). These findings are important for this thesis. The incentives in the Ohlin and West study include retirement plans, group vision and dental and life plans, all of which indicates to the employee that the company is concerned with the employee's total wellbeing. Finally, although the study was conducted on fast-food restaurant employees, the findings of Dienhart (1993) suggest that the employment position of the employee, an intention to leave and intangible work rewards such as feedback, recognition and formal and informal evaluations, are variables influential on the length of employment.

LABOUR TURNOVER THEORY

There are certain variables that appear to be a core set of variables in the study of employee turnover. These emanate from the March and Simon (1958) findings, where the authors identify not only the perceived desirability of movement, but also three main determinants of work satisfaction. First, they suggest that the greater the conformity of the job characteristics to self-image, the higher the job satisfaction. Secondly, they argue that predictability of instrumental relationships of the job promotes job satisfaction, as does compatibility of work requirements with other role requirements. Finally, March and Simon also argue that organizational size influences a person's decision to leave. Each of these variables has, at some stage, been incorporated into a model of employee turnover and so contributes to understanding of employee turnover.

Griffeth and Hom (1995) provide a detailed review of the research into employee turnover, culminating in an integrated model of the key components of the major research. They argue that the withdrawal process is complex and may take the form of a range of behaviours such as, for example, lengthy rest periods or absenteeism. As stated previously, one of the earliest studies into employee turnover is that by March and Simon (1958), investigating the relationship between facets of job satisfaction and employee intentions to leave an organization. Similarly, Porter and Steers (1973) test the facet of satisfaction–turnover relationship together with the concept of met expectations. These authors recommend the use of job previews to prevent unmet expectations. However, this particular theory has been criticized by a number of researchers who argue that the study fails to differentiate between unmet and overmet expectations (Louis, 1980). The Porter and Steers study concludes by urging further research into the decision-making processes.

Labour Turnover Theory in the Hotel Industry

More recent research investigating labour turnover theories within the hotel industry suggests that there are specific factors influencing the trend. These include a concept known as turnover culture (Deery and Shaw, 1999) as well as the impact of internal labour markets (Deery, 1999) on the withdrawal decision-making process. A definition of turnover culture is offered below:

> A turnover culture develops through the acceptance of turnover behaviour by peers, management and the organizational structure. It is more likely to develop in organizations where employees have strong work norms, a positive attitude on life and stress within their work roles. Finally, a turnover culture exists where turnover behaviour is regular, accepted as the norm and may be perceived to be beneficial to both the employer and employee. (Deery 1999, p. 175)

The investigations look at the internal influences on employee turnover and argue that elements of turnover culture and internal labour markets, together with variables such as job satisfaction, organizational culture and job search impact an employee's intention to leave the hotel industry. Figure 4.1 illustrates the hypothesized relationships.

The key findings from this detailed study of labour turnover in the hotel industry argue that an employee's intention to leave is strongly influenced by the following variables:

- organizational commitment;
- job search;
- employee values and norms (dimension of turnover culture);
- promotional opportunity (dimension of internal labour markets);

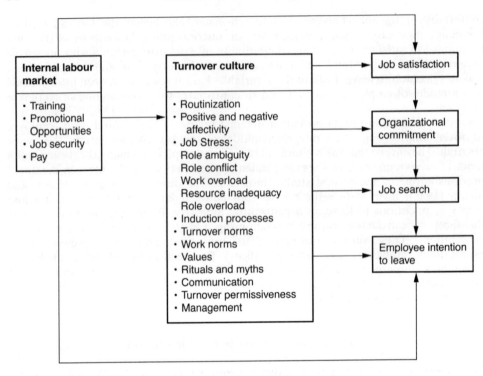

Figure 4.1 Hypothesized model of the organizational influences on employee turnover in the hotel industry
Source: Deery (1999)

- work difficulties (dimension of turnover culture);
- job mobility (dimension of turnover culture); and
- job satisfaction.

The finding that organizational commitment, job satisfaction and job search impact an employee's decision to leave an organization is not new, and it is possible for management strategies to be implemented to increase the level of commitment to the organization and to improve an employee's job satisfaction. The study by Deery (1999) offers some insights into the use for these findings. Hotel management can exploit this knowledge by encouraging pride in working in a particular hotel, or even within a chain of hotels. Behavioural commitment is measured by making greater efforts to work hard in the organization and by not leaving (Iverson and Roy, 1994). Organizations capitalizing on this information could use tangible rewards, such as bonuses, for work well done.

The finding that dimensions of a turnover culture were statistically significant predictors of employee turnover is also important for the hotel industry. In particular the elements of employee values and norms, work difficulties and job mobility were found to impact on an employee's intention to leave. The finding that the culture variable of values and norms is related positively to employee intention to leave is new in the turnover research, but one which might be expected in the study of a turnover culture. This relationship suggests that strong work norms are part of a turnover culture and that turnover behaviour may be indicative of those employees with a strong work ethic attempting to find satisfying and rewarding work. This interpretation of turnover behaviour is supported by the conclusions of Riley *et al.* (1998) which argue that there is high mobility within the hotel industry, also a high level of job satisfaction and commitment to the industry. Turnover behaviour in this instance may indicate a lack of commitment to the organization, but for those who stay within the industry, it represents a commitment to the industry.

The turnover culture dimension of work difficulties also impacts on an employee's intention to leave, supporting previous research by Zohar (1994) on the negative impact of stress on hotel employees. The final dimension of turnover culture that impacts on employee turnover is that of job mobility. This variable combines the elements of myths concerning long-term employment in the hotel industry, items measuring the benefits to both employers and employees of turnover behaviour and the lack of conflict in the perceptions of the employees in their tasks and roles. This finding is again affirmation of the positive aspects of turnover behaviour and an acceptance that this may be the norm within the hotel industry.

The internal labour market variable of promotional opportunity provides support from previous research of the importance of career opportunities. From a management perspective, this finding is important in retaining good staff, and would appear to be a more effective incentive to stay with the organization than, for example, higher pay levels, particularly in the hotel industry.

CASE STUDY: METHODOLOGY

The following case study examines the retention strategies employed by Oberoi Hotels in an Australian-based operation, the Windsor, and two Indonesian-based properties, the Oberoi, Bali and the Oberoi, Lombok, Indonesia. The data for this case study were collected in a number of ways. First, mission statements, human resource records and promotional information were collected to gain an overview of the hotels and their operations. Secondly, the human resource managers of both hotels were interviewed on several occasions in order to gain information on the hotels' human resource practices. These interviews were structured interviews. The general manager of the Windsor Hotel was also consulted on the accuracy of the case studies.

Oberoi Hotels

The Oberoi Group is one of Asia's leading hospitality companies and, as such, is involved in a range of hospitality businesses. These include airline catering, airport bars and restaurants, as well as the flagship company of the group, East India Hotels Ltd. Ten Oberoi hotels are members of 'The Leading Hotels of the World' which is a select group of international hotels judged to be among the best in the world. This case study will discuss three of the Oberoi Hotels: the Windsor in Melbourne, Australia; the Oberoi, Bali; and the Oberoi, Lombok.

The Windsor Hotel is a traditional Victorian building of 116 years' standing which has been classified by the National Trust and is preserved as part of Melbourne's heritage. It is a five-star, medium-sized hotel in the CBD of Melbourne. It employs over

200 staff, and offers a range of services from fine dining to conference facilities. The Windsor has won several awards and was the first hotel in Australia to introduce personalized in-room Hotel Web facilities for all its guests. In order to maintain its high standing in the accommodation sector, staff need to be well trained and know how to offer quality service.

In order to maintain a stable, skilled and satisfied workforce, the Windsor, with an average annual employee turnover rate of approximately 40 per cent, conducts an Employee Attitude Survey each year. The aim of the survey is to establish areas and issues that staff think could be improved. In so doing, the hotel Executive Group believe that issues which may cause staff to leave can be addressed. The areas that the Employee Attitude Survey investigates include job satisfaction, the work itself, the management style of immediate supervisors, department heads and the executive group, as well as training and development and the impact of change on staff.

Using data from the previous years' surveys, the HR manager and the Executive Group have set some priorities in terms of addressing the issues from the surveys. These include improving the management style of supervisors and department heads, improving communication throughout the hotel and concentrating on HR functions such as performance review and succession planning. Included in these priorities, and a successful tool to reduce turnover, has been the use of internal promotion to retain and reward staff. Two of these priorities – the management style and communication – had arisen from previous feedback in the attitudinal surveys and action was taken to improve these areas. Both the survey feedback and the hotel Executive Group confirmed that the style of management was autocratic; it was also thought that the style of management impacted strongly on staff satisfaction and commitment. Using Stephen Covey's *Seven Effective Habits* the hotel ran management development courses to assist in changing the management style to a more consultative type. Daily coaching of the consultative style was also encouraged. The second of the priorities – improving communications – was addressed through the successful application of a government-funded project, Workplace English and Literacy (WEL). This programme ran over a four-month period, using a TAFE provider 1–2 days a week to enhance the English speaking skills of staff. The course also included classes on running meetings and improving the input by staff at meetings.

The results of these and other initiatives have achieved a level of success in improving staff job satisfaction. For example, over a three-year period it was found that employees were gaining job satisfaction through improved promotional opportunities and a sense of greater job security. In terms of the management style at the hotel, employees felt that their supervisors had become more approachable and accessible, were more respectful of staff and that there was a greater sense of fairness in their dealings with staff. The management style of department heads had also improved. For example, the surveys showed that, over the three-year period, department heads were seen to be more competent in their jobs, respectful of staff, more approachable and that there was a great improvement in their communication skills.

However, although the Windsor has improved staff job satisfaction and, at the same time, increased the perceived commitment of the hotel to its staff, the efforts to change the management style have not been entirely successful. Furthermore, the management style was directly and negatively linked to the employees' intention to continue working at the hotel for an extended period of time. When questioned on the preferred management style, staff gave their preferences in the following order: decisive, consultative, democratic and autocratic. However, staff also stated that the key management style of both supervisors and department heads was autocratic, a style they did not want. These findings imply that the strategies to improve the management style to a more consultative one had not been entirely successful. The key question the Executive Group is now grappling with is how best to train supervisors and department heads in the desired management style.

The Oberoi, Bali, is located on Legian Beach on the Indonesian island of Bali. It is set among the traditional rice fields of Bali and is close to some of the ancient temple sites. Situated nine kilometres from the airport, the property comprises 60 Lanai (traditional) cottages and 15 villas. It offers a range of recreational and business services. The Oberoi, Lombok, is located on the coast of Lombok Island, east of Bali. The property, comprising 30 terrace pavilions and 20 villas, is set in a secluded location, 45 minutes' drive from the airport. Again, there is a wide range of recreational and business facilities offered. These two Indonesian Oberoi properties will be discussed together.

The interesting aspect in comparing these two Indonesian properties with the Windsor in Melbourne is the level and 'problem' of employee turnover. In both Indonesian properties, the turnover rate is extremely low. The management initiatives here are not so much concerned with maintaining staff but, rather, to assist staff in dealing with the changes required for continual improvement. Staff, in fact, exhibit strong patterns of loyalty and, with the Indonesian retirement age being set at 50 years, many of the staff stay in the hotels until they retire.

Management strategies to maintain good staff in the Oberoi, Bali and the Oberoi, Lombok, focus on training initiatives, with much of the training dealing with new technology and its uses. With an older workforce than that of the Australian property, the introduction of new systems and methods can be threatening to staff. Training and development programmes, therefore, often deal with issues of change and change management. This requires an awareness and sensitivity, not only to the abilities and skills of the staff, but also to their belief systems. At the same time, management at these properties has been keen to bring in new staff to encourage new ideas and ways. With, often, a limited external labour market from which to acquire skilled staff, management must be careful in its selection of employees. The experience in these Indonesian properties, therefore, is very different from that of the Australian Oberoi property.

In conclusion, these three Oberoi properties provide a range of scenarios in maintaining and developing good staff. In both countries, there are issues of employee turnover; these issues encapsulate the divergent views expressed at the beginning of this chapter. In other words, the question of whether a high or a low turnover rate is beneficial to the hotel industry.

Discussion

The case study of the Oberoi hotels highlights the challenges in maintaining a stable and effective workforce within the hospitality industry. While training staff in key areas such as improved communications has been successful at the Windsor, changing the management style of those in management positions has proved to be much more difficult. Members of the Windsor Executive Group argue that a key means of changing the management style of the hotel managers could be through the staff-selection processes. A strategy for retaining staff through an improved management style could be implemented through more careful selection procedures, where those applicants with a perceived consultative management style could be employed.

While changing hotel management style has been identified as a key to retaining staff in some of the Oberoi hotels, there are other strategies that have used to maintain and develop good staff. These include improving the attitudes of management to staff and improving the competencies and skills of those in management positions. There have also been improvements in facets of job satisfaction such as greater opportunity for promotion, being treated more fairly and greater security of employment. These findings accord with the theoretical findings from research.

The issue of low turnover rates, as exhibited in the Indonesian hotels, raises the need for training of the existing staff. In particular, training in change management and the use of new technologies has been a priority of the Indonesian Oberoi management. Retaining staff is not an issue here, but, rather, the development of staff. However, research into retaining staff in the hospitality industry suggests there are various avenues for keeping good staff. Two key ways are suggested below:

Promoting Organizational Commitment

This strategy, while not new, appears to be one that the Oberoi Group could employ. Staff need to feel proud of their workplace. Employees should be given a clear understanding of the benefits and some of the disadvantages of working in particular organizations. In order to promote job satisfaction, for example, it important that managers listen to work-related problems and be perceived as supportive and reliable. The importance of job design cannot be underestimated in providing job satisfaction; specifically, jobs must not be too arduous, nor should they be overly monotonous and lack variety.

Managing a Turnover Culture

In coming to an understanding of the composition of a turnover culture, it is possible to formulate policies to discourage the incidence of a negative work environment. The choices in dealing with individual components of a turnover culture – in particular, the individual personality predisposition and norms and values – are somewhat limited. While companies are making greater use of personality inventories such as the Myers-Briggs Temperament Indicator and culture inventories, such the OCP (O'Reilly *et al.*, 1991) in order to determine the 'right' person for positions, it is unlikely that most hotels will pursue this strategy. The hotel industry, known for its extensive use of contingent labour, would be unlikely to use such expensive and time-consuming selection processes. While some more innovative hotels have used personality tests for the selection of all staff, including non-supervisory staff, the majority of hotel human resource managers find the cost of such procedures difficult to justify to management. This aspect of turnover culture, therefore, is a difficult component for management to address. However, given that strong work norms are part of this turnover culture, management may be able to harness this strength and try to retain those employees who are not challenged or rewarded by their current work environment.

The implications for management in addressing the structural causes of a turnover culture are more easily identified. The four structural elements of turnover culture are turnover acceptance, job mobility, role stress and work difficulties. If management perceive the existence of a turnover culture as negative, the first element – that of turnover acceptance – can be modified. This would entail the implementation of strong, positive induction programmes, perceived and actual management support within the work setting and tangible rewards for long-term tenure. Equally important in managing or modifying an acceptance of turnover behaviour is to monitor job design. Finally, if a turnover culture is not an organizational characteristic that the organization wishes to encourage, management policies and practices need to clarify such a position to staff.

The other three components of turnover culture also provide strategies for managing a turnover culture. The job mobility element of turnover culture highlights the ambivalence of both management and employees to turnover behaviour. Both groups perceive benefits from turnover, yet there is evidence to suggest that excessive rates of turnover are costly and impair morale (Deery and Iverson, 1996). If turnover rates are to be kept within 'manageable' limits, organizations need to work harder at making the workplace more attractive to employees. This relates to the issue of role stress: workplace stress has become an important issue in the study of occupational health and safety. The constant time pressures and client contact in hotel jobs need to be addressed through the better use of staffing rosters and the use of 'time-out' strategies. Job stress is also linked to the turnover culture concept. The research here suggests that adequate resources for jobs, realistic workloads and committed management would assist in the discouragement of employee turnover.

While this discussion has focused on the findings and use of the concept of a turnover culture, this concept encompasses a range of issues that are important in retaining good staff. It provides the framework for key management strategies that will assist in the retention of staff. Oberoi Hotels has put in place a range of sound management practices to improve work satisfaction and retain staff; the opportunities for further strategies can perhaps be enhanced through investigating whether a turnover culture exists.

SELF-ASSESSMENT QUESTIONS

1. Is employee turnover functional or dysfunctional for the hotel industry? Give reasons for your answer, using examples from the case study.
2. What differences might exist between countries in the strategies used to combat employee turnover problems, either high or low?
3. If employee turnover rates are high, how can they be reduced? Provide some examples of the strategies for retaining staff in hospitality, travel and tourism organizations?
4. How would you define organizational commitment and job satisfaction, both theoretically and operationally, within an international hotel? Develop a model of the determinants of organizational commitment job satisfaction and their relationship to labour turnover.
5. How could an organization determine whether a turnover culture exists? How could the organization change this culture? Would an organization want to promote a turnover culture? Why, or why not?
6. You are the human resource manager in an international hotel. Develop a strategic plan for an international hotel to assist in reducing labour turnover. This plan will need to be presented to the Executive Group and must address the financial implications of the strategies.

REFERENCES

Boles, J., Ross, L. and Johnson, J. (1995) 'Reducing employee turnover through the use of pre-employment application demographics: an exploratory study'. *Hospitality Research Journal*, **19**, 19–30.

Bonn, M. and Forbringer, L. (1992) 'Reducing turnover in the hospitality industry: an overview of recruitment, selection and retention'. *International Journal of Hospitality Management*, **11**, 47–63.

Bowey, A. (1976) *The Sociology of Organizations*. London: Hodder and Stoughton.

Cotton, J. L. and Tuttle, J. M. (1986) 'Employee turnover: a meta-analysis and review with implications for research'. *Academy of Management Review*, **11**, 55–70.

Deery, M. (1999) 'Turnover culture, internal labour markets and employee turnover in the hotel industry: an integrated model'. Unpublished PhD thesis, School of Tourism and Hospitality, La Trobe University.

Deery, M. A. and Iverson, R. D. (1996) 'Enhancing productivity: intervention strategies for employee turnover', in N. Johns (ed.), *Productivity Management in Hospitality and Tourism*. London: Cassell, pp. 68–95.

Deery, M. and Shaw, R. (1999) 'An investigation of the relationship between employee turnover and organizational culture'. *Journal of Hospitality and Tourism Research*, **23**(4), 387–400.

Denvir, A. and McMahon, F. (1992) 'Labour turnover in London hotels and the cost effectiveness of preventative measures'. *International Journal of Hospitality Management*, **11**, 143–54.

Dienhart, J. (1993) 'Retention of fast-food restaurant employees'. *Hospitality and Tourism Educator*, **5**, 31–5.

Griffeth, R. W. and Hom, P. W. (1995) 'The employee turnover process'. *Research in Personnel and Human Resources Management*, **13**, 245–93.

Industry Commission (1996) *Tourism Accommodation and Training* (Report No. 50). Melbourne: Australian Government Publishing Services.

Iverson, R. and Roy, P. (1994) 'A causal model of behavioural commitment: evidence from a study of Australian blue-collar employees'. *Journal of Management*, **20**, 15–41.

Johnson, K. (1981) 'Toward an understanding of labour turnover'. *Service Industries Review*, **1**, 4–17.

Louis, M. (1980) 'Surprise and sense making: what newcomers experience in entering unfamiliar organizational settings'. *Administrative Science Quarterly*, **25**, 226–51.

Manley, H. (1996) 'Hospitality head hunting'. *Australian Hotelier*, April, 8–11.

March, J. and Simon, H. (1958) *Organizations*. New York: Wiley & Sons.

Mok, C. and Finley, D. (1986) 'Job satisfaction and its relationship to demographics and turnover of hotel food service workers in Hong Kong'. *International Journal of Hospitality Management*, **5**, 71–8.

Ohlin, J. and West, J. (1994) 'An analysis of the effect of the fringe benefit offerings on the turnover of hourly housekeeping workers in the hotel industry'. *International Journal of Hospitality Management*, **12**, 323–36.

O'Reilly, C. A., Chatman, J. and Caldwell, D. F. (1991) 'People and organizational culture: a profile comparison approach to assessing person-fit'. *Academy of Management Journal*, **34**, 487–516.

Porter, M. E. (1990) *The Competitive Advantage of Nations*. New York: Free Press.

Porter, L. W. and Steers, R. M. (1973) 'Organizational, work and personal factors in employee turnover and absenteeism'. *Psychological Bulletin*, **80**, 151–76.

Riley, M. (1980) 'The role of mobility in the development of skills for the hotel and catering industry'. *Hospitality*, March, 52–3.

Riley, M., Lockwood, A., Powell-Perry, J. and Baker, M. (1998) 'Job satisfaction, organizational commitment and occupational culture: a case from the UK pub industry'. *Progress in Tourism and Hospitality Research*, **4**, 159–68.

Sparrowe, R. (1994) 'Empowerment in the hospitality industry: an exploration of antecedents and outcomes'. *Hospitality Research Journal*, **24**, 37–46.

Taylor, F. W. (1911) *The Principles of Scientific Management*. New York: Harper Bros.

Timo, N. (1996) 'Staff turnover in hotels'. *Labour Economics and Productivity*, **8**, 43–79.

Wood, R. C. (1992) *Working in Hotels and Catering*. London: Routledge.

Zohar, D. (1994) 'Analysis of job stress profile in the hotel industry'. *International Journal of Hospitality Management*, **13**, 219–31.

5

The Impact of Technology on Human Resources in the Hospitality Industry

Jay Kandampully and Ria Duddy

ABSTRACT

Since the early 1990s, there has been a massive infusion of the application of new technology in almost every aspect of hotel operations and management, with numerous implications for human resources. Contrary to popular opinion, the adoption of technology in the hospitality industry is intended not to replace labour input, but to offer support. Indeed, technology elevates the competitive advantage of a service organization only if it can support the employees and enhance their capacity to offer superior service to the customer. The increasing use of technology in almost every functional area in a hotel has added an information technology component to every manual job. Information technology skills thus represent a new addition to the list of skills traditionally required by hoteliers. Moreover, the relentless update of technology in almost every field has also required firms to seek employees who are both capable and willing to enhance their knowledge on an ongoing basis.

INTRODUCTION

Technology, as discussed in this chapter, encompasses both technical aspects of the business (e.g. computers, machines and other equipment) and all processes and systems that effect an improved result. Technology thus essentially represents a better method or way of doing things, while simultaneously benefiting both the firm and the customer. Moreover, this technology may not be developed by, or be specific to, hospitality, but may have been adopted from various other industries. However, adopting 'alien' technology in a traditionally skill-based profession is not without ramifications, both positive and negative.

This chapter examines the circumstances that render the implementation of technology essential in service organizations. Further, it illustrates how information technology can be effectively utilized to enrich or support a service organization's employees, to improve both the internal and external quality of service. It also outlines a number of technology applications currently utilized by hospitality organizations, and their subsequent implications for human resources. A case study exemplifies the extent to which technology can be implemented without unduly compromising an employee's professional prestige. The objectives of the chapter are, more specifically to:

- demonstrate an awareness of the increasing importance of technology in the hospitality industry;
- outline the contribution of technology in service organizations in terms of how it can assist a firm to enhance the quality of service;
- discuss the importance and benefits of technology with reference to the integration of operations and marketing aspects of a firm;
- identify factors that facilitate acceptance of technology by both customers and employees; and
- describe some of the implications for human resources management associated with the adoption of technology in the hospitality industry.

INFUSION OF TECHNOLOGY

It is estimated that 550 million people (10 per cent of the world's population) were using the internet at the end of 2000 (Sweet, 2000). The application of various forms of information technology (IT) in the hospitality industry has become an essential component for the effective management of today's organizations. Researchers have identified IT as a strategic component that enables firms to gain a competitive advantage in all aspects of their endeavours; whether this be operations, marketing and/ or human resources. Increasingly, hospitality organizations are entering the international arena through alliances and partnerships with various other sectors of the industry. Through this global network they are able to enhance customer-perceived value and to gain a competitive advantage. These strategic alliances have made it imperative for hotel organizations to secure global connectivity – one of the factors pertinent in determining the success of hotel companies (Cline, 1999). Porter (1985) emphasizes the role of IT in a firm's value chain as a means of gaining competitive advantage. The creative use of technology in various service firms thus has the potential to enhance capability, to reduce cost outputs and to maximize personalization and customization (Quinn and Paquette, 1990). For example, the fast-food firm 'Taco Bell' uses information technology to create an environment characterized by access to knowledge, resulting in a narrowing of management hierarchy and facilitating employee empowerment. In utilizing IT, 'Taco Bell' aims to achieve productivity improvement, product freshness, speed of service and, more importantly, to provide services right the first time. Technology can thus prove an effective means of supporting customer-focused hospitality organizations.

CHANGE OF FOCUS TO SERVICES

In the past, the focus of hospitality industry management was primarily concerned with selling accommodation and food and beverage to its customers. Managers have recognized that traditional concepts and foresights that made them successful in the past may prove inadequate if they are to gain recognition, patronage and acceptance from customers who have the luxury of choice in a highly competitive market. Moreover, competing hospitality organizations have recognized that the tangible components of the hotel offer present limited opportunities for differentiation.

Hotels today do not merely represent a home away from home for customers, but also a travelling office for many business customers, a meeting place that promotes exchange of ideas learning etc. for conference customers, a place to practise sporting activities, etc. Thus the traditional core offerings (accommodation, food and beverage) of a hotel may be seen to represent only a small component of the package of experience that customers seek. The non-traditional service components (conference facilities, technology centre, in-room services etc.), in fact, present hotels with an opportunity to differentiate themselves from the competition using various service packages. Moreover, it has become critically important to identify and manage these non-traditional service components, as they constitute the value-adding elements within the package.

TECHNOLOGY AND ITS INFLUENCE ON THE INTEGRATION OF OPERATIONS AND MARKETING

The role of marketing in service organizations such as hospitality differs considerably from the manufacturing industry due to the unique features (intangibility, inseparability of production and consumption, and perishability) inherent to all services. Traditional marketing in the goods manufacturing industry is both physically and conceptually distant from the production process, and thus exists primarily to connect production and consumption. For example, a product may be manufactured in one country and utilized by customers in another. In this case, the production and consumption are not only physically distant from the consumer's sight but, additionally, the customer has no direct influence on the product's manufacture.

In contrast, production and consumption in service organizations (hospitality) is simultaneous. In order to receive the services at a banquet, for example, customers are necessarily required to be physically present. Hence there is often direct contact between employees and customers, and thus the potential customer–employee relationship. In fact, customers rely heavily on employees' recommendations to assist them in their selection of the various services that the firm has on offer. Moreover, in most service interfaces, the production process and the interaction between customers and employees constitutes one of the most effective marketing cues relied upon by customers. Indeed, the human interaction associated with most service delivery commonly reinforces customer trust (Evans and Crosby, 1998). This implies that friendly production and delivery of services communicates a firm's marketing effectiveness. In the hospitality industry, production and marketing should, therefore, be managed as closely interrelated functions. This necessitates that every hotel ~~'~~~ee have both operational and marketing skills. For example, a waiter not only ~~~~~ e customer with food and beverage in a restaurant but, in the process, markets his skills and the organization's superior service. Hotel employees thus serve as part-time marketeers (Gummesson, 1999) of the organization. It is, therefore, imperative that service employees are both encouraged and assigned the responsibility of marketing and selling their organization's various services.

Furthermore, hospitality employees not only assist in marketing the products and services of the hotel, but also serve as relationship managers (the person with whom customers create and develop a relationship). Moreover, the human interaction evident during the service delivery process effectively strengthens the relationship (McKenna, 1991). As a customer relationship grows in scope, more functions of the firm render it to immediate contact with customers (Gronroos, 2000, p. 11). In effect, all departments and employees in a hotel assume the front-line position, based on customers' specific requirements. For example, when a customer's requirement is a room, the receptionist assumes a front-line position; when a customer's requirement is for a TV repair, it is the mechanic from the engineering department who assumes a front-line position. This highlights the importance and contribution of all hotel departments in the management of customer relationships. However, this, additionally, implies the need for ready access to customer and best practice information by all departments and employees. Computer-generated customer information can effectively enhance employees' ability to serve and nurture an ongoing relationship with the customer. Indeed, the customer relationship constitutes the most important and the most valuable contribution of employees in a hotel. This underlies the subcontraction of vendors by organizations such as Taco Bell to undertake non-customer interactive services, enabling employees to focus their energies on serving and developing relationships with their customers (Henkoff, 1994).

NURTURING INTERNAL AND EXTERNAL SERVICES USING INFORMATION TECHNOLOGY

The interrelationship between operations and marketing has direct implications for human resources. Researchers have identified the important role of the 'people' factor and its contribution within a service organization, particularly in relation to the customer's perception of enhanced service value. People in service organizations represent uniqueness in the service offer and contribute to the quality of service. Moreover, employees in hotels are required to work in collaboration by serving and supporting other employees (internal customers). In doing so they collectively fulfil the requirements of the customer. The service outcome received by a customer is thus the end result of various internal services. Hence, effective internal services are prerequisites for external customer satisfaction. It can thus be argued that it is the hotel's employees that maintain the critical balance – the effectiveness of operations and marketing.

Information and its timely access often prove crucial for the effective functioning of the various internal activities in a hotel, criteria that may be said to be particularly pertinent in nurturing employee empowerment. Hospitality firms can effectively utilize IT to support instantaneous access to information and, essentially, to motivate and energize hotel employees to embrace empowerment and perform at exceptional levels of service by facilitating action in any given situation – to serve both internal and external customers. Information technology thus represents a new addition to the list of skills traditionally required by hoteliers. Information available through IT can be utilized to assist inexperienced employees to complete tasks that would not have otherwise been possible, thus reducing the learning curve (Quinn and Paquette, 1990). Within this technology-oriented new business environment, it is thus not experience but immediate access to information that will prove invaluable to employees in the delivery of exceptional service.

The collection, analysis and digital storage of readily accessible information has become a powerful tool that presents junior members of staff in a hotel with an opportunity to assume responsibility for making on-the-spot decisions without the need to consult senior management. Junior members of staff who are equipped with both decision-making information and customer information will be able to modify the firm's service offer to meet, without delay, customers' specific requirements. IT can also assist the sharing of important information between different units of a multi-unit firm, different departments of a hotel and between different levels of staff; this can effect faster and better decision-making throughout the organization (Durocher and Niman, 1993). Indeed, customer data-collection and its dissemination to various hotels within international chains has become common practice in the pursuit of enhanced customer service.

At La Mansion del Rio Hotel in San Antonio, Texas, employees are trained to gather information about customer preferences for their database; this is further analysed and put to use in customer-focused initiatives throughout the hotel (Peppers and Rogers, 2000, p. 115). Technology should be used as a tool, implemented to enhance the effectiveness of employees and the system and, ultimately, reflecting on customer satisfaction (Bensaou and Earl, 1998). Technology, Berry (1995) argues, should be the servant not the master, and engender its users with more control in achieving what they wish to accomplish. Technology, thus, is not intended to replace labour input but to offer support and to elevate the competitive advantage of a service organization by enhancing an employee's capacity to offer superior service.

The adoption of various forms of information technology in the hotel industry has augmented the knowledge required in almost every hotel employee and has become a prerequisite for success in the hospitality job market. The increasing use of technology in almost every functional area in a hotel has added an information technology component to every manual job. This requires hotel organizations to seek employees who are both able and willing to update their knowledge on information technology on an ongoing basis. Indeed, it can be argued that the need for proficiency in information technology has elevated the hospitality labour force from the traditional low-knowledge workplace.

TECHNOLOGY APPLICATIONS

The use of computer-guided technology has become a common feature in the hospitality industry, in production, delivery, marketing and in management. It supports and assists to render user-friendly almost all tasks within a hotel that relate to customers, employees and the management. Some of the commonly used computer-aided tasks in the hotel include:

- on-line reservation system, auto-rate and guest records;
- computerized call accounting, message function and wake-up call;
- smart cards for security and guest deposit-tracking;
- in-room computer, e-mail, fax services for business guests;

- touch screens and electronic hand-held order-takers in restaurants, with a direct link to the kitchen and guest accounts;
- menu-planning, recipe and portion-control systems;
- inventory control and purchase-ordering systems;
- performance assessment, wages and payroll systems;
- recruitment and training systems;
- customer, employee and supplier database;
- customer-satisfaction surveys and research;
- ledger, financial statements, night audit and daily and weekly reporting system;
- cost-analysis of sales levels;
- world Wide Web property-viewing system;
- on-line electronic locking, security, fire and energy management system.

The implementation of technology is particularly evident within the guest-interface side of hospitality, namely front office/reception, reservations and food and beverage outlets. Computerized booking and property-management systems have enhanced the level of customer service and revolutionized accommodation management in most hotel organizations. Hand-held check-in terminals have expedited check-in procedures, benefiting both hotels and their customers. At the Marriott Hotel, Houston Airport, associates use hand-held check-in terminals to check in pre-registered guests at the train station. The associate, equipped with a hand-held computer, can swipe the customer's credit card to verify the reservation, and immediately assign the respective room key. Having checked in, guests can take an elevator from the train station directly to the designated floor of the hotel. Similarly, a check-out facility via in-room video screen is offered by numerous hotels firms. Best Western International, Phoenix, Arizona, computerized their reservation system, which helped them to reduce the check-in procedure to little more than a signature (Hensdil, 1996). Computerized reservation systems thus provide customers with a hassle-free operational process while, simultaneously, reducing the likelihood of reception bottleneck situations and assisting with the elimination of problems associated with human error and consistency of service.

Sheraton Hotels, New York, have introduced a property-management system that directly links their three hotels in the immediate area. This allows the hotels to integrate management and operational functions and to maintain one accounting system. Other benefits derived from a common database include the sharing of computer hardware costs and reduced staffing costs, all while simultaneously achieving more streamlined systems and operations (Hensdil, 1996b). Computerized systems in hotels additionally manifest a potential reduction in time and money spent on training. The Promus Hotel Corporation in Memphis, Tennessee, has developed an integrated management system that facilitates the training of staff and managers. The system is also designed to assist employee clarification, and thus offers online training and user support. Essentially, therefore, technology presents an opportunity to customize internal services for all employees.

Similarly, food and beverage ordering, laundry services and children's games rooms are all becoming part of the technological revolution in hotels. The numerous problems related to a hotel's foodservice operations are universal. Today's hotel chefs are attempting to increase productivity and efficiency while, at the same time, cutting costs and improving the quality of the cuisine. For example, computerized combi-therm ovens can cook at much higher temperatures by forcing steam into the cooking box.

This computer guided-system can maintain a consistent temperature, thereby minimizing the chances of human error.

IMPLICATIONS FOR HUMAN RESOURCES

The change of focus from product to services and the use of technology to enhance services has, indeed, established a new paradigm that recognizes the importance of human input in the quality of service delivery. Services management theory clearly indicates the important role of the human element in the delivery of superior service (Solomon *et al.*, 1985). Further, in the past, labour represented, and was considered by management to be an inevitable cost incurred in the production of goods and services. However, under the present extended definition of resources, labour is valued not in terms of physical assistance but in its creative contribution (customer relationship, innovation, superior service etc.) and potential capacity to enhance the value of a firm's services. Moreover, technology has augmented the knowledge required in almost every functional job in the hospitality industry. Proficiency in IT has become a prerequisite for success in the job market. For example, a hotel receptionist's skill requirement seldom extended beyond that of typing and answering the telephone. However, today's hotel receptionist is expected to demonstrate equal proficiency in a variety of computer programmes, and to possess the aptitude to learn new network systems, reservation systems and property-management systems as they are introduced. These systems, moreover, support employees access to various types of information, and thus allow them to undertake empowered activities.

Access to organizational information (internal and external) is one of the most important components necessary to the nurturing of an employees' self-motivated service activity. Readily accessible information, through IT, has now become standard practice in numerous leading hospitality organizations. Moreover, it can be argued that the IT competency of employees and, more importantly, their ability to creatively utilize such information technology for knowledge-enhancement problem-solving, decision-making and enhancing customer value have become crucial. The focus, therefore, is not just on technology skills, but also in the creative adaptation of information technology to enhance and strengthen management skills within every employee in the hospitality business. It is not the information *per se* that manifests value, but the insight gained, and its potential translation into effective strategies. Thus, information technology facilitates an employee's capacity for effectiveness. It is important, therefore, to offer training or learning opportunities for employees through IT-focused management practices.

Technology innovations within the hospitality industry are often influenced by innovations in other industries. For example, innovations in house security systems in other industries prompted the use of those systems in the hotel industry. However, in spite of the fact that IT-related skills now constitute a fundamental component of the hospitality profession, staff recruitment and training may have to be outsourced. Similarly, assessment of new staff for recruitment may also require IT skill assessment. Thus, human resource management of IT-related issues may have to be outsourced.

Within the new paradigm of service creativity, experience is no longer synonymous with value; it is new knowledge that plays the pivotal role in personal productivity in the technology environment. This knowledge, and the increasing service component, have significant implications both for the labour market (ongoing learning) and the industry (continuous up-skilling). Hence, the aim should be to equip hospitality associates with technology and information on an ongoing basis in an attempt to nurture their creative skills and meet the demands of the market. Hospitality employees as knowledge workers today command a leading role and status within organizations, since it is their respective service creativity that represents the firm's single greatest asset. Moreover, it is on account of this creativity, manifested within each individual employee and the tasks they undertake (how they utilize the information) that renders their services unique and propels the firm to market leadership.

CASE: APPLICATION OF TECHNOLOGY (IT) AT THE BRISBANE HILTON

At the Brisbane Hilton, technology and the human touch have progressed hand-in-hand, with the ratio of each determined by the primary activity and traditional focus of the hotel's respective departments. Information technology is utilized in three predominant contexts: for external communication (with customers); for internal communication (with managers and employees) and; for the provision of in-house services to customers in-room or in-conferences. New technology is also evident in the management and operational functions of various departments including, for example, security and engineering to provide psychological and physical assurance to both guests and staff. Departments such as front office, reservations, sales and marketing have incorporated leading technology to maintain high-level services to the customer.

All staff members employed in these departments are required to demonstrate sufficient knowledge of the hotel's IT systems. This is complemented by the provision of routine training for new IT skill acquisition and enhancement, with a particular emphasis on front office, reservations and sales and marketing departments. All staff members have access to computers and are encouraged to make use of the hotel's learning centre, which facilitates personal development by providing access to the internet and information and employment opportunities at other Hilton properties.

E-mails are used in conjunction with traditional hard copies for information dissemination between the various departments. The use of IT for communication has proved less effective in the context of operational departments such as Kitchen, Restaurant and Housekeeping, where PC use by staff is not prevalent. However, managerial staff often relies on the use of IT through PC for communication and various other managerial activities, such as budgeting, forecasting etc. Creative use of IT when integrated with customer-valued innovation and staff-valued traditional practice will enhance its customer and staff satisfaction. The Brisbane Hilton thus views technology as a tool capable of assisting employees and the organization to enhance the quality of services they offer to customers.

CONCLUSION

It is essentially the employee-generated creative component of service which meets and exceeds the expectations of the customer that proves difficult for competing organizations to emulate. However, creativity is not a design phenomenon, i.e. one cannot expect creativity as an end result of various sets of activities. Creativity can neither be included in a job specification nor training procedures. The creative instinct of a person often becomes apparent when he/she maintains a personal interest (ownership) in the job tasks that they undertake. The attempt of many organizations to instil a quality culture has frequently resulted in policies and practices that stifle initiative and limit the contribution that people can make by setting standards of performance to be reached and financial targets to be met. Hence, the need to introduce mechanisms that engender flexibility and encourage people to take the initiative is imperative.

Technology (IT) is indeed a tool; however, it is the responsibility of management to utilize IT as a vehicle that can effectively uplift employee commitment to that of ownership and creativity. The advent of computers into the workplace dates back to the early 1950s. However, since computers were predominantly utilized to hasten paper-based processes, they failed to effect any fundamental changes in the business process. It is indeed the universally accessible knowledge database via the Internet that propelled technology to leadership. Similarly, in the hospitality industry, the objectives of technology application require a vision beyond that of a task-oriented tool. Technology should be utilized as an effective medium that allows the organization to empower its associates with trust, and to enhance relationships with its internal and external customers. Indeed, it can be argued that creating and maintaining relationships with internal and external customers using technology constitutes the major driver to business success.

SELF-ASSESSMENT QUESTIONS

1. Why has technology become an integral component of the hospitality industry?
2. Describe how technology can be utilized to gain a competitive advantage in a hotel.
3. If you were the general manager of a hotel, in which departments would you consider the implementation of technology a priority, and where would you deem technology less desirable? Justify.
4. As the human resources manager of a hotel, you are asked by your general manager to identify some of the implications for employees (both positive and negative) resulting from the adoption of technology.

REFERENCES

Bensaou, M. and Earl, M. (1998) 'The right mind-set for managing information technology'. *Harvard Business Review*, September–October, 119–28.
Berry, L. L. (1995) *On Great Service: A Framework for Action*. New York: Free Press.
Cline, R. S. (1999) 'Hospitality 2000'. *Lodging Hospitality*, June.
Durocher, F. J. and Niman, B. N. (1993) 'Information technology: management effectiveness and guest services'. *Hospitality Research Journal*, 17(1), 121–31.
Evans, R. K. and Crosby, A. L (1988) *A Theoretical Model of Interpersonal Relational Quality in Enduring Service Sales Relationships*. New York: AMA.
Henkoff, R. (1994) 'Service is everybody's business', *Fortune* June: 48–60.
Gronroos, C. (2000) *Service Management and Marketing: A Customer Relationship Management Approach*. Chichester: Wiley.
Gummesson, E. (1999) *Total Relationship Marketing: Rethinking Marketing Management: From 4Ps to 30Rs*. London: Butterworth Heinemann.

Hensdil, C. (1996) 'Hotels'. *Sheraton Complexing PMS*, **30**, November, 122.

McKenna, R. (1991) *Relationship Marketing: Successful Strategies for the Age of the Customer.* Reading, Mass: Addison-Wesley.

Peppers, D. and Rogers, M. (2000) *One to One Manager Real-World Lessons in Customer Relationship Management.* Oxford: Capstone.

Porter, M. E. (1985) *Competitive Advantage: Creating and Sustaining Superior Performance.* New York: Free Press.

Quinn, J. B. and Paquette, P. C. (1990) 'Technology in services: creating organizational revolutions'. *Sloan Management Review*, Winter, 67–78.

Solomon, M. R., Surprenant, C., Czepiel, J. A. and Gutman, E. G. (1985) 'A role theory perspective on dynamic interactions: the service encounter'. *Journal of Marketing*, **49**, 99–111.

Sweet, P. (2000) 'Strategic value configuration logics and the new economy: a service economy revolution?', in B. Edvardsson, S. W. Brown, R. Johnston and E. E. Scheuing (eds) *Service Quality in the New Economy: Interdisciplinary and International Dimensions.* New York: International Service Quality Association.

6

The Hotel Expatriate in Russia: Competencies for Cross-cultural Adjustment

Norma D'Annunzio-Green

ABSTRACT

As the hospitality industry continues to internationalize, the demands placed on international managers grows. The Russian market-place is one in which there are many challenges, and managers need to be equipped with a set of skills and competencies to enable them to operate effectively. This chapter summarizes the research to date on managerial competencies for international hotel managers, examining these in the context of the Russian market-place. It then proceeds to identify the key managerial competencies identified by a sample of international hotel managers in Russia and discusses these in the context of existing challenges. The chapter concludes that organizations need to focus on the identification and development of these competencies and the subsequent training needs of international managers in order that they are able to adapt to the workplace and cultural challenges of an international assignment in a diverse culture such as Russia.

INTRODUCTION

Travel and tourism is the world's largest industry and generator of employment. It is forecast to add some 100 million new jobs directly and indirectly to the global economy over the next decade (World Travel and Tourism Human Resource Centre, 1998). Within this industry, no area is more important than that of human resource management as people are a central resource to the effective operation of labour-intensive industries (Baum, 1995). In the last twenty years, the travel and tourism industry has seen a 'proliferation of multinational corporations that operate throughout the world' (Pizam, 1997, p. 125). This rapid globalization has brought to the fore an examination of the challenges of human resource management issues in a global environment in industries such as airlines, hotels, restaurants and tour operators. This chapter focuses on the emerging market of Russia as an investment growth area that offers many opportunities to major hospitality operators. It will, more specifically,

- identify the employee resourcing challenges facing multinational hotel operators;
- review the literature which examines managerial competencies for effective cross-cultural adjustment of expatriate managers; and
- present a case study which illustrates the views of British expatriates employed by multinational hotel corporations regarding the key competencies necessary when working in Russia.

THE SIGNIFICANCE OF EMPLOYEE RESOURCING
TO INTERNATIONAL GROWTH

The survey which preceded this text (D'Annunzio-Green, Maxwell and Watson, 2000) identifies the area of employee resourcing as key to sustaining the prolific growth of internationalization highlighted above. One of the main current issues identified by the survey respondents was recruitment and selection of managers with the ability and motivation to work internationally. In addition, one of the top future human resource issues identified was to develop the appropriate managerial competencies to enable international managers to function effectively in diverse cultures. The significance of effective employee resourcing as being key to the success of future international development in the hospitality industry has recently been highlighted by David Wood, CEO of the HCIMA, who stated: 'world-wide the industry already employs one in ten of the global population ... perhaps the most significant problem we face is in recruitment. The millennium time bomb for the industry world-wide is staffing' (Powell, 1999).

There is no doubt, therefore, that increasing internationalization has put pressure on organizations to ensure that their managers have the appropriate competencies to enable them to work productively with others across borders in culturally and nationally diverse strategic alliances and partnerships.

The group of managers who are at the sharp end of these developments are expatriates whose effectiveness is recognized as being a major determinant in the success of international hospitality business activity (Barber and Pittaway, 2000). The term expatriate is defined by Dowling *et al.* as 'a managerial employee who is moved from one country to, and for employment in, another country' (1994, p. 238). The skills and competencies used by these expatriates to manage employees successfully in diverse cultures and adapt to the different work environment is the focus of this chapter. This presents a challenge for expatriates, as although there may be a degree of support offered to them before and during their assignments, they are ultimately responsible for teams of employees in the host country and are charged with developing effective ways of managing the differences which may exist on a day-to-day basis. Mendenhall *et al.* (1995) assert that one of the most difficult tasks of any expatriate manager is to motivate and lead people from cultural backgrounds different from their own. As they go on to discuss:

while leadership is exhibited in all societies, cultural norms influence what kinds of leadership behaviours are appropriate in a particular culture. By definition, leaders stand out from their peers, yet they stand out without pushing the constraints of cultural norms too far. If leaders attempt to behave too differently from cultural norms, they will be rejected: however, if they adhere to all cultural norms to the letter they will not be leaders – for leaders must break some norms to be seen as different. (1995, p. 570)

The challenge of how expatriates manage the delicate workplace balancing act referred to in the quote is influenced by many aspects of employee resourcing, but none more so than the acquisition and development of appropriate managerial competencies to enable the expatriate managers to perform effectively and cope with the inevitable cross-cultural adjustment that will be necessary.

A THEORETICAL PERSPECTIVE ON EXPATRIATE CROSS-CULTURAL ADJUSTMENT

The literature on the management of expatriates and the subsequent adjustment process offers a range of theoretical and empirical evaluations which anatomize the factors influencing the cross-cultural adjustment process (Morley *et al.*, 1997). This serves to heighten the degree of importance afforded to the role of expatriates and acknowledges the complications inherent in an international manager's role once they are asked to operate outside their normal domestic work environment. From this literature emerges many themes, most emanating from the starting point that a focus on expatriate adjustment is an intrinsic factor in the short and long term, if expatriates are to operate at the same level of productivity and performance as domestic managers. The debate surrounding the risk of expatriate failure as an issue does not detract from the almost universal opinion of the importance of expatriate performance to the international multinational corporation (Harzing, 1995; Handler and Lane, 1997; Brewster and Scullion, 1997) and the link between effective performance of expatriates and the process of cultural adjustment (Schneider and Barsoux, 1997; Selmer *et al.*, 1998). The determinants of this relationship can be explained as follows. Viewing cultural adjustment as an opportunity rather than a threat clearly has intellectual, emotional and moral appeal (Schneider and Barsoux, 1997) and, practically speaking, being able to manage this diversity is essential for getting the job done – the challenge that expatriates face and the managerial competencies they require for working with people from different cultures is clearly the key to effective performance. Of course, a manager's performance, whether international or domestic, is dependent on many factors (Armstrong and Baron, 1998) such as:

- personal factors – the individual's skill, competence, motivation and commitment;
- leadership factors – the quality of encouragement guidance and support provided by colleagues;
- systems factors – the systems of work and facilities provided by the organizations;
- contextual (situational) factors – external and internal environmental pressures and changes.

Expatriates have to contend with the adjustment issues from an internal organizational culture perspective, as well as from a national cultural perspective, both of which will wield interrelated challenges. These systems and structures and the environment surrounding them will dictate the accepted ways of managing, and the solutions to these challenges must fit the particular circumstances of the organization. The competencies a manager adopts to cope with this are therefore contingent on the internal and external environment within which he/she operates. This is crucial in helping to understand why certain management techniques, such as teamwork or performance management systems, and certain managerial behaviour, such as consultative or autocratic management styles, cannot safely be transferred from one culture to another without some modifications.

The expatriate adjustment process has many dimensions. Belle and Straw (1989) describe the process as consisting of two interrelated components. The first, referred to as predictive control, involves creating a new set of mental road maps and book of traffic rules. These enable individuals to make predictions about what behaviours and competencies are expected in specific situations, how people will probably respond and what behaviours are appropriate and not appropriate. By enabling expatriates to predict what to do in a variety of situations, these maps and rules allow them to feel a measure of control in the new environment. The next component they discuss is mastery of new behaviour, or behavioural control. This involves attempting to adjust ones own style of managerial leadership to fit the new cultural context. For example,

> it is one thing to know that Chinese communicate more indirectly than Americans but quite another to be able to change one's own style of communication from direct to more indirect. The challenge is equally difficult for the Chinese who must change their indirect style to a more direct one when transferring to the United States. (Black *et al.*, 1999, p. 108)

In this context then, cross-cultural adjustment involves discovering the new cause and effect contingencies in the new culture and mastering the necessary expedient behaviour and competencies.

It is clear from the literature so far that the notion of expatriates being required to change their managerial behaviour and competencies to adapt to new working situations is widely supported and the attitude that a good manager in one country will be a good manager in all countries is disputed as the body of theoretical and empirical knowledge on the dynamics of adjustment have grown. Technical competence, while still important, is not a factor which will single-handedly lead to satisfactory performance in an international setting. An expatriate manager, therefore, must be aware of the need to utilize the most appropriate managerial competencies or indeed adapt those which may have been appropriate in previous work situations to fit the employment context in which he is placed.

MANAGERIAL COMPETENCIES FOR INTERNATIONAL HOSPITALITY MANAGERS

The term 'competencies' was one of the human resource management buzz words of the 1990s with many companies introducing the competency approach to a plethora of HRM techniques such as training and development, performance management and recruitment and selection. Definitions abound, but the discussion in this chapter defines competencies as 'an underlying characteristic of a person which results in effective and/ or superior performance in a job' (Klemp, 1980, p. 99). Behavioural competencies describe typical behaviours observed when those performing the job apply motives, traits and skills to job-relevant tasks and produce job-relevant outcomes (Whiddett and Hollyforde, 1999). At an organizational level and to aid communication with staff, competencies are usually given a title and some form of description. For example, the competency title 'planning and organizing' would be summarized as: 'achieves results through detailed planning and organization of people and resources to meet goals, targets or objectives within agreed time-scales' (Whiddett and Hollyforde, 1999, p. 9). Other commonly used competency titles include team-working, decision-making, managing relationships and influencing. Competencies provide a framework for giving and collecting information about jobs and job applicants and provide examples of behaviours necessary for effective performance in the job. In this context, therefore, what are the necessary competencies to enable an expatriate hotel manager to perform effectively?

There is very little literature specific to the international hospitality industry which examines the managerial competencies required to operate across international boundaries. That which does exist includes: Baum (1995), D'Annunzio-Green (1997), Gliatis and Guerrier (1994), and Jayawardena (2000).

It could be argued that the lack of research in this area may stem from a belief that the very nature of the hospitality industry leads it to attract staff who are enthusiastic about international careers and have themselves developed ways of managing these careers on a global basis. The lack of attention paid to this area in the body of applied hospitality research may signify a lack of concern on the part of organizations with the need to develop specific competencies for international managers. It has been shown, for example, that international staff in hotel companies experience fewer problems in international assignments than in many other sectors. Managers in a sample (Gliatis and Guerrier, 1994) developed positive approaches to managing stress associated with international assignments and clearly enjoyed their lifestyle, essential given the recognized stress of relocation. Another view is that of D'Annunzio-Green (1997) who argues that a prerequisite of a planned approach to developing international managers in the hospitality industry is 'agreement on an appropriate set of competencies and an examination of ways of developing and assessing them' (p. 201). In agreement with this is a more recent study (Jayawardena, 2000) which cites research by the HCIMA and the University of Surrey, identifying the future competency needs of managers in the hospitality industry. Those highest on the list of required skills and competencies were abilities in language, people management, communication and managing cultural differences. Generic research by Iles (1995) further consolidates these areas by identifying five key competencies for successful international managers. As can be seen below these stress the importance of the cultural component as being a crucial area for consideration throughout the selection process:

- cultural awareness – understanding the difference;
- communicative competence – communicating across the difference;
- cognitive competence – acknowledging the stereotypes;
- valuing the difference; and
- gaining synergy from the difference.

General individual attributes

People or relational skills

Perception skills

Ability to tolerate ambiguity

Ability to demonstrate flexible behaviour

Clear goal orientation

Sociability and interest in people

Empathetic and non judgmental

Good communication skills

Figure 6.1 Key competencies required of international managers
Source: CIPD Guide to International Recruitment Selection and Assessment

Technical competence

Previous achievements in home country

Language skills

Motivation

Stress resistance

Independence

Goal orientated personality

Communication skills

Figure 6.2 Selection criteria for international managers in rank order
Source: CIPD Guide to International Recruitment, Selection and Assessment

More recently, the Chartered Institute of Personnel and Development (1999), in recognition of increasing internationalization and the importance of the role of the international manager, conducted an examination of best practice in international recruitment and selection. They summarized the research findings to date (Mendenhall and Oddou, 1988; Abe and Wiseman, 1983; Black, 1990; Clarke and Hammer, 1995; Stoner *et al.*, 1972) which examined key skills and competencies required of international managers and the most common criteria used for selection in rank order. The results can be seen in Figures 6.1 and 6.2.

They conclude from this that organizations 'understate the significance of such relational and intercultural abilities as adaptability and flexibility. Often the very people who are successful in a UK setting – the extremely ambitious, task-oriented, aggressive problem-solvers with a 'time is money' philosophy – are those most destined for failure in another country' (1999, p. 7). This quote emphasizes the importance of consideration by organizations of the selection criteria and necessary skills and competencies required of international managers. The 'domestic = overseas performance' equation should not be relied upon without some consideration of other competencies necessary for successful performance.

Evidence to date on hospitality multinationals' selection criteria and required competencies does show some leaning towards a wider consideration of relevant factors which may influence adjustment and performance in an international setting. British Airways make it a priority to stress the need for flexibility and cultural awareness in their prospective country managers (CIPD, 1999). The application form asks prospective candidates to respond to a challenging critical incident in an international context and tests for a number of competencies such as communication, valuing others and awareness of cultural differences. The latter is measured through a series of job-related tests. Other harder measures include motivation and aptitude for learning a foreign language. Similarly, Inter-continental Hotel Group cite competencies such as: realism about the way people are; an understanding of the differences of culture, behaviour, values and expectations; ability to operate in diverse cultural environments; and ability to cope with plural values; as important characteristics desirable in future internationally mobile general managers (IHG, 1997).

This literature review has shown that there is currently much debate on the importance of the skills and competencies needed by international managers and that there are varying views on what the desired competencies should be. The case study that follows commences by outlining briefly the current environmental and operating climate for hotel operators in Russia, and then goes on to report the findings of a recent research project which asked a number of expatriates their views on the most important skills and competencies required by them as international managers in Russia.

COMPETENCIES REQUIRED BY BRITISH EXPATRIATES WORKING IN THE HOTEL SECTOR IN RUSSIA

The Russian Context

Throughout the 1990s the transformation of Russian management practices to free-market standards has been at the forefront of international issues (May *et al.*, 1998). Many foreign organizations have begun operations in Russia over the last ten years, facilitated in part by the introduction of new laws allowing direct foreign investment. An estimated $4.5 billion in foreign capital had been invested in Russia by the middle of 1995 (EIU *Country Report*, 1995), and Russia offers potential investors the advantages of a highly educated and relatively inexpensive labour force, vast unexploited natural resources and relative geographical proximity to most European countries (Morley *et al.*, 1997). Prospects for investment are increasing as the infrastructure of the market economy is created and as privatization progresses. Many of the western firms who decide to enter the area have, however, encountered significant challenges in managing relations with Russian organizations still carrying values and practices aligned with a centrally controlled system, and 'culture clashes' between Russian and western partners frequently threaten to jeopardize expansion and alliance relations (Barnes, 1997). There is a growing literature on the constraints that Russia's history and culture pose for western investors (May *et al.*, 1998; Shekshnia, 1994, 1998) and given the instability of the free market in Russia, it is imperative that western organizations be prepared for the unique barriers to management effectiveness they may encounter as they expand into Russia.

Tourism in Russia

In January 1990, after more than 10 years of negotiating and with an initial investment of $62 million, McDonald's opened its first restaurant in Moscow in Pushkin Square. Serving 40,000 Soviet citizens, it was for a time the busiest McDonald's outlet in the world (the Beijing restaurant now holds the record). In 1990, McDonald's golden arches – a stone's throw from the Kremlin and Red Square – were the ultimate western consumer symbol in Russia. It brought more Russians – including the 27,000 applicants for the initial crew of 630 – into direct contact with western big business than anything in Soviet history. Now it is possible for virtually any Russian, at least in Moscow and St Petersburg, to witness the full panoply of western consumer goods in chic boutiques located in emporia that have not quite managed to shake their jaded soviet look. Russia is now a market for products and services that 10 years ago would have seemed impossible: London Taxis, cellular telephones, advice on setting up regional business centres, loans to improve roads, railways and airports, yoghurt parlours, Barbie dolls, Mars bars... Holden *et al.*, 1997, p. 142)

As this quote illustrates, there is no doubt that the Russian business environment has changed since the collapse of the Soviet Union, and now western businesses of all types are to be found competing for trade in a once monopolistic economy. The implications of this change are of concern to most sectors contemplating a move towards developing in the Russian market-place and none more so than the tourism industry which has much to gain from the recent developments and much scope for expansion in an environment which was previously inaccessible to all but a minority of curious and culturally adventurous travellers. No one is more aware of these complexities and how they impact on both the work and social setting than expatriate managers who are the linchpins of and a critical success factor in any joint venture in Russia.

During the communist era Russia's government did not consider the tourism industry as an important or effective means of generating hard currency and, more recently, Russia's government has many more pressing concerns on the political agenda, and the industry has subsequently been offered negligible support. The obvious attraction of Russia as a tourist destination, appealing to those in search of cultural adventure and rich history and heritage, coupled with its proximity to Europe, makes it, at first glance, a desirable tourist destination. This is hampered, however, by the declining economy and the much publicized breakdowns in law and order, as well as the danger and expense of travel in Russia. Together, these factors have had a detrimental effect on the leisure and travel sector (Trew, 1997).

The Hotel Industry in Moscow and St Petersburg

The hotel industry in Russia is mirrored by that in Eastern Europe as a whole which, according to Lockwood (1993), has been dominated by large, state-owned hotel companies such as Intourist. The hotel supply consists of three main types – old traditional hotels that were built in a different era but have been left to run down and have lost most of their former splendour; concrete and glass dormitories built post-war; and new hotels built or upgraded to international standards with involvement from international companies.

Table 6.1 Operating performance of deluxe hotels in Moscow and St Petersburg, 1995–8

	Number of international standard rooms	Average occupancy (%)				Average daily rate ($US)			
	1996	1995	1996	1997	1998	1995	1996	1997	1998
Moscow	1348	70	71	64.8	56	251	250	322	335
St Petersburg	950	n/a	n/a	60.7	57.8	n/a	n/a	304	351

Source: Adapted by author from HVS International (1997) and Euro City Survey (1999).

The latest available room count for Russia is 202,033 with 390,931 beds (WTO, 1999) Most of these rooms still resemble the modest requirements provided in the USSR era and it is estimated that only 20–25,000 rooms are suitable for foreign arrivals. Table 6.1 shows the operating performance in terms of average occupancy and average daily rate.

Moscow is ranked among the most expensive business travel destinations in the world and the average daily rate (ADR) of the deluxe hotels is double that of other emerging markets. This is due to the strength of demand and the lack of quality hotel supply due to high market-entry barriers. The 1998 figures do not appear to be too drastically affected by the devaluation of the rouble, although this and the recent incidence of terrorism in the Moscow area has led to a lack of confidence in the destination resulting in many business trips being cancelled or shortened. Up until this point Russian hotels were enjoying a year of very strong growth which explains why the results for the year 1998 were not as bad as might have been expected (Travel Industry Monitor, 1999).

HVS argue that, currently, the business traveller has little alternative to the city centre's five-star hotels as the other hotels offer little in the way of comfort or amenities. There seems to be general agreement (Lockwood, 1993; HVS, 1997; Trew, 1997) that what is needed in the two main cities are acceptable three-star hotels, and business-standard hotels in the regions. Clearly there are plenty of large hotel properties which were developed under the communist regime, but to renovate these would involve a large investment. Trew reports that in the hotel sector relatively few joint-venture projects have been set up despite apparent enthusiasm for foreign investment on the Russian side and strong interest from many international hotel groups anxious to establish a presence in this important potential market. 'Many potential foreign investors and operators say that the environment is just "too difficult" and note the marked reluctance on the Russian side to relinquish any control or succumb to western branding or foreign management' (Trew, 1997, p. 32). These problems coupled with the challenging legal system in respect of property ownership, complicated taxation issues and the bureaucratic difficulties involved in securing a site for development have made foreign parties more guarded and cautious of the Russian market-place.

In-depth, face-to-face interviews were conducted in Moscow, St Petersburg, London and Edinburgh. Seventeen managers were interviewed in five luxury-graded hotel properties and asked a series of questions. The results presented in this chapter relate to one of the questions asked throughout the interview: 'What skills or competencies helped you deal with the challenges you faced as an expatriate manager in Russia?' Each interview lasted between one-and-a-half and three hours. Key themes were then extracted from the data and those that are particularly relevant to the focus of this chapter can be seen below. Four main competencies emerged from the data as being critical for managers dealing with a unique set of challenges and there follows a summary of each theme identified from the interviews with justification and discussion. Actual respondents' quotes are included to clarify and amplify the points made.

Key Competencies Identified by International Hospitality Managers in Russia

An Ability to Build Trust and be Patient

A general consensus among the hotel expatriates was the need to be patient, listen and accept that the adaptation process will take time. The expatriates stressed the need to start off slowly by giving the local staff evidence of their professionalism and technical competence: 'In Russia you must be satisfied with very small steps. You will still reach your goal but it will take you double or triple the time to do so.' Knowing the right approach to adopt was felt to be crucial: 'you don't go in and say, I am the great western manager and now I am going to show you the right way to do things – this attitude doesn't work anywhere and certainly not in Russia'.

Patience as a key competency is stressed in much of the literature (Schneider and Barsoux, 1997; Joynt and Morton, 1999) as expatriates must take time to adjust and adapt to the new culture. Schneider and Barsoux argue that managers must avoid the temptation to continuously benchmark the new culture against the home culture but instead take time to understand the real reasons why local staff perform and view work in a certain way. They refer to the need for expatriates to demonstrate patience and respect as the 'golden rule' (1997, p. 194) of international business.

Building trust was a theme which predominated throughout all interviews. Expatriates identified the existence of strong feelings of mistrust among local staff and local managers which acted as a barrier to effective communication. They acknowledged the cultural divide that existed and recognized the need to employ the right strategies to bridge the gap and gain the trust and subsequent support from local Russian staff. The strategies employed to do this are demonstrated on a simplistic level by one expatriate's quote and validated by others:

> Lots of older Russians will not trust you unless you drink with them – once you have done this you are accepted and they will start to trust you – you will also have great fun in the process.
> 'Let the staff know what you are doing and why. If they know what you are thinking and your words are borne out by subsequent actions then they will grow to trust you – you must provide them with evidence of your trustworthiness and honesty.

As can be seen from this, building trust, or the more challenging task of overcoming mistrust, was approached by trying to build relationships with the local staff through informal friendliness, both off and on the job, and more formal mechanisms of building communication lines. This is discussed more fully in a subsequent section. On a deeper and more complex level, building trust was viewed as the need to understand some key cultural differences that exist in Russia, and the influence of these on accepted working practices. There was no common ground in terms of the best way to obtain this knowledge. Few of the expatriates had been given formal educational or a cross-cultural training pre-assignment. The felt importance of this by the expatriates was mirrored by cautionary advice as illustrated by the following quote:

> The only way you will really learn about the Russian culture is to work here and get
> to know the people. By all means do some homework before hand but be ready to
> open your mental file and adjust the information on a regular basis as you experience
> life here. In my experience no-one will trust you initially and you must find a way to
> break down those barriers over time.

Trust is notoriously difficult to establish when you are working with staff who share a
similar cultural perspective as yourself. It is further complicated, therefore, when
communicating across cultures, leading to high potential for misunderstandings.

An Ability to Manage Change

On an organizational level the expatriates felt pressure to introduce changes in the
hotels in order to raise standards, as well as to justify their positions and perhaps their
salary, so there was a felt obligation to improve operational areas which were not
functioning effectively. The response to this challenge was knowing the right time and
when/how to make the change:

> initially you must keep a low profile and really just assess the situation – it isn't
> rocket science, it's the same everywhere, just a little bit more sensitive in Russia. To
> introduce change in Russia I would wait 4 weeks instead of 2 and would introduce a
> small change at a time rather than all at once – change is a slow process here.

This was felt to be frustrating by some but essential by all. Being open and methodical
about changes was also key but the strategies employed here were quite different from
normal practice. For example, many of the expatriates spoke about having to alter their
common approach due to there being no time for, or acceptance of, the notion of
consultation or the 'Let's explore the problem and come up with a solution' phase: 'You
must make a decision and show your authority and expertise otherwise they may
consider you incompetent'. One manager gave an example of holding a meeting to try
to brainstorm ideas for improvement with his staff. At the meeting he was met with a
stony silence. After the meeting he felt quite despondent until, one by one, many
members of the team came up individually to give him their ideas: 'they were
embarrassed to open up in a group situation but they are really bright and creative
people, it was my job to find a way to tap into this creativity and formal meetings were
not as productive as informal or one to one exchanges'.

Managing change is not a competency that is discussed at any length in the
international literature, although a recent report by the Chartered Institute of Personnel
and Development (1999), identifies flexibility as a key quality in prospective
international managers. Expatriate managers are faced with multiple changes to both
lifestyle and work patterns and must surely be equipped with a range of possible
responses to these changes. The expatriates stressed the fact that many of the Russian
staff had a very parochial attitude towards accepted working practices in the hotels. The
challenge for expatriates was to change the attitudes of these staff to one where they
could see the benefit of a more synergistic approach, drawing on best practice from
both an expatriate and local perspective rather than viewing their way as the best or
only way to operate. Managing this change was seen to be crucial in improving
operating standards and customer service.

An Ability to Manage Relationships

The relationships experienced by the expatriates varied from animosity to acceptance and everything in between. The general consensus was that there is no hard-and-fast rules to help you know how the local staff will react to you – it all depends on the individuals. General opinion was that many expatriates go to work in Russia with a superior attitude which will undoubtedly fail.

> Russians do not like to think you are here to sort out their problems so you must try to couch the issue in clever terms, rather than saying ... this is wrong and it needs to change ... you say ... we had exactly the same problem as this and tried to change it by doing this and this ... this strategy will often be much more readily accepted.

If an expatriate has the attitude that they are there to sort out all the Russian problems then they will not succeed. One of the interesting problems mentioned here was the issue of an expatriate going to work in Russia with unrealistic expectations that the working culture in Russia has changed dramatically over the last few years and, therefore, having expectations that only minimal differences exist. This they cautioned against, and one experienced expatriate explained:

> I have watched many expatriates in different sectors come and go, having built up trust, got to know the Russian people and made changes which were accepted. When a new expatriate comes along, however, it is back to square one – managing people in Russia is so personal and every new expatriate has their own battles and triumphs to experience.

The importance of interpersonal skills is emphasized by another quote: 'Whenever we were looking for new expatriates managers we emphasized the fact that we do not need people who are 200 per cent professional in their job, we need people who are 200 per cent professional in dealing with people – that is more important.'

Managing relationships helps the manager to integrate into the host culture and develop friendships. These friendships may facilitate communication and breaking down any barriers of mistrust which may exist. The last quote above is validated by Schneider and Barsoux (1997) who discuss the dangers of recruiting managers based on technical or conceptual abilities rather than communication skills, thus stressing the need for more people-orientated managers on international assignments such as this.

Flexibility of Managerial Style

Another focal point was the need to adapt to the different manager–staff relationship. At times there was too much respect for hierarchy; staff, basically, worked on the belief that what a manager says or does is right and unquestionable. There was felt to be a real need to encourage questioning ability in staff, the freedom to make suggestions, to question a manager's judgement, to contribute to the debate on issues relating to the workplace and to be open about their opinions:

> Russian staff would rarely say thank you, or complain about a decision. They would feign agreement and go away and immediately grumble behind your back. For this reason large group meetings were very unproductive as people were uneasy about

speaking out. The unpredictability of almost everything I was involved in resulted in feelings of lack of control.

The majority of expatriates reported that their management style had changed to cope with the aforementioned issues – more patient, showing more empathy, being firm and direct, dealing with conflict, de-fusing difficult situations, using a balance of more directive management style and more supportive management style: 'Russian people can be very excitable and emotional so you have to take a firm hand and say ... "it has to be done doesn't it" ... gain agreement to this first and then issue the orders!'

Another view was that the western management style should be adopted as far as possible in a positive sense to show Russians how effective it can be: 'I tried hard not to change my style and force a false impression on those I was working with – I changed the pace and order of what I did but my core managerial style did not alter.'

The readiness to adapt one's managerial style is therefore another key competency. Circumstances may change and the behaviour of locals can be unpredictable, so a quick but appropriate reaction may often be necessary. The feelings of lack of control identified in one of the previous quotes is a natural reaction to uncertainty such as this. All the expatriates interviewed were willing and committed to learning more about the national and corporate culture in which they were working and were prepared, if necessary, to adapt their own style to fit the new operational parameters and norms. At the same time, however, there was a sense of conviction about their own managerial abilities and the benefits of avoiding a parochial or ethnocentric approach in favour of a more synergistic perspective. Achieving this synergy and being able to utilize the strengths of one's own style while being able to adapt when necessary is possibly one of the key competencies required by international managers. As one expatriate stated: '...this often involved striking the balance between a consultative or control-driven approach in order to gain commitment to organizational goals'.

CONCLUSION

It is clear that possessing the right competencies is thought to be of great importance to the managers interviewed. In comparing their responses and the key competencies identified in the literature review, there are some obvious areas of overlap and agreement. The IPD mention, for example, the importance of competencies such as communication skills, building relationships, ability to tolerate ambiguity and flexibility, all of which are confirmed by the international managers interviewed in Russia. Indeed, the expatriates responses were also in alignment with the views of Belle and Straw (1989) and Black (1999) discussed earlier, who stress the need for expatriates to adapt their management style to fit the new cultural context and working situation in which they find themselves, an issue mentioned by many of the expatriates.

But identifying these competencies in themselves is only half the story – more difficult is measuring and developing them in international managers. Pine and Go (1996) support this assertion and argue that the rapid globalization strategy that many companies are pursuing implies the need to upgrade managers' expertise in order that they are capable of meeting the challenges posed: 'The cultivation of competencies and capabilities is moving from the realm of corporate philanthropy to the realm of productivity' (p. 102). This should, they argue, provide the hotel industry with an incentive to support education, training and research in this area. It is clear that providing international managers with support in order to develop the required skills and competencies is essential in what must be one of the most challenging career options in the hospitality industry – that of the international assignment.

ACKNOWLEDGEMENTS

The author acknowledges the help of a Carnegie Trust Research Grant and a Napier University research grant, without which the primary research for this chapter could not have been conducted.

SELF-ASSESSMENT QUESTIONS

1. Debate the advantages and disadvantages of working as an expatriate manager in the hospitality industry from both individual manager and organizational perspectives.
2. To what extent do you agree that the selection criteria for international managers should differ from that for domestic managers? Justify your response with reasons from the text as well as your own opinions or experiences.
3. Take each 'competency title' in Table 6.1 and expand it to provide a 'competency description'.
4. How might a hospitality organization provide initial, ongoing and post-assignment support to international managers working in diverse cultures such as Russia?

REFERENCES

Abe, H. and Wiseman, R. L. (1983) 'A cross cultural confirmation of the dimensions of intercultural effectiveness'. *International Journal of Inter-cultural Relations*, **7**, 53–67.

Armstrong, M. and Baron, A. (1998) *Performance Management: The New Realities*. London: Institute of Personnel and Development.

Barber, N. and Pittaway, L. (2000) 'Expatriate recruitment in South East Asia: dilemma or opportunity?' *International Journal of Contemporary Hospitality Management*, **12**(6), 352–9.

Barnes, J., Crook, M., Koybaeva, T. and Stafford, E. (1997) 'Why our Russian alliances fail'. *Long Range Planning*, **30**(4), 540–50.

Baum, T. (1995) *Managing Human Resources in the European Tourism and Hospitality Industry*. London: International Thomson Business Press.

Belle, N. and Straw, B. (1989) 'People as sculptors versus people as sculpture: the roles of personality and personal control in organizations', in M. B. Arthur, D. T. Hall and B. Lawrence (eds), *Handbook of Career Theory*. London: Cambridge University Press.

Black, J. (1999) 'The relationship of personal characteristics with the adjustment of Japanese expatriate managers'. *Management International Review*, **30**, 119–34.

Black, J., Gregarson, H., Mendenhall, M and Stroh, L. (1999) *Globalizing People Through International Assignments*. Reading, Massachusetts: Addison-Wesley.

Brewster, C. and Scullion, H. (1997) 'A review and agenda for expatriate HRM'. *Human Resource Management Journal*, **7**(3), 32–41.

Chartered Institute of Personnel and Development (CIPD) (1999) *The IPD Guide to International Recruitment Selection and Assessment*. London: IPD Publications.

Clarke, C. and Hammer, M. R. (1995) 'Predictors of Japanese and American managers' job success, personal adjustment, and inter-cultural interaction effectiveness'. *Management International Review*, **35**, 135–70.

D'Annunzio-Green, N. (1997) 'Developing international managers in the hospitality industry'. *International Journal of Contemporary Hospitality Management*, 4 & 5/6, 199–208.

D'Annunzio-Green, N., Maxwell, G. and Watson, S. (2000) 'Human resource issues in international hospitality, travel and tourism'. *International Journal of Contemporary Hospitality Management*, **12**(2, 3), 215–17.

Dowling, P. J., Schuler, R. S. and Welch, D. E. (1994) *International Dimensions of Human Resource Management*. California: ITP.

EIU (1995) *Country Report: Russia* (3rd quarter) Economic Intelligence Unit: London.

Euro City Survey (1999) Pannell Kerr Forster Consultants.

Gliatis, N. and Guerrier, Y. (1993) 'Managing international career moves in international hotel companies'. *Progress in Tourism, Recreation and Hospitality Management*, **5**, 229–41.

Handler, C. A. and Lane, I. M. (1997) 'Career planning and expatriate couples'. *Human Resource Management Journal*, **7**(3), 67–78.

Harzing. A. W. K. (1995) 'The persistent myth of high expatriate failure rates'. *The International Journal of Human Resource Management*, **6**(2), 457–74.

Holden, N., Cooper, C. and Carr, J. (1998) *Dealing with the New Russia*. Chichester: John Wiley and Sons.

HVS International (1997) *The Former Eastern Bloc: Hotel Trends and Opportunities*. London.

IHG (1997) Intercontinental Hotel Group Corporate Management Development Programme Information.

Iles, P. (1995) 'Learning to work with difference'. *Personnel Review*, **24**(6), 51–9.

Jayawardwena, C. (2000) 'International hotel manager'. *International Journal of Hospitality Management*, **12**(1), 67–9.

Joynt, P. and Morton, B. (1999) *The Global HR Manager*. London: Chartered Institute of Personnel and Development.

Klemp Jnr, G. O. (1980) 'The assessment of occupational competence'. Report to the National Institute of Education, Washington, D.C.

Lockwood, A. (1993) 'Eastern Europe and the former Soviet States', in P. Jones and A. Pizam (eds), *The International Hospitality Industry*. London: Pitman, pp. 25–37.

May, R., Bormann Young, C. and Ledgerwood, D. (1998) 'Lessons from Russian human resource management experience'. *European Management Journal*, **16**(4), 447–59.

Mendenhall, M., Punnett, B. J. and Ricks, D. (1995) *Global Management*. Oxford: Blackwell.

Mendenhall, M. E. and Oddou, G. (1988) 'The overseas assignment: a practical look'. *Business Horizons*, **31**(5), 78–84.

Morley, M., Burke, C. and O'Regen, T. (1997) 'The Irish in Moscow: a question of adjustment'. *Human Resource Management Journal*, **7**(3), 53–65.

Pine, R. and Go, F. M. (1996) 'Globalisation in the hotel industry', in R. Kotas, R. Teare, J. Logie, C. Jayawardena and J. Bowen (eds), *The International Hospitality Business*. London: Cassell.

Pizam, A. (1997) Guest editor, in special international edition of *International Journal of Hospitality Management*, **16**(2), 125–6.

Powell, S. (1999) 'Is recruitment the millennium time-bomb for the industry world-wide?' *International Journal of Contemporary Hospitality Management*, **11**(4), 138–9.

Schneider, S. and Barsoux J. L. (1997) *Managing Across Cultures*. Hemel Hempstead: Prentice-Hall.

Selmer, J., Torbiorn, I. and de Leon, C. (1998) 'Sequential cross-cultural training for expatriate business managers: pre-departure and post-arrival'. *International Journal of Human Resource Management*, **9**(5), 831–40.

Shekshnia, S. (1994) 'Managing people in Russia: challenges for foreign investors'. *European Management Journal*, **12**, 298–305.

Shekshnia, S. (1998) 'Western multinationals HRM practices in Russia'. *European Management Journal*, **16**(4), 460–5.
Stoner, J. A., Aram, J. D. and Rubin, J. (1972) 'Factors associated with effective performance in overseas work assignments'. *Personnel Psychology*, **24**, 303–18.
Travel Industry Monitor (1999). Russia Report.
Trew, J. (1997) *International Tourism Reports: No. 3: Russia*. London: Travel and Tourism Intelligence.
Whiddett, S. and Hollyforde, S. (1999) *The Competencies Handbook*. Wiltshire: Institute of Personnel and Development.
World Travel and Tourism Human Resource Centre (1998) *Steps to Success*. **2**(1), March.
WTO (1999) *Tourism Market Trends Europe 1989–1998*. World Tourism Organization Commission for Europe, 34th meeting, Tashkent, Uzbekistan, 19–22 April.

Part II Employee Development

7

Human Resource Strategy and Development for Quality Service in the International Hotel Sector

---

Gillian A. Maxwell and Samantha Quail

ABSTRACT

Until relatively recently, the role of employees in hotel and tourism service offerings was generally undervalued in the UK, especially at a strategic level. With the advent of human resource management in the past couple of decades, however, the contribution of employees – and their management – in this context has achieved greater recognition and organizational status. One catalyst for this promotion in organizational standing is the drive for quality service. This chapter discusses the contemporary organizational contribution of human resource management and development in relation to quality service. The Hilton Group plc, with its UK-driven launch of a renewed quality offensive across the globe, is the case study used to exemplify the development of human resource strategy and employee development for quality service in the international hotel sector. The singularly important conclusion that is drawn is the co-dependency between human resource management and development on the one hand, and quality service on the other.

INTRODUCTION

In 'the age of service competition' (Gronroos, 1994, p. 5) that is international hospitality and tourism, the customer reigns supreme. Such is the power of customers that the term 'service management' is increasingly used to emphasize management imperatives in this age of service competition and market forces. Gronroos (1994, p. 7) isolates five key characteristics of service management:

(1) It is an *overall management perspective* which should guide decisions in all areas of management;
(2) It is *customer driven* or market driven;
(3) It is a *holistic perspective* which emphasizes the importance of intraorganizational, cross-functional collaboration;
(4) Managing *quality is an integral part* of service management; and
(5) *Internal development* of the personnel and reinforcement of its commitment to company goals and strategies are strategic prerequisites for success.

This chapter focuses in on four aspects of these characteristics, in particular in its discussion of the connections that human resource management and development have with quality service in the international hotel sector. Market orientation (2 above), intraorganizational, cross-functional collaboration (3 above) and managing quality (4 above) can be considered as the touchstones for the discussion which, as the case study highlights, also includes internal development of employees as a strategic prerequisite for success (5 above).

The aim of the chapter is to map the relationship of human resource management and development with quality service in the international hotel sector. Worsfold (1999, p. 346), for one, has called for 'a research agenda [that] should seek to examine the links between human resource management and service quality'. Integral to the chapter aim is discussion of three related subjects, namely:

- the organizational contribution of human resource management and development in the hotel and tourism sector;
- the drive for quality service in hospitality and tourism; and
- the examination of an international case, the Hilton Group plc, which illustrates the conceptual and operational fusion between human resource management and development with quality service.

THE ORGANIZATIONAL CONTRIBUTION OF HUMAN RESOURCE MANAGEMENT AND DEVELOPMENT

human resource management (HRM) in its widest sense can essentially be seen as an employee-centred approach to management, although there is a myriad of definitions of the term. Interest in HRM has endured over the past twenty years or so since its inception in the US (Beaumont, 1994). To say that HRM across all industry has had something of a chequered history during this period may be an understatement. From optimism about the possibilities of, and prospects for, HRM in the 1980s (Armstrong, 1988; Guest, 1989), there have been questions over the extent of the uptake of HRM in industry as a whole in the 1990s (Armstrong and Long, 1994; Legge, 1995).

A key part of the great HRM debate is the strategic role of HRM. Indeed, a strategic focus is often claimed to be a distinguishing feature of HRM (Armstrong, 1992). In practice, however, it seems evident that the intrinsic merits of HRM are often considered less important in organizations than other functional aspects, like finance and marketing. The advent of service management may yet galvanize interest in the organizational contribution of HRM however, for the contribution of HRM towards customer satisfaction is gradually being recognized (Schneider and Bowen, 1993; Schneider, 1994; Lengnick-Hall and Lengnick-Hall, 1999).

Another dimension of the interest in HRM is the organizational uptake of employment management initiatives over the last decade that reflect, if not constitute, an HRM approach. Examples here include empowerment, flexible work, team-working and learning organizations. In some contrast, employment practices which can be seen to largely contradict an HRM approach have also formed part of employee management in the same period. Examples here would include down- and right-sizing, and business process re-engineering. human resource development (HRD), in particular, is an integral part of HRM: Keep (1989, p. 111) states simply that 'training and development should be regarded as central to anything that can be sensibly termed HRM'. In all service organizations (and hospitality and tourism companies are no exception) this centrality is clearly important, as 'people are the only organizational resource that can shape and create the ways in which all other business resources are used' (Torraco and Swanson, 1995, p. 18). The Hilton case study outlined later in this chapter underlines this point.

Like HRM, however, the term 'human resource development' (HRD) has been variously defined. Garavan's (1991, p. 17) definition of HRD is helpful here as it links employee development to strategy: '[HRD is] concerned with the management of employee learning for the long term keeping in mind the explicit corporate and business strategies.' Indeed, much of the literature on HRD makes a case for strategic HRD (e.g. Harrison, 1992; Stewart and McGoldrick, 1996). Garavan (1991) identifies nine key characteristics of strategic HRD:

- integration with organizational missions and goals;
- top management support;
- HRD plans and policies;
- line manager commitment and involvement;
- complementary HRM activities;
- expanded trainer roles;
- recognition of culture; and
- emphasis on evaluation.

Arguably, these characteristics could be applied to HRM, thus distinctions between HRM and HRD can become rather fine. In short, 'HRM and HRD are not mutually exclusive and form a close symbiosis to support organizational objectives' (Wilson, 1999, p. 18). Again, the Hilton case illustrates this point.

Locating hospitality and tourism in the HRM/D debate is not always straightforward. The volumes of mainstream HRM literature have a tendency to concentrate on industry as a whole or the manufacturing sector in the US or UK. Guerrier and Deery (1998) state that, in the hospitality context, researchers increasingly borrow from the mainstream literature in applications to hospitality although the converse rarely occurs. There is a relatively modest amount of contextually specific literature on HRM as a management approach in the hospitality and tourism sector, and much of this centres on hotels. Within the hotel segment of the literature, there is some debate about the extent of the uptake of HRM (Hoque, 1999; Nickson *et al.*, 2000). Wood (1992), Price (1994), Baum (1997) and Goldsmith *et al.* (1999), for example, have also researched personnel/HRM approaches in the context of hospitality and tourism in the UK. What their studies generally reveal is less a demonstrable than a potential contribution of

HRM. As regards research on strategic HRM specifically, Lucas (1995) asserts that there is negligible evidence of strategic approaches to HRM in the UK hotel sector, while Lashley and Watson (1999) indicate this is a minority element of research activity in hospitality and tourism.

In short, despite a couple of decades of debate about, and practice in, elements of HRM, the conclusion that HRM – and HRD – has largely failed to achieve its potential in industry as a whole and in hospitality and tourism in particular seems inescapable. Where there are exceptions to this general rule, they seem to be in larger organizations (Hoque, 1999). A recent exceptional example is Hyatt International's emphasis on training and career development across the group's 73 hotels, which is not typical of the industry's 'less than five-star employment practices' (Robinson, 1998, p. 22). Notably, Hyatt's vice-president of human resources attributes the success of the group's HR practices to strategic support of the contribution of human resources while implicitly recognizing that this support is unusual: 'We are blessed with a board which gives great support to human resources' (*ibid.*, p. 22).

Similarly, many of the recent employment practices that may be said to reflect an HRM approach, if not constitute HRM itself, in the hospitality and tourism sector are manifest in large organizations. Examples include empowerment in Marriott (Maxwell, 1997) and in McDonald's Restaurants, TGI Friday's and Harvester Restaurants (Lashley, 1997), and the Commitment to Excellence programme of customer-care training in Forte Hotels (Arkin and Johnson, 1999). Each of these examples links customer satisfaction to employee satisfaction and, therefore, managing quality to human resource management and development initiatives.

THE DRIVE FOR HOSPITALITY AND TOURISM QUALITY SERVICE

Quality control, like HRM, emanated from the manufacturing sector and became a part of services literature in the early 1980s (Kandampully, 1997). Because quality management has its origins in tangible products, applying quality concepts and practices to intangible services or experiences in the hotel sector, for example, proved somewhat problematic initially (Maxwell, 1994; Brush, 1997). In tourism especially, delivering quality across tangible and intangible elements represented a departure from conventional, manufacturing-orientated approaches to total quality management (Gronroos, 1982). At the heart of quality service is the difficulty in ensuring consistency due to the variability of the human element. Kamdampully (1997, p. 6) spells out the directions of this variability and the centre stage part played by employees in quality service:

a) the quality of service performance varies from one service organization to another;
b) the quality of service performance varies from one service performer to another;
c) the quality of service performance varies for the same performer from one occasion to another.

As 'service performers' – employees – are central to service quality, so, too, is their management. This centrality is likely to be accentuated as service competition and the focus on customer perceptions and expectations intensifies in hospitality and tourism and industry overall. Lewis (2000, p. 28) argues that 'as the 21st century unfolds it is clear that most people accept that service will play an increasingly important part in the economy'. Atkinson (2000, p. 8) goes further in asserting the importance of service performer/customer exchange in that: 'Customer perception of service delivery will be imperative and will shape their choice of supplier or service provider. Service excellence will need to take on a new mantle of one to one partner relationships with the customer, the consumer and end-user.'

To remain competitive, therefore, hospitality and tourism providers must continue to meet, if not exceed, customer expectations, which are themselves dynamic (Atkinson, 2000). In the UK hospitality and tourism industry for instance, with its dubious record on quality, improving quality service is a must (Maxwell *et al.*, 2000). Where any co-ordinated, macro-approach to quality is initiated here, it is often driven by public sector initiatives which hospitality and tourism organizations then seek to observe.

Improving quality service in international hospitality and tourism brings with it the added challenge of cross-cultural service encounters in branded organizations. Critical to global success in cross-cultural service translations, according to Ulrich and Black (1999, p. 45), 'is being able to tell between what is core to the business – what should be standardised throughout operations – and what isn't'. These authors use the example of Disney in Paris deviating from the usual company line on alcohol provision for reasons of French national culture to illustrate their assertion. Weiermair (2000) highlights that quality service failure in the international market is exacerbated and can result in not only negative and emotional responses from customers but also in cultural conflicts. He advocates that the key to quality service in the international market is an appropriate blending of 'global, national and local cultures, of globally and locally valid service qualities. . .[to] create tourism and destination specific cultures' (*ibid.*, p. 407). Such blends, arguably, create an important role for managing diversity, particularly in the hotel sector, as a service quality opportunity (Maxwell *et al.,* 2000). Again, this represents a linkage between HRM and quality service.

One standard organizational response to the imperative of quality service is measuring 'service quality levels and identifying errors' (Fache, 2000, p. 356). Such forensic measurements rely more on consistency of, and conformity in, service delivery which can act to inhibit the innovation (*ibid.*) that may be increasingly needed, as discussed above. One way of tuning into changing customer expectations in tourism in order to allow customization and innovation in service delivery is through Kandampully's (1997) process flow in dynamic service quality. This 'interactive feedback communication process' (*ibid.*, p. 12) stresses the importance of the interplay between customers, service deliverers and organizational strategists in quality service. Beyond its primary purpose of quality service, the model has potential HR benefits which underline the nexus between service quality and HRM/D, namely,

- a better understanding between management and employees;
- improved morale among managers and employees; and
- the development of strong and positive corporate culture, engendering commitment and participation from every member of the organization towards the common goal. (Kandampully, 1997, p. 12)

An example of the interplay between customers, service deliverers and organizational strategists in quality service, and of the co-dependency between HRM/D and quality service, is offered in the Hilton case study below.

CASE STUDY: THE HILTON GROUP PLC

Methods

The purpose of the empirical research is to map the relationship between HRM/D and service quality in an international case organization. Thus the research is both relatively broad and potentially multifaceted. Because the qualitative case study method of research lends itself readily to more intricate topics, where depth of investigation is required above quantitative volume of data, it supports the research purpose. The case in point here, the Hilton Group plc, is an instrumental case study (Stake, 1994). It is used to signal the issues inherent in developing human resource strategy for quality service in the international hotel sector. human resource development is one of the main dimensions.

Access to Hilton International Hotels, through 2000 and 2001, was developed through the good (England-based) offices of the Human Resource Vice-president (HR VP) for Hilton UK and Ireland. Material provided for the research included company communication and training videos, HR policy and training manuals, and quality system information. Preliminary face-to-face, unstructured interviews were held with the unit HR manager and HR VP (UK and Ireland) in the Glasgow Hilton in Scotland. Thereafter, semi-structured telephone interviews were held with Hilton's HR VPs (see company structure below), including the HR VP for the UK and Ireland, around the world. In the Europe, Middle East and Africa region, the regional training manager represented the HR VP. Finally, a semi-structured telephone interview was conducted with the customer service development manager (UK and Ireland).

Company Structure

Hilton International is the hotel part of the Hilton Group plc business that comprises hotels, betting and gaming, and Living Well fitness centres. It is not to be confused with the Hilton Hotel Corporation (HCC) of the US, although the Hilton Alliance does bind the two Hilton organizations in some ways and permits the usage of the 'H' logo for Hiltons around the world. The Hilton Group plc consists of some 500 hotels across the world, employing over 60,000 staff in 50 countries. All of these hotels are operated by management contract or wholly owned by Hilton. Most Hiltons are sited by airports or in city centres. Headed by a main board and chief executive, the Hilton Group plc is divided into four global regions: UK and Ireland; Europe, the Middle East and Africa; Asia Pacific; and the Americas. In each region, area presidents and executive teams run their operations.

In the UK, there are four operating regions: Scotland; the Midlands and West; London; and the South East and South Coast. These regions are encouraged to set up their own operating teams including HR, finance, sales and revenue, working in a cross-functional collaboration. The decentralized, organizational structure in the Hilton Group, in the words of the UK HR VP, Gordon Lyle, 'relies fundamentally on a clear brand direction – a strong frame – in values and behaviours'. The teams are currently at an early stage of development as their formation follows the £1.4bn integration of Hilton and Stakis plc in the UK in 1999 (to a company known at the time in the UK hotel units as 'Stilton'). At the time of the integration there were 80 Hilton hotels in the UK and 54 Stakis hotels.

The integration of the two organizations meant a rationalization of two different organizational cultures. Hilton was characterized by professionality, and being 'systematised and process-led'. Stakis, on the other hand, was more characterized by its company 'personality', engendering customer loyalty by being 'accessible and intuitive', making service mistakes but overcoming them in a friendly manner. In the period February to July 1999, the senior jobs in the new, integrated organization were filled in an organic way, mainly with the senior people from the Stakis organization. It was recognized that there was then a need to create a new organizational culture, part of which was to make the Hilton Group in the UK 'a number-one employer, the first choice in the hotel business'. The development of the new culture was derived from an extensive market research exercise that was conducted in 1999 in order to establish what customers expect and want from the Hilton brand.

Service Quality through Equilibrium

The result of the market research was clear identification of the contemporary Hilton brand. Part of this is physical, the tangible aspects of the service offering in hotel units. As a result of specification of the tangible standards, thirteen of the Stakis units were considered unrepresentative of the brand Hilton customers expect, so are now being disposed of along with a handful of Hilton hotels. The other part of the contemporary Hilton brand is intangible, the quality service element. Hilton customers expect a very high standard in this respect in that:

- staff will deliver a service;
- staff will deliver that service well and on time; and (most emphatically)
- staff will deliver the service with a smile.

For the HR VP for Asia, Rosie Holis, quality service '*is* the customer package ... we [Hilton] are not in the race if we are not delivering quality service'. Thus quality service depends heavily on employees, particularly those at the front line of customer contact. To differentiate Hilton service and meet Hilton customer needs, the brand-new concept of 'Hilton time' being 'restorative' was developed. Putting this concept into practice means the implementation of a quality service strategy named Equilibrium. Essentially, Equilibrium aims to ensure all Hilton customers experience a stay at/visit to Hilton that balances their wider life needs of work and leisure in a restorative way. Achieving such a balance – an equilibrium – may mean relaxation for stressed business people or excitement for under-stimulated guests: These groups could, respectively, make use of the rest or rumpus rooms to be made available in all Hiltons. Equilibrium is summed up within Hilton as 'putting back in a little of what life takes out' and, importantly, is attuned to individual guests through 'brand promises'. Product icons reflecting Equilibrium include goldfish swimming across the television screens as guests enter their bedrooms, and seasonally selected essential oils in bathrooms. In addition, service standards and exchanges constitute the restorative, quality experience.

In large measure, therefore, Hilton quality service is related to the behaviour of staff, mainly with guests but also with each other to create – directly and indirectly – the right type of organizational culture which will encourage appropriate employee/guest exchanges. The main challenge identified by Hilton in developing this quality of service is expressed by the HR VP for the UK and Ireland as 'an organizational cultural belief issue: Do we really believe in it [Equilibrium approach to quality]?' Closely related to this challenge are two other important considerations, both of which signal the role of HRM/D.

First, there is the development of the Equilibrium service culture throughout Hilton's four global regions. The role of the UK and Ireland region is pivotal here: the Equilibrium strategy was not only developed here as a result of the Stakis merger, but it was also launched here – in the Glasgow Hilton – in January 2000. From its initiation in the UK, Equilibrium was presented last year to the other three Hilton regions, and advertised by Jeff Goldblum, the actor, to represent the new Hilton brand and image. Given the decentralized organizational structure, the senior management teams in each region were able to decide whether or not to adopt Equilibrium. Europe, Middle East and Africa had its official launch in January 2001. The Americas region launched Equilibrium to its General Managers in May 2001 and to its regional hotels in August 2001. Asia Pacific, having had a working party to 'explore the philosophy of Equlibrium', had its launch in September 2001.

The second important consideration in the implementation of Equilibrium is adapting the Hilton brand around the world to specific locations, which is seen as an issue of national culture: 'quality in Japan is not necessary quality in London', as Gordon Lyle illustrates. Beyond the standard Hilton company specifications of quality, local unit managers are expected to ensure their staff provide more localized dimensions of quality, a new approach for Hilton. In Asia especially, the translation of Equilibrium across a diverse range of cultures in different countries represents an important and complex challenge, from the underpinning philosophy through to language dimensions (Esprit (see below) means ghost in Chinese, for example). In the Americas region, there is a difference between the expectations of North and South American customers, with the former generally enjoying a higher and more structured/pressurized standard of living, and the latter with less affluent but more relaxed lifestyles.

Thus the Equilibrium initiative is inextricably linked to employees and, as a consequence, their management. The bridge between customer service quality – Equilibrium – and the service performers in Hilton is the Esprit HRM initiative which complements Equilibrium.

Service Quality through Esprit

The contribution of HRM in the new service quality drive at Hilton is recognized formally in a newly devised, Stakis-orientated, HRM policy initiative called Esprit. This initiative builds on the four, interrelated Hilton core values as expressed in a Hilton training manual:

- Customer: to know who are customers are and provide them with the product and service they want;
- Quality: that the customer is provided with an exceptional product by exceptional staff in terms of service and flexibility;
- People: to work together and enjoy being part of a team, pulling together to provide excellent service;
- Profit: to ensure that sales are maximized in answering the customer's needs and that costs are controlled without compromising quality.

Esprit has been designed to embrace demonstrably the key principles of employee recognition, respect and reward. The regional training manager for Europe, the Middle East and Africa, Andrea Kluit, sums up the fundamental role of staff in Esprit: 'Esprit puts employees in front. There will be no guest delight without employee delight.' Recognizing the contribution of employees is not only important from an organizational perspective; it is, according to Andrea Kluit, also important because 'employees more and more expect training, a good working environment etc., and not just a job'. Thus Hilton employment packages have to take account of internal and external factors.

HRD is seen as crucial to Equilibrium and, therefore, to Esprit also. 'At the root of employee development is a real understanding of what makes a good service giver at co-worker level,' asserts Gordon Lyle. He continues that quality service 'starts with recruitment but relies more on appropriate [employee] development ... Esprit training aims to change behaviours to deliver Hilton moments.'

New recruits are encouraged to understand Equilibrium from a guest perspective, and feel positive about it before they officially join the company, by experiencing part of its service offering courtesy of Hilton (staff are also encouraged to act as mystery customers when they stay at Hiltons for preferential rates). Esprit training begins formally with The Spirit of Hilton, 'My First Day' (induction) training. Part of this orientation explores the new employee's views on their Hilton experience. It also sets out Hilton standards and moments. Examples of Hilton moments include employee initiative in providing food bowls and dog biscuits for guests with dogs and, in a more extreme case, a night manager staying with the sister of a guest who had been hospitalized with a heart attack. More Spirit of Hilton training is carried out in the employee's department before a personal development planning day is spent with the HR department, covering sales technique and customer care, for example. At each of the three stages, employees are invited to complete a questionnaire to evaluate the effectiveness of the training.

When the Spirit of Hilton training is completed, employees develop an individual training record, a Technical and Behavioural Skills record, which includes assessments, review and industry-accredited training. After twelve weeks, employees take part in an Esprit workshop. This workshop checks understanding of, and commitment to, Hilton core values, Hilton brand standards (generic and departmental) and Hilton moments. On successful completion of this programme, employees become members of the Esprit Club which then entitles them to a range of employee benefits. Thereafter, employees can tailor their own training through Hilton's Pathfinder training ladder. In sum, staff (or 'Hilton people', as they are called within the company) entry into Esprit depends of the fulfilment of four specific conditions:

- completion of the Spirit of Hilton Programme;
- attendance at an Esprit Workshop;
- completion of Technical and Behavioural Skills Training; and
- participation in a one-to-one review with a manager.

Recognition is afforded to staff through the certification of achievement, employee of the month and year schemes and Star Bond scheme, for example. This last scheme rewards Hilton moments through staff nominations to build teamwork. Nominations are heard by staff consultative committees in each hotel and Star Bond vouchers awarded according to the perceived value of the Hilton moment. For example, being cited personally (and favourably) in a guest's letter could earn the member of staff a couple of Star Bonds which can be used for retailing.

Esprit training is based on technical and behavioural skills to support the identified brand standards and provision of Hilton moments. It is continuous to keep Equilibrium alive through all training and team meetings. In addition to directly supporting Equilibrium, continuous, individually centred employee development is recognized as important to individual motives too:

> Good people need to grow intellectually and materially. So employee development has to be available to people [employees] so that they can feel they can do things. Some people [employees] may not want to progress but they have a choice. Employee development is not a company responsibility but an individual [one]. The company facilitates development. (Gordon Lyle)

The Esprit system is expected to be adapted locally. In Europe, the Middle East and Africa, a Championing Quality in the Teams programme, bringing quality awareness back to hotels, launched Esprit at the beginning of 2001. The current round of appointments of training managers or co-ordinators in each hotel in this region underlines the commitment to employee development. In Asia there are four 'champions' of Esprit and Equilibrium, each representing different countries in the culturally diverse region. In the Americas region, Esprit is being managed by the Esprit Committee comprising the regional HR VP, two HR directors, two general managers and an area director for sales and marketing. Here, the goal is to have all hotels qualify for Esprit membership by mid-2002. Generally, the regional HR VP, Edwin Zephirin, considers that the North American employees will take more persuading about Esprit as it 'takes more time to gain their hearts ... there is less loyalty than in the countries in South America and the Carribbean'. In some contrast, employees in South America are 'naturally more personal, intuitive givers of service', the very essence of Hilton moments.

In short, Equilibrium identifies Hilton quality and Esprit delivers it. Then, as the customer service development manager (UK and Ireland), Jason George, points out, quality has to be measured and audited.

Measuring and Auditing Quality

There are five main company measures of quality in the Hilton Group: the systems of Richey, GSTS, Grip, balanced score cards, and mystery customers, each of which will be outlined in turn. (In addition to these, individual hotels may have their own measures, for example in their restaurants.) The Richey system is that of an external company that specializes in international hotel. Except in the UK and Ireland, representatives of Richey visit each Hilton twice a year, unrecognized and armed with a definitive list of the Hilton quality standards, physical and people. They use all the available facilities, then only at the time of their check-out do they reveal themselves to meet the hotel general manager. At this meeting they outline the positive and negative aspects of their experience. Around four to six weeks later, a detailed and substantial report is submitted to the general manager that measures adherence to every standard listed and yields a total percentage score for the service and facilities. These reports allow cross-hotel comparisons to be made.

GSTS is the guest satisfaction tracking system which measures (genuine) guests' perceptions of service. Again, this is administered by an external company. After every stay at a Hilton, guests receive a letter from the area president requesting that an enclosed questionnaire on their experience is completed and returned. Around 20–25 per cent of questionnaires are usually returned. These form the basis of three-monthly reports on the customer perceptions. Although this measurement is relatively superficial due to its standardization, it allows another comparison between hotels. In contrast, the Grip system is a more personalized approach. This system of feedback is administered within hotels. A questionnaire is left for guest completion in bedrooms, which guests can either leave in their bedrooms or at the front office. The unit general manager follows each completed questionnaire as appropriate and replies personally to the respondent guest. Also administered within hotels is the balanced score-card system. This system is derived directly from the Hilton core values of customers, quality, people and profit, as outlined earlier. Specific measurements of each value can be made every month; for example, the percentage of staff joining the Esprit club. The score card balance lies in customer experiences, staff performance and resultant profit. Again, league tables are produced on the basis of this data.

Finally, the mystery customer approach is used in two ways: first, when a mystery guest stays at a Hilton Hotel and uses all its services, these services are marked against the company brand standards; and secondly, a mystery phone call is made to the Conference and Banqueting Sales department and the Room Reservations department. The call response is measured against company brand standards too. Again externally administered, this system results in reports on set standards observed and experienced; for example, on response times to queries, and includes a transcript of the mystery call. In the UK and Ireland, eight mystery audits a year are carried out, together with eight test (telephone) calling exercises to specific hotel departments such as conference and banqueting (sales) and room reservations. Points are awarded during each visit for standards met and for Hilton moments created by staff. The target is the achievement of a minimum of 85 per cent of quality standards and a score of 75 per cent in Hilton moments in each visit. When this minimum is met in two consecutive visits, the hotel gains its entry to the Esprit Club. HR managers in hotels are then subject to evaluation of their achieving the identified People Standards, their functional brand standards.

DISCUSSION AND CONCLUSIONS

Hilton's performance is determined by the interaction of its core values – customer, quality, people and profit – in each hotel. These values are clearly interrelated but must be co-ordinated in a such a way that the fundamental imperative of ensuring quality customer service results in profit. Thus the customer offering is the priority in order to achieve the end of profit, through the means of quality staff performance. In Equilibrium, Hilton has adopted a new strategic approach to ensuring quality which explicitly combines its service offering with employee performance, through the Esprit initiative. Therefore, it bases its quality drive on three essential dimensions: customers; service deliverers; and strategists, in Kandampully's (1997) terms. Importantly in the international arena (Ulrich and Black, 1999; Weiermair, 2000), the Hilton approach to quality service is adapted to national cultures.

Unlike many service quality initiatives, Hilton's Equilibrium and Esprit was initiated in the UK commercial sector (Maxwell *et al.*, 2000) and was precipitated by some organizational restructuring after the integration with Stakis. The restructuring focused the need to identify changing customer expectations (Atkinson, 2000) and led to the market research exercise that was the very basis of Equilibrium and Esprit. Hilton can, therefore, be described, in Gronroos's (1994) terms, as being market driven in its holistic perspective that recognizes intraorganizational collaboration, where managing quality and employee development are integral. HRM and HRD are critical to the quality drive, contributing at strategic and operational levels, but are secondary to the quality service focus. HRM is not seen as important in itself, but is important because it, with HRD, supports – even defines – customer satisfaction (Schneider and Bowen, 1993; Schneider, 1994; Lengnick-Hall and Lengnick-Hall, 1999). The Hilton case, in sum, illustrates that driving and striving for quality service has promoted the organizational status of HRM overall, and that there is a co-dependency between human resource management and development on the one hand, and quality service on the other.

ACKNOWLEDGEMENT

The authors would like to express their thanks to Gordon Lyle, Hilton HR Vice-President, UK and Ireland, for his invaluable support and assistance.

SELF-ASSESSMENT QUESTIONS

1. Present a case for adopting strategic human resource management and development initiatives in hotel organizations, indicating the (potential) business benefits.
2. Discuss the imperatives of service quality in the international hotel sector.
3. How can human resource development support service quality?
4. In the context of international hospitality and tourism, should HRM strategy be central to business strategy?

REFERENCES

Arkin, A. and Johnson, R. (1999) 'Coming up roses'. *People Management*, **5**(20), 14 October, 46–7, 49.

Armstrong, M. (1988) *A Handbook of Personnel Management Practice*. London: Kogan Page.

Armstrong, M. (1992) *Human Resource Management: Strategy and Action*. London: Kogan Page.

Armstrong, M. and Long, P. (1994) *The Reality of Strategic HRM*. London: Institute of Personnel and Development.

Atkinson, P. (2000) 'The strategic imperative: creating a customer focused organization'. *Change Management*, October, 8–11.

Baum, T. (1997) 'Policy dimensions of human resource management in the tourism and hospitality industries'. *International Journal of Contemporary Hospitality Management*, **9**/5/6, 221–9.

Beaumont, P. B. (1994) 'The US human resource management literature: a review', in G. Salaman (ed.), *Human Resource Strategies*. London: Sage Publications.

Brush, R. (1997) 'Managing quality organizations in the US hospitality sector', in M. Foley, J. Lennon and G. Maxwell (eds), *Hospitality, Tourism and Leisure Management: Issues in Strategy and Culture*. London: Cassell.

Fache, W. (2000) 'Methodologies for innovation and improvements of services in tourism'. *Managing Service Quality* (special edition on hospitality, tourism and leisure), **10**(6), 356–66.

Garavan, T. N. (1991) 'Strategic human resource development'. *Journal of European Industrial Training*, **15**(1), 17–30.

Goldsmith, A., Nickson, D., Sloan, D. and Wood, R. C. (1999) *Human Resource Management for Hospitality Services*. London: International Thomson Business Press.

Gronroos, C. (1982) 'Towards a third phase in service quality research challenges and future directions'. Report presented at the AMA Services Marketing Conference, Vanderbilt University, Nashville, TN, cited in J. Kandampully (1997).

Gronroos, C. (1994) 'From scientific management to service management: a management prespective for the age of service competition'. *International Journal of Service Industry Management*, **5**(1), 5–20.

Guerrier, Y. and Deery, M. (1998) 'Research in hospitality human resource management and organizational behaviour'. *Hospitality Management*, **17**, 145–60.

Guest, D. (1989) 'Personnel or human resource management: Can you tell the difference?' *Personnel Management*, **21**(1), January, 48–51.

Harrison, R. (1992) *Employee Development*. Institute of Personnel Management. London.

Hoque, K. (1999) 'New approaches to HRM in the UK hotel industry'. *Human Resource Management Journal*, **9**(2), 64–76.

Kandampully, J. (1997) 'Quality service in tourism', in M. Foley, J. Lennon and G. Maxwell (eds), *Hospitality, Tourism and Leisure Management: Issues in Strategy and Culture*. London: Cassell.

Keep, E. (1989) 'Corporate training strategies: the vital component?', in J. Storey (ed.), *New Perspectives on Human Resource Management*. London: Routledge, pp. 109–25.

Lashley, C. (1997) *Empowering Service Excellence: Beyond the Quick Fix*. London: Cassell.

Lashley, C. and Watson, S. (1999) 'Researching human resource management in the hospitality industry: the need for a new agenda?' *International Journal of Tourism and Hospitality Research*, **1**(1), 19–40.

Legge, K. (1995) *Human Resource Management: Rhetorics and Realities*. London: MacMillan Business.

Lengnick-Hall, M. L. and Lengnick-Hall, C. A. (1999) 'Expanding customer orientation in the HR function'. *Human Resource Management*, **38**(3), 201–14.

Lewis, J. (2000) 'Are you being served?' *Personnel Today*, August, 28–9.

Lucas, R. (1995) *Managing Employee Relations in the Hotel and Catering Industry*. London: Cassell.

Maxwell, G. (1994) 'Human resource management and quality in the UK hospitality industry: where is the strategy?' *Total Quality Management*, **5**(3), 45–52.

Maxwell, G. (1997) 'Empowerment in the UK hospitality industry', in M. Foley, J. Lennon and G. Maxwell (eds), *Hospitality, Tourism and Leisure Management: Issues in Strategy and Culture*. London: Cassell.

Maxwell, G., McDougall, M. and Blair, S. (2000) 'Managing diversity in the hotel sector: the emergence of a service quality opportunity'. *Managing Service Quality* (special edition on hospitality, tourism and leisure), 367–73.

Maxwell, G., Ogden, S., and Russell, V. (2000) 'Approaches to enhance service quality orientation in the UK: The role of the public sector', in *Service Quality Management in Hospitality, Tourism and Leisure*, ed. by Kamdampully *et al.*, Haworth Press (forthcoming).

Nickson, D., Wood, R. C. and Hoque, K. (2000) 'HRM in the UK hotel industry: a comment and response'. *Human Resource Management Journal*, **10**(4), 88–94.

Price, L. (1994) 'Poor personnel practice in the hotel and catering industry: Does it really matter?' *Human Resource Management Journal*, **4**(4), 44–62.

Robinson, J. (1998) 'Four-star treatment'. *Personnel Today*, 23 April, 22–3.

Stake, R. E. (1994) *The Art of Case Study Research*. London: Sage.

Schneider, B. (1994) 'HRM: a service perspective: towards a customer-focused HRM'. *International Journal of Service Industry Management*, **5**(1), 64–76.

Schneider, B. and Bowen, D. E. (1993) 'The service organization: human resources management is crucial'. *Organizational Dynamics*, spring, 39–52.

Stewart, J. and McGoldrick, J. (1996) (eds), *Human Resource Development: Perspectives, Strategies and Practice*. London: Pitman Publishing.

Torraco, R. J. and Swanson, R. A. (1995) 'The strategic roles of human resource development'. *Human Resource Planning*, **18**(4), December, 10–22.

Ulrich, D. and Black, J. S. (1999) 'Worldly wise'. *People Management*, **5**(21), 28 October, 42–6.

Weiermair, K. (2000) 'Tourists' perceptions towards and satisfaction with service quality in the cross-cultural service encounter: implications for hospitality and tourism management'. *Managing Service Quality* (special edition on hospitality, tourism and leisure), 397–409.

Wilson, J. P. (ed.) (1999) *Human Resource Development: Learning and Training for Individuals and Organizations*. London: Kogan Page.

Wood, R. C. (1992) *Working in Hotels and Catering*. London: Routledge.

Worsfold, P. (1999) 'HRM, performance, commitment and service quality in the hotel industry'. *International Journal of Contemporary Hospitality Management*, **11**(1), 340–8.

8

The Benefits of Training for Business Performance

Conrad Lashley

ABSTRACT

Attempts to calculate the business benefits of training are notoriously difficult. Some studies have suggested there are no positive and robust links between training and business performance. This chapter argues that attempts to link the costs of training to the gains often fail because they use a narrow range of financial measures when considering returns from a training investment. At root they treat an investment in people in the same way as they consider an investment in physical facilities and capital plant. Training is about changing the behaviour of the trainee, and measure of training benefits have to start with a consideration of the behavioural change that may or may not have occurred. Using this approach, consideration of the benefits of training need to engage with a balanced score-card approach to business performance appraisal. The model developed in the chapter suggests that both employee performance and satisfaction, together with service quality and customer satisfaction, have to be included in measures of the benefits of training. Consideration of this wider set of measures may lead to the more downstream financial benefits. The chapter includes research using one benchmark organization as a case study to demonstrate that even within one organization there can be considerable variation in training provision which, in turn, leads to variations in restaurant performance.

INTRODUCTION

The chapter reports upon a study commissioned by the Hospitality Training Foundation (Eaglen *et al.*, 1999). Specifically, the study proposed an industrial training benefits and cost model, and the model was applied to McDonald's Restaurants Ltd as a case study. The chapter summarizes the findings including both data gained from the company's records and from semi-structured interviews with a range of company personnel.

This research project was commissioned in a context where the hospitality industry, with some notable exceptions, has a poor training record. Prior studies of training in the hospitality industry (HCTC, 1995) show that over 40 per cent of employer organizations reported that they had not undertaken training activities in the previous twelve months. Only one quarter of firms trained all employees and the majority of training activity is related to meeting statutory requirements as, for example, with food handling and health and safety.

In many ways the nature of the research question reflects a very British phenomenon. Nationally, there is a long history of managerial amateurism across all industry (Ashton and Felstead, 1995) and British companies tend to invest less in training than many of their international competitors. Against this background many hospitality industry managers are themselves inadequately trained and are not naturally convinced of the value of an investment in training activities. This situation is further compounded by a financial establishment which has been accused of short-termism and a failure to account for the value of training and investment in people (Armstrong, 1995).

Attempts to measure an investment in training and the benefits ensuing from it are notoriously difficult to establish. While training costs can be estimated and measured, the precise financial yield from a training investment is much more complex. The linkages between an independent variable factor like the level of training activity, and dependent variables, such as business benefits, are hard to establish because successful business performance is frequently due to a cluster of factors and will vary between organizations and service types. Even where a linkage can be established, say between the level of training activity and the level of staff turnover, it is not certain in which direction the relationship flows (Kochan and Osterman, 1998).

This project attempts to minimize some of these difficulties by using a case study approach which allows researchers to control some operational variations. McDonald's Restaurants Ltd has a highly developed, systematic and standardized approach to job design, training and employee development. It is an organization which prioritizes employee and manager training as key aspect of business practice (Boella, 1992, p. 113). In addition, the company has an extensive management-information system which allows exploration and comparison of restaurant performance where there appear to be variations in training practice and the subsequent performance of the unit.

MAKING THE CASE FOR THE BENEFITS OF TRAINING

Evaluation of the benefits of training is complex, not least because notions of what constitutes 'training' and potential benefits in terms of subsequent changes in 'business performance' are often contested terms. This section, therefore, begins by exploring the terms 'training', 'business performance' and 'benefits analysis'. In their highly regarded review of training in small businesses, Curran *et al.* (1996) provide a useful typology of training as follows:

- formal off-the-job training, i.e. instruction that takes place outside the workplace but is designed to enhance skills and knowledge related to employment;

- informal off-the-job training, i.e. activities that improve skills and knowledge but do not lead to formal accreditation or are not part of a systematic programme;
- formal on-the-job training, i.e. instruction that takes place at the place of employment with the intention of raising skill levels;
- informal on-the-job training, i.e. those activities that improve skills and knowledge relating to an employee's tasks, but which involve few organizational inputs.

In the research being discussed here the emphasis is focused upon formal and informal skills-related training which is on the job. This includes both initial and continuing training. It is recognized that there are a number of points of degree between formal and informal training. Thus, 'standing next to Nellie' is a well-known phrase, but may cover different approaches to training. At one end Nellie may be a person who has been trained to train others working to a structured brief. On the other hand the training may be unstructured and involve merely watching an experienced worker do the job, or, at its most extreme, may involve the trainees learning by doing the job and having mistakes corrected by fellow workers and supervisors. Thus we define *informal training* as taking place in organizations which have no systematic approach to the design, delivery, monitoring and evaluation of employee performance and development.

Understanding Benefits and Costs

Attempts to identify the benefits to be gained from an investment in training are difficult to prove (Wade, 1995). In the first instance it is difficult to isolate training as the key independent variable in managing a business unit which leads to specific gains in business performance. Is it training which is leading to improvements in productivity, for example, or are changes the result of improved employee motivation because the employee values training? What effect does the employment environment make? Do high levels of unemployment result in employees feeling grateful to have a job and thereby improve productivity (Kochan and Osterman, 1998)?

Even if it is possible to link benefits in business performance it is not always possible to identify the direction in which the causal relationships flow. Is training, therefore, an independent or a dependent variable? Does employee training lead to a reduction in staff turnover, or does reduced staff turnover result in the build up of a 'stock' of trained employees?

Even when these difficulties are overcome, the calculation of the benefits from an investment in training which will yield a tangible and financially measurable set of business performance improvements is at best simplistic (Parry, 1996). Indeed the question is itself a bi-product of a particular set of assumptions to be found in abundance in the United Kingdom. During the planning stage for the research discussed in this chapter a senior executive of one major international company said: 'Why are you even asking the question? Of course training produces benefits in business performance. You don't need to prove it, its the way you do business. Its an act of faith. Its like why you send your child to university. You know the benefits will out-weigh the costs.' However, there are many British line managers who are far from convinced that the time and costs of training result in measurable benefits in business performance which ultimately impact on sales, profits and business value.

This study attempted to build a systematic model that

- provides a fair sample of the benefits of training;
- assumes that training ultimately 'aims to change behaviour' and benefit analysis should be chiefly concerned with changes in performance as a result of the training;
- is methodologically robust; and
- can be used to apply in contexts other than the case study organization(s).

In addition to these measures of validity linking the costs of training with measures of performance, it is necessary to speculate on the *costs of not training*. Hall (1975) provides a declaration that senior managers in non-training organizations need to sign a declaration if they are to support claims that training is unnecessary in their organization. The list of items (p. 39) includes an array of issues such as the need to train new recruits, improve worker competence, meet challenges for the future, business growth, new technology, and to develop the potential of employees. In addition to these circumstances of everyday organizational life which Hall argues ensure that training will be a necessity for all organizations, he goes on to argue that inadequate training is likely to generate additional costs to the business:

- *Loss of new recruits* – the lack of induction training and the use of staff 'poached' from elsewhere are likely to fuel high levels of staff turnover;
- *Inability to recruit staff* – depending on the state of the labour market it may become increasingly difficult to recruit staff who are untrained;
- *Reduced service quality* – low-skilled and untrained staff have a direct impact on service quality in many hospitality service organizations. In some cases this is linked to and reinforced by insufficient staff;
- *Low staff morale* – untrained staff are ill-prepared for the requirements of service jobs and this adds stress and discontent; and
- *Reduced output* – in addition to reductions in the quality of output, there is likely to be a reduction in absolute output by untrained service staff.

To this list it is possible to predict other costs that arise from not training employees, or at least relying on informal training methods which result in employees largely self-training through personal experience, watching others, error, or unstructured coaching.

- *Extended period of learning to be competent* – new employees take longer to become competent in the job. For each extra shift needed for the employee to become competent there is a loss of output.
- *Additional wastage and equipment damage* – unstructured training both extends the period during which wastage is produced and increases the level at which wastage is produced. In addition, unstructured and ill-trained employees increase the damage to equipment and property, through the use of incorrect or inefficient procedure.
- *Increased accidents and unsafe practices* – untrained workers lead to increased accidents. Employers are required to provide some basic training for safe working practices for all employees and a basic training in food hygiene for those producing or serving food. Failure to provide this training is itself likely to cause extra accidents and incidents as well as increase the chance of prosecution and fines.

BUSINESS PERFORMANCE MEASUREMENT

It is now widely recognized that 'business performance' needs to be understood as a more comprehensive notion then merely in terms of static – and largely historic – financial data such as profitability ratios (Geanuracos and Meiklejohn, 1993). For as Brander Brown and McDonnell (1995, p. 7) argue, 'the traditional use of profit-based performance measures by many organizations has been criticized on a variety of fundamental grounds – for instance, their relative incompleteness and lack of accuracy and neutrality (1), their encouragement of short-termism (2) and their lack of "balance"'. This is illustrated by Eccles (1991, p. 132) who observes that 'many ... companies' strong financial records deteriorate because of unnoticed declines in quality or customer satisfaction ...' There is now an emerging consensus that, given the characteristics of service sector businesses, notably arising from the intangibility, heterogeneity, simultaneity and perishability of the service offer, business performance measurements must be differentiated between manufacturing and services (Brignall *et al.*, 1991; Fitzgerald *et al.*, 1994). As a consequence, a number of approaches to performance measurement have been developed, which incorporate both 'hard' measures – such as financial performance – and, critically, 'soft' measures, such as employee satisfaction (Stone, 1996).

In the context of examining the potential benefits of training for business performance, it is instructive to review briefly the range of items included within the more holistic approaches and to consider the rationale for their inclusion. The commentary that follows is not designed to provide a toolkit for implementing performance-measurement systems but, rather, to highlight the key dimensions of such a notion.

One means of measuring business performance that has gained currency in recent years is the 'balanced scorecard' approach. Its central feature is the development of objectives and measures for four categories or perspectives: financial; customer; internal processes; and innovation and learning. Within each category, a range of indicators, or monitors, are developed within the context of particular organizations (Roest, 1997; Dinesh and Palmer, 1998). The customer perspective may, for example, include a customer-satisfaction index. The innovation and learning category may be measured through regular staff attitude surveys and/or numbers of suggestions made by employees relating to operational improvements. The internal business perspective might include time staff spend with customers, and the financial category would itemize performance according to measures such as profitability (Kaplan and Norton, 1993). Although the specific means of evaluating each category would vary between businesses depending upon their particular objectives; the approach serves to emphasize that business performance is more than short-term financial performance.

Other commentators discuss related approaches for business performance measurement (Eccles, 1991; Geanuracos and Meiklejohn, 1993; Wholey, 1996). Since these represent variations of the main theme of the balanced scorecard approach, they need not be considered here. The input-process-output model developed by Fitzgerald *et al.* (1994) is, however, worthy of comment because it was created in the context of service organizations and reinforces effectively the connections between various activities of the business. It is the latter which confirms the appropriateness of adopting a broad conception of business performance.

Fitzgerald *et al.* (1994) argue that there are six generic performance dimensions: competitive performance, financial performance, quality of service, flexibility, resource

Table 8.1 Performance measures across six dimensions

	Dimensions of performance	Types of measure
Results	Competitiveness	Relative market share and position Sales growth Measures of the customer base
	Financial performance	Profitability Liquidity Capital structure Market ratios
Determinants	Quality of service	Reliability Responsiveness Aesthetics/appearance Cleanliness/tidiness Comfort Friendliness Communication Courtesy Competence Access Availability Security
	Flexibility	Volume flexibility Delivery speed flexibility Specification flexibility
	Resource utilization	Productivity Efficiency
	Innovation	Performance of the innovation process Performance of individual innovations

Source: Fitzgerald *et al.* (1994, p. 8)

utilization and innovation. The key element of their proposition is that these dimensions may be divided into two categories: resultant and determinant factors. They present a persuasive case for perceiving competitive and financial performance indicators as the result of the other factors that, therefore, determine business performance. As can be seen from Table 8.1, a number of measures may then be developed that relate to both determinants and results. In the context of this study, it is important to appreciate the possibility that training may impact upon the determinant measures and, thereby, influence competitiveness and financial performance.

The Benefits of Training

Estimating the benefits of training – particularly in the context of potential contributions to improved business performance – is clearly difficult to gauge. This is

Table 8.2 Benefits of training

- Improved productivity
- Reductions in labour turnover
- Reductions in waste
- Quality improvements
- Greater organizational commitment
- Reductions in accidents
- Greater flexibility
- Improved ability to accept change

not surprising given the variety of forms of training undertaken within the hospitality industry and because other variables impact upon training activity; for example, the quality of the training provision, the existing skills and capabilities of trainees and the duration of training programmes.

In addition, it is self-evident that a wide array of influences impact upon the business performance of an organization. For example, economic climate, levels of investment, marketing and promotional activities, to name but three. The problems of ascribing changes to training activity are described at the end of this section. Nevertheless, considerable effort has been expended which has sought to identify the impact of training on the performance of enterprises. In many cases, these relate to the determinant factors, i.e. those which contribute to competitiveness and financial performance, discussed earlier in this review. The main themes identified in the literature are contained in Table 8.2 below. It is interesting that some commentators have, in the past, referred to these as the 'costs of not training' (Hall, 1975).

A significant proportion of the literature on training is predicated on an acceptance that training leads to improved business performance. Thus, while advocating greater training activity and claiming to provide means of evaluating training or best practice in programme design, offer little evidence to support propositions (see, for example, Holcomb, 1998). Such literature offers little insight for the purposes of this project and is, therefore, given little attention. Instead, more robust evaluations of the impact of training on determinants of business performance are reviewed. The research study drew heavily on the recently funded DfEE project which was charged with reviewing the benefits of training for employers (Green, 1997). It discusses each of the themes identified in Table 8.2.

It is important to consider the nature of the benefits in relation to training and the impact of training on individual performance. In other words, if training ultimately aims to change behaviour, then the measurement of benefits must be concerned with those benefits which are associated with the behaviour of job-holders under scrutiny. Thus, improvements in productivity, reductions in staff turnover, improvements in employee satisfaction, reduced wastage etc. are the results of changes in individual actions; hopefully as the result of training received; and where insufficient training has been received it is expected that performance will be less satisfactory. This can be modelled and calculated as in Table 8.3.

Table 8.3 Modelling the benefits of training

Benefits formula	Benefits
(Optimum work output level formally trained – optimum work output level informally trained) × 12 months (or some other appropriate time period)	(a) Absolute productivity gain
(Number of weeks to reach OWO informally trained – number of weeks to reach OWO formally trained × the proficiency gap (output formally trained – output of informally trained)	(b) Productivity gain from improved learning speed
(Number of leavers under informal training – number of leavers under formal training) × average replacement costs	Reduced staff turnover costs
Levels of wastage under informal training – levels of wastage in formal training	Reduced levels of wastage
Service quality measures after formal training – service quality measures after informal training	Improved service quality
Measure of employee satisfaction in formal training context – measure of employee satisfaction in informal training context	Increased employee satisfaction
Number of days lost through employee accidents in informal training – number of days lost through employee accidents in formal training	Reduced employee accident rate
The pool of peripheral employees ÷ the range of job types covered	Benefits of flexibility through training
(The numbers accepting change ÷ the total number of employees) × 100	The benefits of training on acceptance of change
Total benefits	

MCDONALD'S RESTAURANTS LTD

McDonald's Restaurants Ltd operate quick-service restaurants in a manner which has been described as a 'production line' or 'service factory' approach to service delivery. That is, the production and delivery of the company's services are informed by Weberian 'formal rationality' and have much in common with Taylor's approach to factory production. Production and service tasks are routinized and require minimal discretion by operational crew. Operating manuals and procedures specify not just product standards but also a detailed breakdown of service times and targets.

In these circumstances, training crew to perform tasks in 'the one best way' is an essential feature of delivering the company's highly standardized and uniformity-dependent (Lashley, 2000) offer to customers. Production and service operations are tightly defined and the subject of detailed training programmes. Crew are trained against these standards and a management-development programme supports manager training for each stage of the management hierarchy up to unit management.

The company's approach to training is based on personal competencies that are described as 'a combination of knowledge, skills and behaviours critical to job success'. Training documents encourage individuals to develop and work through their own Personal Development Plan, supported by a Personal Development System Appraisal. Furthermore, company documents stress the opportunities to develop through the company's training programmes. These training programmes, therefore, provide a mapped set of stages through which an individual can foresee their own progression and development.

The key elements of the McDonald's approach to training are:

- all crew are trained including full and part-time employees;
- training is competence based;
- ultimately training aims to develop a flexible workforce capable of undertaking all crew jobs;
- much crew training involves learning to do the job in 'the one best way';
- competencies are defined for each task in *Observation Check Lists*;
- completed training is rewarded through the *five star badge* and pay increases;
- training is delivered through *training squad* (crew members trained to train);
- Observation Check Lists are also used to monitor ongoing employee performance;
- unit managers are accountable for training and are monitored through the *training log* and training audits to ensure that crew training is being administered correctly and OCLs are being completed to plan. The Human Resource and Training computer system enables both unit managers and regional executives to monitor training in each restaurant.

A sample of twelve business units (restaurants) were identified by the organization for more detailed training activity analysis, based on their scorecard criteria and categorized as relatively, 'high' (*Alpha*) or 'low' (*Beta*) performers, over the first nine months of 1998. The definition of 'high' and 'low' involved an assessment of each unit's 'training' grades. That is, the company's own criteria for determining the extent to which each restaurant complied with the company's standard approach to training. Monitoring of restaurant performance includes the number of fully trained crew and the updating of the Observation Check Lists. In each case, restaurants are graded out of a maximum score of 100. Identification of two sets of restaurants reflecting better than, and worse than average performance against the company's standards involved both the current numerical grade and the judgement of senior training personnel. Thus we can identify restaurants which had consistent performance over a prolonged period. Table 8.4 lists the restaurants which were selected for study and identifies the company's recorded training grade for each restaurant as at 1 November, 1998.

The research team attempted to look beyond the figures to explore the extent of training activity through the number of fully trained crew who were available in each restaurant. The figures in Table 8.4 do show that the number of trained staff in the first group of restaurants was consistently higher in the first group than in the second group. Similarly, the number and extent of the backlog of performance reviews was consistently greater in the restaurants where training audits showed lower grades. The number of training squad on duty did vary between restaurants. However, there was no clear difference between the two sets of restaurants.

Table 8.4 Training in the restaurants

Units	Overall training grade	Average crew numbers	Fully rotatable crew	Fully trained crew (%)		Training squad	Out- standing OCLs	Employee satisfaction training (%)
Alpha 1	92.00	35	21	15	71	6	8	64
Alpha 2	91.00	71	46	35	76	5	9	56
Alpha 3	93.00	33	15	10	67	3	7	66
Alpha 4	85.00	54	27	13	48	3	15	63
Alpha 5	85.00	46	26	15	58	6	15	80
Alpha 6	93.00	41	33	20	61	3	7	71
Beta 1	76.00	72	38	19	50	8	26	55
Beta 2	80.00	34	26	8	31	4	19	36
Beta 3	74.00	70	39	16	41	4	26	46
Beta 4	80.00	47	27	13	48	3	23	39
Beta 5	72.00	44	26	13	50	3	27	38
Beta 6	54.00	49	35	13	37	5	36	44

Employee comments gathered via the employee survey data did show clear differences between the two sets of restaurants. The company's Employee Satisfaction Survey asks a suite of questions relating to 'performance and training' and the responses were in the first cluster of restaurants were generally above the regional average of 57 per cent for this group of questions. All the restaurants in the second group registered lower levels of employee satisfaction with training and performance review in their restaurants. Similarly, responses from 'rap sessions' tended to be more negative about training in the restaurants where training audits recorded lower grades. There is a sense that under the pressure of business the OCL performance reviews can slip in all restaurants, but the crew in the second cluster were particularly critical of the training system. In response to the question 'How are new staff initially trained?' the following comments were registered:

- 'They are not. They get thrown in at the deep end, never trained by a manager.'
- 'With great difficulty – not enough people on to train new crew properly. Difficult when busy. No consistency, new crew are rotated too quickly.'
- 'New crew train themselves. Rotation is poor. Dining area staff are always on the till. OCLs are completed erratically. Crew have to pester for OCLs to be conducted.'
- 'New crew are left on station without training. Lose people because they aren't trained. Crew said they have been left in the kitchen on their own in the kitchen in the first week.'
- 'The training is good but a lack of rotation.'

Interview with unit managers included two activities to establish the priority that each unit manger placed on training within the unit. At the beginning of the interview the manager was asked: 'Please list the five most important factors which influence successful restaurant management.' At the end of the interview managers were given a list of ten factors including, 'trained staff' and asked 'Please rank the following factors in order of importance to successful restaurant management'. In response to this last question most managers ranked employee training in the top three position, and this was common among managers in both categories of restaurants. However, manager responses to the unprompted question were different. Managers in the restaurants that had above-average training grades tended to include staff training in their list, while managers in the second group were less likely to mention training as an important factor. Furthermore, interview responses tended to confirm that a key feature differentiating the two restaurants was the general approach to managing recruitment and training. In most cases, these managers took direct responsibility for managing training progress, or delegated as a core responsibility to the First Assistant. These managers were also more likely to take part in the recruitment and selection of staff. The following response was typical: 'I involve myself in the selection and recruitment of staff because careful selection reduces staff turnover.' Where restaurants had a lower training profile, managers often complained, 'I just can't recruit enough staff'.

In summary, the findings showed:

- There are differences in the training audit grades for the two sets of restaurants;
- Lower than average trainers had
    - a lower proportion of fully trained staff;
    - a larger backlog of OCLs;
    - registered below-average responses to the training section on employee satisfaction survey;
    - more critical employee comments about training on RAP Session reports; and
    - managers who seemed to give employee training lower priority.

The Benefits of Training McDonald's Crew

This study has shown how training is seen as a central aspect of the way that McDonald's conducts operations. The whole approach stems from both the company's history and the nature of the service offer to customers. Presentations by company executives about the problems in the 1950s when expansion via franchisees, unsupported by tight operating standards, resulted in high levels of customer complaints and confusion about the diversity of different products in different branches.

These early experiences have created a strong cultural commitment to uniformity and standardization. Training is central to standardization. If customers are being sold uniformity services and products are produced by 'one best way', therefore, training crew in the one best way is fundamental. Table 8.5 shows some of the variations possible, even within the controlled environment of McDonald's. Whilst there are some overlaps, the general picture is that the restaurants with the better training grades also have lower levels of staff turnover, more satisfied employees and better service, quality and cleanliness scores.

One of the benefits of using McDonald's as a case study has been the consistent approach to define both Crew tasks and ensuring that employees work to the 'one best way'. This approach is fundamental in delivering the 'uniformity-dependent' (Lashley, 2000) offer to customers. Without tight control over the training of employee performance the company would find it is difficult to deliver the standardized product and service offer which customers are buying into. It is not surprising, therefore, that variations between units do not display huge variations in productivity and output levels. However, there are variations even in the most structured training environment;

Table 8.5 A comparison of some internal audit grades within the two groups

Rest code	Training grade	Crew turnover	Crew opinion survey	Mystery service score	Mystery quality score	Mystery cleanliness score
Alpha 1	91.00	64.72	64.00	88.10	97.00	94.90
Alpha 2	93.00	68.75	65.00	83.60	96.40	88.00
Alpha 3	92.00	44.22	65.00	92.00	100.00	98.30
Alpha 4	85.00	55.65	81.00	82.90	90.70	95.10
Alpha 5	85.00	63.34	68.00	88.90	93.60	90.70
Alpha 6	93.00	89.30	66.00	92.10	96.80	95.60
Beta 1	80.00	145.26	33.00	80.90	93.10	85.40
Beta 2	80.00	166.81	35.00	87.40	96.20	96.70
Beta 3	74.00	141.00	43.00	84.10	88.40	86.90
Beta 4	76.00	143.91	51.00	74.40	96.80	84.50
Beta 5	72.00	151.28	38.00	72.80	90.90	82.70
Beta 6	54.00	128.91	49.00	76.00	87.40	90.00

local unit managers can have a significant impact on the general quality of the training delivered in the restaurant. Where the company's training grades were below average, restaurants registered lower scores across the array of measures, as Table 8.6 shows.

Table 8.6 The benefits of training McDonald's crew

Benefits formula	Benefits
(a) Absolute productivity gain	728 more transactions per annum per crew
(b) Productivity gain from improved learning speed	12–51 fewer transactions per crew
Reduced staff turnover costs	Consistently lower staff turnover at £450 per head minimum – averaged £19,500 lower per restaurant
Improved service quality	Better than average service quality grades – service averaged 10 percentage points better
Increased employee satisfaction	Better-than-average employee-satisfaction grades and ratings of employee attitudes – averaged 27 per cent better on survey
Benefits of flexibility through training	More flexible workforce to plan the restaurant's activities
Reduced levels of wastage	Nominal estimate of an extra £10.00
Reduced employee accident rate	Difficult to detect variations in study
Total benefits	

CONCLUSION

The aim of the research discussed in this chapter was to devise a means of identifying the benefits of training that could be applied in an industrial setting. The development of such an approach was informed by a comprehensive review of existing research. This review encompassed not only the academic literature but also any relevant studies undertaken on behalf of various agencies with an interest in the hospitality industry or training generally. A key feature of the project was that the utility of the model was tested and refined by applying it in the context of a hospitality retail organization, McDonald's Restaurants Ltd. The choice of organization was deliberate: McDonald's has a systematic approach to training and maintains comprehensive data relating to training and business performance.

A challenge inherent in any study such as this is that a number of factors influence aspects of the phenomenon being studied. In this case, although estimating the costs of training is relatively straightforward, attempting to gauge its benefits is more problematic. Clearly, a variety of variables – of which training may be one – impact on the business performance of an organization. Inevitably, therefore, it was not possible to measure precisely any resultant financial benefits associated with expenditure on training. Nevertheless, as this study demonstrates, it is possible to identify training benefits.

The literature review confirmed the perception that crude mechanisms purporting to measure the financial benefits of expenditure on training was not possible. Instead, any positive influence of training should be conceptualized in terms of its impact on wider business performance indicators, the so-called determinants of financial performance. More specifically, business performance is more appropriately considered to be a variety of factors that contribute to the sustainability of the organization. The impact of training on service quality, or staff attitudes, are important examples of determinants of sustainable financial performance. This kind of conceptualization is useful also because it helps *explain* how training may impact positively on business performance.

The findings of this study suggest that there are numerous benefits to be obtained from training. Although it is inappropriate to quantify such benefits, the foregoing has presented varied evidence that is supportive of the notion that training leads to improvements in service quality, staff satisfaction, and functional flexibility. In addition, there is evidence of training's impact on staff turnover and productivity. Based on these observations, it is clear that the benefits derived from training contribute significantly to the sustainability and growth of McDonald's Restaurants Ltd. There are few reasons for supposing that such benefits would not apply equally elsewhere in the hospitality industry.

SELF-ASSESSMENT QUESTIONS

1. Why is it important to measure the benefits of employee training in hospitality service operations?
2. What are the difficulties associated with a traditional cost and benefit analysis for an investment in training?
3. Why does a 'balanced score card' approach to managing organization performance more readily lend itself to training benefit assessment than more traditional financial measurement? What arguments would you use to senior managers for the introduction of a balanced score card approach?

4. What were the key benefits from the case study comparing restaurants in the McDonald's case study?
5. Given the case made for the benefits from an investment in training, identify the costs being incurred by firms who do not train employees effectively. That is, make a case for the cost of not training.

REFERENCES

Armstrong, P. (1995) 'Accountancy and HRM', in J. Storey (ed.), *Human Resource Management: A Critical Text*. London: Routledge.

Ashton, D. and Felstead, A. (1995) 'Training and development', in J. Storey (ed.), *Human Resource Management: A Critical Text*. London: Routledge.

Boella, M. (1992) *Human Resource Management in the Hospitality Industry*. London: Stanley Thornes.

Brander Brown, J. and McDonnell, B. (1995) 'The balanced score card: short term guest or long term resident? *International Journal of Contemporary Hospitality Management*, **7**(2/3), 7–11.

Brignall, T. J., Fitzgerald, L., Johnston, R. and Silvestro, R. (1991) *Performance Measurement in Service Businesses*. London: CIMA.

Curran, J., Blackburn, R. A., Kitching, J. and North, J. (1996) *Establishing Small Firms' Training Practices, Needs, Difficulties and Use of Industry Training Organizations*. London: HMSO.

Dinesh, D. and Palmer, E. (1998) 'Management by objectives and the balanced scorecard: Will Rome fall again?' *Management Decision*, **36**(6), 363–9.

Eaglen, A., Lashley, C. and Thomas, R. (1999) *Benefits and Costs Analysis: The Impact of Training on Business Performance*. Leeds: Leeds Metropolitan University.

Eccles, R. G. (1991) 'The performance measurement manifesto'. *Harvard Business Review*. January–February, 131–7.

Fitzgerald, L., Johnston, R., Bignall, S., Sylvestro, R., and Voss, C. (1994) *Performance Measurement in Service Businesses*. London: CIMA.

Geanuracos, J. and Meiklejohn, I. (1993) *Performance Measurement: The New Agenda*. London: Business Intelligence.

Green, F. (1997) *Review of Information on the Benefits of Training for Employers*. Research Report No. 7. London: DfEE.

Hall, N. (1975) *Cost-Benefit Analysis in Industrial Training*. Manchester Monographs 6.

HCTC (1995) *Training: Who Needs It?* London: Hotel and Catering Training Company.

Holcomb, J. (1998) *Training Evaluation Made Easy*. London: Kogan Page.

Kaplan, R. S. and Norton, D. P. (1993) 'Putting the balanced scorecard to work'. *Harvard Business Review*, September–October, 134–47.

Kochan, T. and Osterman, P. (1998) 'The mutual gains enterprise', in C. Mabey, G. Salaman and J. Storey (eds), *Strategic Human Resource Management*. London: Sage.

Lashley, C. (2000) *Hospitality Retail Management: A Unit Manaager's Guide*. Oxford: Butterworth-Heinemann.

Parry, S. B. (1996) 'Measuring training's ROI'. *Training and Development*, May, 72–77.

Roest, P. (1997) 'The golden rules for implementing the balanced scorecard'. *Information Management and Computer Security*, **5**(5), 163–5.

Stone, C. L. (1996) 'Analysing business performance: counting the soft issues'. *Leadership and Organization Development Journal*, **17**(4), 21–8.

Wade, S. (1995) *Measuring the Impact of Training*. London: Institute for Personnel and Development.

Wholey, J. S. (1996) 'Formative and summative evaluation: related issues in performance measurement'. *Evaluation Practice*, **17**(2), 145–9.

9

Multi-site Management: HRM Implications

Steven Goss-Turner

ABSTRACT

The profile of the contemporary tourism and hospitality sector is dominated by international brands and chains. The subsequent growth of managerial structures and systems has in part been characterized by a need to develop a middle management layer of area or regional managers. Such managers form the level of supervision immediately above unit managers and are a crucial interface between the units and the strategic hierarchy of the organization. The multi-site management position is a career development aspiration for many unit managers who see management development in such a role to be essential in reaching the operations management apex. Literature and research studies are reviewed in this chapter in order to gain a picture of the role of the multi-site manager, the attributes and competencies required and the human resource management issues and implications for employee development. A case study is then utilized to contextualize some of the results of recent primary research, and to illustrate the many factors which can affect the nature of the job and role. Conclusions are drawn regarding the inherent tensions of the multi-unit manager position, from issues concerned with management development to the inescapable outcome that, as organizations rely more on standardized branded offerings, so the multi-site manager's role is one of strategic implementation rather than strategic formulation.

INTRODUCTION

The traditional structure of the tourism and hospitality sector has been one of predominantly small to medium-sized enterprises, often owner-managed, providing a particular locality with a range of appropriate services and attractions (Lee-Ross, 1999). However, in terms of international profile, customer recognition and corporate profitability, the industry began to change from the 1950s with the development of large-scale groups or chains which dedicated their long-term business strategy to international expansion, exemplified by the Holiday Inn brand, founded in 1952, and now a truly global presence due to its commitment to a brand-extension strategy (Parker and Teare, 1992, p. 113). Such brands or chains experienced further acceleration of their development in the 1970s and 1980s, offering strongly marketed products and services, especially in fast food and restaurants, the licensed trade, roadside dining, branded hotel chains and tourism complexes (Jones, 1996). Many of these branded operations have secured an increasing market share through their consistency of standards and quality, and the ability of the customer to recognize and be attracted by the presence of the business in many destinations throughout the world.

This expansion had inevitable consequences for the organizational structure, with the firms becoming increasingly large, multi-site companies, standardizing operations and influencing the supply chain from central production to more prescribed service-delivery systems. Many such organizations adapted the principles of mass production and modern retailing, connecting the service sector more closely to forms of industrialization as in the seminal work of Levitt (1972) and Schmenner (1986). This structural change led to a growing hierarchy of management in order to control complex networks of outlets, including the appointment of multi-site managers, responsible for a number of similar businesses, e.g. fast-food outlets, each unit manager reporting directly to the area or regional manager (Ball, 1996, p. 181).

This chapter explores the employee development issues and challenges facing both the organizations and individual multi-site managers as such tourism and hospitality-based companies continue to expand both nationally and internationally in a sector constantly subjected to the merger and take-over scenario of consolidation. The chapter has the objectives of establishing the characteristics of multi-site organizations and reviewing management and organizational development aspects; reviewing the literature pertaining to such organizations; assessing the key human resource management (HRM) themes emanating from empirical research within a sample of companies; forming conclusions regarding the implications for training, management development and human resource planning.

LITERATURE REVIEW

As with the Holiday Inn example mentioned above, the USA was the focus and origin of many of the subsequently global chains of service firms, as personified by twentieth-century brand symbols such as Hilton, Sheraton, McDonald's and Burger King. It is therefore not surprising that most of the pertinent literature on the subject of multi-site management and the service sector was developed by US researchers and writers. Of notable relevance is the work of Olsen *et al.* (1992), which devotes considerable attention to the development of multi-unit hospitality organizations, including a review of the HRM implications. Their definition of a multi-unit (multi-site) firm is a useful starting point: 'an organization that competes in the industry with more than one unit of like concept or theme'. Olsen *et al.* point to the problems of managing a dispersed operation across many geographical boundaries, and the subsequent challenges associated with quality control, in particular the supervision of the skills and attitudes of service-delivery employees. They also raise the issue of the span of control, i.e. the number of unit managers reporting directly to a multi-site manager, their research indicating that this can vary between two and fifteen. As spans of control have gradually increased in scope and size, so multi-site managers need alternative forms of management development in order to give them the skills necessary to supervise a much larger number of unit managers. There is also reference to the typical hierarchical structure and the position of the multi-unit manager within that structure. Literature on this subject focuses on the first-line area or regional management level, positioned between single-unit management and senior executive responsibility (Goss-Turner, 1999, p. 39).

In reviewing the US literature, factors which emerge as significant include the link between HRM development in multi-unit firms and the organizational life-cycle considerations of introduction, growth, maturity and decline, a link well established by Sasser *et al.* (1978), when extending the concept of the product life-cycle into a service firm life-cycle. The implication of this and other research (Greiner, 1972; Kimberley and Miles, 1980) is that HRM will develop along with the organization in the areas of recruitment, selection, training and development, and in compensation and benefits. This concept gains insight when a new start business is considered, and its ensuing life-cycle (see Schuler and Jackson, 1987; Tyson, 1995). The founder will normally be the creative, entrepreneurial drive behind the first outlet, attracting the most compatible, like-minded talent available but often lacking HRM professionalism and experience. Growth of the firm, including the opening of more identical concepts elsewhere is associated with a need to develop more systematic HR approaches and, ultimately, consideration of manpower planning, management development and succession planning. The appointment of multi-site managers is a natural component of this process.

Tyson (1995) enhances the work of Schuler and Jackson by relating the life-cycle scenario to both business strategy and HR approach. At the early stages of foundation and growth, it is suggested that innovation is the key business strategy, and that a flexible *ad hoc* form of HRM is most beneficial. With growth, quality enhancement and consistency of standards is the optimum strategy, while the HR philosophy must begin to concentrate on vision, values and the development of a team culture and career development. This style of HRM has been termed the 'soft' approach, whereas in maturity and possible decline, the business strategy emphasizes cost reductions and efficiency gains, the 'hard' variety of HRM (Storey, 1992). A similar analysis is given by Fombrun (1984), pointing to the subjective and unsystematic HR/recruitment practices at introductory stages in contrast with the increasing use of standardized criteria during growth, and by the time that a multi-site operation is reached, far more systematic assessments for recruitment, selection and development. Again, the multi-site management role is associated closely with this move towards more systematic procedures and the drive for standardization and consistency.

Other US studies have concentrated on the personal qualities and types of behaviour required of multi-unit managers, in quick-service restaurants (Muller and Campbell, 1995), on career-development factors (Lefever, 1989), and on the component parts of the job (Umbreit, 1989). Literature from the UK has focused on strategic and operational developments and service-development issues connected with multi-site management (Teare, 1996), and there have been a number of studies covering the operational systems aspects of the contemporary hospitality industry (Kirk, 1995), and about what hospitality managers actually do at unit level (Lockwood and Guerrier 1990). The impact of empowerment has also been addressed in connection with multi-site firms, analysing the knock-on effects of the de-layering of hospitality organization structures and, therefore, the nature of the roles of the different layers of management, including the impact on the multi-unit manager position. Lashley (1997) has contributed to the understanding of the concept of empowerment within a service-industry context, relating particularly to research within the Harvester Restaurants chain. In Harvester, the empowerment of service employees via more self-managing work groups and the redistribution of responsibilities led to a de-layering of two managerial levels. The removal of a layer above the regional/area manager and directly below the managing director increased the accountability of the regional management positions.

The implications of empowerment initiatives for the role of middle management is also considered by Simons (1995) who points to the need for robust control systems in order to avoid the danger of control failures due to a more remote management style, as in the situation often observed in de-layered, de-centralized organizations, where the multi-site manager is made responsible for a span of control of twenty units when previously he had only twelve directly reporting unit managers. His framework, directly related to the multi-unit manager role and the multi-site organization, consists of four dimensions: diagnostic control systems, the multi-unit management responsibility for checking that goals and targets have been achieved effectively and efficiently; beliefs systems or core values, such as empowering unit managers to be innovative; boundary systems, providing clear parameters of the job; and, finally, interactive control systems, like regular face-to-face meetings or on-site business reviews to assess performance, issues and future plans and actions. The perspectives put forward by both Lashley and Simons impact on the topic of this chapter by assisting in the understanding of the role of the multi-unit manager within the wider managerial hierarchy, particularly focusing on the inherent tensions between the actual job and the range of tasks required, and the changing pattern of development required for such managers.

These inherent tensions arise from the aim to integrate successfully the three crucial service-delivery elements: the employees; the customers; and the form of control systems utilized. This challenge is particularly significant to multi-national companies, dealing with a branded operation in many different countries and cultures. A global brand like Pizza Hut must be organized in such a way that quality, standards and the meeting of customer expectations are ensured across the globe. The multi-site manager role in this organization has a major impact in effecting and implementing corporate strategy and decisions, and in ensuring that the highly prescribed standards are attained. As a result, a large part of the job is in checking the unit operation in detail, every possible aspect of the offering being inspected systematically against the so-called 'red roof evaluation' pro-forma, a detailed checklist for the area manager to complete at an on-site visit. During the author's own field research, this approach could be markedly contrasted with the philosophy of Pizza Express, a much smaller but highly successful UK-based restaurant chain. Although now expanding internationally, initially this chain grew within a reasonably confined area of the south-east of England. The multi-unit manager role was much less defined and inspectorial, there being a philosophy of entrepreneurial flair unhindered by too many systems and procedures, a scenario still prevalent within a relatively youthful company.

HRM implications of the developing multi-site firms in the hospitality industry have been at the heart of recent studies involving researchers from both the University of Surrey and the University of Brighton.The significance of the role of multi-unit manager has been consistently stressed by those national and international companies participating in the research. Such managers are the most influential interface between corporate strategic management and the operational outlets in which the service encounter takes place. The demands on this manager are in some ways unique. This manager, whilst responsible for unit managers of like concept and operation, is only rarely present at the operation, is physically distant, often quite remote, and direct control is only occasionally and briefly possible (Jones, 1999). Similarly the multi-unit managers themselves may well be located far from their peers and superiors. Co-ordination and collaboration is therefore relatively difficult. Research into a representative sample of hospitality companies (UK national and global chains) was undertaken, exploring the role and responsibilities of the multi-unit manager and the major HRM and management development implications. Conclusions from these studies give us key themes and issues for both the firms and the management.

Goss-Turner and Jones (2000) conclude that there are four key aspects of the first-line, multi-unit management level: job scope; organizational congruence; geographic density; and unit conformity. Within job scope, i.e. the range of tasks and responsibilities, there was great variance, polarized between those with a very tightly defined set of tasks geared towards inspection, to a broader concept within which the manager would have accountability for development of the business and innovation. International, mature restaurant chains with global brand significance tended towards more rigorous control in standardizing the offering and achieving high margins through such control. Multi-site management roles within firms at an earlier growth stage, and less international, were characterized by a broader range of duties. Interestingly, those companies with a strongly branded set of products, such as the major pubs groups, although national rather than international, also followed a pattern of ever more narrowly defined job scope.

For international firms, organizational congruence was important, i.e. the extent to which all managerial levels share a common vision and purpose. In the global franchised hotel brands, Marriott, for example, there were clear and formal systems of developing all employees in the culture and values of service inherent in the base company's strategic underpinning. Such international firms are also attempting a congruence of systems (such as information technology, appraisal and management development), and culture (such as values, beliefs and service).

Geographic density, i.e. the number of units in an area or region relative to the size of the area, is again a key difference between large, mature multinationals and the developing, less-mature nationals. For example, international hotel firms have a low relative density, requiring an even more mobile and experienced international manager to take on the area role, skilled in multicultural awareness and with strong personal attributes of self-motivation. As for unit conformity, i.e. the extent to which units within an area are identical or not, there was a definite trend towards 'streaming' by brand rather than geographical division due to the effectiveness and efficiency gains to be achieved from a regional manager always reviewing identical units. However, even here a factor such as size and scope of business might dictate another approach. For example, TGI Friday's restaurants operate by geography and by low density as their restaurants are such large profit centres, whereas groups like Scottish & Newcastle Retail and, in another study, Bass (Preece, Steven and Steven, 1999) were moving towards managers having more units to manage of an identical brand, rather than by the more traditional approach of a geographical area of outlets.

In a study of further HRM implications of these characteristics of multi-site firms, Goss-Turner (1999) concludes that the multi-unit manager role is predominantly an implementer of policy, not a creator of policy. This is largely a function of the role being so clearly placed between the strategy-makers in the boardrooms and the operational front-line unit managers. It is also because all the companies in the research had strategic expansion plans, mostly involving international expansion, of their already tightly branded concepts, sometimes within strictly controlled global franchises. As a result, such organizational development involving growth, consolidation and brand extension, requires the implementation and maintenance of absolute standards. There is, therefore, a need for inspection, checking and systematic control. However, this scenario also presents challenges in the management development of multi-site managers towards the more senior strategic positions within the organization. Several companies had identified that a large training gap was being created between area/ middle management and senior/executive management. In some cases this was being addressed by putting some multi-site managers on executive management development programmes at major international business schools to prepare them better for future, more strategic roles.

From an overall HRM perspective, the aspect of the role which appears to give the multi-unit managers themselves the greatest satisfaction is the ability to 'make a difference', motivating unit managers to improve and to be successful, sharing good and bad practice across their area, attempting to find a balance between a high level of prescription due to branding with the need to encourage a high level of commitment to the values and philosophy of the company (Walton, 1985). One international hotel regional manager was typical of those managers who saw their job as a combination of the need to implement strategic imperatives with a need to motivate the managers in the units:

> The job entails firstly maintaining the brand – we do have an identity and maintaining that identity in terms of our standards in the customer's mind and in their perception. I also want to stretch the managers as much as I can by getting them to achieve, such as the 'Investors in People' in every hotel, giving them objectives, ensuring they are ambitious over their business plans. But of course you can never take your eye off the profit level, and implementing company policy.

This dual approach is a clear indication of the possible development of managerial competencies required within the multi-site firm, analysed in a detailed study of change within Bass (Preece, Steven and Steven, 1999), as a subtle combination of implementer and controller of strategy, with the 'make a difference' attributes of influencer, coach, guide and facilitator of communication.

PIZZA EXPRESS PLC

Research Methodology

Pizza Express plc was one of the original research companies participating in the studies carried out by the University of Brighton and the University of Surrey in 1996/97. This entailed the interviewing in a semi-structured format of a number of key individuals within the company, the HR director and two regional or multi-site managers. The research design was essentially qualitative and deductive, a non-positivistic stance, the primary need being to explore the experiences of the managers involved and examine the outcomes for HRM. Documentation analysis supplemented the interviews. The semi-structured interview schedule was divided into five sections of questions, with prompts and areas for exploration, and a common framework to assist later analysis, when all the companies involved were comparatively analysed (Goss-Turner, 1999, pp.

39–57). The five sets of questions were constructed under the headings of organization structure; roles and responsibilities; skills and development; career development; and the documentation check. Subsequent research with Pizza Express plc has been in the form of follow-up discussions with two of the original interviewees and examination of the Pizza Express website and annual reports.

The Company

Pizza Express plc was founded in 1965 in London, by Peter Boizot, an entrepreneur who wanted to change the perception of the pizza from the product already being imported via US-based firms. In particular, he introduced more traditional Italian recipes, including a thinner crust base and more authentic sauces and toppings. Following a steady but relatively slow early growth the company began to expand within London and the South east region of England, and at the start of 1993, the number of restaurants in the chain stood at 45. Since that watershed, the past seven years has seen the company experience a rapid and sustained growth, supported financially by a stock-market flotation. In 1999 the company had a group turnover of £127 million and a pre-tax profit of £29 million (Pizza Express website).

During the early period of growth, the expansion was through franchise within the UK, a strategy which was later changed with the majority of franchises being bought back. This move was prompted by the challenge of rapid expansion and a need to ensure consistency of quality and standards across the increasing number of Pizza Express restaurants. In recent years, with a developing strategy of international expansion, the company has reintroduced the business format of franchising, but only in overseas locations, where it is felt necessary to have the involvement of an entrepreneur with detailed knowledge of the area, language, culture and consumer behaviour. By June 2000, the number of restaurants in the group had risen to more than 250. There are now some twenty restaurants outside the UK. This expansion overseas has seen openings in western Europe (e.g. France, Switzerland), eastern Europe (e.g. Poland, Russia), the Middle East (e.g. Egypt, Dubai), Japan and the US capital of Washington D.C.

Organizational Development

As a result of the earlier UK expansion, the original entrepreneurial approach to organizational structure began to change as it was clear that a new level of management was required between the board and the growing number of unit managers. The new position created was entitled Regional Operating Manager (ROM), this firm's equivalent of a multi-site manager. By 1997, six regional operating managers were appointed, all reporting directly to the managing director. The outlets were divided into regions purely on a geographical basis, as the restaurants have similarity in size, offering and turnover. Each ROM controlled between fifteen and eighteen units at this stage, all normally within easy travelling distance. There also developed an interim multi-site management role between restaurant manager and ROM – that of senior manager, an individual who supervised the running of perhaps two or three outlets situated very near to each other. Whilst the number of units under the management of a ROM increased steadily, this new development position of senior manager, reporting directly to the ROM, lessened the direct impact on workload.

This simple operational structure was supported by a small head office group of functional specialists, from HRM, to food-buying and quality, to transport management, property development and finance. However, the culture of this company has always been to concentrate effort on the units and the customer, and in developing both managers and employees who accept autonomy and accountability, possess an individualism of personality, and – even at ROM level – undertake their duties with a freedom from excessive control and administrative systems. As a result it was often mentioned in the research study in 1997 that different ROMs had almost completely different approaches to running their region. The company's Personnel and Training Director put it thus:

> Yes, we do have a culture, and it's a very strong culture – it's difficult to define – we really have in the six different regions, six different companies, each one of the Regional Managers is totally different, and the culture in the region reflects the style and personality of that particular multi-unit manager – the culture here is very strong at that regional level rather than over the whole company, compared with some companies who have a very strong corporate culture.

This approach maintained the spirit of entrepreneurialism within the company, there being relatively few critical measures of success of a ROM other than the normal business ratios such as cost of sales and labour cost, certainly no exhaustive checklists and site-visit evaluation systems. Indeed, in 1997 there were still few job descriptions, which were seen by senior management as a symbol of excessive restriction and control rather than the culture of accountable autonomy which the culture wished to develop. There was a standard menu and service-delivery system, but creativity and innovation were actively encouraged within the confines of the brand. The personnel and training director again:

> There are aspects of the operation that cannot be altered, principally the menu, the concept, but out-with that constraint, the managers can come up with ideas, and the test we ask them to apply is to ask themselves, 'Is this a Pizza Express idea?'– and if their answer is 'yes', and then they start putting roast beef and yorkshires on the menu as a special, then they're with the wrong company.

ROMs interviewed as part of the original research project had been promoted within the company and perceived no problems with regard to how their personal managerial style fitted with their role in the organization. Internal development and progression was a feature of the firm, and those interviewed believed that they had been promoted because their approach was consistent with what the firm was looking for in an area manager, as discussed by one ROM:

> The firm is a very hands-on company and if you're not one of those hands-on types of managers, then you're in the wrong job. I don't have a job description, though my objectives are discussed with the MD, which are all about improving standards and pushing to increase sales, but as to how we do that, it's up to the individual Regional Manager.

This element of being involved with the operation rather than a remote administrator type of ROM extended to HRM considerations regarding the recruitment and selection of ROMs, with both of those interviewed concurring that it would be an absolute requirement to have managed a Pizza Express restaurant before being considered for the position of multi-unit manager. This view was endorsed by the Personnel and Training Director, who felt that whatever your background outside the company, you would need to spend at least six months acclimatizing to the company's informal and somewhat unstructured approach. He went on to stress that though a strong brand, it was more important to possess excellent behavioural skills compatible with the culture than to be an excellent technical operator or manager:

> It's not just the technical skills but the culture of the company – the skills are very easy to grasp – it's a simple operation, but what is difficult to grasp is the approach – it took me – coming from a much more structured and systemised firm, a very long time to get my head around how things are done here.

Goss-Turner and Jones (2000) propose a typology of alternative approaches to area management based on the Surrey and Brighton research studies (see Figure 9.1).

They suggest that there is 'the archetype' multi-unit management approach, a mature, single-brand organization, typified by McDonald's, strongly branded identical units with tightly defined tasks for area managers, highly suited to international expansion strategies. The area manager would have narrow job scope, the firm a high degree of organizational congruence with high geographic density so that area managers can visit regularly and control closely. Secondly, there is 'the multi-brand manager', with more than one concept, tightly branded, applying identical managerial systems in each brand. While the job scope is still narrow, there is more flexibility and variety as more concepts are involved in mature companies. High congruence is difficult to attain, geographic density remains high, as the firm's structure is predominantly

Multiple brands	Multi-brand manager	Business manager
Number of concepts		
	Archetype	Entrepreneur
Single brand		
	Mature	Dynamic
	Approach to maturity	

Figure 9.1 Typology of alternative approaches to area management

Source: Jones, P. and Goss-Turner, S. (2000) 'Multi-unit management in service operations: alternative approaches in the UK hospitality industry'. *Tourism and Hospitality Research*, **2**(1), 51–66.

region- or area-based on a critical mass of outlets rather than on streamed brands. This approach is difficult to position in the international market-place. Thirdly, 'the business manager', responsible for more than one brand, and working within a more dynamic environment, with more opportunity for creative solutions and actions within broad policy guidelines and goals. This approach can be readily applied to international hotel companies for example. Finally, there is 'the entrepreneur', with each area manager responsible for one concept, tightly branded, but with an autonomy to develop the business, to be innovative where appropriate, and always within the cultural norms of the firm. Organizational congruence is driven by adherence to values and cultural issues, job scope is relatively broad within a dynamic environment which eschews a global system of control. The organizational life-cycle can affect all such classifications, particularly the stage of maturity reached by the firm.

While it is clear from this case study that at the time of the original research Pizza Express plc firmly fitted into 'the entrepreneur' typology, as a dynamic, single-brand environment, subsequent developments may begin to question its placement within this approach. As discussed earlier, the past two years have seen early but growing fulfilment of a strategy of international expansion, in response to a mission declaring that Pizza Express plc intends to become a global pizza brand growing to more than 400 restaurants within the next five years (Pizza Express website). It has been established that development of an international dimension would be a significant challenge for a single-brand, multinational, yet entrepreneurial firm. The company has reviewed its business format for overseas outlets, re-introducing the concept of franchising outside of the UK, developing opening teams to develop sites and new businesses in collaboration with the local franchisee, who with local knowledge and contacts is in a better position to make a major success of the business in as short a time as possible.

Recent structural developments, in an update of the original 1997 research study, illustrate that growth and globalization are inevitably accompanied by more structure and system. In the UK, the ROM position has disappeared as another layer of management has had to be introduced. Reporting directly to the managing director are now three regional directors, covering areas described as north, south and central and Greater London. In turn each regional director is responsible for about six area managers who are responsible for up to twelve units. Internationally, with the units so globally spread as indicated above, the company has moved towards the appointment of franchise consultants, specialists in their field who are responsible for development and quality monitoring within a set of countries. Although an emphasis is still placed on individuality and personality of both area managers and regional directors, the company is clearly on a path towards much closer elements of control and more organization-wide managerial systems. The structure at head office gives credence to this assertion, as there now exist central support services concerned with 'communications management', 'quality control' and 'systems', with a planned move to a new purpose-built site targeted for early 2001. There is an increasing need for more systematic management development programmes and succession planning within the enlarged structure.

DISCUSSION AND CONCLUSIONS

This chapter has reviewed some of the HRM implications of an ongoing phenomenon, namely the continuing development of larger, multi-site firms within an ever more international and branded hospitality and tourism industry. It has been established that this has increased the need for, and significance of a position of multi-site management, immediately above the front-line operations management and between operations and senior/strategic executive levels. As such it has been found to be a very important career development position for many unit managers, but essentially an implementer of strategy rather than a creator. Training gaps are evident, not only in the move from unit manager to multi-site manager, but also in the need for more strategic management training if such *implementers* of policy are to eventually become *creators* of policy. Further it has been discussed that the role in many strongly branded chains has the potential to be a largely controlling and checking role, with the proviso that there is still an opportunity for any area or regional manager to exercise his/her specific skills as a motivator and a coach to unit management. There is still the need to encourage and energize, to gain a high level of commitment to the values and beliefs of the company.

The latitude of this level of management is also determined by the size and stage of development of the firm's life-cycle. It has been found that the larger, more mature companies display a control-oriented, structured approach, while smaller, more youthful, more entrepreneurial firms tend towards a strategy which emphasizes mission, values and culture. Organizational development in recent years is also directly affecting the role, as head office support has in many companies been diminished in downsized and de-layered organizations. In the short term this may mean that the multi-unit managers need a broader range of management skills, to compensate for the reduced number of head office functional specialists. It was discovered in the field research that such managers are much more involved with HRM, marketing and financial management issues than they used to be. Such managers will need more training and development in HRM matters such as recruitment, selection and performance appraisal. Recruitment plans may be affected, with some hospitality and tourism firms perhaps recruiting more from outside their firm, even the industry, as more traditional technical skills are replaced by more generic management competencies. There is evidence from the licensed trade that there are indeed successful multi-site managers joining the major pubs groups from high-street retailers.

One aspect which will need to be the focus of future research pertains to the longer-term career development and succession planning aspects of multi-site managers. While there may be many more opportunities to become an area manager in the large branded chains, the decentralization of many such companies is leading to smaller head-office support functions. This has a direct impact on future career development prospects, as many area managers in the past have aspired to more specialist, centrally based roles. It is possible that such managers may have to stay in post longer than previously was the case, due to the flatter structure of such organizations. This clearly has implications for HRM, succession planning and compensation and benefits if motivation is to be maintained.

With regard to training and development, the Surrey and Brighton research project uncovered two significant challenges at crucial positions within the managerial succession. First, it is imperative that there is more systematic training of unit managers identified as possessing the potential for multi-unit management appointments, particularly in those competencies, such as HRM, marketing and financial management which will be needed to a much greater extent in the multi-site role. Add to this the motivational ability required across a large number of units and unit managers in a geographically spread area, and it is clear that the skills of being a top-class unit manager are very different from those required in the area role. Secondly, it must be accepted in most firms that the multi-unit role is one of implementation of standards, and that positions higher up the organization will require additional and enhanced skills in the area of strategic formulation and corporate-level decision-making. Succession plans must influence management development programmes to ensure that this gap in the training cycle is bridged.

SELF-ASSESSMENT QUESTIONS

1. Why has the position of multi-site manager become so significant within branded hospitality and tourism chains?
2. What key characteristics within the role of multi-site manager have been identified by literature and previous studies?
3. What is the relationship between management style and the role of the multi-unit manager?
4. What do you understand by job scope, organizational congruence, geographic density and unit conformity and how do they impact upon the role of the multi-site manager?
5. What do you consider to be some of the key competencies required of the multi-site manager?
6. What are the key issues outlined in the typology of alternative approaches to area management proposed by Goss-Turner and Jones (2000)?
7. What longer-term implications for HRM need to be considered by multi-site hospitality and tourism firms?

REFERENCES

Ball, S. (1996) 'Fast food sector', in P. Jones (ed.), *Introduction to Hospitality Operations.* London: Cassell.

Fombrun, C. J., Tichy, N. M. and Devanna, M. A. (1984) *Strategic Human Resource Management.* New York: John Wiley.

Goss-Turner, S. (1999) 'The role of the multi-unit manager in branded hospitality chains'. *Human Resource Management Journal,* **9**(4), 39–57.

Goss-Turner, S. and Jones, P. (2000) 'Multi-unit management in service operations: alternative approaches in the UK hospitality industry'. *Tourism and Hospitality Research,* **2**(1), 51–66.

Greiner, L. E. (1972) 'Evolution and revolution as organizations grow'. *Harvard Business Review,* **50**, 37–46.

Jones, P. (1996) (ed.), *Introduction to Hospitality Operations.* London: Cassell.

Jones, P. (1999) 'Multi-unit management: a late twentieth-century phenomenon'. *International Journal of Contemporary Hospitality Management,* **11**(4), 155–64.

Kimberley, J. R. and Miles, R. H. (1980) (eds), *The Organizational Life Cycle.* San Francisco, CA: Jossey-Bass.

Kirk, D. (1995) 'Hard and soft systems: a common paradigm for operations management'. *International Journal of Contemporary Hospitality Management,* **7**(5), 13–16.

Lashley, C. (1997) *Empowering Service Excellence.* London: Cassell.

Lee-Ross, D. (1999) *HRM in Tourism and Hospitality.* London: Cassell.

Lefever, M. M. (1989) 'Multi-unit management: working your way up the corporate ladder'. *Cornell Hotel and Restaurant Administration Quarterly,* **30**(1), 60–7.

Levitt, T. (1972) 'The production line approach to service'. *Harvard Business Review,* September/October, pp. 41–52.

Lockwood, A. and Guerrier, Y. (1990) 'Managers in hospitality: a review of current research'. *Progress in Tourism, Recreation and Hospitality Research*, **2**, 151–67.

Muller, C. C. and Campbell, D. F. (1995) 'The attributes and attitudes of multi-unit managers in a national quick service restaurant firm'. *Hospitality Research Journal*, **19**(2), 3–18.

Olsen, M., Ching-Yick Tse, E. and West, J. J. (1992) *Strategic Management in the Hospitality Industry*. New York: Van Nostrand Reinhold.

Parker, A. C. and Teare, R. (1992) 'A brand extension strategy for Holiday Inn Worldwide development'. in R. Teare and M. Olsen (eds), *International Hospitality Management*. London: Pitman Publishing.

Pizza Express plc website: http://www.pizzaexpress.co.uk/

Preece, D., Steven, G. and Steven, V. (1999) *Work, Change and Competition: Managing for Bass*. London: Routledge.

Sasser, W. E., Olsen, R. P. and Wycoff, D. D. (1978) *Management of Service Operations*. Boston, MA: Allyn and Bacon.

Schmenner, R. (1986) 'How can service businesses survive and prosper?'. *Sloan Management Review*, spring, 21–32.

Schuler, R. S. and Jackson, S. E. (1987) 'Organizational strategy and organizational level as determinants of HRM practice'. *Human Resource Planning*, **10**(3), 125–41.

Simons, R. (1995) 'Control in an age of empowerment'. *Harvard Business Review*, March/April, 80–8.

Storey, J. (1992) *Developments in the Management of Human Resources: An Analytical Review*. Oxford: Blackwell Publishers.

Teare, R. (1996) 'Hospitality operations: patterns in management, service improvement, and business performance'. *International Journal of Contemporary Hospitality Management*, **8**(7), 63–74.

Tyson, S. (1995) *Human Resource Strategy*. London: Pitman.

Umbreit, W. T. (1989) 'Multi-unit management: managing at a distance'. *Cornell Hotel and Restaurant Administration Quarterly*, **30**(1), 52–9.

Walton, R. E. (1985) 'From control to commitment', in K. Clarke, R. H. Hayes and C. Lorenz (eds), *The Uneasy Alliance*. Boston: Harvard Business School Press.

10

Performance Management in International Hospitality and Tourism

Bruce Millett

ABSTRACT

In international hospitality and tourism, where customer service is critical and the performance of staff is a central management issue across cultural and national boundaries, there is an obvious need to align human resource management in general, and performance management in particular, to the strategic requirements of service-oriented firms. The use of performance management as a competitive tool is paramount for hotel managers and, hence, their perspectives on such a tool provides valuable insights to managers in other types of service-oriented firms. After reviewing the literature in this area, this chapter describes and discusses the use of performance management at the Marriott Hotel on Australia's Gold Coast as a case study, with implications for other organizations operating within the broader context of international hospitality and tourism.

INTRODUCTION

The question for human resource management (HRM) is how it can add value (Stewart, 1996), particularly during a time when organizations have to rely increasingly on the knowledge, skills and commitment of all staff to stay competitive in the twenty-first century. In general, organizations are operating in uncertain and dynamic environments and must be more responsive to customer needs. This situation requires innovative approaches to HRM that encourage employee flexibility, adaptability and commitment to the organization (Guest, 1987) and that promote HR as a business partner (Beatty and Schneider, 1997).

131

This is particularly so in international hospitality and tourism where customer service is critical and the performance of staff is a central management issue across cultural and national boundaries. There is an obvious need to align HRM in general, and performance management in particular, to the strategic requirements of service-oriented firms. The competitive advantage of a hotel can depend on the relationship it has with each employee, for obvious reasons. Positive, negative and mediocre contributions impact on the quality of the service delivery to guests. It is, therefore, critical that hotel executives take personal responsibility for a performance-management system that supports all staff in feeling good about their work and achieving a positive sense of self-efficacy.

In very general terms, performance management is a system that is specifically developed to manage employee performance (Kramer, McGraw and Schuler, 1997). It is a system of integrating all aspects of the employment relationship that impact an employee's ability to perform (Williams, 1998). It is also a communication process that is ongoing and involves a partnership between the employee and the person responsible for the work of that employee (Bacal, 1999). This relationship, coined as a partnership to de-emphasis the control and hierarchical aspects of management, is a central feature of the system. In a more functional sense, performance management is 'a set of practices through which work is defined, reviewed and rewarded, and employee capabilities are developed' (Stephen and Roithmayr, 1998, p. 229).

The purpose of this chapter is to describe and discuss the use of performance management at the Marriott Hotel on Australia's Gold Coast as a case study, with implications for other organizations operating within the broader context of international hospitality, travel and tourism. There are two reasons for this. First, the hotel industry is highly competitive and focused on the quality of service delivery. The use of performance management as a competitive tool is paramount for hotel managers and, hence, their perspectives on such a tool could provide valuable insights to managers in other types of service-oriented firms. The changing dynamics of the market-place are stimulating the need for integrating HRM strategies and functions with bottom-line performance criteria.

Second, there is a dearth of publications on HRM in general, and performance management in particular, in the hotel industry. Unfortunately, researchers have either focused on manufacturing or looked at HRM and the performance relationship in more generic terms, rather than investigating the issues of HRM practices in service industries specifically (Hoque, 1999). However, interest in HRM within the hotel industry has increased (see Buick and Muthu, 1997). From what accounts are available of the service industry, the theme has been one of poor practice and a lack of interest in HRM among managers (see, e.g., Price, 1994; Lucas, 1996). Price adds that practices in the hotel industry were at odds with the theory and ideals of HRM.

This chapter is divided into a number of sections. First, the elements of the performance management cycle are identified and discussed in relation to the current research. The cycle provides a useful conceptual framework for discussing the performance-management process and is well supported by the literature. Secondly, a case study of the Marriott Resort on the Gold Coast in Australia is used to demonstrate a particular application of performance management in an international hotel chain. While a single case study has its limitations, it does provide a source of rich data for focusing discussion on a range of significant issues in managing staff performance in the service sector. Data for this case were collected from company documents and interviews with a number of senior staff working for the Marriott chain. Thirdly, the practices and issues relating to the influence of HR support programmes and managerial behaviour are discussed. Finally, the chapter is summarized and a number of implications for managers are identified.

THE PERFORMANCE-MANAGEMENT CYCLE

The concept of performance management is not new (Stephen and Roithmayr, 1998). The scientific management movement that emerged in the early part of the twentieth century as a result of the work of Frederick Taylor and others, focused on identifying an ideal way of doing work. However, the current re-focusing on and re-conceptualization of the concept has been brought about by the significant changes in the economic, business and social context since Taylor.

Although there is no single prescribed model in use (Clark, 1998), performance management is an umbrella term generally described as an iterative cycle of activity combining a number of common elements. It is a cycle of activity where the employment relationship is influenced through a continuous process of goal-setting, performance measurement and feedback (see, for example, Story and Sisson, 1993; Ainsworth and Smith, 1993; Clark, 1998; Stephen and Roithmayr, 1998). Figure 10.1 illustrates such a process as having four identifiable elements.

First, the employment relationship is the central feature of a performance-management system, and it is based on the psychological contract. While an employee generally signs a formal agreement of employment at the outset, the psychological contract is a set of expectations and understandings that develop between an employee and an organization, specifying what each expects to give and receive from each other during the period of employment (Hiltrop, 1995). These expectations are implicit and informal (Greenberg and Baron, 2000). Clear expectations are essential to a positive performance- and service-oriented relationship. Managing the psychological contract is

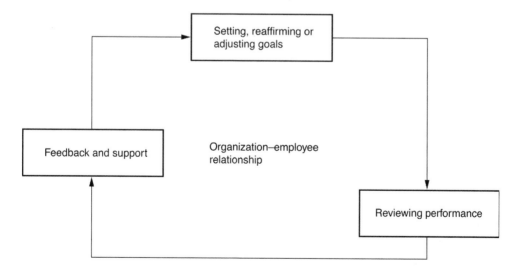

Figure 10.1 The performance management cycle

a particularly sensitive issue now that hotels are taking quality service more seriously (Harrington and Akehurst, 1996).

Secondly, goal-setting is the logical starting point for any performance management system and its importance within the hospitality sector is documented (Merrit and Berger, 1998). It represents the mechanism by which the vision, mission and goals of the business are translated into the more specific objectives that an individual has to achieve. For many front-line employees, the linkage with business objectives can be set out in terms of the position statement listing the particular functions to be carried out. In terms of managerial or professional positions, the goals can be interpreted in relation to broader areas of responsibility. Goal-setting provides the vital link between each individual and the organization. In this way, goals can be viewed as a cascade of objectives, from broad intentions to narrow prescriptions. George Odiorne (1979) promoted the virtues of management-by-objectives (MBO) as a method of linking performance planning with appraisal, and developing a more effective and productive relationship between employees and employers.

Those organizations that implement goal-setting as part of their performance management system tend to be more profitable than organizations that do not (Terpstra and Rozell, 1994). Merritt and Berger (1998) interviewed 22 managers and executives in the hospitality industry to determine the utility of goal-setting. Their results indicated that goal-setting provided a great opportunity for these people to manage both themselves and their subordinates. Some of the benefits of goal-setting that were obvious from this study included directing actions, fostering the development of potentially innovative strategies, connecting short- and long-term plans, focusing the efforts of the team and managing stress by avoiding burnout, and stimulating positive feelings.

Another important point is that goal-setting can support employees' beliefs in their own capabilities (Gellatly and Meyer, 1992). No incentive will motivate employees with low self-efficacy because they will not strive for rewards they believe are unattainable. What the goal-setting process does is commit individuals to goals they believe they can reach. However, self-efficacy is only one aspect in setting direction for employees. Another issue that can arise for hospitality managers is the tension between personal priorities and the hotel's priorities (Merritt and Berger, 1998). The goal-setting process needs to ensure that there are positive returns for both the employee and the hotel, and any potential areas of conflict needs to be identified and clarified.

The third major component of the performance cycle is appraisal. Although performance appraisal is only one component of a performance-management system (Bacal, 1999), it is now seen as a significant part, rather than a marginal or peripheral aspect of the HRM portfolio (Thornhill *et al.*, 2000).

Even without a formal system of appraisal, managers make probation, promotion, training, discipline and dismissal decisions on the basis of some sort of appraisal, even if it is no more than plain old 'gut feeling'. From a review of various definitions of performance appraisal, a number of critical elements can be identified:

- Performance appraisal requires some process to identify the criteria on which job performance can be based. Normally, appraisal systems rely on some form of job evaluation to provide a description of the job requirements and the criteria on which job performance is to be based.
- Performance appraisal requires an appropriate format for utilizing the performance criteria and evaluating the incumbent's performance for the job(s) in question.
- Performance appraisal should have a developmental aspect to it. What this aspect

means is that some effective mechanisms should be put in place to correct performance deficiencies and develop further competencies for the staff member concerned.

(Millett, 1998)

There are different ways to appraise a staff member and the selection of an appropriate method will depend on the circumstances of the organization and the preferences of those who are designing the appraisal system. Table 10.1 illustrates the main methods of appraisal.

A study of 389 hotels in the United States revealed that respondents conducted regular performance appraisals (Woods *et al.*, 1998) and the two most popular forms of appraisal were management-by-objectives and behaviourally anchored rating scales. In their study of hotels in Hong Kong, Cheung and Law (1998) found that performance appraisals were commonly used with the major benefits of motivating employees by providing recognition of their efforts and to help employees map out a career path and give guidance to needed training and development. It was also reported that the results of performance appraisals were not being fully utilized.

Fourthly, an essential element of any performance system is providing effective feedback on current achievements so that the organization and the individuals in it can learn constructively and take positive steps to take corrective action or develop new goals and strategies. Feedback is a vital component of goal-setting because it provides an opportunity for encouragement (Merritt and Berger, 1998). Employees and managers need continuous and relevant feedback to determine the impact of their actions. The employment relationship is central to the exchange of constructive feedback. In their study, Woods *et al.* (1998) reported that respondents raised two issues relating to appraisal feedback. It was found that, in general, managers were not reviewing the results with their employees. A second concern suggests that the annual review is too infrequent for meaningful feedback.

Another important aspect of this performance cycle is that it is played out in two different contexts. It is a formal mechanism, as well as an informal set of activities and interactions. The formal process involves measuring performance through an appraisal technique appropriate to the organization and each employee. It also involves a meeting between the employee and a manager. Such a meeting is held once or twice a year, depending on the needs of the organization. The informal process involves the day-to-day activity and discussions between an employee and managers about work-related issues. While many employees see the informal process as the 'real' process, performance management must be viewed in terms of these two contexts as they co-exist in action.

PERFORMANCE MANAGEMENT AT THE MARRIOTT

Marriott International is a leading accommodation, food and facilities management company that employs over 200,000 people in more than 30 countries worldwide. The company had its origins in the United States when J. Willard and Alice Marriott opened a nine-seat root beer stand called The Hot Shoppe in 1927. Today, it has developed into a well-known corporation with a strong market share in the hospitality and lodging industry, and has achieved annual sales in excess of US$8 billion.

Table 10.1 Methods of appraisal

Method	Description
Ranking	Employees in a section are ranked in an order of performance.
Grading	Employees are graded on a scale such as superior to unsatisfactory. Graphic rating scales are used to rate employees on various performance dimensions such as initiative, quality and quantity of work.
Critical incidents	Actual incidents are recorded as evidence of performance.
BARS	Behaviourally Anchored Rating Scales are used to determine the level of competency (behavioural statements) achieved for a particular job.
Essays	Where jobs (such as senior executive positions) are difficult to describe in specific and detailed dimensions, it is useful to write more qualitative statements about achievements and short-comings.
MBO	Management by Objectives is an important mechanism for promoting personal dialogue between staff and management and provides the ability for negotiating goals.
360 degree	While most systems of measurement rely on one source of information, such as the immediate supervisor, this method involves multiple sources including peers and subordinates.

Source: Adapted from R. Stone (1998)

The Surfers Paradise Marriott Resort is located on the Gold Coast in Australia and represents one of the preferred destinations for guests looking for 5-star convenience while staying on the coast. The hotel's performance-management system is an integral part of working with the 450 associates who assist in operating the resort 24 hours a day, seven days a week, and who are critical to developing and maintaining the resort's reputation. Approximately half of the associates are employed on a casual or part-time basis.

While the performance-management system at the Marriott can be portrayed by the iterative cycle described in Figure 10.1, the case has highlighted the fact that these activities do not occur in a vacuum. The performance of each individual occurs in the context of the mission of the Marriott, the HR programmes that provide support and guidance, the behaviour of managers in dealing with performance issues and the balanced scorecard system that focuses attention and activity on performance outcomes and strategic direction. These four factors are depicted in Figure 10.2.

Performance at the Marriott is described in terms of the balanced scorecard which is a customer-focused planning and process improvement system, translating strategy into an integrated set of financial and non-financial measures (Chow *et al.*, 1998). There are many examples of organizations using the balanced scorecard (see Birchard, 1995; Kaplan and Norton, 1996; Kurtzman, 1997). For example, the Hilton hotel chain introduced the balanced scorecard as a mechanism to link its strategic priorities to employee performance (Huckestein and Duboff, 1999). It communicates the organizational strategy to employees through four typical components: the customer's perspective about the organization, the internal business perspective concerning what areas in which the organization, the innovation and learning perspective about the organization's ability to improve and create value for customers and, finally, the financial perspective concerning the sources of capital (Chow *et al.*, 1998).

The Marriott is committed to the balanced scorecard approach and has four universal performance measures that guide the work of all staff – who are referred to as

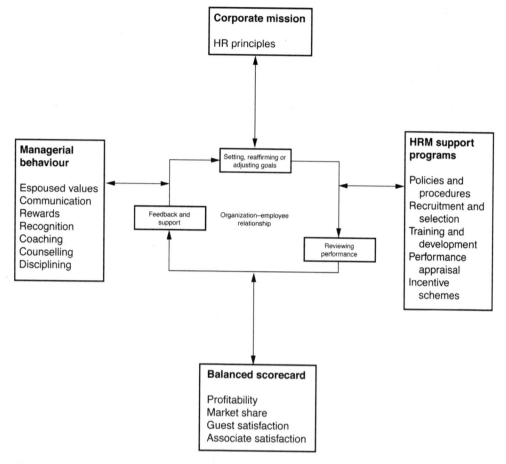

Figure 10.2 Performance management at the Marriott

associates as a mark of respect for their valued contribution to the organization. The four measures are:

- guest satisfaction: surveys are done on a continuous basis to identify the general level of satisfaction and the areas of concern for guests;
- associate satisfaction: associates are surveyed at least once a year on a range of issues relating to the performance of the organization;
- market share: figures are compiled on a continuous basis and displayed on strategically located notice boards in the administrative backrooms of the hotel; and
- sales: progressive figures are made available on a monthly basis.

While each of these measures can be seen as specific outcomes of the performance-management system, the results are used in combination to assess the total performance profile of the resort. The company places a deal of emphasis on the associate satisfaction ratings that are conducted once a year. These ratings, as well as the other three measures, provide important feedback during the performance appraisal of managers in particular.

The corporate mission, and the principles relating to associates, also provides important guidelines for managing performance. The Marriott corporate mission is to be the worldwide leader in the consistent delivery of high levels of products and services to quality-tier lodging guests. The management principles and values espoused by the corporate executive emphasize a strong commitment to associates. Those principles are embedded in the following strategies that are promoted throughout the company worldwide:

- increasing the profitability of the company by empowering associates;
- treating associates in the same manner as the company expects them to treat the customers;
- breaking down the barriers to better teamwork;
- ensuring a management culture that is action-oriented, always flexible and never bureaucratic;
- improving communication through listening, asking and speaking up;
- maintaining an innovative, restless business spirit, constantly seeking new opportunities to grow;
- recognizing the efforts of associates and celebrating them;
- encouraging all associates to contributing to the decision-making process at all levels and treating them as partners in the business; and
- sharing the company's vision and goals with associates and asking associates to share their aspirations with the company.

The corporate mission, the balanced scorecard and the guiding principles relating to associates provide an important framework for managing associates on a daily basis. Connecting the strategic vision and goals of the organization with the work of employees is a critical aspect of any programme of improving performance. For example, at the ANA Hotel in San Francisco, management adopted a quality improvement training programme in an effort to deliver customer satisfaction and increase profitability (Allison and Byron, 1996). The hotel's management estimated that at least 25 per cent of the training curriculum needed to focus on educating staff on the hotel's vision, values and strategic goals. With this information ingrained in the curriculum, staff would be in a better position to understand that any continuous improvement effort needed to align with the hotel's overall goals.

Two other important aspects of the performance management system at the Marriott are HR support programmes and managerial behaviour. They will be discussed in the following sections.

HR Support Programmes

The HR director and his staff, support associates and line managers through policies and procedures, recruitment and selection, training, performance appraisal and incentive schemes. The Marriott Hotel chain is a large international company and one of the keys to its success is the development of policies and procedures that assist HR managers around the world in developing a clear, relevant and consistent set of guidelines for all employees to follow. The HR director has various corporate and in-house publications to assist him. While it is a neglected point in the HRM literature, these policy and procedure documents are critical to effective recruitment and selection, training and development and performance appraisal.

Employee selection for virtually every position at Marriott hotels entails an assessment-of-fit to the profile developed for that position (Dube and Renaghan, 1999). Before any appointment is made, applicants are interviewed twice over a ten-day period. According to the HR director, the hotel's philosophy is 'they want all associates to be successful', hence there is a lot of time and effort that goes into making sure the candidate is comfortable with the hotel and the hotel being sure the candidate will be successful at the Marriott.

Attitude is seen to be very important in this process. Good staff are hard to come by in hospitality and, according to one executive, management want to ensure that they 'don't let good people slip through their fingers'. In their survey of best practice in the United States' Lodging industry, Dube and Renaghan (1999) found that success at the Marriott and the Four Seasons hotels could be attributed to hiring people who are motivated to service guests.

When candidates are selected, they are put on a three-month probationary period, during which time they receive an intensive orientation into the company. As the HR director points out: 'it is none of this two day and it's all done nonsense; we insist on the "Marriott ways – first 90 days" orientation programme'. Initially, it involves a half day with the HRM department on the formal requirements of the hotel. There is an induction with the relevant department. This is a formal session using a checklist of information that each associate must be familiar with.

After one month, there is a 'Welcome to Marriott' day where associates are introduced to the executive team with lunch in the restaurant. This is part of a one-day formal training session on various topics such as sexual harassment and safety and health issues. After three months, there is a final half-day training session followed by a celebration where each new associate gets to stay in the hotel as a guest, free of charge. The associate is able to provide feedback from a guest's perspective and also appreciate what this may mean as an associate of the hotel. The final aspect of the 'Marriott ways – first 90 days' programme is the associate's first appraisal. This acts as a learning tool, as well as confirmation that the orientation has been successfully completed.

While the hotel seeks to recruit the best people, it is subject to the supply and demand dynamics of labour in the local region. For example, maintaining quality in food and beverage services can be dependent upon the availability of top chefs and waiters in the area. Also, finding maintenance engineers with the right attitude towards service is an ongoing dilemma in the five-star section of the industry. Nankervis's (1993) survey found that Australian hotels experienced difficulties with the calibre of job applicants and with their unrealistic career expectations.

Effective training is a central feature of best practice hotels (see, for example, Barrows, 2000; Dube *et al.*, 1999; Dwyer *et al.*, 1998). Marriott is recognized in the industry for the quality of its training programmes. Training is an integral part of maintaining good associate relations, and achieving high levels of customer service through a participative style of management. Managers are responsible for their own development, as well as the development of associates. Marriott's responsibility is to supply the necessary opportunities and developmental programmes.

There is a range of training programmes available to associates. One such programme is 'Spirit to Serve'. It involves four modules of eighteen hours in total. The managers conduct the training in an experiential learning format. Other programmes include the Advanced Management Skills course and the Foundations of Leadership course that includes topics such as Stephen Covey's seven habits of successful people, train the trainer, and navigating through change. The hotel also uses a buddy system where new associates are assigned to experienced staff. This mentoring system is critical in areas such as functions and catering, where high standards are demanded.

Some associates are reluctant to undertake training in their own time. This presents a challenge for the HR director to not only fund the essential programmes on the job, but also to find the time to run such programmes within the current hectic work schedules. There are difficulties inherent in shift work for supporting associates. The manager responsible for housekeeping staff on late night and early morning duty, expressed some concern over her ability to support associates and deal with performance-related issues because of the lack of direct contact with them.

Each year, all associates are appraised. However, the appraisal process varies according to their employment category within the hotel. Grade 1 to 3 employees – that includes managers and other staff on the higher remuneration scales – are subject to a 'Leadership Performance Process'. This incorporates an aspect of goal-setting in the formal performance-appraisal process. Goal-setting applies mainly to managerial staff because the areas of responsibility are much broader and the priorities within those responsibilities can change from time to time and, hence, negotiation becomes a relevant aspect of managing their performance. After the information from the balanced scorecard is compiled for the year, these associates are assessed on the past twelve months' achievements, and their goals for the coming twelve months are negotiated. Performance is evaluated equally on achievement of business goals and the demonstration of key competencies. A three-point scale is used. For managers, in particular, the guest and associate surveys are very important to their assessments. The senior members of the management team have their salary package tied to the performance assessments.

Grade 4 and 5 associates, who are on the lower levels of the remuneration scales, are assessed using a less complex assessment form. There is no specific goal-setting component in the formal process of appraising this group. The assessment is related to the more specific requirements of their job/position statement that tends to be relatively fixed. A four-point rating scale is applied to twelve factors that include such items as teamwork, initiative and knowledge of work. The assessment form seeks to identify areas where the associate can improve through constructive advice or development options. It also allows the person being reviewed and the reviewer to make general comments about any aspect of performance and the appraisal process.

Rix (1990) maintains that many appraisal systems become moribund, resented and discredited. At worst, appraisals can be concerned with making retrospective judgements about such subjective aspects of performance as personality and attitude. English (1991) adds that many appraisal systems are poorly designed, so that a supervisor is obliged to find at least one fault per review. At the Marriott, there was a concern expressed over the relevance of the rating system for grade 4 and 5 associates. Some of the attributes assessed were questionable in terms of their relationship with an individual's performance. Also, the inconsistency of managers in their assessment of associates was an issue and this applied to both systems of appraisal. However, the current system was seen as relatively effective in helping to focus discussion on improving an individual's performance.

While the HR staff put a great deal of emphasis on recruiting associates with the right attitude towards service, incentive schemes are deemed to be necessary to recognize good performance and to motivate ongoing acts of service excellence. Various incentive schemes have been tried with mixed success. For example, front-desk associates have been offered a bonus scheme during periods of low occupancy. The bonus applies to any increased sales which may come from convincing guests to upgrade rooms or to transfer to a room with an ocean view. One of the issues identified with providing incentive schemes was the ability to keep changing the incentive schemes in order to maintain their potency. Incentive schemes have a limited life-span. Issues can arise with the removal of incentives. For example, housekeepers were being paid for any extra rooms serviced over their normal allocation. When this arrangement was abandoned, the housekeeping section expressed their disapproval.

Investigating the motivational preferences of Caribbean hotel workers, Charles and Marshall (1992) found that hotel workers in seven hotels in the Bahamas were motivated most by higher wages, but differences in age, organizational level and number of years in the same job position also influenced workers' motivational preferences. They concluded that managers need to use creative, monetary-based incentives and that motivational strategies should suit different groups of workers.

Managerial Behaviour

While the HR support programmes are designed to directly influence the performance of associates, the case highlights the significant influence that managers have on the performance of their subordinates. Leadership is a critical managerial issue for any organization (Millett and Marsh, 2001) and the behaviour of managers is important to sustaining the culture and values that the Marriott executive management team aspire to. The values are apparent in the principles identified above and, in essence, they are based on a strong belief in the contribution of associates which translates into attracting loyal customers by investing in associates (Sullivan, 1999). The HR director expressed it as 'you treat your associates as you would treat your guests'.

The chairman and president of the Marriott organization explained that the basic philosophy at Marriott is to make sure their associates are very happy, and that they enjoy their work so they take care of customers and have fun while they are doing it. Their business is based on associates going the extra mile – which can be lending a guest a pair of cufflinks or it can be more dramatic, such as in the US invasion of Panama, where Marriott staff risked their lives to hide American guests in the laundry room dryers (Sambrook, 1992). While the hotel has not adopted a formal quality-assurance system, the philosophy of quality management is engrained into the Marriott culture. As one senior executive commented: 'We don't talk about it. We just practice it.'

The performance-management system operates in the context of these espoused ideals and the managers at the Marriott are clear about their priorities. They want every associate to be successful and if an associate has a problem, then it gets attended to. The need for managers to continuously act out these ideals is critical to enhancing the Marriott brand name. They do this by communication and involvement, by giving rewards and recognition to top performers, and by coaching, counselling and, on occasions, disciplining associates.

The general manager of the hotel takes a direct interest in the associates and manages by walking around (MBWA). He takes an interest in everyone's performance appraisal. His intention is not to interfere in the work of departmental managers, but to get to know associates. He is often seen strolling through the hotel and shaking hands with staff from all sections. He practises the Marriott philosophy of 'no manager is too busy to talk to an associate'. Every two months, the resort manager selects 24 associates for a lunch with him. This is part of a strategy to improve communication and to again reinforce his appreciation for the work that they do. The management team has a social night out several times a year. These activities are reinforced by what Lee-Ross (1993) reports as a close link between management style and employee motivation.

Marriott has a worldwide associate appreciation week to celebrate success. During this week, associates do things for the community such as charity work. In one American resort, associates banded together and helped to rebuild a house for a couple after it had been gutted by fire. More importantly, the week is a time where executives demonstrate their appreciation of the work of associates. They put on uniforms, wash dishes and do the basic jobs of the resort. The resort manager provides free meals in the cafeteria during this week.

Managers are trained in how to counsel and coach associates effectively. They are also required to be competent in disciplining staff. These three skills are seen to be an important aspect of managerial behaviour and how managers can influence the performance of associates. This can be viewed in the context of Nankervis's (1993) survey that found Australian hotels experienced difficulties with high rates of absenteeism and sick leave.

Sometimes, however, incidents occur where managers are put to the test. In one instance, an associate was guilty of striking another. Under normal circumstances this situation is not tolerated by Marriott regulations. However, the associate was not dismissed because the manager responsible at the time failed to intervene appropriately. Such situations can be complex, with more than one person at fault. The organization has a duty of care to associates, so proper training for managers in this regard is critical. While the Marriott has its regulations to cover such situations, managers need to understand the relevance of local law in each circumstance. In this case, dismissal could have resulted in a claim of vicarious liability in the courts because of the failure of the hotel management to take appropriate action.

Each executive will have a particular style or approach to managing a hotel. While some managers are more visible than others, it does not mean that visibility necessarily equates to effectiveness. Various executives at the Marriott, for example, have to balance their local responsibilities with their regional and corporate responsibilities. The Marriott on the Gold Coast is part of a large international chain of hotels and, from time to time, the hotel manager and the HR director may be away from the hotel for periods of time because they have responsibilities covering the South-East Asian region. The priorities of managers are another consideration in terms of their ability to contribute to the performance management system.

SUMMARY AND CONCLUSIONS

The Marriott organization appreciates the value of its associates and places a lot of emphasis on having a performance management system that encourages and supports positive and effective behaviour. From the case described above, it is apparent that the current system is designed to reflect the values espoused by corporate management and to guide and integrate practices across cultural boundaries to ensure that the brand name of Marriott is not only protected, but enhanced in the top end of the hospitality and tourism industry globally.

In the United Kingdom, the Institute of Personnel Management (1992) undertook a major study of performance management and established a number of advantages for its implementation. First, it can offer a greater degree of involvement by all employees in realizing the organization's vision. Secondly, it can encourage delegation of appropriate decision-making responsibilities in the hands of line managers and employees for more effective and responsive action. This also clarifies the areas of accountability for line managers. Finally, it offers a mechanism for linking rewards to performance.

These advantages are confirmed indirectly by the fact that hospitality managers have increasingly adopted empowerment and teamwork and accepted the need to devolve responsibility as steps towards continuous improvement (Gilbert and Guerrier, 1997). Dube *et al.* (1999) point out that the champions in their study of best practice in the US lodging industry reached a successful level of market orientation through the implementation of innovative human resources practices, especially employee training and rewards, job design, information sharing and employee empowerment and involvement. From housekeeping and maintenance to front-desk operations and revenue management, employees were seen to be the key to successful adoption of best practices to improve customer satisfaction and financial performance. The case study of the Marriott at the Gold Coast provides the following set of implications for managers in the industry:

- Whatever the size of the operation, a clear set of goals, performance criteria and value statements need to be communicated and understood throughout the organization as a fundamental integrating mechanism. This establishes a framework throughout the organization for high-performance expectations and for the development of an environment that supports those expectations.
- Open and honest commitments to support and recognize the efforts of staff are fundamental principles for achieving quality in the provision of services.
- A balanced scorecard approach can provide the focus for managing employee performance within a culture of openness and integrity.
- Performance management needs to be developed and managed as an integrative system involving various HR programmes.
- The impact of managers on employee performance should never be underestimated and frank and open discussions about such an impact should be encouraged. In the case of the Marriott, this is assisted by the use of the associate survey in the performance-management process.

In his study of hotels in the United Kingdom, Hoque (2000) concluded that there had been genuine and positive change in relation to HRM practices. While there are still improvements to be made in the way employees are utilized in a quality-oriented and service-related environment, service industry managers can benefit by observing the way that Dube *et al.*'s champions respond to the market-place through a genuine commitment to working with their people. The Marriott provides a specific example of managing people effectively by paying attention to detail, working through an integrative system, and living out their espoused ideals about quality service.

SELF-ASSESSMENT QUESTIONS

1. Is performance management the same as performance appraisal?

2. What are the major components in the performance-management cycle?
3. Do you think it is practical to use a balanced scorecard approach in the international hospitality and tourism industry?
4. Discuss the appropriateness of the Marriott's commitment to its associates.
5. Identify the issues you believe are critical to the success of managing performance in a hotel.

REFERENCES

Ainsworth, M. and Smith, N. (1993) *Making It Happen: Managing Performance at Work*. Sydney: Prentice-Hall.
Allison, J. and Byron, M. (1996) 'Aligning quality improvement with strategic goals at ANA Hotel San Francisco'. *National Productivity Review*, 15(2), spring, 89–99.
Bacal, R. (1999) *Performance Management*. New York: McGraw-Hill.
Barrows, C. (2000) 'An exploratory study of food and beverage training in private clubs'. *International Journal of Contemporary Hospitality Management*, 12(3), 190–7.
Beatty, R. and Schneider, C. (1997) 'New human resource roles to impact organisational performance: from "Partners" to "Players"', in D. Ulrich, M. Losey and G. Lake (eds), *Tomorrow's HR Management*. John Wiley and Sons, New York, pp. 69–83.
Birchard, B. (1995) 'Making it count'. *CFO: The Magazine for Senior Financial Executives*, October, 42–51.
Buick, I. and Muthu, G. (1997) 'An investigation of the current practices of in-house employee training and development within hotels in Scotland'. *Service Industries Journal*, 17, 652–8.
Charles, K. R. and Marshall, L. H. (1992) 'Motivational preferences of Caribbean hotel workers: an exploratory study'. *International Journal of Contemporary Hospitality Management*, 4(3), 25–9.
Cheung, C. and Law, R. (1998) 'Hospitality service quality and the role of performance appraisal'. *Managing Service Quality*, 8(6), 402–6.
Chow, C., Ganulin, D., Haddad, K. and Williamson, J. (1998) 'The balanced scorecard: a potent tool for energizing and focusing healthcare organisation management'. *Journal of Healthcare Management*, 43(3), May/June, 263–80.
Clark, G. (1998), 'Performance management strategies', in C. Mabey, G. Salaman and J. Story (eds), *Human Resource Management: A Strategic Introduction*. Oxford: Blackwell, pp. 125–52.
Dube, L. and Renaghan, L. (1999) 'Strategic approaches to lodging excellence'. *Cornell Hotel and Restaurant Administration Quarterly*, 40(6), December, 16–26.
Dube, L., Enz, C., Renaghan, L. and Siguaw, J. (1999) 'Best practices in the U.S. lodging industry: overviews, methods, and champions'. *Cornell Hotel & Restaurant Administration Quarterly*, 40(4), August, 14–27.
Dwyer, L., Murray, P. and Mott, R. (1998) 'Continuous improvement in hospitality: a case study approach'. *Australian Journal of Hospitality Management*, 5(1), autumn, 19–31.
English, G. (1991) 'Tuning up for performance management'. *Training and Development Journal*, 45(4), April, 56–60.
Gilbert, D. and Guerrier, Y. (1997) 'UK hospitality managers past and present'. *Service Industries Journal*, 17, 115–32.
Gellatly, I. and Meyer, J. (1992) 'The effects of goal difficulty on physiological arousal, cognition, and task performance'. *Journal of Applied Psychology*, 77(5), 694–704.
Greenberg, J. and Baron, R. (2000) *Behaviour in Organizations*. Sydney: Prentice-Hall.
Guest, D. (1987) 'Human resource management and industrial relations'. *Journal of Management Studies*, 24(5), 503–21.
Harrington, D. and Akehurst, G. (1996) 'Service quality and business performance in the UK hotel industry'. *International Journal of Hospitality Management*, 15(5), 283–98.
Hiltrop, J. (1995) 'The changing psychological contract: the human resource challenge of the 1990s'. *European Management Journal*, 13(3), September, 286–94.

Hoque, K. (1999) 'Human resource management and performance in the UK hotel industry'. *British Journal of Industrial Relations*, **37**(3), September, 419–43.

Hoque, K. (2000) *Human Resource Management in the Hotel Industry*. London: Routledge.

Huckestein, D. and Duboff, R. (1999) 'Hilton Hotels: A New Approach to Creating Value for All Stakeholders'. *Cornell Hotel and Restaurant Administration Quarterly*, **40**(4), August, 28–38.

Institute of Personnel Management (1992) 'Performance management in the UK'. London: Institute of Personnel Management.

Kaplan, R. and Norton, D. (1996) 'Using the balanced scorecard as a strategic management system'. *Harvard Business Review*, January/February, 75–85.

Kramer, R., McGraw, P. and Shuler, R. (1997) *Human Resource Management in Australia*. South Melbourne: Longman.

Kurtzman, J. (1997) 'Is your company off course? Now you can find out why'. *Fortune*, February, 128–30.

Lee-Ross, D. (1993) 'Two styles of hotel manager, two styles of worker'. *International Journal of Contemporary Hospitality Management*, **5**(4), 20–4.

Lucas, R. (1996) 'Industrial relations in hotels and catering: neglect and paradox?' *British Journal of Industrial Relations*, **34**, 267–86.

Merritt, E. and Berger, F. (1998) 'The value of setting goals'. *Cornell Hotel & Restaurant Administration Quarterly*, **39**(1), February, 40–9.

Millett, B. (1998) 'Performance management: a strategic human resource function', in K. Parry and D. Smith (eds), *Human Resource Management: Contemporary Challenges and Future Directions*. Toowoomba: USQ Press, pp. 95–114.

Millett, B. and Marsh, C. (2001) 'The dynamics of strategic learning in an era of industry restructuring', in R. Wiesner and B. Millett (eds), *Management and Organisational Behaviour*. Brisbane: John Wiley and Sons, pp. 185–196.

Nankervis, A. (1993) 'Service quality and productivity in the hotel industry'. *Tourism Training Australia*, Sydney.

Odiorne, G. (1979) *MBO 11: A System of Managerial Leadership for the 80's*. Belmont: Fearon Pitman Publishers.

Price, L. (1994) 'Poor personnel practice in the hotel and catering industry: does it matter?' *Human Resource Management Journal*, **4**(4), 44–62.

Rix, A. (1990) 'Performance appraisal: a look back in anger'. *Employee Relations*, **12**(3), S1–S2.

Sambrook, C. (1992) 'Marriott: a name to contend with', *Marketing*. Oct. 8, pp. 16–18.

Stephen, A. and Roithmayr, T. (1998) 'Escaping the performance management trap', in M. Butteriss (ed.), *Re-Inventing HR: Changing Roles to Create the High-Performance Organisation*. Toronto: John Wiley and Sons, pp. 229–48.

Stewart, T. (1996) 'Taking on the last bureaucracy'. *Fortune*, April, p. 105.

Stone, R. (1998) *Human Resource Management*. Brisbane: John Wiley.

Storey, J. and Sisson, K. (1993) *Managing Human Resources and Industrial Relations*. Buckingham: Open University Press.

Sullivan, J. (1999) 'Human Resources Propel the Future of Foodservice', *Nation's Restaurant News*, Dec 20, **33**(51), p. 72.

Terpstra, D. and Rozell, E. (1994) 'The relationship of goal setting to organisational profitability'. *Group and Organization Management*, **19**(3), 285–94.

Thornhill, A., Lewis, P., Millmore, M. and Saunders M. (2000) *Managing Change: A Human Resource Strategy Approach*. Harlow: Financial Times/Prentice-Hall.

Williams, R. (1998) *Performance Management: Perspectives on Employee Performance*. London: Thomson Business Press.

Woods, R., Sciarini M. and Breiter D. (1998) 'Performance appraisals in hotels'. *Cornell Hotel and Restaurant Administration Quarterly*, April, 25–9.

11

Tourism Training in Developing Countries: A Commercial Solution to Training Needs

J. John Lennon

ABSTRACT

This chapter examines the area of human resource development, particularly vocational training, in the context of developing economies. In both of the countries examined – the Republic of Fiji and the Republic of South Africa – tourism had been identified as a critical aspect of economic development. Accordingly, the need for trained labour in the growing hospitality and tourism industries has become a concern for government. As education budgets are rarely adequate to suffice fundamental needs, this chapter considers two planned approaches which focus on the creation of a hotel school environment. The hotel schools considered in both cases utilize the environment of an operating hotel to both generate revenue to sustain training and provide a realistic work environment. Such a development option was seen as equally valid by national government and development agencies in both contexts and the planning models merit further application.

INTRODUCTION: EDUCATION AND TRAINING IN A DEVELOPMENT CONTEXT

In recent years, significant aid and development funding for tourism training has been allocated by organizations such as: International Labour Organization, United Nations Development Programme and World Tourism Organization and various Directorate Generals (DGs) of the European Union. Tourism for many developing countries is seen as a highly attractive development option generating significant earning through overseas currency and serving to attract international investment. This initial attractiveness does, of course, bring with it many unwanted social and environmental aspects, which can be harmful to development and can significantly impact on host nations.

A fundamental need for any nation developing or extending its tourism appeal is the development and training of service and production employees for employment in hotels, resorts, tourist attractions, travel and related infrastructure. However, in many developing countries training for these sectors is often relatively unsophisticated and lacking in industry credibility. Skilled and experienced labour is invariably a scarce resource and funding for vocational education is invariably limited. In many developing countries education priorities are clearly focused on primary level (from 4 to 11 years) wherein fundamental skills and abilities such as reading and writing are the focus of education development policy. Consequently, the most significant elements of education finances and budget allocations are directed at this aspect of learning development. Vocational education that offers sector-specific skills for operational/supervisory positions in sectors such as tourism and hospitality are very limited. Minimal budget allocation is usually focused on the post-16-age group. As a result, tourism and hospitality employers in emergent destinations in developing countries are confronted with employees who are fundamentally unskilled and require considerable investment in training and development. Numerous attempts to deal with this situation have been attempted. This chapter considers the application of the commercial hotel school concept in both Fiji and South Africa – contrasting locations which evidence significant demand for trained and educated labour in the tourism industry.

FIJI: MAIN ECONOMIC ACTIVITIES AND EMPLOYMENT

The nation of Fiji consists of over 300 islands located in the South Pacific. In 1997 it had a population of 779,000 (ESCAP, 2000) with an estimated adult literacy rate of 87 per cent. Life expectancy and infant mortality rates, along with GDP per capita, place it among the upper quartile of developing countries. Some 70 per cent of the population live on the main island of Vitu Levu with Suva the government capital being host to a number of international aid agencies, development banks and the EU delegation for the South Pacific.

Fiji is primarily an agrarian society with agriculture, forestry and fishing comprising 21.1 per cent of gross domestic product (GDP). Sugar remains central to agriculture and employs about 25 per cent of the labour force, contributing just over 11 per cent of GDP (Horner, 1996). Sugar constitutes 38 per cent of total exports, most of which was until 2000–1 sold to the EU on a preferential price basis. The production of sugar remains labour-intensive and would not be commercially viable without subsidies arising from the Lome Protocol (Horner, 1996). Such preferential access is ultimately a source of vulnerability since agricultural subsidy constitutes a major difficulty in the reduction of global trade barriers and, as such, has been targeted by the General Agreement on Tariff and Trade (GATT) negotiations.

Invariably, any improvements in production efficiency will involve reduction in the demand for labour and will result in increased unemployment in the medium to long term. Real growth in employment is most likely to be in garment manufacture, which has grown considerably, following the introduction of tax-free status for factories in 1988. The non-preferential trade region established under SPARTECA has allowed access to the lucrative markets of Australasia, the USA and the EU. However, as the

Bank of Hawaii economic commentary noted: 'Preferential access to large markets such as Australia, New Zealand, the European Union and to a lesser extent the United States, will aid Fiji's economy in the short run, but Fiji will not be able to compete economically unless it builds its economy with capital and a skilled work force' (Bank of Hawaii, 1996, p. 34).

However, all preferential trade relationships enjoyed by the island nation are currently threatened by the political reaction to the 2000 coup which saw many of the old ethnic tensions within Fiji remerge in an unpleasant and damaging manner (see below).

Tourism has become a major source of employment in Fiji; it has generated approximately 25 per cent of gross foreign exchange receipts and earns approximately 24 per cent of GDP (Kroner, 1996). According to the World Travel and Tourism Council (WTTC, 2000a) travel and tourism was expected to generate US$824.7 million of economic activity in 2000, growing to US$1531.7 million by 2010. Travel and tourism demand was expected to grow in real terms by 44.5 per cent per annum between 2000–10. In 2000, travel and tourism was estimated to be responsible for the generation of 92,300 jobs or 21.2 per cent of total employment.

Fiji was seen by some internationally as a potentially very strong trading nation and the period to late 1999 saw some very positive reports on growth. The Bank of Hawaii in assessing Fiji noted: 'Fiji is a potential showcase among the South Pacific's economies because of its large land mass, natural resources, work force and infrastructure, and its capacity for growth' (Bank of Hawaii, 1996, p. 39).

Such forecasts and figures may now, of course, be seen as somewhat optimistic following the 2000 coup led by the native Fijian George Speight and his supporters. This saw the democratically elected Fijian Indian prime minister taken hostage and resulted in the Fijian army taking control following a period of rioting and civil unrest in Suva and some other centres of population.

Prior to the 2000 coup it was anticipated that tourism would contribute a further 270,000 jobs by 2005 (direct, indirect and induced), seventy per cent of these jobs to be located in hotels and resort properties in the Nadi Bay area, the Coral Coast, the Mamanucas and Yasawas Islands (Deloitte and Touche, 1997). Travel agents, airlines, retailers, arts and crafts producers, restaurants, car rental outlets, tourist sites, tourist guides and dive operations were all predicted to benefit from this expansion. Yet the instability of the country and the clear ethnic tensions that are present had already caused social and trade-related problems some thirteen years earlier. Indeed, tourist demand was severely affected by the 1987 coup and, following this, Fiji experienced a flight of capital and human resources as many of the Fiji Indian population emigrated. This caused a considerable shortage in professional, technical, managerial and clerical workers in both the public and private sectors (Kay, 1996). Emigration had returned to more manageable proportions before the 2000 coup, although primary indicators are that a second flight of capital and human resources is currently ongoing.

In assessing the demand for skilled labour the ethnic tensions remain an important factor that has to be considered. However, The European Union DG VIII in its development of a major training and education plan for Fiji in 1997–99 accepted certain generalizations about the demand for education and training prior to the 2000 coup. These were that:

- skills shortages were most acute in the hospitality and tourism sectors (Deloitte and Touche, 1997; Canberra Institute of Technology, 1996);
- the majority of employment will be in the private sector and this will create demand

for new forms of education and training;
- rapid technological change will continue demonstrating the needs for continuous education; and
- growth in the manufacturing sector will continue to stimulate demand for general and specialized education and training.

Fundamentally, the potential for tourism was seen as considerable, and given the concentration of tourism facilities in the Nadi area on the main island of Vitu Levu, priority was given to this area. Nadi is also the location of the main international airport for the South Pacific and the area benefits from a drier, sunnier climate than other parts of the island. Given this recognition of the critical importance of tourism, the Fiji Tourism Development Plan (Deloitte and Touche, 1997) and the related EU planning exercise for human resource development (IBF, 1997a, Tourism Council of the South Pacific, 1997) were to be proactively linked.

The Fiji Tourism Development Plan

The Fiji Tourism Development Plan incorporated a major element of development funds to the training and education elements. Building quality services in the South Pacific in order to develop realistic competitive advantage is dependent upon the education of the workforce. Such difficulties have been recognized in previous investment in training developments (Hall and Page, 1996). However, the 1997 Tourism Development Plan incorporated a vision of improved tourism to Fiji, which was predicated upon targeted marketing and appropriate infrastructure support. The Belgium-based consultancy; IBF International Consulting were contracted to deliver the operational planning scenario for regional education and training. The multi-skilled team led by the author of this chapter were charged with the development of a regional training facility for the South Pacific that was both economically viable and environmentally sustainable (IBF, 1997a and b).

Given the problems with trade and the economy discussed earlier, this project was seen as vital to reaffirming the island's pivotal position as a regional training centre for the South Pacific and was in accordance with international reportage on the need for consolidation in training and the demand for state-of-the-art training facility development (ILO, 1997).

The development scenario was relatively simple: concentrate on the tourism sector through the training of individuals in the context of a realistic work environment based in a Nadi Campus. This was to be achieved by the development of a hotel school incorporating:

- 25 bedroom hotel with native Bure accommodation;
- four conference and meeting rooms (capacity 100 persons);
- restaurant for 60 covers; and
- bar for 40 covers.

These accommodation and food-and-beverage facilities allowed the host institution, the Fiji Institute of Technology (FIT), to generate revenue. Regional students from the surrounding nations were to be accommodated on site (in student accommodation for some 250 residents) and this gave opportunities for staged learning in the organization.

First-year students would, initially, cater for their peers and provide accommodation service for them before progressing to hotel-based training with 'live' customers in years two and three of their education. Given the relatively limited knowledge of hotel services among such students a staged introduction to practical areas is vital prior to industrial placement or career commencement in the hospitality and tourism sector.

Retained income and profit was to be used to catalyse the development of other aspects of the campus including information technology facilities and the extension of library content and facilities. Revenue generation centres included:

- hotel accommodation;
- hotel food and beverage;
- staff restaurant operation;
- student catering;
- student accommodation; and
- training activities in partnership with industry.

An outline plan prepared by Nigel Hall Architects is included below and illustrates the integration of learning and training facilities.

The linkage of this facility to an existing institution, FIT, was logical in terms of course support and the building of a realistic work environment on an existing educational resource. Given such development, FIT had the potential to be one of the most important tertiary vocational education and training providers within the South Pacific. Indeed, in 1997–99 a number of factors were positively facilitating this development. These included:

- the proactive role of the government (particularly in its identification of key sectors for investment and financial incentives to stimulate the economy);
- the government's recognition of the significance of tourism to a diversified economy in Fiji;
- the tourism potential of the archipelago; its proximity to Australasia and the emergent Pacific Rim economies;
- the outstanding natural beauty of the islands and the charm and friendliness of the native peoples;
- the relatively developed state of the infrastructure of the major islands;
- the use of the English language within the islands; and
- the potential for FIT to act as a major provider of regional training and education.

FIT was the driving force behind technical and vocational education in Fiji. It primarily serviced educational demand from the main island of Vitu Levu, although, increasingly, there was a need to extend provision to the outlying islands and more remote areas within the region. The relationship between the Fiji National Training Council (FNTC), a main employers group, and FIT had improved considerably in the years to 1997–8, and the two organizations were working in partnership to develop a more comprehensive and coherent strategy for meeting the nations industrial needs. FNTC were represented on FIT's academic and governing council and they had expressed a very strong interest in contributing finance and manpower to the development of Nadi campus Hotel training operation.

FIT had been striving to improve relationships with industry. All FIT courses involved a period of industrial secondment and this has resulted in improved liaison

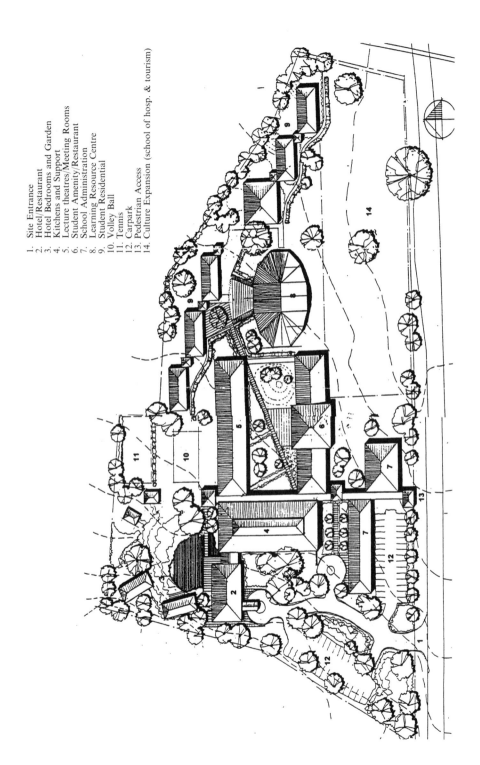

1. Site Entrance
2. Hotel/Restaurant
3. Hotel Bedrooms and Garden
4. Kitchens and Support
5. Lecture theatres/Meeting Rooms
6. Student Amenity/Restaurant
7. School Administration
8. Learning Resource Centre
9. Student Residential
10. Volley Ball
11. Tennis
12. Carpark
13. Pedestrian Access
14. Culture Expansion (school of hosp. & tourism)

Figure 11.1 NADI campus: indicative masterplan

between FIT and industry. However, adequate preparation of students, particularly in high-guest contact industries such as hospitality and tourism, was seen as crucial in establishing the credibility of the student output. Thus an existing resource was being extended in an innovative and positive way, the most sustainable feature being the revenue-generation aspect which allowed for a growth in further education vocational training for this sector in the context of a developing country. The validation and proof of the acceptance of the concept was the planned allocation of some Fiji $4.4 million of EU structural funds for the development of what was to be titled the Nadi Centre for Hospitality, Tourism and Commerce.

Sadly, following the Coup of 2000 and the introduction of a military-based government this innovative and realistic work environment development has been suspended.

THE TOURISM INDUSTRY AND THE REPUBLIC OF SOUTH AFRICA

In Africa, international tourist arrivals reached 20.6 million in 1996 with earnings of US $8 billion. The top destination was the Republic of South Africa (RSA) which was chosen by more than 25 per cent of visitors to the continent. According to Kessel Feinstein Consulting (1998) the industry is worth R 24 billion annually which constitutes between 4–5 per cent of total Gross Domestic Product (GDP). WTTC estimates for RSA are even more buoyant with travel and tourism anticipated to generate US$ 15 billion of economic activity and growing at a rate of 7.2 per cent annually (WTTC, 2000b). Travel and tourism employment is estimated at 742,300 jobs or 7.5 per cent of total employment which constitutes one in every 13.3 jobs in RSA, with a forecast growth of 9.3 per cent of employment or one in every 10.8 jobs by 2010 (WTTC, 2000b).

The growth in tourism has created, and will continue to create, a massive training and education need in the hospitality and tourism industries. Based upon future growth estimates for the industry employment is estimated to grow from 300,000 in 1997 to 600,000 by 2004. Currently, an estimated 35,000 to 50,000 students are required to be trained/educated each year with some 80 per cent of this figure required for the hospitality sector. Currently, only 5,000–6,000 are enrolled in quality establishments leaving employers with a massive shortfall in trained and educated labour (BMI, 1997). This leaves hospitality employers with little option but to recruit untrained labour. Consequently, the quality of service and, most particularly, guest service deteriorates.

A familiar scenario of an expanding industry and a dearth of trained labour to fuel that industry is evident. Yet in South Africa the huge problem of unemployment estimated at 20–25 per cent increases the requirement to absorb those without work into employment to increase stability and position the economy for growth. The hospitality industry is notoriously labour intensive and the logic of focusing on this sector in terms of policy and development incentives is clear.

Any attempt to service this massive training need must reinforce the sustainable development strategies, which are being progressed in the RSA. Indeed, it is encouraging to see that many agencies associated with developing the South African tourism product are adopting an approach to development, which is based on the principles of environmental, as well as economic, sustainability (Government of South Africa, 1997). There is a commitment at all levels to encourage local communities, government and parastatal agencies, as well as the private sector, to take a stake in the improvement and protection of the South African natural resources (Woodward, 1997; Holt-Biddle, 1996).

The next section of this chapter considers the application of the hotel school framework to the South African context. The author was once again involved in the training and development plans for the operation and this more ambitious application provides an ideal foundation for revenue generation in the context of a limited education development budget. The project is located in the north of the country and aims to provide for the shortfall in appropriately qualified and trained personnel to work in this growing sector at a local level. Furthermore, this project aims to explore ways of delivering training by means of a partnership between the RSA's providers and UK institutions.

The feasibility of demand for such a school is evident in the severe skill shortages apparent in the hospitality and tourism sector. Training and education has been recognized as critically important to the future of the South African economy. Recent legislation, such as the Skills Development Bill (1997) provides clear justification for growth and development of such as school. However, investment in the vocational education sector is often seen as a lower priority than investment in the woefully inadequate primary and secondary provision. Accordingly, any development that is both economically and environmentally sustainable gains greater support in the context of a transitional economy.

The Training Project builds on the successful planning exercise, which was utilized in Fiji and described earlier. The obvious use of a similar context in the South Africa context was the starting base of the Mpumulanga Project.

The Training and Education Project in Mpumulanga

This project constituted a much more ambitious commercial operation (100-bedroom hotel, 150-cover restaurant, 100-cover café) with a training and educational establishment which was planning a 200–300 student intake per year. Once again the commercial mode of operation allows the hotel and other facilities to generate revenue and profits which can then be invested in upgrade and development of the fledgling educational facility.

Once again, the relevance of a realistic environment of a 'live' hotel is the ideal learning facility for students from a developing transitional economy. It gives students with a limited experience of the tourism sector a fast-track and highly appropriate training mode which makes them highly attractive to employers. The consequent and planned generation of employment in tourism helps in the development of the economic stability of the nation. The crucial role of tourism as an employment generator has been recognized consistently at the most senior levels of the European Union and has been reflected in the allocation priorities of development funds (DG XXIII, COM (1997) 322, DG XIII (1998)). This proposed school would provide skilled labour for the emergent hotel, tourism and conference industry as well as the national parks and related game reserves. Mpumulanga is of course the location of the world famous Kruger National Park.

The School was also planned to develop the Mpumulanga province as a key source of employees for the RSA tourism industry in the medium to long term. The potential for this School as a Southern African training establishment was also seen as considerable. Furthermore, the relatively unusual and entrepreneurial design could act as a blueprint for future development of similar establishments throughout Southern Africa.

The South African training operation will be developed in line with sustainable best practice in business development and would have sensitivity to environmental and ecological issues related to tourism. Recent research on ecotourism in South-East Asia has shown that an understanding of the complex relationship between people, resources and tourism is critical in the development of appropriate management strategies in protected areas (Ross and Wall, 1999) It is also possible that the school will incorporate a Centre for Eco-tourism and Sustainable Tourism Business Development. This would have the following key aims:

- to conduct research and development in new environmental technologies;
- to advise on and communicate best practice in applying the principles of sustainable development; and
- to underpin training and education with environmental/sustainable best practice principles.

Initially, training is planned to be undertaken in partnership with UK education and training staff who will provide curriculum, learning methods and design input to the development of the school. The plan being that within a period of three to five years the school would be sustainable and independent at the operational training level with a diminishing partner role for UK institutions. The task of the UK partners then becomes to develop the managerial and research potential of the school. This second stage is anticipated to take a further three years and will culminate in the establishment of a full campus environment offering training and education from the operational through to the managerial/specialist levels with a strong environmental/sustainable approach to tourism development underpinning growth.

Thus the project was planned to combine environmental and economic sustainability in a country that desperately needs to deal with massive youth unemployment and maximize its tourism potential. The project is currently at the final stages of financial feasibility and it is anticipated that construction will commence in late 2002.

CONCLUSIONS

The commercial merger of training and trading represents a realistic context for the rapid development of education and training in the developing world. In countries where tourism is a pivotal industry it represents one of the only real alternatives for development and if political stability is assured it can offer a highly sustainable platform for human resource-development.

SELF-ASSESSMENT QUESTIONS

1. What are the major training advantages offered in the development of realistic work environments in the two cases analysed?
2. To what extent are such approaches valid in all countries wherein tourism and hospitality development is seen as important for economic development?
3. Compare and contrast the Fijian and South African projects via a brief SWOT analysis of each.

REFERENCES

Bank of Hawaii (1996) *Fiji: Economic Profile and Investment Trends.* Internal reportage.

BMI (1997) *Tourism Training Needs in South Africa: A Situational Analysis to Assist in the Formulation of a Tourism Training Strategy.* South Africa: BMI.

Canberra Institute of Technology (1996) *Fiji Institute of Technology Study on the Feasibility of a School of Hospitality and Tourism for the Fiji Institute of Technology.*

COM (1997) 322 of 02.07.1997 *Report from the Commission to the Council on Community Measures affecting Tourism.*

Deloitte and Touche Consulting and Tourism Council of the South Pacific (1997) *Fiji Tourism Development Plan.*

DG XXIII October 1998 *Report of the High Level Group on Tourism and Employment.*

Economist Intelligence Unit (1995) *International Tourism Report*, **2**, pp. 5–22.

ESCAP (2000) *Fiji Statistics.* Statistics Division, United Nations Economic and Social Commission for Asia and Pacific, New York.

Government of South Africa (1997) *Tourism in Gear – A National Strategy to Implement the Tourism White Paper 1997–2000, Final Discussion Document*, April.

Hall, C. and Page, S. (1996) *Tourism in the Pacific: Issues and Cases.* London: International Thompson Business Press.

Holt-Biddle, D. (1996) 'The new South Africa: ecotourism flavour of the year?' *The Ecotourism Society Newsletter*, **6**(1), 1–2.

Horner, S. (1996) 'Country Report: Fiji', in *ACP-EU Courier*, No. 160, November–December, 9–25.

IBF (1997a) Republic of Fiji European Commission VII Development Fund. *Study for the Project Identification, Feasibility Study and Preparation of Project Dossier for the Proposed Project for the Upgrading of the Fiji Institute of Technology*, Part 1, Brussels: IBF.

IBF (1997b) Republic of Fiji European Commission VII Development Fund. *Study for the Project Identification, Feasibility Study and Preparation of Project Dossier for the Proposed Project for the Upgrading of the Fiji Institute of Technology*, Part 2, Brussels: IBF.

ILO (1997) *Employment Promotion Through Integrated Human Resource Development Programmes.* Fiji: International Labour Organization.

Kay, R. (1996) *Fiji: Economic and Political Overview* (http://www.aloah.com/~rkay/economy.html).

Kessel Feintstein Consulting (1998) *South African Tourism Trends: An Interim Update of Tourism Talk* (4th Edition). Kessel Feintstein Consulting, Republic of South Africa.

Kroner, E. (1996) 'Fiji-EU co-operation: a comprehensive package', in *ACP-EU Courier*, No. 160, November–December, 24–5.

Ross, S. and Wall, G. (1999) 'Evaluating ecotourism: the case of North Sulawesi, Indonesia'. *Tourism Management*, **20**(6), 677–82.

Tourism Council of the South Pacific (1997) *Tourism in the South Pacific*, (internal planning document) TCSP, Suva, Fiji.

Woodward, S. (1997) 'Cashing in on the Kruger: the potential of ecotourism to stimulate real economic growth in South Africa'. *Journal of Sustainable Tourism*, **5**(2), 166–8.

WTTC (2000a) *Tourism Satellite Accounting Research Fiji.* Washington: World Travel and Tourism Council.

WTTC (2000b) *Tourism Satellite Accounting Research South Africa.* Washington: World Travel and Tourism Council.

Part III Employee Relations

12

Building Organizational Commitment in International Hospitality and Tourism Organizations

Debra F. Cannon

ABSTRACT

Organizational commitment has, typically, been defined as the relative strength of an individual's identification with a particular organization and degree of involvement of the individual in the organization. The concept of organizational commitment has importance to varied industries and professions, including hospitality and tourism, primarily because of the negative relationship found between commitment and potentially costly behaviours such as absenteeism and turnover. This chapter provides a review of research on organizational commitment starting with the early studies that established a theoretical foundation for the concept. More recent studies incorporating international organizations are included as well as research that has focused on organizational commitment in the hospitality industry. A hypothetical international company in the travel and tourism sector is presented in the case study that presents cultural diversity issues in creating a work environment that aims to maximize organizational commitment.

INTRODUCTION

The role of human resources in hospitality and tourism organizations has never been more important than it is now. Increasingly, hospitality and tourism businesses are global in scope, working with multicultural employees and guests and competing in entirely new arenas in which service demands are escalating. Involved, enthusiastic employees, committed to the values and goals of their respective organizations, are a vital ingredient to the success of any hospitality and tourism business.

For many organizations in this industry, turnover rates in the triple digits are common place and routinely accepted. Iverson and Deery (1997) referred to this phenomenon in the hospitality industry as a 'turnover culture' which has become evident in many companies. Although there may be a myriad of reasons for this culture, many employers have rationalized the high turnover rates, according to Iverson and Deery, based on a high presence of part-time and casual labour, low job security in some segments and low wages and skill levels in certain job positions. The turnover issue is complicated even further today as many countries face serious labour shortages, particularly involving qualified applicants. Widespread acceptance of the identified 'turnover culture' could threaten to undermine the very essence of the hospitality and tourism industry, providing quality service through its most important resource – employees.

As organizations face multiple human resource challenges, the concept of 'organizational commitment' becomes increasingly germane. Having received attention in management and organizational behaviour literature since the 1950s, organizational commitment has been described as employees who exceed the formal requirements of the employer organization (March and Simon, 1958; Grusky, 1966) and 'the strength of a person's attachment to an organization' (Grusky, 1966, p. 489).

Since the work of these earliest theorists, the concept has been embraced by numerous researchers, with over 500 studies published on the topic of organizational commitment from the mid-1970s to the end of the 1990s. The attention on organizational commitment in research has been fuelled by the many positive organizational outcomes associated with this concept. In fact, in later research, it was determined that organizational commitment was one of the most reliable predictors of turnover intentions (Johnston *et al.*, 1990). As the review of the literature section will explain, significant relationships have been established between organizational commitment and additional positive employee behaviours that would, typically, be advantageous to hospitality and tourism organizations. Organizational commitment has also been found to be a more stable and enduring measure of employee attitude as compared to other constructs such as job satisfaction (Mowday *et al.*, 1984; Williams and Hazer, 1986).

While research on organizational commitment in the hospitality and tourism industry has not been abundant, the findings based on studies conducted in other fields are relevant. The antecedent variables associated with organizational commitment in previous research will be delineated in this chapter. Research that has involved international subjects will also be highlighted in showing some of the cultural issues that have emerged as related to organizational commitment. The research directly involving subjects from the hospitality and tourism sector will also be discussed. The hypothetical case study included in this chapter allows the reader to apply the research findings in establishing a work environment in a travel and tourism business to maximize organizational commitment.

The objectives for this chapter include the reader being able to accomplish the following points:

* define the concept of organizational commitment;
* discuss the theoretical foundation for organizational commitment;
* differentiate between three types of organizational commitment;
* delineate at least five positive outcomes associated with organizational commitment;

- identify the antecedent relationships found in research between at least five personal variables and organizational commitment;
- identify the antecedent relationships found in research between at least five job and work place variables and organizational commitment;
- discuss the research that has been conducted in the hospitality and tourism industry on organizational commitment;
- explain approaches to use in a travel and tourism business to maximize organizational commitment among employees.

EXPLORING ORGANIZATIONAL COMMITMENT

The concept of organizational commitment was significantly developed by the work of Mowday *et al.*, (1982). These authors delineated three components of organizational commitment which included: (1) a strong belief in and acceptance of the organization's goals and values; (2) a willingness to exert considerable effort on behalf of the organization; and (3) a definite desire to maintain organizational membership.

A common element among many organizational commitment studies is the presence of an exchange involving a type of psychological contract between the employee and employer (Angle and Perry, 1983; Mowday *et al.*, 1982). This concept of employee – organizational exchanges has earlier roots in March and Simon's inducement-contributions theory (1958), Becker's theory of side bets (1960), the investment model (Rusbult, 1980) and the exchange theory (Homans, 1961). The values and needs that the employee brings to the organization are of paramount importance in considering the employee–employer exchange. When an employee's expectations, based on his or her values and needs, are met, the level of commitment to the organization is expected to increase.

Some of the research involving exchange theories has concentrated on tangible benefits such as insurance and pension plans contributing to greater commitment (Goldberg *et al.*, 1989). According to this perspective, the attachment of rewards other than income, such as an attractive benefits plan, fulfils employee expectations and needs and makes leaving the organization more difficult. The exchange process may also be more passive with factors such as age, tenure and educational level contributing to the investment and reward value of the resources associated with the organization involved (Brief and Aldag, 1980).

Another theoretical approach in organizational commitment research has been tied to role theory. There are three primary aspects of role theory that influence commitment: job scope or challenge, role conflict, and role ambiguity. One basic hypothesis incorporating role theory is that an increase in the number of different operations required in a job (job scope) increases the level of challenge to the employee and, therefore, increases commitment (J. M. Stevens *et al.*, 1978). Role conflict, on the other hand, and role ambiguity tend to be adversely related to organizational commitment (Morris and Sherman, 1981; Stevens *et al.*, 1978).

More recent research has focused on the different types of organizational commitment. Allen and Meyer (1990) have delineated three major components and corresponding scales. As described by Wahn (1998), the first component of affective commitment refers to the emotional attachment of employees to the organization and encompasses identification with, and involvement in, the organization. This is the tie between the employee and organization because the individual wants to be there. The continuance component refers to the costs that employees associate with leaving the organization. This tie is based on the employee perceiving that he or she actually needs to remain with the organization. Thirdly, the normative component refers to employees' feelings of obligation to remain with the organization or the tie based on the individual perceiving that he or she ought to be there. Research using these three components has shown different consequences of the different commitment types. For example, continuance commitment has been found to be negatively correlated with turnover but may also be associated with poorer job performance (Meyer *et al.*, 1989), lower levels of organizational citizenship (Shore and Wayne, 1993) and a greater likelihood to comply with organizational pressures to behave unethically (Wahn, 1993).

Crosby *et al.* (1994) also differentiated between two types of organizational commitment: passive and active. Passive commitment relates to resistance to outside influences and includes aspects such as training, employee benefits and employee welfare. Active commitment, on the other hand, pertains to what the employee says about the organization and the dedication of the employee to organizational goals and objectives. According to Hoffman and Ingram (1992), both passive and active commitment can affect customer satisfaction and the willingness of the employee to remain with an organization.

Organizational commitment has been linked to a number of positive work-related behaviours. For example, Hrebiniak and Alutto (1972) considered the variable to be evidenced by an unwillingness to leave the organization for incremental increases in pay, status, professional autonomy or increased social interactions. A significant inverse relationship has been found between commitment and employee punctuality, attendance and turnover (Mobley, Horne and Hollingsworth, 1978). In a meta-analytical study, Brown and Peterson (1993) found that commitment has a dominant negative impact on turnover intentions (-0.78) and most of the influence on job attitudes and role stressors is mediated by commitment. In another meta-analysis of 61 studies, Lee and Ashforth (1996) found a weighted correlation of -0.43 between organizational commitment and emotional exhaustion. There have been mixed results, however, regarding the relationship between organizational commitment and job performance (Mathieu and Zajac, 1990; Reichers, 1985). Some studies have found a positive relationship (DeCotiis and Summers, 1987) such as Bateman and Organ (1983) who referred to commitment as 'organizational citizenship' encompassing altruism, co-operation, performance in a crisis and generalized compliance. Others have found no relationship of significance (Angle and Perry, 1981) or even a negative relationship when individuals feel a significant extrinsic investment (time, pension, pay scale) in the organization (Allen and Meyer, 1990). Brown and Peterson (1993), however, found considerable evidence to suggest a positive relationship between the variables. The logic is based on high levels of performance, engendering the belief that the company will provide future success opportunities which result in higher commitment levels to the organization (Singh, 2000). Organizational commitment has also related positively to participation, power, teamwork and professionalism (Welsch and LaVan, 1981).

Steers (1977) developed one of the earlier models of organizational commitment encompassing antecedents and consequences of commitment. Steers delineated three groups of major categories that influence the development of commitment. These groups included personal characteristics, job characteristics and work experiences. Numerous studies have been conducted in trying to identify antecedent variables. Steers concluded that of the three groups, work experiences were most directly associated with organizational commitment. Table 12.1 illustrates a sample of the studies conducted on antecedents of organizational commitment and the findings from these works using the three category groupings delineated by Steers.

Table 12.1 Summary of research on organizational commitment

Variable related to organizational commitment	Study findings	Study (author/date)
Personal Characteristics		
Age	Positively related	Hrebiniak & Alutto (1972); Morris & Sherman (1981); Michaels (1986);
Tenure with the organization	Positively related	Koch & Steers (1978); Stevens *et al.* (1978)
Education	Negatively related	Koch & Steers (1978); Angle & Perry (1981); Morris & Sherman (1981);
Central life interest in Work	Positively related	Dubin *et al.* (1975)
High need for achievement	Positively related	Steers (1977)
Intrinsic need strength	Positively related	Lawler (1973); Hackman & Oldman (1976)
Acceptance of the Protestant work ethic	Positively related	Buchanan (1974); Kidron (1978)
Marital status and number of children in the family	No significant relationship found	Ritzer & Trice (1969)
Gender	Females were higher in continuous commitment;	Wahn (1998)
Job characteristics		
Task identity, job challenge, job scope, opportunities for social interaction, amount of feedback provided, autonomy	All positively related	Sheldon (1971); Buchanan (1974); Marsh & Mannari (1977); Steers (1977); Hunt *et al.* (1985);
Participation in decision-making	Positively related	Rhodes & Steers (1981); Pierce & Dunham (1987)
Role ambiguity	Negatively related	Jones (1986)
Job complexity	Positively related	Pierce & Dunham (1987)
Work experiences		
Organizational concern for employees; positive, warm, supportive organizational climate	Positively related	Buchanan (1974); March & Mannari (1977); Steers (1977); Mathieu & Zajac (1990); Luthans *et al.* (1992)
Supervisory ability	Positively related	Morris & Sherman (1981); Michaels & Spector (1982)

Table 12.1 *continued*

Variable related to organizational commitment	Study findings	Study (author/date)
Leadership initiates structure and consideration behaviour	Positively related	Pierce & Dunham (1987)
Managerial adherence to organizational ethical values	Positively related	Fritz *et al.* (1999)
Company-provided training when the training is perceived as effective	Positively related	Chang (1999)
Perceived fairness in the assignment of work tasks	Positively related	Witt (1993)
During the lay-off of employees, perception that it was handled fairly	Positively related for hourly and management employees	Grunberg *et al.* (2000)
Company being unionized	Negatively related	Stanley & Cooper (1972) Kochan (1975);
	No relationship found	Stevens *et al.* (1978)
Employees experiencing their company being acquired through a hostile acquisition	Negatively related	Del Vecchio (1999)
Employee's perception of flexible work hours	Positively related with female managers; no significant relationship with male managers; Positively related with managers who had children under 18 years of age living at home	Scandura & Lankau (1997)

INTERNATIONAL PERSPECTIVES OF ORGANIZATIONAL COMMITMENT

While most of the research on organizational commitment was initially conducted in the United States and western Europe, the 1990s heralded an increasing number of studies involving subjects from other parts of the world. Although not based in the hospitality industry, this research is of great significance to various professions in demonstrating cultural influences on organizational commitment as well as a number of basic relationships that seem to be universal in importance to employees.

Sommer *et al.* (1996), in researching certain demographic antecedents to organizational commitment, found similarities to western study results. Korean subjects who were in higher positions, had longer tenure in the same job, and were older had higher levels of organizational commitment. Korean subjects did vary, in comparison to the prevalent finding in western studies, in that no significant relationship existed between organizational commitment and either organizational tenure or level of education. Sommer *et al.* concluded that the influence of the Korean culture could have accounted for the insignificant relationship involving organizational tenure and educational level. The significant relationships found between organizational commitment and level of accomplishment and contribution to the organization were consistent with Korean values.

Chang (1999) also noted cultural differences in Asian countries where long-term employment is expected more so than in western countries and employees are more committed to their respective companies. Chang, in his study of Korean researchers, however, did find affective commitment greater when the employer is perceived as providing internal promotion opportunities, proper training, and supervisors are effective in offering career counselling. Continuance commitment was greater when the company was perceived as proactively trying to prevent layoffs. The presence of 'career commitment' played a moderating role in this study with the researchers identifying their careers as separate from the organizations in which they worked.

Ngo and Tsang (1998) concluded from their study of 772 managers in Hong Kong that work values and norms of a country can impact employee perceptions of work attitudes. These researchers found a strong relationship between career advancement and organizational commitment, reflecting the culture's emphasis on personal achievement. Tan and Akhtar (1998), in studying 147 employees of a Chinese-owned bank in Hong Kong, also found strong cultural ramifications. These researchers found a stronger presence of normative commitment which was consistent with a Confucian-based managerial ideology. Chen and Francesco's study (2000) of 333 manufacturing and service employees and managers from 36 companies in Mainland China included hotel workers. The employer organizations were located in the cities of Guangzhou and Shanghai. The results of this study showed no significant relationship between organizational commitment and age, gender, education or tenure. As with Sommer *et al.* (1996), there was a significant relationship between organizational commitment and level of position with employees higher in the hierarchy displaying greater commitment. Chen and Francesco (2000) concluded that these findings, although consistent with a previous study, reflected different cultural connotations. A very important characteristic in the Chinese culture involves the personal relationships found in organizations known as 'guanxi'. Guanxi refers to the 'network of personally defined reciprocal bonds' (Redding *et al.*, 1993, p. 656) that enhances an individual's functioning in business settings and in a larger societal context. Chen and Francesco linked the guanxi relationship to the higher organizational positions involving good relationships with involved supervisors and thus resulting in greater organizational commitment.

Other international studies on organizational commitment have included Hoon's study (2000) in Singapore of general managers, human resource directors and assistant vice-presidents in a variety of business firms. A significant positive relationship was found between human resource practices and organizational commitment, particularly involving layoff procedures that were clearly and fairly stated, accurate measure of job performance, and training and career development opportunities. Chiu and Ng (1999) found in their study of 300 managers in Hong Kong that organizational commitment was significantly linked to family and work-related factors for both men and women. 'Women-friendly' workplace policies, however, were found to have a positive impact only on women and only on their affective commitment levels.

Additional studies have involved other countries in an analysis of workplace behaviours and organizational commitment. With a sample of non-management employees in Malaysia, Zin (1996) showed a significant positive relationship between organizational commitment and the perception of greater participation in decision-making among employees. Varona (1996) found a significant positive relationship between employee satisfaction with communication within the organization and organizational commitment. Federico's study involved 307 subjects from three

Guatemalan organizations including the faculty of a private school, the staff of a children's hospital and employees of a food factory.

ORGANIZATIONAL COMMITMENT IN HOSPITALITY AND TOURISM ORGANIZATIONS

In comparison to the vast number of studies on organizational commitment, few have focused specifically on the hospitality and tourism industry. Paxson and Umbreit (1992) noted the absence of research on this topic although the benefits associated with long-term organizational membership, reduced turnover, lower absenteeism and increased quality of products and services would be advantageous to hospitality and tourism businesses.

In one of the earliest studies on organizational commitment, DeCotiis and Jenkins (1986, p. 73) surveyed 784 managers in a full-service restaurant company in the United States. The study measured the managers' agreement with statements regarding commitment related to management practices. This study concluded that management practices did impact organizational commitment. Commitment was found to be highest when:

1. decisions were made as far down the company ranks as possible;
2. people were told the whys and hows of change;
3. people were informed about how the company was performing;
4. employee input was sought;
5. people's individuality was respected; and
6. the focus of leadership styles was on helping people to perform.

One of the management practices found by DeCotiis and Jenkins that negatively affected organizational commitment was overly close supervision. Commitment decreased among the managers when they felt that they were being controlled and not allowed to make their own decisions.

Often portrayed as a consuming industry with erratic and lengthy work hours, many of the existing hospitality studies on organizational commitment have included quality-of-life issues. Farber and Susskind (1992) explored the relationship between level of organizational commitment and alternative work schedules and non-work activities. The sample consisted of 153 hourly hotel employees in the United States. The results of this study showed that the schedule type did not have significant effects on the worker commitment for respondents with children. Respondents without children who worked flexible schedules, however, did experience higher levels of organizational commitment as compared to respondents without children working standard rigid schedules.

The Farber and Susskind research also analysed the effects of involvement in 38 specific non-work activities. Employees without children, who prioritized personal appearance maintenance activities, such as exercise, displayed a higher level of organizational commitment with flexible work schedules. Family-related chores and taking care of financial responsibilities were significant for employees with children.

Cannon (1992) researched hotel employees in an analysis of the relationship between organizational commitment, job satisfaction and factors that interfered with work. Using role theory as the theoretical foundation, this study focused on inter-role conflict

(Bobbitt *et al.*, 1978) specifically between work and personal roles of the subjects. The following conflict variables were analysed: medical problems, family responsibilities, transportation difficulties, personal activities/hobbies, home-maintenance responsibilities and personal/family problems. The final sample in this study consisted of 300 subjects employed in twelve different urban hotels in a major south-eastern convention city in the United States. The employees ranged from entry-level positions in housekeeping and stewarding to front-office agents, reservation agents and concierges to departmental assistant managers and managers.

Through multiple regression, job satisfaction and overall interferences to working were found to be significant predictors of organizational commitment in this study with a significant positive relationship existing between job satisfaction and commitment and a significant negative relationship existing with work interferences. Through using stepwise regression analysis, it was found that certain work interferences were significant negative predictors of organizational commitment. These included medical problems and childcare responsibilities ($R^2 = .0719$, p < .001). Education was a significant determinant of a number of work interferences including medical problems and childcare responsibilities with employees having more formal education indicating lower levels of interference with their jobs.

In Cannon's research, significant differences did exist between the three levels of employees. Organizational commitment and job satisfaction were highest for management employees and lowest for housekeepers and stewards (p < .001). Hotel housekeepers and stewards experienced significantly higher levels of work interferences due to childcare (p < .001), personal/family problems (p < .001) and medical problems (p < .05). The implications of this study reinforced employers addressing work policies and practices that can reduce role conflicts among employees in building organizational commitment among the workforce.

In a follow-up analysis of the data from the 300 hotel employees, intrinsic and extrinsic job factors were related to organizational commitment in the three levels of represented employees (Cannon, 1994). Job factors utilized were from the Minnesota Satisfaction Questionnaire (Betz *et al.*, 1966). This analysis showed a significant relationship between both intrinsic and extrinsic job factors and organizational commitment for employees ranging from entry-level, hourly positions to management. In using a multiple regression analysis, significant predictors or organizational commitment (p < .001) included satisfaction with steady employment (extrinsic), satisfaction with one's supervisor (extrinsic), and opportunities for advancement (intrinsic). For front-office and reservation agents and concierges, the significant predictors (p < .01) included satisfaction with one's boss (extrinsic) and satisfaction with job autonomy (intrinsic). An extrinsic factor, satisfaction with one's boss (extrinsic), was the only significant predictor (p < .001) for assistant managers and managers in the sample.

In another US hotel study on organizational commitment, 7504 hourly and 94 salaried employees of a particular lodging organization were surveyed in analysing the relationship between job satisfaction and organizational commitment (Smith *et al.*, 1996). In researching the relationship between job satisfaction and organizational commitment among these employees, a two-step analysis was performed. The first step involved a factor analysis which yielded eleven factors which had questions loaded at 0.4 or above as pertaining to job satisfaction. These factors, with eigenvalues of 2.0 or higher, were labelled into categories, including organization support, supervisor relations, immediate work environment, attitude towards general management and attitude towards the executive committee. These four factors accounted for 40.8 per cent of the variance in overall job satisfaction. A multiple regression was performed in the second step. Level of overall job satisfaction, used as the independent variable, was correlated with the dependent variable: 'I would choose to work here if faced with the same decision again.' There was a positive correlation with a R^2 of 0.103 and a 'F'value of 742.18, with a significance level of $p < .001$. The second dependent variable was: 'I would not accept a job at another company, doing the same job as here, with the same pay and benefits.' There was a positive correlation with overall job satisfaction with a R^2 of 0.053, a 'F'value of 450.95 and a significance level of $p < .001$.

Enz and Inman (1992) compared levels of commitment among part-time and full-time employees in the food-service industry. With 125 subjects employed in a full-service restaurant in the Northwestern part of the United States, levels of commitment were analysed for the following: organizational beliefs of restaurant cleanliness, cost control, honesty in guest relations, quality presentation of food and service and high food quality. This study found no significant differences in the commitment levels for these variables between part-time and full-time employees. The demographic factors of age, gender and job type were controlled in this study to avoid confounding effects.

Borchgrevink (1993) analysed the relationship between employee burnout and organizational commitment focusing on non-managerial, non-supervisory line and entry-level food-service workers. Burnout was found to be negatively associated with organizational commitment in this sample of 63 employees of a foodservice company in the Midwest area of the United States.

Sparrowe (1993) studied the hypothesized outcomes of employee empowerment which included organizational commitment. The sample included hotel front-desk clerks, housekeeping personnel, restaurant servers and cooks from 36 hospitality organizations in the United States. The results indicated employee empowerment to positively impact organizational commitment and negatively impact employee intentions to leave their jobs. Positive relationships were also found between organizational commitment and pay satisfaction and the employee liking and respecting his or her supervisor.

CASE STUDY: ADVENTURE TRAVEL

Having graduated eight years ago with a hospitality management degree, you are venturing into a new career opportunity as Director of Human Resources for Adventure Travel. This entrepreneurial company, started in the 1990s, brought together an energized, talented group of previous hotel and airline executives who wanted to experience the growth of the dynamic travel segment of ecotourism and adventure excursions (Nelson and Shock, 1998). Based in Europe, you will oversee smaller offices in South America, Asia and Africa. With a site manager in each office location, in total the corporation now has approximately 50 employees with an additional 50 to 75 employees who work on a part-time or contractual basis as personal guides and liaisons in various countries. Although you contract with numerous hotels, transportation services and food providers, the Adventure Travel staff are personally there with every travelling group to ensure that top-quality service and products are delivered. Staff members are called upon to handle anything from the most minor difficulty to major crises involving weather or travel conditions.

In your first week, after thoroughly reviewing the strategic plan, a meeting is held with the management team to discuss Adventure Travel's short- and long-term goals.

The company's mission statement reflects personalized, world-class quality service for individuals, groups and corporations planning destinations in some of the most exotic and remote areas of the world. Not to be confused with economy travel, clients of this corporation pay top-market prices and, in turn, expect all of the comforts and amenities delivered in some of the most challenging environments. Your goals, delineated with the team and individually with the corporation's president, include the following:

1. recruiting and selecting multi-talented individuals who can provide the highest level of service to guests from around the world;
2. developing training processes to support the organization's service performance; and
3. creating policies and processes to support employees in maximizing their performance and in their retention with the corporation so that strong employee loyalty is built.

You have numerous recruiting ideas based on your previous years working in the hospitality industry as a corporate recruiter and your background in employee selection and training techniques is very sound. However, as you sit at your desk and consider how to positively impact employee retention and performance through human resource policies and processes, you feel less sure of the appropriate action steps. How does one build loyalty particularly when employees are spread over the world and are quite diverse? How do you establish strong linkages between the full-time staff as well as the part-time guides who are so essential to the personal service encounters with guests? This is a growing company but is still small particularly in comparison to large corporate structures that may have the advantage of comprehensive benefit plans and multiple career growth options.

You have been given two weeks to develop action plans for the designated goals. At the quarterly corporate meeting you will be presenting these plans to the directors of other functional areas as well as the owners of the company. Knowing that organizational commitment has been positively linked to employee retention and other desired employee outcomes, you review the research literature on this subject and analyse possible applications for Adventure Travel.

•   What process will you follow to determine these plans?
•   What are action plans will you outline and why?

Human Resources Response

As Director of Human Resources for Adventure Travel, you are in a pivotal position to impact the success of this company through the linkages established with employees. As you sit at your desk and feel almost overwhelmed by the enormous distance between you and the site locations of your company, take comfort in the realization that there are more similarities than differences between the company's internationally dispersed employees. Judging from studies on organizational commitment from around the world, there are many job and workplace characteristics that are seemingly universal in building and maximizing organizational commitment among employees.

One of the foremost things as you contemplate organizational policies and processes for Adventure Travel, is to recall the important impact of employees being involved in the decision-making process. Numerous studies have found a significant positive relationship between employee empowerment and involvement in the decision-making process and organizational commitment (Rhodes and Steers, 1981; DeCotiis and Jenkins, 1986; Pierce and Dunham, 1987; Sparrowe, 1993; and Zin, 1996). Although requiring a great time and monetary investment, there could be tremendous benefits in arranging to personally visit each site location and meeting with every full-time and part-time employee. These visits could serve several purposes including personally getting to know the individuals that will directly determine the success of the company and to ascertain what is meaningful to these individuals and what they expect from their employer, as related to the exchange theory of organizational commitment. The personal visit also addresses the importance of forming relationships with the employees as individuals (as compared to someone known only through e-mails, faxes and memorandums). In some countries (i.e. the Asian locations) this may help in addressing cultural preferences (Chen and Francesco, 2000), but certainly for all of the site locations, the visit reinforces the importance of employees and their involvement in the organization.

In terms of the content of your proposed plan, the visit to the site locations could be instrumental in delineating employee needs, expectations and individual goals as well as offering a forum for ideas to maximize the success of Adventure Travel. The site visits will also offer an opportunity to discuss the mission and goals of Adventure Travel. Commitment without a cause is futile. Employees want to know the mission of their organization and the direction in which it is headed. This connection is more than just providing employees with a written copy of the organization's mission statement. It involves explaining what the mission statement entails, the philosophy it reflects and the steps planned to achieve the company's goals. Clarifying the mission and ideology of Adventure Travel is important now and will be important at regular intervals throughout the company's existence. Keeping employees abreast of company information has been related positively to organizational commitment if employees actually perceive that there is effective and regular communication (DeCotiis and Jenkins, 1986; Federico, 1996).

In that the site locations for Adventure Travel are located throughout the world, the site managers will play a crucial role in developing and maximizing the commitment of employees. The site managers are the role models for what the entire organization represents. Their commitment to daily 'put life' into the mission and ideology is essential. The adage 'Walk your talk' must be clearly represented. From service-oriented behaviours toward employees to providing effective training and career counselling to following ethical standards (DeCotiis and Jenkins, 1986; Chang, 1999; Fritz *et al.*, 1999, Hoon, 2000), each individual site manager's role is a critical link in developing commitment among employees as are the entire management and supervisor staff.

Organizational commitment research has shown the importance of creating a positive, supportive workplace in which the concern for employees is evident (Buchanan, 1974; March and Mannari, 1977; Steers, 1977; Pierce and Dunham, 1987; Mathieu and Zajac, 1990; Luthans *et al.*, 1992). The hiring and developing of site managers with leadership styles that are conducive to establishing such working environments is particularly critical in this global company. Processes and policies, initiated through the corporate office, that consistently reinforce the importance of employees and their role in the success of Adventure Travel will be equally important in sustaining the positive environment of each site location.

Organizational commitment research has also emphasized the importance of employees perceiving task identity, a personal connection between their efforts on the job and the results accomplished. Employee perceptions of being challenged, achieving autonomy in their work and having meaningful feedback regularly provided have also been significantly and positively related to organizational commitment (Sheldon, 1971; Buchanan, 1974; Marsh and Mannari, 1977; Steers, 1977; Hunt *et al.*, 1985). Again, much of these important job factors must be addressed through effective supervision as well as through appropriate job design. In the case with Adventure Travel, most of the employees work very independently in their roles as guides and because of the wide job scope of tasks involved, there is a high level of autonomy. Task identity can be consistently reinforced by illustrating the connection between efforts made by employees and the resulting positive guest experiences. These examples, reinforcing the mission of the company, can be effectively communicated throughout the company through newsletters, electronic messages and recognition events. Task identity and recognition also relate to the strong connection found in some cultures between organizational commitment and perceived personal achievement (Ngo and Tsang, 1998). The feedback mechanisms may be more difficult involving full- and part-time employees but processes can be designed to regularly provide written performance feedback as well as informal appraisals. The accuracy of this feedback will be essential as has been shown in studies around the globe (Tsang, 1998; Hoon, 2000).

Although Adventure Travel is a small company, it is a growing organization. Realistically portraying career opportunities will be important to both incoming and existing employees for this appears to be one of the universal determinants of organizational commitment (Chang, 1999).

Lastly, in designing company benefits, research on organizational commitment has shown possible connections to benefits addressing quality-of-life issues and some of the role conflicts experienced in the hospitality industry (Cannon, 1992; Farber and Susskind, 1992). Adventure Travel may want to consider flexible benefits that allow employees throughout the company to select those most appropriate for their individual needs. If the company's size does not allow this approach, surveying employees to determine their most prevalent needs regarding benefits would be highly recommended.

DISCUSSION AND CONCLUSIONS

With the hospitality and tourism industry's need to retain employees and maximize quality results, the concept of organizational commitment is most pertinent. There is an obvious need for more research on organizational commitment in hospitality and tourism businesses around the world. An increasing number of international studies are being conducted on organizational commitment and this pattern certainly needs to continue involving the hospitality and tourism industry.

Organizational commitment is not a static concept. It can be assumed that many of the changes being experienced by hospitality and tourism companies will have an impact on organizational commitment and this provides numerous research opportunities. For example, how has the limited labour market in many parts of the world affected organizational commitment? How have changing work values impacted this concept? The findings of research from decades past may be quite different in today's organizations with the growing presence of 'Generation X' employees. How have the changing demographics of workforces around the world affected organizational commitment in hospitality and tourism businesses? How are gender issues related to organizational commitment, particularly involving advancement opportunities for females past the glass ceiling? How have the numerous mergers and acquisitions, particularly in the hotel segment, impacted the commitment level of involved employees? As hospitality companies are dealing with more expatriates and issues of repatriation, how is organizational commitment impacted?

More research is needed in reflecting the organizational commitment variances within any one organization. From lower-skilled, entry-level workers to corporate-level executives, this is a rich area for research on the determinants of commitment among the population segments in many hospitality and tourism companies. More attention on the desired 'exchanges' that would be perceived as meaningful between employees and employers is also warranted. This type of information could impact operational aspects from employee work schedules to benefit plans. The companies that address changing needs and expectations will be those that are the most competitive in recruiting and retaining quality-oriented individuals in the labour market.

SELF-ASSESSMENT QUESTIONS

1. Discuss how the definition of 'organizational commitment' has changed from the early 1980s to the early 1990s.
2. Explain the theoretical connection between organizational commitment and the exchange theory. Include both tangible and non-tangible factors that might be included with this theory.
3. Explain the cultural variations found in antecedents and determinants of organizational commitment.
4. In summarizing the research on organizational commitment in the hospitality and tourism sector, what antecedents and determinants were found to be significant?
5. In applying the material on organizational commitment to your expectations as a current or future employee in hospitality and tourism, what could a company offer that would maximize your commitment level?

REFERENCES

Allen, N. J. and Meyer, J. P. (1990) 'The measurement and antecedents of affective, continuance, and normative commitment to the organization'. *Journal of Occupational Psychology*, **63**, 1–18.

Angle, H. L. and Perry, J. L. (1981) 'An empirical assessment of organizational commitment and organizational effectiveness'. *Administrative Science Quarterly*, **26**, 1–14.

Angle, H. L. and Perry, J. L. (1983) 'Organizational commitment: individual and organizational influences'. *Work and Occupations*, **10**, 123–46.

Bateman, T. S. and Organ, D. W. (1983) 'Job satisfaction and the good soldier: the relationship between affect and employee "citizenship"'. *Academy of Management Journal*, **26**, 887–95.

Becker, H. S. (1960) 'Notes on the concept of commitment'. *American Journal of Sociology*, **66**, 32–42.

Betz, E., Weiss, D. J., Dawis, R., England, C. W. and Lofquist, L. H. (1966) 'The concept of work adjustment'. *Minnesota Studies in Vocational Rehabilitation*, **20**, 1–13.

Bobbitt, H. R., Breinholt, R. H., Doktor, R. H. and McNaul, J. P. (1978) *Organizational Behaviour: Understanding and Prediction*. Englewood Cliffs, NJ: Prentice-Hall Inc.

Borchgrevink, C. P. (1993) 'Burnout among non-managerial hospitality employees'. *Annual CHRIE (Council of Hotel, Motel and Institutional Education) Conference Proceedings*, 123.

Brief, A. P. and Aldag, R. J. (1980) 'Antecedents of organizational commitment among hospital nurses'. *Sociology of Work and Occupations*, **7**, 210–21.

Brown, S. P. and Peterson, R. A. (1993) 'Antecedents and consequences of salesperson job satisfaction: meta-analysis and assessment of causal effects'. *Journal of Marketing Research*, **30**, 63–77.

Buchanan, B. (1974) 'Building organizational commitment: the socialization of managers in work organizations'. *Administrative Science Quarterly*, **19**, 533–46.

Cannon, D. F. (1992) 'Determinants of organizational commitment among hotel employees'. *Annual CHRIE (Council of Hotel, Motel and Institutional Education) Conference Proceedings*, 245–6.

Cannon, D. F. (1994) 'Intrinsic/extrinsic predictors of work attitudes among hotel employees'. *Annual CHRIE (Council of Hotel, Motel and Institutional Education) Conference Proceeding*, 88.

Chang, E. (1999) 'Career commitment as a complex moderator of organizational commitment and turnover intention'. *Human Relations*, **52**, 1257–78.

Chen, Z. X. and Francesco, A. M. (2000) 'Employee demography, organizational commitment, and turnover intentions in China: Do cultural differences matter?' *Human Relations*, **53**, 869–80.

Chiu, W. C. K. and Ng. C. W. (1999) 'Women-friendly HRM and organizational commitment: a study among women and men of organizations in Hong Kong'. *Journal of Occupational and Organizational Psychology*, **72**, 485–502.

Crosby, L., Grisaffe, D. and Marra, T. (1994) 'The impact of quality and customer satisfaction on employee organizational commitment'. *Marketing and Research Today*, **22**(1), 23–4.

DeCotiis, T. A. and Jenkins, J. M. (1986) 'Employee commitment: money in the bank'. *The Cornell Hotel and Restaurant Administration Quarterly*, **26**(4), 70–5.

DeCotiis, T. A. and Summers, T. P. (1987) 'A path analysis of a model of the antecedents and consequences of organizational commitment'. *Human Relations*, **40**, 445–70.

Del Vecchio, G. A. (1999) 'Determinants of job satisfaction and organizational commitment after an acquisition'. *ProQuest Digital Dissertations*, Publication number AAT-9926486, 1221.

Dubin, R., Champoux, J. E. and Porter, L. W. (1975) 'Central life interests and organizational commitment of blue-collar and clerical workers'. *Administrative Science Quarterly*, **20**, 411–21.

Enz, C. and Inman, C. (1992) 'A comparison of attitudes and work practices of part-time and full-time workers in the food service industry'. *Annual CHRIE (Council of Hotel, Motel and Institutional Education) Conference Proceeding*, 19–21.

Farber, B. and Susskind, A. (1992) 'Alternative work schedules and non-work activities: Their effects on hotel worker commitment'. *Annual CHRIE (Council of Hotel, Motel and Institutional Education) Conference Proceeding*, 4–6.

Fritz, J. M., Arnett, R. C. and Conkel, M. (1999) 'Organizational ethical standards and organizational commitment'. *Journal of Business Ethics*, **20**, 289–99.

Goldberg, W. A., Greenberger, E., Koch-Jones, J. And O'Neil, R. (1989) 'Attractiveness of child care and related employer-supported beliefs and policies to married and single parents'. *Child and Youth Quarterly*, **18**, 23–37.

Grunberg, L., Anderson-Connolly, R. and Greenberg, E. S. (2000) 'Surviving layoffs: the effects on organizational commitment and job performance'. *Work and Occupations*, **27**, 7–31.

Grusky, D. (1966) 'Career mobility and organizational commitment'. *Administrative Science Quarterly*, **10**, 488–503.

Hackman, J. R. and Oldman, G. R. (1976) 'Motivation through the design of work: test of a theory'. *Organizational Behaviour and Human Performance*, **16**, 250–79.

Hoffman, K. D. and Ingram, T. N. (1992) 'Service provider job satisfaction and customer-oriented performance'. *Journal of Services Marketing*, **8**, 14–26.

Homans, G. C. (1961) *Social Behaviour: Its Elementary Forms*. New York: Harcourt, Brace & World.

Hoon, L. S. (2000) 'A managerial perspective of the objectives of HRM practices in Singapore: an exploratory study'. *Singapore Management Review*, **22**, 65–80.

Hrebiniak, L. G. and Alutto, J. A. (1972) 'Personal and role-related factors in the development of organizational commitment'. *Administrative Science Quarterly*, **17**, 555–72.

Hunt, S. D., Chonko, L. E. and Wood, V. R. (1985) 'Organizational commitment in marketing'. *Journal of Marketing*, **49**, 112–26.

Iverson, R. and Deery, M. (1997) 'Turnover culture in the hospitality industry'. *Human Resources Management*, **7**, 71–82.

Johnston, M., Parasuraman, A., Futrell, C., and Black, W. (1990) 'A longitudinal assessment of the impact of selected organizational influences on salespeople's organizational commitment during early employment'. *Journal of Marketing Research*, **27**, 333–44.

Jones, G. R. (1986) 'Socialization tactics, self-efficacy, and newcomers' adjustments to organizations'. *Academy of Management Journal*, **29**, 262–79.

Kidron, A. (1978) 'Work values and organizational commitment'. *Academy of Management Journal*, **21**, 239–47.

Koch, J. L. and Steers, R. M. (1978) 'Job attachment, satisfaction and turnover among public employees'. *Journal of Vocational Behaviour*, **12**, 119–28.

Kochan, T. A. (1975) 'Determinants of the power of boundary units in an interorganizational bargaining relation'. *Administrative Science Quarterly*, **20**, 434–52.

Lawler, E. E. (1973) *Motivations in Work Organizations*. Belmont, CA: Wadsworth.

Lee, R. T. and Ashforth, B. E. (1996) 'A meta-analytic examination of the correlates of the three dimensions of burnout'. *Journal of Applied Psychology*, **81**, 123–33.

Luthans, F., Wahl, L. K. and Steinhaus, C. S. (1992) 'The importance of social support for employee commitment: a quantitative and qualitative analysis of bank tellers'. *Organization Development Journal*, **10**, 1–10.

March, J. G. and Simon, H. A. (1958) *Organizations*. New York: Academy Press.

Marsh, R. M. and Mannari, H. (1977) 'Organization commitment and turnover: A prediction study'. *Administrative Science Quarterly*, **22**, 57–75.

Mathieu, J. E. and Zajac, D. M. (1990) 'A review and meta-analysis of the antecedents, correlates, and consequences of organizational commitment'. *Psychological Bulletin*, **108**, 171–94.

Meyer, J. P., Paunonen, S. V., Gellatly, I. R., Goffin, R. D. and Jackson, D. N. (1989) 'Organizational commitment and job performance'. *Journal of Applied Psychology*, **74**, pp. 152–6.

Michaels, P. (1986) 'Testing the antecedent and outcomes of organizational commitment and overall job satisfaction'. Unpublished doctoral dissertation, Tuscaloosa, AL: University of Alabama.

Michaels, C. and Spector, P. (1982) 'Causes of employee turnover: a test of the Mobley, Griffeth, Hand and Meglino model'. *Journal of Applied Psychology*, **67**, 53–9.

Mobley, W., Horner, O. and Hollingsworth, A. (1978) 'An evaluation of precursors of hospital employee turnover'. *Journal of Applied Psychology*, **63**(4), 408–14.

Morris, J. H. and Sherman, J. D. (1981) 'Generalizability of an organizational commitment model'. *Academy of Management Journal*, **24**, 512–26.

Mowday, R. T., Koberg, C. S. and McArthur, A. W. (1984) 'The psychology of the withdrawal process: a cross-validation test of Mobley's intermediate linkages model of turnover in two samples'. *Academy of Management Journal*, **27**, 79–94.

Mowday, R. T., Porter, L. W. and Steers, R. M. (1982) *Employee-organizational Linkages*. New York: Academic Press.

Nelson, K. S. and Shock, P. J. (1998) 'The tourism industry: travel motivation and economics', in R. A. Brymer (ed.), *Hospitality and Tourism: An Introduction to the Industry*. Dubuque, IA: Kendall/Hunt Publishing Co., pp. 34–44.

Ngo, H. Y. and Tsang, A. W. N. (1998) 'Employment practices and organizational commitment: Differential effects for men and women?' *International Journal of Organizational Analysis*, **6**, 251–66.

Paxson, C. and Umbreit, T. (1992) 'What organizational commitment research can teach us about turnover'. *Annual CHRIE (Council of Hotel, Motel and Institutional Education) Conference Proceeding*, 191–3.

Pierce, J. L. and Dunham, R. B. (1987) 'Organizational commitment: pre-employment propensity and initial work experiences'. *Journal of Management*, **13**, 163–78.

Redding, S. G., Norman, A. and Schlander, A. (1993) 'The nature of individual attachment to the organization: a review of East Asian variations', in M. D. Dunnette and L. M. Hough (eds), *Handbook of Industrial and Organizational Psychology*. Palo Alto, CA: Consulting Psychology Press.

Reichers, A. E. (1985) 'A review and reconceptualization of organizational commitment'. *Academy of Management Review*, **10**(3), 465–76.

Rhodes, S. and Steers, R. (1981) 'Conventional vs. worker-owned organizations'. *Human Relations*, **34**, 1013–35.

Ritzer, G. and Trice, H. (1969) 'An empirical study of Howard Becker's side-bet theory'. *Social Forces*, 475–9.

Rusbult, C. E. (1980) 'Commitment and satisfaction in romantic associations: A test of the investment model'. *Journal of Experimental Social Psychology*, **16**, 172–86.

Scandura, T. A. and Lankau, M. J. (1997) 'Relationships of gender, family responsibility and flexible work hours to organizational commitment and job satisfaction'. *Journal of Organizational Behaviour*, **18**, 377–91.

Sheldon, M. E. (1971) 'Investments and involvements as mechanisms producing commitment in the corporation'. *Administrative Science Quarterly*, **16**, 142–50.

Shore, L. M. and Wayne, S. J. (1993) 'Commitment and employee behaviour: comparison of affective commitment and continuance commitment with perceived organizational support'. *Journal of Applied Psychology*, **78**, 774–80.

Singh, J. (2000) 'Performance productivity and quality of frontline employees in service organizations'. *Journal of Marketing*, **64**(2), 15–34.

Smith, K., Gregory, S. and Cannon, D. F. (1996) 'Becoming an employer of choice: assessing commitment in the hospitality workplace'. *International Journal of Contemporary Hospitality Management*, **8**, 3–9.

Sommer, S. M., Bae, S. H. and Luthans, F. (1996) 'Organizational commitment across cultures: The impact of antecedents on Korean employees'. *Human Relations*, **49**, 977–93.

Sparrowe, R. (1993) 'Empowerment in the hospitality industry: An exploration of antecedents and outcomes'. *Annual CHRIE (Council of Hotel, Motel and Institutional Education) Conference Proceeding*, 128.

Stanley, D. T. and Cooper, C. (1972) *Managing Local Government under Union Pressure*. Washington, D.C.: Brookings Institute.

Steers, R. M. (1977) 'Antecedents and outcomes of organizational commitment'. *Administrative Science Quarterly*, **22**, 46–56.

Stevens, J. M., Beyer, J. and Trice, H. M. (1978) 'Assessing personal, role, and organizational predictors of managerial commitment'. *Academy of Management Journal*, **21**, 380–96.

Tan, D. and Akhtar, S. (1998) 'Organizational commitment and experienced burnout: An exploratory study from a Chinese cultural perspective'. *International Journal of Organizational Analysis*, **6**, 310–33.

Varona, F. (1996) 'Relationship between communication satisfaction and organizational commitment in three Guatemalan organizations', *Journal of Business Communication*, **33**, 111–40.

Wahn, J. C. (1998) 'Sex differences in the continuance component of organizational commitment'. *Group & Organization Management*, **23**, 256–66.

Welsch, H. P. and LaVan, H. (1981) 'Interrelationships between organizational commitment and job characteristics, job satisfaction, professional behaviour and organizational climate', *Human Relations*, **34**, 1079–89.

Williams, L. J. and Hazer, J. T. (1986) 'Antecedents and consequences of satisfaction and commitment in turnover models: a reanalysis using latent variable structural equation methods'. *Journal of Applied Psychology*, **71**, 219–31.

Witt, L. A. (1993) 'Reactions to work assignments as predictors of organizational commitment: the moderating effect of occupational identification'. *Journal of Business Research*, **26**, 17–30.

Zin, R. M. (1996) 'Moderating effects on the relationship between participants in decision-making and organizational commitment: a Malaysian case'. *Singapore Management Review*, **18**, 65–82.

13

Occupational Health and Safety Risks and Management Issues in the Hotel and Fast-Food Sectors

Megan Tranter

ABSTRACT

Occupational health and safety (OHS), as discussed in this chapter, has become an important issue for workers, employers and clients in the hotel and fast-food sectors of the international hospitality and tourism industry. OHS is recognized in most countries as a legal and ethical obligation to minimize harm to workers and other parties that may be affected by the undertakings of an organization. Certainly, its role in human resource management has long been accepted. Hotels and fast-food restaurants have particular characteristics that may place workers at higher risk of ill health, disease or injury. These include high levels of casual and part-time employment; young workers; relatively low levels of formal education; short job tenure and relatively low-skilled occupations. Workers within the sector are also much less likely to be members of a trade union, affecting negotiation of conditions. These workforce characteristics, along with inherent OHS hazards in the sector, further exemplify the importance of managing risk in a systematic way to protect all workers.

INTRODUCTION

The notion of occupational health and safety (OHS) is not new to hotels and fast-food restaurants. However, while high-profile events such as homicide or electrocution in fast-food venues receive media attention, this should not negate the day-to-day hazards that exist in all workplaces. Indeed, given the nature of the industry with high levels of young and inexperienced workers, casual employment contracts and a constantly changing environment, it is perhaps not surprising that OHS management is a key challenge for the human resource manager. There are also many insidious hazards that can impact on health, including exposure to chemicals; non-ionizing radiation from outdoor work; fatigue and shiftwork; slips, trips and falls; lower back injury from manual handling; and exposure to airborne contaminants from substandard indoor quality. For some developing countries, where sexual exploitation is a form of work within the hotel, tourism and catering industry (Black 1995), transmittable disease and occupational violence become real issues.

This chapter aims to introduce and discuss a variety of occupational health and safety hazards that can be found in hotels and fast-food restaurants, as well as to relate these to human resource management practices. Strategies for managing risk and developing an occupational health and safety management system are presented and supported with a case study of how cultural change improved health and safety standards in a multinational fast-food restaurant chain.

Since 1972, when the Robens' Committee released its report into the United Kingdom's approach to health and safety at work, OHS has gained much needed attention. This report was a watershed for occupational health and safety as it identified the need to manage risk in the workplace, rather than relying on rules and prescriptive regulations that were slow to respond to changes in industry and technology that consequently led to the introduction of hazards. Other concerns that were identified included:

- imposing responsibilities or a *duty of care* to employers to ensure the health and safety of workers, where practicable;
- recognizing that workers also held a *duty of care* to act in a way that did not endanger themselves or others;
- the need to adopt a systems approach for management to identify and control risks; this should incorporate safe premises, a safe working environment, safe equipment and employment of trained and competent workers; and
- providing adequate training, instruction and supervision to perform the work safely and without risk to others.

This approach to OHS has been termed *Robens' style regulation* or *self-regulation*. Self-regulation is characterized by a reduction in the number and detail of regulation (except for particularly hazardous work), the presentation of information and guidance that employers can use to assess risk and the need for consultation with workers to minimize risks in the workplace. Most countries have some form of regulation of the work environment, although its enforcement does vary markedly.

OHS HAZARDS IN THE HOTEL AND FAST-FOOD SECTORS

Management of risks at work is a topic that has been hotly debated in terms of its outcomes and costs. This is particularly true in hotels and fast-food restaurants, where most OHS incidents do not result in fatality, but may, nonetheless, have serious and long-term consequences, impacting on a worker's quality of life and career prospects. Owing to the diverse nature of the industry, a wide variety of OHS hazards can be found. These hazards are, typically, categorized as chemical, biological, ergonomic and

CHEMICAL	BIOLOGICAL	ERGONOMIC	PHYSICAL
• Acrolein and formaldehyde from cooking fume generated by frying oil • Allergic reaction (e.g. occupational asthma, dermatitis) from latex gloves or vegetable dust • Side-stream smoke from environmental tobacco smoke • Caustic acid from oven cleaners • Perchloroethylene from dry-cleaning operations • Chlorine used in pools • Pesticides for gardening • Carbon dioxide used to carbonate drinks • Hypochlorite disinfectant used for cleaning beer lines	• Blood-borne disease from broken glassware, sporting accidents • Contaminated wastes from bed linen • Sexually transmitted disease • Insect transmitted disease such as Ross River Fever of Dengue Fever in tropical regions • Legionella from water coolers and spa pools	• Slips, trips and falls • Manual handling of bed linen, boxes, trays • Use of visual display terminals • Occupational violence • Shiftwork • Stress • Fatigue	• Noise from discos and fast-food drive-thru head sets • Cold stress from walk-in freezers • Contusions from kitchen equipment • Lacerations from sharp objects • Heat stress in laundries and kitchens • Ultraviolet and infra-red radiation from outdoor work • Cluttered work areas • Electricity • Burns from hot equipment • Steam from pressure vessels such as espresso machines • Fire from hot oil or overheated appliances

Figure 13.1 Examples of occupational health and safety hazards in hotels and fast food restaurants

physical (Figure 13.1). According to the United Kingdom's Health and Safety Executive (1998) most major injuries to workers in the hotel and catering industry of the United Kingdom occur in the kitchen, residential accommodation, bar and canteen/ restaurant. Recent research into OHS experiences of adolescent workers in the fast-food industry (Mayhew 2000) identified the major incidents as minor burns and lacerations, slips/trips/falls, manual handling incidents, occupational violence, customers overdosing on heroin and collapsing on site. The Department of Employment, Training and Industrial Relations (DETIR) (1999) in Australia, have further identified the hazards in the fast-food, restaurant and café industry as manual handling, work environment, plant, heat and indoor air quality.

Manual handling includes lifting, lowering, pushing, pulling, carrying, holding and dragging (Kroemer and Grandjean, 1997) that can result in wear and tear on the back (especially the intervertebral discs). With many tasks of the hotels and fast-food sector involving this nature of work, it is not surprising that manual handling injuries make the largest contribution to non-fatal injuries. Several risk factors have been identified as influencing the level of stress placed on the body during lifting. These variables include horizontal position of the load; height and range of lift; method of lifting; frequency of lifting; object size, weight, stability and whether the load is difficult to grip (Sanders and McCormick, 1992). Some examples of manual handling problems in hotels and fast-food restaurants include reaching to clean ovens, stoves and deep fryers; carrying rubbish; lifting boxes of foodstuffs and vegetables; and carrying luggage. Slips, trips and falls are a major cause of injury (Le Poidevin, 1998) and, typically, occur in areas such as slippery floors (kitchens, swimming-pool surrounds, bathrooms, laundries), stairways and working in cluttered areas.

The work environment refers to the physical and psychological aspects of work that may affect health or safety. Workers may be exposed to the extremes of heat, such as excessive heat and humid conditions in tropical environments, laundries (Tranter, 1998) and kitchens. Low levels of air movement and poor ventilation typically accompany these areas. Cold conditions such as working outdoors at ski resorts, or indoors in cold rooms, may exposure workers to the risk of numbness of the extremities, frostbite or trench foot. For those workers who are involved in scuba diving, possible health effects from working in hyperbaric conditions include decompression sickness, vertigo or dental and ear barotrauma. Exposure to excessive noise may arise from noisy kitchen equipment (e.g. sirens, buzzers, release of pressure, metal-on-metal clashes); from the headset of fast-food, drive-through areas; in discos and from live entertainment bands. Biological hazard sources include contaminated wastes from linen; exposure to viruses such as HIV and Hepatitis from broken glass contaminated with blood, intravenous needles and other skin-penetrating injuries. Hazardous chemicals, such as sodium hydroxide (in some oven cleaners), sodium hypochlorite (pool chlorine), pesticides, hypochlorite disinfectant (used as a beer line cleaner), perchlorethylene (a solvent used in dry cleaning) and carbon dioxide (for gaseous drinks), all present the potential for adverse acute and chronic health effects.

Psychological hazards at work include occupational violence (verbal abuse, threats, harassment and physical assault), shiftwork, fatigue and boredom. Within the hotel industry, the significance of mental well-being has been acknowledged by a hotel (Borger, 2000), which employs a 'wellbeing manager' for a range of wellness issues, but including workplace and everyday life stress.

Exposure to plant and equipment in hotels and fast-food restaurants can be particularly hazardous. Moving parts may cause lacerations, bruises and contusions. Workers are especially susceptible to cuts from knife accidents (to the non-knife holding hand) and electrocution from inadequately earthed equipment during cleaning (NIOSH, 1984). Some other hazards associated with plant include fire and explosion, noise and vibration from gardening equipment. The use of pressure vessels, such as espresso machines, should also be treated with caution. Burns from cooking, removing and handling food, making beverages from urns and espresso machines is a significant cause of minor and major injury to workers in the sector.

Indoor air quality is a complex issue with a myriad of contributing agents. The main chemical contaminants that contribute to inadequate indoor air quality include dusts (such as fibreglass and asbestos), carbon monoxide, environmental tobacco smoke, fried food smoke and microbiological hazards (e.g. *Legionella pneumophila* in cooling towers). Cooking fumes from frying oil contains hazardous compounds such as acrolein, formaldehyde and polycyclic aromatic hydrocarbons (Vainiotalo and

Matveinen, 1993). Some workers also experience allergic contact dermatitis from food handling (e.g. plants, vegetables, flour) or wearing latex gloves (Diepgen and Coenraads, 1999; Shum and English, 1998).

HUMAN RESOURCE ISSUES AND OHS RISKS

When reviewing OHS hazards in the hotel and fast-food sector, it is important to consider human resource factors that may contribute to risks and their management in the workforce. Within the sector, children symbolize a low-paid and vulnerable segment of the workforce (Mizen *et al.*, 1999; Banco *et al.*, 1997). Research by Chautard *et al.* (1999) indicates that 75.6 per cent of workers in the fast-food industry in France are aged between 18 and 25 years. Children have a higher risk of work injury than adults (Richter and Jacobs, 1991). A study of young workers in the United States of America (Windau *et al.*, 1999) indicated that retail-trade industry accounted for about three-fifths of serious non-fatal injuries and illnesses of youth workers, with restaurants contributing to more than 50 per cent of these incidents. In addition, research involving young New Zealand workers identified higher occupational injury rates in part-time and inexperienced workers, with risk factors including the absence of safety training and the non-use of personal protective equipment and machine guarding (Alsop *et al.*, 2000).

From an ergonomic perspective, children may not have the strength or physical dimensions to work with the same tools and environment as adults. In addition, exposure to hazardous substances on their developing bodies can cause long-term health effects. Factors bound up with information and training can also place young workers at higher risk (Forssman and Coppée, 1974).

Work in the hospitality industry is also often precarious in nature and workers are called in for contingency measures (Whitehouse *et al.*, 1997), with the International Labour Organization (1999) identifying the prevalence of precarious work as increasing and occurring worldwide. In Australian hotels, Timo (1999) identifies that some employees involved in food, beverage and bar work hold at least one other regular job. This can have impact on fatigue, the effects of multiple and different exposure patterns and tracking worker health for chronic effects (Aronsson, 1998). It is also apparent that much employment within hotels and fast-food restaurants is not unionized or has no collective strength, especially in small businesses, and have flexible workforces due to market demands (Buultjens, 1998; Buultjens and Luckie, 1997). In some developing countries such as Kenya, Philippines, Mexico and Sri Lanka (Black, 1995) child workers work in the hotel, tourism and catering industry. However the work is often menial, the children are low-skilled and employment is casual or short-term.

MCDONALD'S FAST-FOOD RESTAURANTS

Background Information

McDonald's fast-food restaurants are one of the hospitality industry's greatest icons, with nearly 28,000 restaurants in 119 countries on six continents (McDonald's Corporation, 2000). In Australia the company is one of the largest employers of young, casual workers – a group considered to be at high risk for occupational health and safety incidents. To meet its legal and social obligations, McDonald's Australia has implemented a systems approach to manage occupational health and safety for its franchised and company-owned stores, which has considered the importance of cultural change and catering for the demographic needs of the organization. This case study analyses the components of the programme and its accomplishments to date.

The success of McDonald's fast-food restaurants internationally is nothing short of remarkable. The first McDonald's opened in Des Plaines, United States of America (USA) in 1955. Business expanded rapidly, with 200 restaurants opened throughout the USA by 1960. In Australia, McDonald's Australia opened its first restaurant in 1971, with the first franchisee-operated restaurant opened a year later. With more than 700 franchised and company-owned restaurants in all states and territories of Australia, McDonald's Australia is a significant employer of young and casually employed workers who may be at risk of ill health or exposure to an unsafe environment. In Australia, McDonald's consists of both franchised and company-owned restaurants. This poses additional issues in managing health and safety, as the complex arrangement of franchising means that franchisees are actually the employers of many of the restaurants, although McDonald's has an overall duty to provide safe systems and procedures for their franchisees.

Management of risks at work is a constant challenge for McDonald's Australia due to its multi-state operations, combination of franchisee-operated and company-owned (McOpCo) stores, and workforce characteristics. However, the company has recognized its obligations and is striving towards best practice through integration of risk-management principles into all aspects of management. This goal is being realized by embracing cultural change with commitment from top-level management and consultation with all levels within the organization.

Occupational health and safety management (or *workplace safety*) in McDonald's Australia has undergone considerable change in recent times. The watershed occurred in March 1996, with the fatality of a 19-year-old worker through electrocution at a regional restaurant (CCH, 2000). This was the first (and only) fatality that McDonald's Australia had been faced with, and led to the company critically reviewing its approach. Prior to 1996, external consultants, line-management and employee-relations personnel were responsible for workplace safety-related issues. However, since 1996, a National Workplace Safety Manager and team have been appointed to promote a risk-management culture within the organization. The team includes qualified occupational health and safety professionals, as well as operations personnel to combine the strengths of operational knowledge with risk-management experience.

The Approach to Risk Management

In its bid to manage risks to health and safety, McDonald's Australia has adopted a systems approach to identify hazards, evaluate the magnitude of risk, control the risk and monitor performance. This approach has been fully supported by top management, with the chief executive officer (CEO) showing a strong commitment through his personal involvement in developing strategies and policy, as well as his affirmation of the importance of managing workplace safety risks in all aspects of business.

All McDonald's Australia stores exhibit the OHS policy, which is regularly revised and has, most recently, taken on a contemporary design, aimed at attracting the attention of workers. The policy demonstrates the organization's commitment to workplace safety, as well as providing information about worker and employer responsibilities. These obligations are identified and reinforced during training of franchisees, managers (including line management) and workers. As a consequence, workplace safety is integrated into all management functions using a risk-management approach. The organization has also identified the importance of setting goals and targets for workplace safety, and aligning strategies to meet these objectives. While the minimum performance standard has been identified as meeting legislative requirements (in Australia, these differ among the eight states and territories), *best practice* has been the ultimate performance goal for the organization.

In Australia, the approach to deal with workplace-safety issues involves the management of risk. McDonald's Australia uses various strategies that focus on the workplace being a safe and healthy place for workers, customers and contractors. The approach to hazard identification is chiefly driven by individual stores, although supporting information, such as a 'safety toolbox' (containing resources such as policies, procedures, incident reporting forms), videos and checklists, are provided to the stores.

The process of developing and reviewing resources for workplace safety at McDonald's Australia adopts a co-operative approach to empower workers, considering the workers' and management's values, beliefs and needs, in order to encourage a sense of ownership of workplace safety. The approach involves consultation (with stores, management and workers), trial and then making changes. During the trial process, the intervention is tested in a small number of stores, followed by management review of its success.

In order to ensure incidents are investigated and reviewed, McDonald's Australia uses a uniform incident-reporting system that encompasses food safety, occupational health and safety incidents and visits by government authorities. This simplification of paperwork allows individual stores to readily identify the one-page form and easily complete it. The rationale of using a consolidated form is its 'user-friendliness' while still allowing adequate information to be collected regarding the nature of the incident for future review.

McDonald's Australia prides itself on its communication and interpersonal skills within the organization and with its customers. Workplace safety communication is achieved at two levels – within individual stores (via workplace safety committee meetings) and with support departments in the company's head office. From a national perspective, the company's workplace safety team provides advice and additional information to stores to assist their meeting legal and best practice standards. Written materials such as brochures, 'Safety Alert' notifications of extraordinary hazards and newsletters with particular safety themes are regularly sent to stores.

Training is a cornerstone of McDonald's Australia and workplace safety certainly has not missed out on this front. Workplace safety is incorporated into every aspect of training through the identification of possible risks that may arise during the performance of tasks. This has been achieved through the organization's structured training programme for crew and management, which has been especially targeted to the receiving audience. For instance, a recently reviewed safety induction video included a motivational speech by a young, Australian racing car driver who draws parallels between his profession and the importance of workplace safety.

From a systems aspect, one of the most significant strategies where McDonald's Australia has found success has been through the use of an externally audited proprietary occupational health and safety management system known as SafetyMAP. This system was developed in Australia and uses various criteria to assess elements of an organization's occupational health and safety management system. In a process spanning eighteen months, McDonald's Australia successfully achieved the requirements for the advanced level of SafetyMAP, which encompassed a review of 139 elements relating to issues such as commitment, documentation, contractors and monitoring standards, in its McOpCo stores in one state. Verification of the company's systems was obtained by an external auditor and included a review of documentation, as well as audits of a selection of stores to ensure the systems were indeed effective and operational.

In preparation for the assessment, a multi-functional team was established to ensure a comprehensive approach was taken. A further objective of this style of approach was to allow expert advice to be obtained from various business units when considering a large number of issues and promote lateral-thought processes. Senior and top management supported the process and were involved throughout many developmental and implementation stages of the process.

Measuring Success and the Future of Workplace Safety in McDonald's Australia

McDonald's Australia uses various positive and negative performance indicators to determine the success of its occupational health and safety management system. Indicators such as the Lost Time Frequency Incident Rate (LTFIR), type of incident and number of days lost (due to injury or ill health) per store per year are examples of negative-performance indicators that the organization utilizes in its reporting systems. Various positive indicators, including perception surveys (of workers and management), identification of hazards and conducting workplace safety committee meetings, are seen as motivational tools to improve the profile of workplace safety in stores and in the organization.

After massive cultural changes that identified and reinforced the importance of managing occupational health and safety risks in McDonald's Australia, the organization has recognized the future need to consolidate its current systems and ensure these systems are practicable throughout the entire company. Opportunities for streamlining operations to promote uniformity and efficiency will also need to be realized to allow continual improvement for workplace-safety management. With an ongoing expansion of restaurants and products in Australia, the importance of a robust process for store and product design lies central to the growth of the business.

Case Conclusion

McDonald's Australia is an example of an organization, operating under various regulatory authorities, which has shown the success of implementing a systems approach to occupational health and safety management. While organizational idiosyncrasies allow this integrated approach to work for them, it is, nonetheless, quite an achievement when considering the organization employs significant numbers of 'at risk' employees due to their chiefly young and casualized workforce.

DISCUSSION AND CONCLUSIONS

Managing OHS risks in the international hospitality and tourism industry to improve conditions at work is a process involving commitment and co-operation, to develop a system that is sustainable. However, the conundrum facing many organizations is how to logically and practicably handle these issues. Clearly, the style and approach adopted will depend upon the nature and size of the business, and the conditions in which it operates. Similarly, the culture of the company and country will affect the perception of the optimal way to improve conditions affecting the health and safety of workers.

For some employers, legal obligations are certainly a strong motivator to improve conditions at work. The prospect of significant fines and/or imprisonment, along with common law suits resulting in multi-million dollar settlements is a significant deterrent to many organizations. From an ethical standpoint, public perception of the morality of an event or situation combined with industrial-relations reasons may further sway employers to manage OHS risks (Tranter, 1999). Figure 13.2 illustrates some costs of occupational illness, disease and injury that can be used to implore management to manage risks appropriately.

One further point to reinforce the need to manage OHS risks lies in the continual change that the international hospitality and tourism industry faces. From a human resources perspective the largest of these changes relate to the labour force and use of technology. As work hours increase, employment patterns change to more precarious or contingent work, the age of workers becomes lower and more women become employed. The introduction of new technologies such as computerization, telecommunications, new methods of preparing and cooking foods, has led to concern by the International Labour Organization (1997) that occupational health and safety conditions may deteriorate unless appropriate training also accompanies these introductions.

INDIVIDUAL	WORKPLACE	COMMUNITY
• Lost income	• Compensation	• Social security payments for injured
• Lost benefits of superannuation, holidays and bonuses	• Rehabilitation	• Burden on public health care system
• Physical trauma and injury	• Lost productivity	• Family stresses impacting on community
• Hospital expenses	• Decreased worker morale	
• Funeral charges	• Sabotage	
	• Client relations	
	• Public perceptions	
	• Wasted inputs	
	• Damaged equipment	
	• Repair and maintenance costs	
	• Clean up costs	
	• Investigation of incident	
	• Legal ability or prosecution	
	• First aid costs	
	• Industrial conflict	

Figure 13.2 Costs of occupational illness, disease and injury

Clearly, adverse effects of risks to which an organization is exposed need to be eradicated or minimized. Management strategies typically focus on the physical working environment, monitoring and treatment strategies to identify susceptible workers, and behaviour modification (Bohle and Quinlan, 2000). However, it has been acknowledged that a comprehensive OHS programme or management system (OHSMS) is the best vehicle to create and maintain a safe and healthy work environment. A system such as this typically includes obtaining commitment from top-level management, line management and employees. This can be expressed in a number of ways, although it is most commonly seen as a policy and objectives that take into account legislative requirements and information about OHS risks. Specific responsibilities for OHS may be imposed (these can be related to individual or organizational performance reviews) and employee involvement and consultation occurs. Consultative arrangements may include holding OHS committee meetings, electing OHS representatives (to represent employees) and informing employees of changes to process or equipment that may affect their health or safety at work.

A strategy for managing risks should also be implemented. This process, known as *risk management*, is used by most managers and workers in the hospitality, hotel and tourism industry, although it may not be formalized. It should be an integral component of the management process within an organization along with human resource, environmental and quality management. Put simply, risk management is a systematic process that involves anticipating and identifying hazards, assessing the magnitude of risk, controlling the risk and reviewing the performance of the control measures. One useful method to identify OHS hazards is known as the *walkthrough survey*. This involves walking through the workplace and asking questions such as 'How many people are exposed to the hazard', 'for how long', and 'what are the likely health effects?'

Part of this process should also incorporate measurable objectives, set priorities and allocate resources. Many large organizations develop policies and procedures at this stage for specific hazards (e.g. first aid standards, personal protective equipment, emergency evacuation) and provide appropriate information in a systematic way to ensure all personnel (including visitors) are aware of procedures.

In order to monitor standards, the performance of the OHSMS should be regularly measured and evaluated. Some suggested strategies include regular inspections of the workplace, periodic review of OHS policies and procedures and ensuring corrective actions have been implemented and are effective. This may include reviewing workplace injuries, illnesses and incidents. In most countries, organizations are required to report certain incidents to regulatory authorities. However, it is important that all incidents are investigated to reduce the likelihood of a recurrence of similar incidents. For instance, a number of kitchen hand employees may suffer lacerations to the hand. The cause is identified as a malfunctioning tomato slicer, which can then be taken from service for repair and replacement of the cutting blades.

While many businesses within the international hospitality and tourism industry are small, it is none the less, important to manage OHS risks in all organizations. However, a work injury or disease which permanently disables a small-business owner or a key worker can seriously harm the financial viability of the business. Injuries to customers or clients can also damage the reputation, and thus future earnings, of the business. For the human resource manager, dealing with OHS issues may become an additional responsibility. By considering the people, equipment, materials and work environment in the organization, it is possible to manage the risks.

ACKNOWLEDGMENTS

The author would like to thank Natalie Berney and the staff of McDonald's Australia for their co-operation in interview for the collection of information for the case study.

SELF-ASSESSMENT QUESTIONS

1. Make a list of the benefits of managing OHS risks in the international hospitality, travel and tourism industry. Identify the stakeholders and factors that may influence the perception of these benefits.
2. Compare and contrast the strengths and limitations in utilizing a risk-management approach to OHS.
3. Identify human resource issues that may impact on the management of OHS risks in the international hospitality, travel and tourism industry.
4. Discuss the major health effects associated with any two of the following hazards: manual handling; chemical exposure; plant; indoor air quality.

REFERENCES

Alsop, J., Gafford, J., Langley, J., Begg, D. and Firth, H. (2000) 'Occupational injury in a cohort of young New Zealand adults'. *Journal of Occupational Health and Safety: Australia and New Zealand*, **16**(2), 107–16.

Aronsson, G. (1998) 'Contingent workers – some issues on a research agenda'. ISEOH 1998 Post Congress Workshop, Helsinki, 26 September.

Banco, L., Lapidus, G., Monopoli, J. and Zavoski, R. (1997) 'The Safe Teen Work Project: a study to reduce cutting injuries among young and inexperienced workers'. *American Journal of Industrial Medicine*, **31**(5), 619–22.

Black, M. (1995) *In the Twilight Zone: Child Workers in the Hotel, Tourism and Catering Industry*. Geneva: International Labour Office.

Bohle, P. and Quinlan, M. (2000) *Managing Occupational Health and Safety: A Multidisciplinary Approach* (2nd edn). Melbourne: Macmillan Publishers.

Borger, H. (2000) 'The interview'. Interview with Lucy Tuttle and Katie Benson, *CCH's Australian OHS Occupational Health and Safety Magazine*. CCH, Sydney, February, 19–22.

Buultjens, J. (1998) 'The impact of size on employment relations in registered clubs', in R. Harbridge, C. Gadd and A. Crawford (eds), *Current Research in Industrial Relations*. Proceedings of the 12th AIRAANZA Conference, Wellington, New Zealand, 3–5 February, 55–63.

Buultjens, J. and Luckie, K. (1997) 'Flexibility in the hospitality industry: Is deregulation necessary?' *Current Research in Industrial Relations: Proceedings of the 11ᵗʰ AIRAANZ Conference*. Brisbane, 30 January–1 February 1997. Association of Industrial Relations Academics of Australia, 89–99.

CCH (2000) *CCH's Australian OHS Occupational Health Magazine*. CCH Australia Limited, Sydney, April/May, p. 4.

Chautard, G., Cuvillier, F., Grimaud, I. and Richoux, C. (1997) 'Le travail dans la restauration rapide à Paris'. *Documents pour le médecin du travail*, 72, 4th quarter, 337–46.

Department of Employment, Training and Industrial Relations (Qld) (1999) *Workplace Health and Safety in the Fast Food, Café and Restaurant Industry: A Guide to Risk Management.* Queensland: Department of Employment, Training and Industrial Relations.

Diepgen, T. L. and Coenraads, P. J. (1999) 'The epidemiology of occupational contact dermatitis'. *International Archives of Occupational and Environmental Health*, **72**(8), 496–506.

Forssman, S. and Coppée, G. H. (1974) *Occupational Health Problems of Young Workers.* Geneva: International Labour Office.

Health and Safety Executive (1998) *Key Fact Sheet on Injuries within the Hotel and Catering Industry Reported to Local Authorities 1991/92 to 1996/97.* Merseyside: Health and Safety Executive.

Kroemer, K. H. E. and Grandjean, E. (1997) *Fitting the Task to the Human* (5th edn) London: Taylor and Francis.

International Labour Organization (1997) 'New Technologies and Working Conditions in the Hotel, Catering and Tourism Sector', *Report for discussion at the Tripartite Meeting on the Effects of New Technologies on Employment and Working Conditions in the Hotel, Catering and Tourism Sector.* Geneva: International Labour Office.

International Labour Organization (1999) *World Labour Report Industrial Relations (Democracy and Social Stability) 1997–98.* Geneva: International Labour Office.

LePoidevin, J. (1998) 'Preventing slips and trips in the food industry'. *Health and Safety at Work*, **19**(3), 16–18.

McDonald's Corporation (2000) *Financial Press Release: McDonald's Reports Year to Date May Sales*, 06/09/2000, http://www.McDonald's.com/corporate/press/financial/2000/06092000/index.html, accessed 1 August 2000.

Mayhew, C. (2000) 'Adolescent worker occupational health and safety'. *Journal of Occupational Health and Safety: Australia and New Zealand*, **16**(2), 137–43.

Mizen, P., Bolton, A. and Pole, C. (1999) 'School age workers: the paid employment of children in Britain'. *Journal of Work, Employment and Society*, **13**(3), 423–38.

NIOSH (1984) *NIOSH Alert: Preventing Electrocution of Workers in Fast Food Restaurants.* Publication No. 85–104, West Virginia: NIOSH.

Richter, D. and Jacobs, J. (1991) 'Work Injuries and exposures in children and young adults: review and recommendations for action'. *American Journal of Industrial Medicine*, **19**(6), 747–69.

Sanders, M. S. and McCormick, E. J. (1992) *Human Factors in Engineering and Design* (7th edn) London: McGraw-Hill Inc.

Shum, K. W. and English, J. S. C. (1998) 'Allergic contact dermatitis in food handlers, with patch tests positive to compositae mix but negative to sesquiterpene lactone mix'. *Contact Dermatitis*, **39**(4), 207–8.

Timo, N. (1999) 'Contingent and retentive employment in the Australian hotel industry: reformulating the core-periphery model'. *Australian Journal of Labour Economics*, **3**(1), 47–64.

Tranter, M. (1998) 'An assessment of heat stress among laundry workers in a Far North Queensland hotel'. *Journal of Occupational Health and Safety – Australia and New Zealand*, **14**(1), 61–63.

Tranter, M. (1999) *Occupational Hygiene and Risk Management: A Multimedia Package.* Alstonville: OH&S Press.

Vainiotalo, S. and Matveinen, K. (1993) 'Cooking fumes as a hygienic problem in the food and catering industries'. *American Industrial Hygiene Association Journal*, **54**(7), 376–82.

Whitehouse, G., Boreham, P. and Lafferty, G. (1997) 'From casual to permanent part-time?: non-standard employment in retail and hospitality'. *Labour and Industry*, **8**(2), 33–48.

Windau, J., Sygnatur, E. and Toscano, G. (1999), 'Profile of work injuries incurred by young workers'. *Monthly Labor Review*, **122**(6), 3–10.

14

The Structure of Employee Relations in Multi-national Hotels in Australia

Nils Timo and Michael Davidson

ABSTRACT

The Australian hotel industry is dominated by large multinational enterprises (MNEs) that compete on price and quality. Despite the size and importance of MNEs in the industry, employee relations practices remain relatively undeveloped. MNEs in the Australian hotel industry have generally adopted two strategies: cost minimization based on flexible forms of labour, and standardization involving standardizing hotel services and products that require minimum investment in terms of labour and training. These operate in tandem in order to achieve a competitive edge based on cost-sensitive and standard-quality (service) using a flexible labour model. The inherent implications for employee relations are discussed in this chapter.

INTRODUCTION

Over the past decade, human resource management (HRM) has come to be viewed as a dominant paradigm within which analysis of the changing nature of work has been located. In particular, labour relations and management practices have been scrutinized by researchers seeking to identify strategies that contribute to a firm's competitive advantage (Kochan *et al.*, 1986). Schuler and Jackson (1987) have argued that competitive strategies may be improved if firms adopt strategic HRM/industrial relations (HRM/IR) and labour-flexibility practices and integrate these with broader competitive strategies of the types proposed by Porter (1990). According to Guest (1987, p. 829), strategic HRM is 'synonymous with the adoption of certain practices of the "high trust" variety including career planning, quality circles, team working, employee consultation and empowerment' linked to broader business strategies based on quality.

However, the idea of a 'strategic' approach to HRM derives intellectual origins from research drawn from managerial models of work and flexibility that often involve a strong element of craft and job tenure and strong domestic labour regulatory systems. Multinational enterprises challenge traditional approaches to labour regulation by their capacity to diffuse transnational employee relations practices that may not always be in the interest of labour (Ritzer, 1993). Whereas Lane (1991) suggests that while there are a broad range of employee relations practices available to MNEs, they tend to reflect the influence of national regulatory labour systems. Ramsay (1997), however, sees increasing internationalization and growth of MNEs as raising questions about the ability of labour to influence managerial decision-making effectively. In the hotel industry, increasing debate has focused on the extent to which hotel employee relations are being reshaped by 'high trust' practices (Hoque, 2000).

This chapter examines the employee relations practices adopted by MNEs operating in the Australian hotel industry. In so doing, it attempts to identify trends in employee relations, work organization and labour utilization. But, first, what is meant by the term, employee relations? There is no simple definition as it has often been used interchangeably with industrial relations or human resource management, though it tends to be associated with an approach at odds with conventional notions of industrial relations that looks at the regulatory framework for employees. According to Bennett (1994, p. 1) the term includes a range of 'strategies used for managing relations between a firm and its employee'. The term is used here to describe the way in which work and jobs are structured and organized as well as including both external and internal factors that shape work organization and labour utilization.

We argue that there are many paths to achieving competitive advantage. In the Australian context, hotel production systems and competitive strategies are more likely to be linked to a flexible labour force that is located in a system of work that is standardized and routinized. We argue that Australian MNE hotels are dominated by a production strategy that uses HRM to engender low-trust strategies based on the use of flexible labour as part of a broader cost-minimization strategy. Common perceptions of working practices in the hotel industry typically include work intensification, high labour turnover, casualization, poor career prospects, low pay and low levels of unionization (Guerrier and Lockwood, 1989; Price, 1994). On this basis, the chapter addresses three questions in the context of the Australian hotel industry.

- How are hotel employee relations structured and organized?
- In what way have hotels used standardization of services and labour?
- If hotels have adopted particular types of labour-management practices, what implications are there for hotel employee relations strategies?

INTERNATIONALIZATION AND THE GROWTH OF MNES IN THE AUSTRALIAN HOTEL INDUSTRY

Over the past three decades, tourism has emerged as a significant global industry, growing by about 7 per cent per annum. The hotel industry is becoming increasingly internationalized, with a rapid rise in the importance of MNEs and the importance of global branding (Dunning and Kundu, 1995). The demand for hotel accommodation is price sensitive and contextual (where push–pull factors operate, such as location or destination-specific, weather, political stability, currency fluctuations). Hotels are increasingly competing in a range of market sectors (such as business, conference, tourist or recreational) with a number of chains having close commercial ties to travel and touring companies. Hotel accommodation is often bundled according to various pricing regimes involving airline and/or travel agent discounting and leveraged with organized tours, shopping excursions, entertainment and other packaged recreational activities. International hotels contribute significantly to domestic economies both in terms of revenue and job creation.

Australia has about a 1 per cent share of the total world tourist trade but, significantly, has over 7 per cent of the world's long-haul trade (Timo, 1996a). The Asia-Pacific region is emerging as having the highest rate of growth in tourism in the world and is a vital part of the Australian hotel industry. This rapid growth in overseas tourism, especially from Japan, Asia and Europe during the past decade, promoted a surge in building infrastructure such as hotels, resorts, golf courses and retail facilities (*ibid.*). This expansion saw a substantial increase in the supply of hotel accommodation, accounting for just under £300 million (sterling, see note p. 198) in capital investment during 1997–98 (Australian Industry Commission, 1996). By 1999, Australian hotels provided 191,147 beds, employed 71,468 workers and had turnover in excess of £533 million (Australian Bureau of Statistics (ABS), 1998, Table 1). There are important implications for employment. In the case of tourism-dependent states such as Queensland, employment in tourism has become the largest employer of young people, growing by 13.3 per cent during the period 1994 to 1999 (Morgans, 1999). Queensland is a major international tourism destination that includes the Great Barrier Reef as well as Tropical Island tourist resorts.

The Australian hotel industry is dominated numerically by small to medium-sized businesses with just over 86 per cent, or 3732 hotels employing twenty or fewer workers. Medium-sized hotels – that is those employing between 20 and 99 workers – accounted for 477, or 11.0 per cent, and larger hotels – that is those employing 100 or more workers – represented 105, or only 2.4 per cent of all hotels according to the ABS survey. MNE hotels in the four- and five-star category exert, proportionately, a greater influence, as they accounted for 45.8 per cent of all hotel workers employed. They paid 59.1 per cent of gross wages and represented 49.7 per cent of gross hotel income (ABS, 1994, Table 4.2, latest figures; ABS, 1998, Table 1.0).

Historically, the Australian hotel industry was built on a tradition of pubs owned and operated by the major breweries. They were mainly small businesses employing up to twenty workers, usually on a regular casual basis. Hotels provided hospitable services as well as accommodation as a regulatory requirement under state liquor laws that required pubs to provide a limited number of rooms, often up to twenty at each establishment in order to ensure accommodation to the weary (and thirsty) traveller. In the early 1970s, there was a temporal shift in employment practices. First, there was the advent of the motor lodge or motels accommodating the automobile traveller that provided budget-style accommodation. Secondly, with the increasing popularity of Australia as a destination for overseas travellers and the introduction of the long-haul and relatively cheap flights on 747 'jumbos', there was a substantial increase in inbound tourists. This was accompanied by an extensive building programme involving construction of large, integrated hotels (providing a range of services, fine dining restaurants, entertainment and four-to five-star accommodation) that was operated by international hotel chains. By the mid 1970s, major international hotels such as Conrad, Hyatt, Accor, Hilton, Ritz-Carlton, Sheraton, Oberoi, Intercontinental, Marriott and others established a presence in Australia. Pro-development state governments actively encouraged the growth in hotel construction, particularly in Queensland during this period despite the protests of the conservation lobby. With a relatively small domestic market, these global brand hotels have struggled to maintain a competitive edge over domestic and international competitors (Australian Industry Commission, 1996).

Generally, MNE hotels in Australia employ between 100 to 400 employees and this figure can fluctuate by up to 50 per cent during peak (July to December) and off-peak (February to June). Australian MNE hotels reflect organizational structures adopted by the parent chain adopting a complex bureaucratic structure and are organized according to a departmental management structure. This reflects a pattern of management adopted by international hotel chains often referred to as departmentalization (Lucas, 1995). Some Australian MNE hotels have sought to alter the traditional organizational structure, principally through industrial-relations processes, such as enterprise bargaining, to allow them to have more flexible labour arrangements.

COMPETITION AND PRODUCT MARKETS

In seeking new promotional opportunities, many hotels have sought to differentiate from competitors by providing higher quality and a more personalized service. This involves a degree of standardization (discussed later on). For example, on Australia's Gold Coast, competition between MNE hotels is considerable. They all offer similar levels of service and services, therefore price is the major competitive factor. MNE hotels tend to be relatively autonomous in relation to marketing and operational issues; however, corporate head office influences marketing directions and revenue issues. These hotels have sought to gain a competitive edge by reducing the amount of rework (e.g. minimizing service failure) by adopting a model of work organization based on product standardization. This uses routine operating procedures and work methods that are controlled through the use of company-wide standardized operating manuals in the context of flexible labour supply as discussed further on.

THE AUSTRALIAN HOTEL LABOUR MARKET

The Australian hotel labour market has a number of defining characteristics. For example, the hotel labour market is relatively unstable with higher levels of turnover than most manufacturing industries (KPMG, 1991; Benson and Worland, 1992; Timo, 1996a). More than half of all hotel employment is on a casual or contingent basis, which is far higher than the OECD average (Buuljens, 1997; Timo, 1999). A hotel labour-market survey conducted by Norris *et al.* (1995) found that hotel workers (excluding maintenance engineers and chefs) are lower paid, earning on average only 73 to 86 per cent of the all-industry average. In addition, they found that most hotel jobs had few skill barriers to entry and were attractive to young workers looking for travel and excitement.

The Australian Industry Commission (AIC, 1996, now part of the Australian Consumer Competition Commission, or ACCC) has concluded that hotel work is generally low-paid and labour-intensive. The demand for skills (excluding cooks and chefs) was low, with only 11 per cent of hotel workers requiring trade qualifications as compared to an all-industries average of 16.4 per cent. The IAC found that 70.6 per cent of hotel workers had no post-school qualifications, as compared to 52.9 per cent for an all-industries average (IAC, 1996, p. 257, Table 13.8). A survey of hotel training needs by Tourism Training Australia (TTA) showed that hotel workers are relatively young – aged 25 years and under – and highly mobile. The TTA survey found that future growth in hotel employment was expected to be in semi-skilled occupations, particularly in kitchen work (27.1%), food attendants (26.5%), cooks (17.1%, bar attendants (12.2%) and porters and house attendants (4.1%). Skilled and supervisory positions were only expected to increase by 3.6 per cent (TTA, 1997). Norris *et al.* (1995, pp. 57–8) have concluded that the demand for hotel jobs exceeded supply by almost two to one, thus reducing pressure on hotels to either increase wages or reduce labour turnover.

HOTEL PRODUCTIVITY, HRM AND EMPLOYEE RELATIONS

Australian hotels are seen as having, on average, higher operating costs. The most recent (and only) study on operating costs – that undertaken by the Tourism Task Force in its report *Labour Costs and Training* (1992) found that Australian hotels have one of the highest labour cost components as a percentage of revenue, at 37.2 per cent, compared to North America (34.7%), Europe (31.2%), United Kingdom (28.3%) and Far/East Asia (25.8%). Yet, on a proportion of employees per available room, Australia was found to have the second lowest proportion of employees per room at 0.67 (as compared to Europe of 0.048), followed by North America, 0.68, then United Kingdom, 0.95, and Far/East Asia, 1.16). Despite the higher domestic labour costs, the study found that Australian hotels are generally cheaper and enjoy higher retail sales/ revenue per employee at £11,715 per employee (second to Europe at £16,901). This is followed by the United Kingdom (11,560), North America (11,129) and Far/East Asia (7,636) and suggests that Australian hotels have higher productivity per employee (1992, pp. 13–14).

Linking and measuring HRM practices and productivity outcomes in hotels presents a number of problems. First, productivity lacks an agreed definition and benchmark. Secondly, productivity and quality is the outcome of both management choice and guest expectations; they are, therefore, contingent. Finally, productivity is integrally bound up with labour utilization (Timo, 1996a; Nankervis, 1993). The characteristics of service work that hotels are engaged in includes the sale, production and consumption of a service almost simultaneously. This generally involves hotel workers in a high degree of emotional work (Lucas, 1995), characterized by a high levels of human contact that becomes central to meeting consumers' expectations and satisfaction level. The level of service quality in hotels is largely a subjective matter and influenced by these staff–customer interactions. There is a considerable degree of uncertainty in managing service quality.

To date, perhaps the most useful study of the impact of HRM practices on hotel productivity is that of Prais *et al.* (1989) that examined training and skill development. They attributed greater productivity with fewer staff in German hotels – as compared to UK hotels – to different approaches to human capital. German hotels had higher levels of trade skills, 35 per cent, as opposed to 14 per cent in British hotels, and departmental staff were better trained and educated and more directly involved with departmental decision-making. The German hotel vocational courses were broader and emphasized greater cross-skilling; and German hotels were less reliant on part-time and casual employees (19%) as opposed to British hotels (41%). The authors concluded that labour productivity contributed to German hotel prices being up to 20 per cent lower than in Britain (Prais *et al.*, 1989).

Hoque (2000) cites the benefits of flexible working in hotels to increase productivity. He traces the development of a range of HRM techniques such as training, teamwork and performance-related reward systems, as issues relating to increased productivity. An organizational climate must be created making hotel employees aware that productivity is important. These practices are more effective where they form part of an induction process and on-the-job training programmes (Davidson, 2000). Improved training, multi-skilling and creation of long-term, permanent jobs are seen as contributing to long-term skill development and improved labour productivity (Baker and Riley, 1994; IAC, 1996).

METHODOLOGY

Data here has been drawn from a range of industry and academic sources. Importantly, it includes data on workplace employment-relations practices from a survey of formal workplace agreements. This is approved by industrial relations tribunals covering four- to five-star hotels on the Agreements Database and Monitor (ADAM) and collected by the Australian Centre for Industrial Relations Research and Training (or ACIRRT) at the University of Sydney. The industry classifications used by ADAM are defined in accordance with the Australian and New Zealand Standard Industry Classification, adopted by the Australian Bureau of Statistics (ABS). The number of hotel agreements were 116 (n = 116) and the 'all other industries' category was 6909 (n = 6909). The agreements were collated electronically using a standard code developed by ACIRRT in order to categorize workplace agreements according to a range of industrial relations and HRM variables.

FINDINGS

The Structure of Hotel Employee Relations

In order to understand how hotel employee relations are structured and organized, it is necessary to understand the external and internal influences on how hotel tasks and labour needs are allocated. First, historically, the balance between managerial prerogative and the negotiating power of collective labour in the employment relationship has been mediated by Australia's highly centralized system for establishing and regulating employment and working conditions. This has been achieved through federal and state-based industrial tribunals that set industrial awards covering industries and occupations. The federal tribunal (known as the Australian Industrial Relations Commission or AIRC) sets wages policy (through national wage case decisions) which would normally be followed by state industrial tribunals. By the late 1980s there were approximately 7000 awards operating in Australia.

Awards concentrate on 'hygiene' factors associated with conditions of work, rewards and factors that may minimize employee dissatisfaction. Awards impose legally binding minimum wages and employment conditions that have become the substance of internal labour markets. Tourism awards covering hotels generally link hours of work and payment systems whereby a typical working period such as weekend work, late-night work and public holidays are compensated by higher rates known as penalty rates. Hotel awards also prescribe hours of work, shift arrangements, days off and rostering requirements. The rules set by awards have gradually weakened since the mid-1990s through various government attempts to deregulate the industrial-relations system through the introduction of enterprise bargaining and non-union agreement-making. By September 1999, it is estimated that there were 11,420 current workplace agreements covering 1.3 million workers (Petzall *et al.*, 2000). While awards set comprehensive details regarding employee wages and conditions, the quantity and quality of the work performed is rarely spelled out.

MNEs hotels in Australia have generally adopted unitarist approaches to employee relations allowing each hotel to determine and implement its own individual policies. Yet they continue to rely on collectivist forms of labour regulation provided by the award system. For example, only 2.6 per cent (n = 3) of hotel workplace agreements surveyed (n = 116) sought to replace the application of hotel awards (ACIRRT, ADAM, Hotel Agreement Survey, 2000). Hotel MNEs have generally adopted and adapted to this award system through applying cost-minimization strategies that have involved structuring hotel labour markets according to numerically flexible ('just-in-time') labour. In addition, reducing the amount of rework necessary through standardization of tasks and emotional content of hotel labour controls labour costs.

Employee Relations and the Importance of Hotel Task Structure

Outwardly, Australian hotels appear to be structured bureaucracies. However, behind this façade they are essentially organic structures built upon a departmental structure. There is an absence of a clear-cut authority structure in hotels. Rather, labour and tasks are allocated according to function and department (Timo, 1996a). Departmental managers exert considerable control over the allocation of tasks and labour. For example, the executive chef is often solely responsible for allocating tasks in the kitchen and the control of labour. Departmentalization encourages unitarist managerial styles and informal rule-making that shapes the pattern of labour use. This enables a range of informal work practices to develop at department level between the manager/supervisor and individual employee. Hotel employment relations are dominated by a strong individualist approach to employee governance. 'Visible' and *being there* styles of management give rise to employee relations practices characterized by informality, paternalism and authoritarianism, reflected in a *my people* approach to employee relations.

This impacts on hotel labour use in two significant ways. First, departmental procedural flexibility allows employment practices and working-time arrangements to be restructured at departmental level in order to match labour supply with changes in demand. This may involve changes to rostering, starting and ceasing times, shift-working, taking of leave or rostered days off, working of overtime, timing of meal breaks and breaks between one shift and the next etc., to be decided directly between the supervisor and the employee. For example, 25.9 per cent (n = 30) of hotel workplace agreements delegated hours-of-work arrangements to individual department level compared with only 16.0 per cent (n = 1103) of all industry agreements (ACIRRT, ADAM Hotel Survey, 2000). Secondly, rewards and favours are distributed according to this informal system through individual bargaining (e.g. access to overtime, favourable rosters or days off etc.). Only 2.6 per cent (n = 3) of hotels provided a systematic approach to individual performance or merit pay, as opposed to 4.7 per cent (n = 334) for all industry agreements. Further, only 1.7 per cent (n = 2) of hotel agreements made provision for bonus payments based on performance as compared to 8.3 per cent (n = 441) for all-industry agreements (ACIRRT, ADAM, Hotel Agreements Survey, 2000). Due to the lack of structure in relation to key performance indicators and performance pay, the effect has been to engender employee loyalty and commitment to the manager of the department in order to access management favours. Individual loyalty was highly regarded. In return for employee loyalty, departmental managers were expected to reciprocate by 'looking after' their employees. This point is crucial in understanding how employee relations practice is structured and why existing departmental managerial practices go largely unchallenged.

It is difficult to assess the impact of these informal arrangements on hotel employees. First, they were often not prepared to complain about them (and then usually only after having left the service of the employer). Secondly, the informal negotiation over rewards and arrangement of working-time preferences are accepted workplace norms. Female hotel workers generally preferred flexible starting/ceasing times that coincided with family commitments, whereas male employees preferred blocks of working time to maximize leisure time or income. However, the extent to which management dedicates time and effort towards building effective workplace relations with employees remains an open question. A major source of dissatisfaction among employees interviewed was the perceived lack of equity over the allocation of rewards and, at times, the lack of fairness in the way that grievances were dealt with. Employee failure to 'fit in' at this level could also lead to isolation and encourage exit behaviour (Davidson, 2000).

Cost Minimization and Numerically Flexible Labour

It has been argued that firms operating in highly unstable and competitive product markets are more likely to adopt contingent and numerically flexible workers (Atkinson, 1987; Rubery, 1987; Tilly, 1992). A number of studies of the hotel industry have identified issues such as casualization, lack of permanency, low skill, low pay and weak HRM practices (Price, 1994). Other studies have emphasized gender, weak training systems, numerical flexibility and the replacement of regular employment by atypical forms of employment (Bagguley, 1987; Kelliher, 1989; Guerrier and Lockwood, 1989). Similar studies of the Australian hotel industry have shown a high degree of commonality (Benson and Worland 1992; Sonder and Underhill 1994; Timo, 1996b and 1999).

A central problem of efficiency in the hotel trade is the utilization of capacity in the face of irregular customer/guest arrivals and different levels of demand during operating hours over the day, week and season. In this context, labour in hotels is structured according to 'derived' demand and the adaptability in labour costs by the matching of labour inputs (paid hours) to customer demand. According to ACIRRT, ADAM Hotel Survey (2000) 58.6 per cent (n = 68) of hotel agreements provided for the flexible use of casual and part-time staff as compared to 34.7 per cent (n = 2397) of all-industry agreements. Casual work comprises more than half of all hotel jobs and most jobs are offered, initially at least on a casual basis to see whether the employee 'works out' (Timo, 1999; Australian Industry Commission, 1996, p. 253).

Using flexible labour not only forms part of a cost-minimization strategy, it also has a number of HRM functions. Using casual engagements as ports of entry not only maintained control over staffing levels but also extended more control over employee behaviour and discipline through the promise of work as a reward (or withdrawal of it as a form of punishment). Yet casual employment has a number of transaction costs. Casual employees are seen by hotel management as being less committed and motivated; not as well-skilled or trained, and are therefore more prone to higher turnover and multiple-jobs holding (reducing their availability).

New Forms of Work Organization

Departmentalization can often reduce internal career ladders and promotional opportunities due to lack of vacancies. They collectively place limitations and barriers in the internal labour market that force workers to seek opportunities for advancement elsewhere. The most important of these influences is the scope, or lack of it, for training within any single hotel. This encourages mobility and turnover that, in turn, affects quality. The lack of training opportunities and career movement within the organization contributes to a 'culture' of mobility (Timo, 1999). Hoque (2000) has identified a range of new HRM practices such as team-working, quality circles, job redesign, communication and performance pay systems in hotels. However, Australian MNEs, apparently, remain reluctant to fully implement these practices.

Australian MNEs have found the flexible labour market model more effective in reducing pressure to adopt new HRM practices and have traded off functional flexibility in favour of a continued reliance on numerical flexibility. For example, only 4.3 per cent (n = 5) of hotels had introduced teamwork, as compared to an all-industry average of 12.9 per cent (n = 891). Where teams have been introduced, these have been mainly limited to housekeeping and room attendants. Workers have become responsible for their own quality and checking. Team-working has been accompanied by middle management and supervisory delayering that reduced upward mobility. Whilst MNEs such as the Sheraton have sought to reduce the employment of casuals in their teams, the result has been more flexible, part-time work arrangements. In addition, the reliance upon flexible forms of labour reduces the scope for functional flexibility and cross-skilling. Cross-skilling is often discouraged because it leads to potential conflict between departments over access to suitable workers. Departmental managers are often reluctant to 'let go' of their better workers in other departments in case they do not come back.

Instead of performance pay systems, all of the hotels surveyed (n = 116) have sought in their agreements to control payroll costs by absorbing weekend payments and special rates into an all-up hourly rate through the introduction of annualized wages. This serves to break the connection between payment systems and hours of work, thereby treating all hours the same, irrespective of when and how often weekends or public holidays are worked. To work effectively, this annualized system of wages needs equitable rostering to ensure equal treatment of working patterns for all employees. Except for higher skilled trades such as cooks and chefs, few over-award or use performance pay systems.

The Importance of Standardization

Outwardly, it appears that Australian hotel management have adopted employee relations practices that mitigate against efficiency and organizational success of the kinds suggested by Porter (1990) and Hoque (2000), such as quality leadership, better integrated business and HRM strategies. Yet there is a kind of logic among Australian MNE hotel management thinking. They appear to have adopted two strategies. First, as discussed above, Australian hotels have organized the task structure in a self-regulating and autonomous manner where departmental managers exert a great deal of control over labour use and reward allocation. This enables departmental managers to adjust and reshape the content of labour on a just-in-time basis.

The second strategy is to standardize the emotional content of hotel service. According to Leidner (1993) management can use two strategies to overcome obstacles to routinizing the service interaction or service encounter. The first is to standardize the service–recipient behaviour. The other is to personalize routinization in standard ways that Pine has labelled 'mass customization' (*ibid.*, p. 36). This involves routinizing not only the service provided but also the interaction between producer and consumer.

The process of standardization can be masked in a number of ways so that individual brand names can assert their own identity and offer differentiated service options within a single hotel. For example, the hotels offer executive and business floors that provide additional service at little extra additional cost but at a substantially increased room rate. In these circumstances the hotel consumer is offered a limited range of additional services by the hotel. This process of mass customization masks a larger reality associated with routinization and standardization of hotel services.

However, the capacity of hotels to standardize service is dependent upon a range of factors. First, there is a reliance on hotel workers' discretion in order to up-sell these bundled and customized hotel products. Quality becomes a key factor in the service encounter. Customization is likely to be especially important where the service interaction forms part of the product being sold (e.g. fine-dining restaurant service, valet and butler services). Secondly, the more difficult or complex the interactive task, the more likely it is that things can go wrong. This means that the task is likely to be more varied, or difficult to execute, and the more difficult it will be to control and predict worker discretion and performance. Under these circumstances, ensuring the quality of the interaction between service provider and service consumer is not merely a matter of specifying and 'programming' hotel workers' attitudes and demeanour (such as socially pleasing behaviours), it is also about reducing uncertainty through task routinization.

How do MNEs ensure the delivery of a consistent and predictable service in the context of departmentalization and a highly flexible and casual workforce? Hotels have adopted a range of contradictory yet effective approaches. First, as observed earlier, hotel work has been restructured, where possible, to standardize the range of services provided, whereby guests choose from a limited range of bundled services. Secondly, in order to offset the unpredictable nature of a low-cost, flexible labour force, hotels have sought to standardize the emotional content and context in which the service is produced and consumed. This has involved transforming the hotel worker by restructuring the workers' task as well as emotional labour content into something more effective. Achieving predictability and certainty becomes a major goal here. In order to achieve this, MNE hotels have developed extensive codes of practice or hotel rules in employee manuals that aim to incorporate into the worker's contract of employment a range of additional obligations.

The process of standardization can occur at the level of task and organization. In terms of tasks, hotel manuals specify in detail the way in which a task is to be prepared and delivered (the kitchen is a good example of where tasks are clearly defined and spelt out in detail, similarly with housekeeping and front office). In addition, the emotional content can be made more predictable through controlling and setting constraints on individual behaviour by distinguishing between acceptable and non-acceptable behaviours. In terms of the organizational level, hotel employee manuals set constraints

Box 14.1 Working task and emotional content standardization

The characteristics of a successful employee at our Resort include the following:

- A strong desire to work at the Resort
- Enjoys working with people
- Believes the customer is an important part of his (her) job
- Understands, through training, the operators perceptions of quality
- Committed to career and a career path
- A positive attitude towards the success of the product
- Determination to achieve a high level of service
- Friendly, professional and approachable
- Involvement in the establishment of work procedures
- A team player

The overall financial objectives for the Resort are to realise significant capital gain and achieve acceptable financial returns for the owners. These objectives are supported by effectively minimising waste in all areas of the operation and constantly improving quality in all areas of the Resort. This pursuit of constant improvement will result in lower costs as a result of less rework, fewer mistakes, fewer delays and better use of facilities and staff.

Source: *Resort Employee Relations Handbook*, from a large MNE Integrated Resort, North Queensland, November, 1998.

on forms of behaviour such as non-smoking, standards of personal appearance and hygiene (e.g. no visible tattoos, body piercing etc.), uniforms and neatness; as well as modifying and regulating individual behaviour, such as rules about courtesy to guests, personal habits, physical appearance (e.g. a ban on beards for men), mode of address to guests and setting a range of interpersonal behaviour.

Hotel employee manuals also list a set of standardized repertoire of greetings, questions that might be asked and the required answers, and social pleasantries (like 'Have a nice day'). In-house training serves a major function in inculcating these behaviours as well as ensuring ongoing compliance in order to ensure replication and predictability. The hotel employee relations manual becomes an important mechanism for ensuring not only social control, but acts as the 'glue' that holds departments together by stipulating corporate standard rules of behaviour and conduct. An extract from one MNE hotel's employee manual describes the hotel's ideal type of employee, illustrated in Box 14.1.

Standardization is also an important organizational variable. For example, the consistent public perception of MNE corporate image and brand name ensures that consumers come to link a type of hotel service with a particular hotel chain or group. The standardization of service interaction, procedures, service expectations, and homogenization of products are used to promote a corporate image or product in order to ensure consumer acceptance (not dissimilar to the way in which the McDonald's Corporation is able to project a standard image associated with a core product). Standardization and replication become key competency areas for HRM staff. Feedback from hotel HRM managers during this research suggests that a majority of their time is spent drafting organizational procedures, training notes and employee relations manual entries.

MNEs have used an additional range of mechanisms in order to engender compliance and motivation. These include newsletters, notice boards, regular address by departmental manager, pre-/after-work meetings, and 'employee of the month' schemes, subsidized meals and induction programmes. Ultimately, on the surface, these forms of employee incorporation appear to foster employee involvement and empowerment. However, they aim to ensure that the staff are made familiar with the views of management and designed to foster a sense of common interest and incorporation, and not concerned with collective power sharing. While union membership is higher among MNEs due to their larger employment size, workplace union activity is low (except in one case during the Olympic Games in Sydney, when staff at one hotel went on strike over Olympic loadings, usually about £70 per week for the two weeks of the games). This reflects a number of factors, such as weak union representational structures, casualization, a young and mobile workforce, and hostile management. Union membership is estimated to be less than 1.5 per cent of the hotel labour force overall.

DISCUSSION AND CONCLUSIONS

It is argued here that despite the size and importance of MNE hotels in the Australian hotel industry, employee relations practices remain relatively undeveloped when compared to other service and manufacturing industries. This is due to the way in which MNEs have chosen to structure their employee relations. MNE hotel operators have generally adopted two contradictory strategies to employee relations. The first is a cost-minimization strategy based on flexible forms of labour, principally using a high level of casual employees to match demand. The second is standardization of hotel services and products that require minimum investment in terms of labour and training (and less rework). Standardization allows hotels to deliver a level of acceptable service reliability by low-cost and numerically flexible labour. Flexible labour can be unpredictable and by using standardization of work procedures ensures task replication and minimum reworking. For the hotel consumer, this means a competitive price and standardized quality that ensures that the hotel consumer connects a 'brand' name with a particular level of service and experience. For hotel management, it allows a degree of control and certainty in labour use and quality. While this chapter focuses on Australian MNE hotels, it raises broader issues concerning the divergent paths that different sectors of the hotel industry may adopt towards achieving competitive advantage.

This chapter has sought to examine the way in which hotel employee relations are structured in Australian MNE hotels and has argued that they have adopted a two-pronged strategy involving using numerically flexible labour as well as standardizing hotel services. Standardization is a key strategy for ensuring not only a competitive edge based on a very competitive product market, but also as a means of controlling often unpredictable behaviour and quality by a numerically flexible workforce. Rather than being peripheral to hotel operations, standardization plays a key role in broader cost-minimization strategies adopted by Australian MNE hotels.

ACKNOWLEDGEMENTS

The authors gratefully acknowledge the continuing assistance of hotel managers in this research and the staff of the Australian Centre for Industrial Relations Research and

Training (ACIRRT) who conducted the survey of hotel agreements drawn from the ADAM agreements database.

NOTE:

Pound sterling conversion as at December 2000 was 0.375 pence to $AUS.

SELF-ASSESSMENT QUESTIONS

1. How useful is the term 'employee relations' to understanding labour management?
2. Describe the link between employee relations and work organization.
3. What are the advantages or disadvantages in standardizing hotel managerial practices and employment relations?
4. Quality service and mass-customerization don't mix! Discuss.

REFERENCES

Atkinson, J. (1987) 'Flexibility or fragmentation: the UK labour market in the 1980s'. *Labour and Society*, **12**, 87–105.

Australian Industry Commission (1996) *Tourism Accommodation and Training*. IAC Report No. 50. Melbourne: Australian Government Printing Office.

Australian Bureau of Statistics (1994) *Hospitality Industries Australia, 1991–1992*. Catalogue No. 8674.0. Canberra: Australian Government Printing Office.

Australian Bureau of Statistics (1998) *Tourist Accommodation, Australia*, December, Catalogue No. 8635.0. Canberra: Australian Government Printing Office.

Australian Centre for Industrial Relations Research and Teaching (2000) *'Hotel Agreements Survey on ADAM (Agreements Database and Monitoring)'*. Sydney: University of Sydney.

Bagguley, P. (1987) 'Flexibility, restructuring and gender: changing employment in Britain's hotels'. *University of Landcaster Region Group Working Paper*, No. 24, May. Lancaster: University of Lancaster.

Baker, M. and Riley, M. (1994) 'New perspectives on productivity in hotels: some advances and new directions'. *International Journal of Hospitality Management*, **13**, 297–311.

Bennett, R. (1994) *Employee Relations*. London: Pitman.

Benson, T. and Worland, D. (1992) 'Hotel international', in R. Lansbury and D. Macdonald (eds), *Workplace Industrial Relations: Australian Case Studies*. Melbourne: Oxford University Press, pp. 96–125.

Buuljens, J. (1997) 'Casual employment in the hospitality industry: a situational analysis', in P. Brosnan and E. Underhill (eds), *Precarious Employment: Conference Proceedings No. 2*. Center for Research on Employment and Work. Brisbane: Griffith University, pp. 93–106.

Davidson, M. (2000) 'Organisational climate and its influence upon performance: a study of Australian hotels in South-east Queensland'. Unpublished paper. Gold Coast: Griffith University.

Dunning, J. and Kundu, S. (1995) 'The internationalisation of the hotel industry: some new findings from a field study'. *Management International Review*, **35**, 101–33.

Guest, D. (1987) 'Human resource management and industrial relations'. *Journal of Management Studies*, **25**, 503–21.

Guerrier, Y. and Lockwood, A. (1989) 'Core and peripheral employees in hotel operations'. *Personnel Review*, **18**, 9–15.

Hoque, K. (2000) *Human Resource Management in the Hotel Industry: Strategy, Innovation and Performance*. London: Routledge.

Kelliher, C. (1989) 'Flexibility in employment: developments in hospitality industry'. *International Journal of Hospitality Management*, **8**, 157–66.

Kochan, T., Katz, H., and McKersie, R. (1986) *The Transformation of American Industrial Relations*. New York: Basic Books.

KPMG Peat Marwick Management Consultants (1991) *The Tourism Labour Market: Constraints and Attitudes*. Report prepared for Tourism Training Australia, Sydney.

Lane, C. (1991) 'Industrial reorganization in Europe: patterns of convergence and divergence in Germany, France and Britain'. *Work, Employment and Society*, **5**, 515–39.

Leidner, R. (1993) *Fast Food, Fast Talk: Services Work and the Routinisation of Everyday Life*. Berekely, CA: University of California Press.

Lucas, R. (1995) *Managing Employee Relations in the Hotel and Catering Industry*. London: Cassell.

Morgans Stockbrokers (1999) 'Five years of the Queensland economy'. *Economic Strategy Briefing*. Brisbane: Morgans Stockbrokers.

Nankervis, A. (1993) 'Productivity service excellence and innovation in South East Asian hotels'. Department of Employment Relations. Sydney: University of Western Sydney (Nepean).

Norris, K., Stromback, T. and Dockery, A. (1995) *How Tourism Labour Markets Work*. Commonwealth Department of Tourism, Research Report No. 1. Canberra: Australian Government Publishing Service.

Petzall, S., Timo, N. and Abbott, K. (2000) *Australian Industrial Relations in a South East Asian Context*. Melbourne: Eruditions.

Pine, B. (1993) *Mass Customisation: The New Frontier in Business Competition*. Harvard: Harvard Business School Press.

Porter, M. (1990) *The Competitive Advantage of Nations*. London: Macmillan.

Prais, S., Jarvis, V. and Wagner, K. (1989) 'Productivity and vocational skills in service in Britain and Germany: hotels'. *National Institute Economic Review*, November, 52–72.

Price, L. (1994) 'Poor personnel practice in the hotel and catering industry: Does it matter?' *Human Resource Management Journal*, **4**, 44–62.

Ramsay, H. (1997) 'Fools gold? European works councils and workplace democracy'. *Industrial Relations Journal*, **28**, 314–22.

Ritzer, G. (1993) *The McDonalidaztion of Society*. Thousand Oaks, California: Sage.

Rubery, J. (1987) 'Employers and the labour market', in D. Gallie (ed.), *Employment in Britain*. Oxford: Blackwell, pp. 251–80.

Schuler, R. and Jackson, S. (1987) 'Linking competitive strategies with human resource management practices'. *Academy of Management Executive*, **1**, 207–19.

Sonder, L. and Underhill, E. (1994) 'Penalty rates in the hospitality industry: economic and social implications of change'. Paper presented to the 8th AIRAANZ Conference. Sydney: Australian Center of Industrial Relations Research and Teaching (ACIRRT), University of Sydney.

Tilly, C. (1992) 'Dualism in part-time employment'. *Industrial Relations*, **31**, 330–47.

Timo, N. (1996a) 'Employment relations and management in the hotel and tourism industry: case studies'. Unpublished PhD thesis. Toowoomba: University of Southern Queensland.

Timo, N. (1996b) 'Staff turnover in hotels'. *Labour Economics and Productivity*, **8**, 43–81.

Timo, N. (1999) 'Contingent and retentive employment in the Australian hotel industry: reformulating the core-periphery model'. *Australian Journal of Labour Economics*, **3**, pp. 47–64.

Tourism Task Force (1992) *Labour Costs and Training*. Sydney: Tourism Task Force.

TTA (1997) 'Workforce 2020'. Report prepared for the Australian National Training Authority. Canberra: Tourism Training Australia.

15

A Feeling for Empowerment?

Conrad Lashley

ABSTRACT

Employee empowerment is usually referred to as a way of managing employees in a systematic way. It is frequently discussed as an approach to management that implies participation, or at least consultation, between employees and managers. It is a total approach involving culture shift and best suited to the learning organizations required of service businesses in the new millennium. This chapter argues that these total and systematic approaches often assume a shift in the relationship between employees and management in general. Managers and employees work together in ways quite different from the traditional command and control structure. At root, they assume a relational definition of empowerment. In these circumstances, command and control organizations, and particularly those depending on 'one best way' approaches to operational systems and service delivery have limited opportunities to adopt empowerment, because the opportunities for delegated decision-making among the workforce are limited. However, given a more motivational definition of empowerment, individuals can be developed and empowered to take on additional responsibility and authority.

INTRODUCTION

Empowered employees are supposed to feel in greater control (Conger, 1989), have a greater sense of personal power together with the freedom to use that power (van Oudtshoorn and Thomas, 1993) and a sense of personal efficacy and self-determination (Alpander, 1991). They feel that they have power and can make a difference. They feel they have choices and can exercise choice (Johnson, 1993). Unlike disempowered or powerless employees, empowerment provides employees with a sense of autonomy, authority and control (*ibid.*) together with the abilities, resources and discretion to make decisions. Empowerment, therefore, claims to produce an emotional state in employees from which positive attitudes to the organization, additional commitment and increased effort stem (Johnson and Redmond, 1998).

The increasing requirement of employees in hospitality and tourism – indeed in all service-sector organizations – to manage their emotions in meeting customer-service expectations intensifies the inputs which employees bring to the work (Hochschild, 1983). In front-line service jobs employees not only have to provide the physical labour and skills required for serving the customer, they must also supply the appropriate emotions and body language which will encourage customers to feel welcome, wanted and delighted. The provision of emotional labour has intensified, particularly in the service sector, as firms have recognized that effective competitive strategy via service quality enhancement requires employees to provide more than standardized and scripted interactions with customers. Effective service delivery requires employees to genuinely feel a commitment to the customer, which goes 'beyond smiling' (Adelmann *et al.*, 1994) and this requires the employee to manage their feelings so as to achieve the required state (Hochschild, 1983).

While these general ambitions are clearly stated in the literature, there is little discussion of how the state of empowerment might be created, nor the contextual factors likely to enhance or inhibit its development. Similarly, the processes through which employees develop attitudes which are more positive to the organization and its management are rarely discussed. Finally, how do employees cope with the additional stresses and pressure required of managing feelings for commercial purposes? This chapter attempts to provide some discussion of the concepts which help to develop an understanding of how empowerment might bring about these changes, and highlights those contradictions both within the conceptual models themselves and within the realities of organizational life which might inhibit the required changes.

This chapter is, therefore, largely conceptual in nature. It is not informed by dedicated research activity, though it is influenced by a number of consultancy and 'paid for' research projects undertaken by the author. The paper takes as read that empowerment is a term which has a variety of meanings and managerial intentions (Lashley, 1996; Collins, 1999; Holden, 1999), and is often introduced in forms which have much in common with initiatives which claim to enhance employee involvement and participation. That said, a defining feature of claims for empowerment is that employees *feel* empowered and experience an altered emotional state.

AN EMOTIONAL STATE

Aspirations for empowerment aim to change employees' feelings of personal power and control, together with more positive attitudes to the organization and increased commitment to its policies and goals. It is hoped that empowered service employees will display sufficient confidence to do whatever is necessary to meet customer service needs. They will understand and manage potential tensions between organizational commitments to customer service quality, brand rigidities and profits, and will be loyal employees who will 'pay back' training costs by remaining with the organization. Much of the more evangelical and normative literature takes these benefits as axiomatic. Empowerment of employees will result in the desired outcomes (Barry, 1993; Johnson, 1993). There is little by way of an explanation of how these changes in working relationships will result in changes in feelings, attitudes and behaviour.

Conger and Kanungo (1988, p. 471) do, however, attempt to provide some explanations of the 'empowerment process' and signal up those contextual factors which are likely to influence the development of feelings of powerlessness and feelings of empowerment in organizational life. First, they draw a distinction between concepts of empowerment which are *relational* and those which are *motivational*. Relational constructs stress the power relationships between managers and employees. This relates to the debates in the literature relating to employee participation and democracy (Marchington *et al.*, 1992; Poole, 1986 and 1989). They state that this focus has led to the development of approaches to the relationship between employees which equate, even out or redistribute power between managers and employees. Techniques that involve more participation and involvement of employees, are said to be empowering and they have been identified as meaning the same as participation and involvement. The key problem, they suggest, is that these meanings do not address the experiences of empowered employees. Hence, empowerment can be used as an operational rhetoric to cover quite different degrees of involvement, forms, levels, ranges of issues to be covered and power to influence decisions (Potterfield, 1999). Table 15.1 lists some of the variations in empowerment using the literature to analyse the nature of the relation aspects of empowerment. This framework helps to analyse empowerment as a 'political' process.

Empowerment as a motivational construct relies more for an understanding of empowerment through individuals' internal needs for power and control (McClelland, 1975) and feelings of personal efficacy (Bandura, 1986). Under this model, individuals perceive themselves as having power when they are able to control events or situations and deal effectively with the environments they encounter. Conversely, individuals are likely to feel powerless in situations where they cannot influence decisions, or where they do not have the time, resources or skills to be effective. From a motivational perspective, power is intrinsic, based on a need for self-determination, and managers should adopt techniques which strengthen employees' needs for self-determination and personal efficacy. Sparrowe (1994) adds that to be effective in generating feelings of empowerment, the empowered have to both value that which they have been empowered to do and feel that their empowerment encompasses meaningful actions.

Table 15.1 Analysing the relational aspects of empowerment

Degree of involvement	Directive – tell, tell and sell
	Consultative – tell and test, seek
	Participative – joint problem solving; delegation
	Direct – all employees
Form of involvement	Indirect – representatives of employees
	Financial – shares, profits, bonuses
	Tasks – how tasks are done
Level of involvement	Department – who does what; tactical issues
	Corporation – business strategy and goals
	Service delivery – meeting customer needs, complaints
Range of issues involved	Employment issues – pay and conditions of employment
	General organization conduct – general purpose and aims
	Making the decision stick
Power	Who makes the final decision – recommending or deciding?

Source: Lashley (1997)

Under this motivational construct of empowerment, employees are enabled through the development of employees' personal efficacy. Implicitly, this means that employee perceptions of their ability to cope in situations and where they value success by exercising a range of judgements and skills becomes paramount. Effective management needs to be aware that heightened motivation to complete organizational tasks and aspirations to achieve organizational goals, such as increased customer satisfaction, will be achieved through the development of a 'strong sense personal efficacy' (Conger and Kanungo, 1988, p. 474). Using the motivational construct, Conger and Kanungo define empowerment 'as a process of enhancing feelings of self-efficacy among organizational members through the identification of conditions that foster powerlessness and through their removal by both formal organizational practices and informal techniques of providing efficacy information' (p. 474).

For Conger and Kanungo, relational models of empowerment may or may not provide necessary conditions for the empowerment of employees. Thus a redistribution of power over organizational resources with more participative forms of empowerment may provide an environment in which employees develop a sense of personal efficacy, they are not guarantees of feelings of empowerment in themselves.

While this view of empowerment can be criticized because it takes for granted much about organizational life and plays down the tensions inherent in empowerment (Cunningham and Hyman, 1999), it does provide a useful explanation of how empowerment 'should' work. It provides a model against which organizational practices can be compared with experiences of the empowered. If the analysis of empowerment is to move beyond the face value of initiatives which are labelled 'empowerment', it must provide a robust model of the conditions in which employees develop their sense of personal efficacy.

Conger and Kanungo identify feelings of powerlessness as the key target of initiatives designed to empower employees. Although this may be an important motive, and one consistent with the suggestion that empowerment is a necessary ingredient to the management of organizations in modern, internationally competitive economies, it is not the only motive. Hospitality and tourism organizations have a particularly urgent need to engage employees on an emotional level. The nature of service requires that employees are committed to delighting the customer and this requires the display of the appropriate emotions of welcome, care and concern for customer needs. To be most effective, employees need to both believe in their own efficacy and their central significance in making the service encounter a success, and in summoning up the appropriate feelings required of the interaction. The 'empowering process' has a key role in developing feelings of efficacy and in managing the feelings required.

Conger and Kanungo's representation of the five stages in the process of empowerment is useful. The five stages involves consideration of those aspects of the organization and its operation which are leading employees to feel disempowered, the use of techniques to remove or redress these feelings of powerlessness; increasing communications with employees sharing success in performance; encouraging employees to reflect on their new experiences; and long-term behavioural change.

This focus on the motivational concept of empowerment does allow a consideration of the possibility of employees developing a sense of personal efficacy even in situations where there has been no alteration to relational power. The notion of 'empowerment via commitment' (Lashley, 1995), or Lockwood's (1996) 'enabling empowerment' are consistent with this. Organizations can develop this sense of personal efficacy in employees if there is an organizational commitment to identifying those policies and practices which create barriers to its development. Changes are made so as to overcome the barriers and employees are encouraged to track their development.

Again, this model can be criticized because it fails to recognize some of the contradictions inherent in the empowerment of employees, particularly in branded hospitality and tourism organizations. For example, many organizations that have introduced employee empowerment have done so in circumstances where the organization is making a tightly defined branded offer to its customers. In these cases, employees may be encouraged to 'delight the customer' by meeting customer service needs as they arise, but they may not do anything 'out of brand', where customers might become confused because they are getting different experiences in different establishments. In these situations empowered employees are in a difficult position and have to manage the tension inherent in their relationship to both customers and the organization.

These reservations limit the overall utility of their observations, but Conger and Kanungo do provide a model for understanding how personal efficacy might be developed at an individual level. Whilst recognizing the significance of content, theorists, in suggesting that discomfort with disempowerment may stem from inner-need states – for example, the need for power (McClelland, 1975) and the need for self-actualization (Maslow, 1954) – they look to process theory for explanations of how variations in the strengths of these needs might occur. Lawler's (1973) expectancy theory and Bandura's (1977, 1986) self-efficacy theory suggest that feelings of empowerment will develop through employees' evaluations of the situations in which they find themselves. Put simply, this assumes a two-stage process empowerment to result in changes in employee behaviour. First, the employee has to believe that their efforts will result in an improvement in their performance and, secondly, that their improved performance will produce valued outcomes.

Thomas and Velthouse (1990) also suggest that employee expectancies are likely to be key to the development of feelings of empowerment. They suggest a four-dimensional model based on a cognitive assessment of their own *competence* to operate effectively in the situation, the *impact* which they as individual employees can make to effective performance, the *meaningfulness* which they attach to the tasks which undertake as empowered employees and the *choice* which they can exercise. In other words the state of empowerment is likely to be a consequence of the individual's assessment of their ability to be effective, that they can make a difference in a task which they perceive as worthwhile, and that they have some degree of freedom to act as they see fit in the situation.

Taking these models it is possible to conceive a practical set of stages through which empowerment is achieved via progressive involvement in making decisions. Figure 15.1 below briefly summarizes the changing roles of the team leader and team member through the developmental process. Figure 15.1 provides a model of practical steps that team leaders can adopt with individuals or teams. It can be used to explain a systematic approach and, therefore, can be helpful when considering the steps needed to bring about the emotional state of empowerment through relational changes. It provides a model that can be used to show how 'empowerment' as a systematic approach needs to engage and progressively develop team members through the variety of forms of empowerment discussed earlier. In addition, this model is helpful when considering empowerment as a motivational concept aimed at individual employees in essentially command and control contexts.

Hence empowerment can be achieved without a systematic approach to empowerment. Team leaders and managers in all organizations can use the motivational concept of empowerment to bring people on and develop them to take on to make more of the

Level 1 – *Waits to be Told*

Typically the team member has never performed the task before. They wait too be told and shown how to complete the task.

The team leader is demonstrating, explaining, training and giving feedback to the employee and will be present throughout the time the task is being done.

High	Team member waits
Team member authority and responsibility	
Low	
	Team leader instructs

Level 2 – *Asks What to Do*

The team member is aware that a task needs doing or that there is a way of getting round a problem, but does not know how to do it. They ask what needs to be done and are shown the task.

The team leader is involved in demonstrating, explaining, training and giving feedback, though this would be reduced because the employee has at least a basic grasp of the issue to be undertaken.

High	Team member asks
Team member authority and responsibility	
Low	
	Team leader explains

Level 3 – *Recommends What to Do*

The team member is familiar with the job or task and is confident enough to make recommendations for correction or improvement. They are still not skilled, experienced or knowledgeable enough to take action themselves.

The team leader should now be receiving and deciding on the suggestion, getting the team member working on the task and giving feedback on their efforts, and will need to spend less time on direct supervision of their work.

High	Team member recommends
Team member authority and responsibility	
Low	
	Team leader explains

	High	Team member checks back
Level 4 – *Takes Action, Reports Immediately*		
The team member is confident and familiar with task, but will not have completed it without supervision in the past. They now need to do the task, but check back that they have done it correctly.	Team member authority and responsibility	
The team leader is confirming correct action, or preventing an action that might cause damage to the unit or a loss of confidence in the team member. Minimal supervision of the person undertaking the task.	Low	

	High	Team member reports routinely
Level 5 – *Takes Action – Reports Routinely*		
The team member is skilled, knowledgeable and confident enough to get on with the task and do whatever is needed. They will not need to inform you of their actions immediately, though will routinely report to you.	Team member authority and responsibility	
The team leader needs to provide feedback on a regular basis so that team member is informed about their progress and their motivation levels are maintained. There is virtually no direct supervision of the team member, though you will be indirectly monitoring progress.	Low	Team leader monitors progress

Figure 15.1 Five stages in individual empowerment

decisions. In many organizations, the 'one best way' approach to the service offered to customers limits the opportunities for individual flair and creativity, but the model shows that individuals can be encouraged to take on more responsibility and authority.

THE CASE OF MCDONALD'S RESTAURANTS

McDonald's Restaurants is an organization that has developed many of its managers from within the organization. Over 50 per cent of unit managers started working for the

Table 15.2 Elements of crew training in McDonald's Restaurants

Key area	Elements/OCLs
	Fries
Fried products	Fillet, pies and veg. deluxe
	Chicken products
	Buns and dressings
Grilled products	Regular grills
	Quarter grill
	Backroom
Hygiene and backroom	Hygiene and food safety
	Safety
	Direct draw
Counter and dining areas	Counter
	Dining area
	Sausage and bacon batch cooker
	Breakfast assembler
Breakfast	Hash browns and McMuffins
	Pancakes
	Scrambled eggs/round eggs
Additional training tests	Fire, health and safety test
	Health and safety
	Food hygiene test A–E

organization as crew. Even allowing for students who start working for the organization during their course and subsequently join the firm as management after their course, the number of graduates within unit management is in the order of 30 per cent. The vast majority of current management personnel have been developed through the application of a model of personal empowerment.

Crew and managers are trained to do the full range of production and service tasks in the restaurant. Although some employees have personal preferences and skills which mean they do specialized jobs either in the 'kitchen' or on the 'counter', most employees seem to like the variety which this approach to training allows. Certainly from management's perspective, functional flexibility has considerable advantages when staffing the restaurant for the extensive opening periods that are typical of most of the company's properties. One the benefits is that for some employees, expanding the range of tasks they can do is empowering. Certainly it provides an important start point in the building blocks suggested in Figure 15.1.

Training squad and floor managers have the primary responsibility for training crew at shop-floor level. Training squad are crew members who are fully trained in all the restaurant's production and service skills, as well as having successfully completed the company's 'Learning to Train' module. This module provides important guidance in training to train, and is also undertaken by all management personnel. The availability of a pathway for crew to become training squad and, ultimately floor managers, are important ingredients in the development of opportunities and ultimately personal empowerment.

After the initial probation period, the training approach involves the crew member working alongside either a training squad member or a floor manager. Initially, they are shown how to do the job and given an explanation of why the job is done that way.

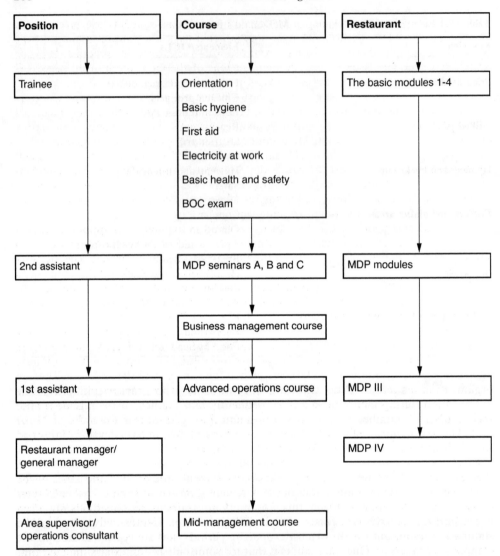

Figure 15.2 Salaried management flow chart of training

After this short introduction they work with the *trainer*, and make corrective action where needed. To be judged competent on a job the crew member has to score over 90 per cent on an Observation Check List for a specific work station. On completion of the full training programme, the crew member will have been rewarded with their five stars. Hence Five Star Crew are those members of staff who have completed the full training. Observation check lists play an important role in both defining and monitoring crew-member performance. As we have seen they are used to check competence after initial training. Observation check lists are also used to monitor employee performance in each restaurant. Every crew member should be observed against each task in each six-month period. Scores are then graded and averaged over the full range of jobs, and crew who achieve above 90 per cent in the total number of assessments are given a pay increase of up to 15p per hour. OCLs are conducted by the restaurant management's personnel, though there are some examples of variations in practice between restaurants. The key issue is that the management of the OCL monitoring process is seen as an important performance indicator of line-management performance. The process of monitoring not just employee performance but employee development gives the company an insight into the way individual managers develop their crew members and, thereby, the levels of employee empowerment. Unlike many competitor organizations, the company actively encourages managers to be developmental.

Figure 15.2 shows how the McDonald's Restaurants programme of management development matches against the career development of unit managers. This confirms the components of the development programme as comprising self-study modules, including work outputs undertaken in the restaurant, and courses requiring attendance at both the regional and national training centres.

The modules and courses track the progress of an individual from appointment as a management trainee through appointment as a second assistant, through to appointment as a first assistant and ultimately to restaurant manager. The step-by-step aspect to management development is an important feature of the company's approach to developing management talent, and in the context of this discussion, to building a personal sense of empowerment flowing from training, performance reviews and coaching from other managers.

As we have seen, unit managers are encouraged to develop and empower subordinates through the organizational hierarchy. Interviews with crew and managers reveal a common understanding that the organization offers opportunities, though, interestingly, these ambitions tend to be aimed at the next level in the structure. Thus, in response to the question 'What do you want to be doing in six months' time?' new crew wanted to achieve their 'five-star badge', Five-star crew wanted to be training squad, and they, in turn, wanted to be floor managers. Floor Managers wanted to be shift running floor managers. While all these roles are essentially undertaken by hourly-paid staff, a similar pattern emerges when interviews are undertaken with management trainees, second assistants, first assistants and unit managers.

Recent interviews with managers in the company confirm that the importance of the model of development and personal empowerment outlined in Figure 15.1 is to their own personal development. In several cases interviewees discussed individuals who been inspiring or strongly committed to developing them. Interestingly, despite the company's attempts to monitor and encourage this approach, the approach was not completely universal. There are some managers who find this approach difficult, and many crew are only interested in 'just coming in for the money'. While any large organization will have difficulty achieving consistency throughout every unit, the company's systems of monitoring, and its generally developmental culture, presents an impression shared by many organization members that it is possible to develop skills and talents through the company. Empowerment in these circumstances refers to a more internal and motivational concept than a relational one.

CONCLUSION

This chapter has argued that empowerment as a management approach to running service organizations covers different types of arrangements and different forms in practice. At root, all forms of empowerment are judged on the extent to which they produce feelings of being empowered. Indeed a common problem experienced in the practical introduction of empowerment is that mangers fail to address the development of these feelings in the supposedly empowered.

On another level, consideration of the motivational model of empowerment allows individual team leaders to consider empowering people without the introduction of empowerment as a system. Personal-development plans and the design of an organization structure that clearly demonstrates pathways to development encourage individuals to think of their future with the firm. So even where many decisions and policies are fixed at the centre, individuals can be developed and encouraged through empowerment to become more skilled and confident in themselves and in their abilities.

The systematic approach to training and development of crew, together with a clear set of stages in management development at McDonald's, provides an example of how this empowerment can take place even in an organization traditionally thought to be 'disempowering', because work systems are highly prescriptive and undertaken in 'one best way'. By seeing empowerment as chiefly a motivational concept the company has been able to develop a sense of personal efficacy and personal effectiveness that brings many grass-roots employees through to management positions.

SELF-ASSESSMENT QUESTIONS

1. Describe the differences between motivational and relational definitions of empowerment.
2. Why is feeling empowered an important defining feature of all initiatives that claim to be empowering?
3. Show how feelings of empowerment can be developed by individual managers.
4. Some people argue that command and control organizations with restricted working arrangements and job design cannot empower their employees. Do you agree? Explain why.
5. Design a management development training programme that would build skills in empowering others. What are the essential ingredients?

REFERENCES

Adelmann, M. B., Ahavia, A. and Goodwwin, C. (1994) 'Beyond Smiling: social support and service quality', in R. T. Rust and R. L. Oliver (eds), *Service Quality: New Directions in Theory and Practice*. London: Sage.

Alpander, G. (1991) 'Developing managers' ability to empower employees'. *Journal of Management*, **10**, 13–24.

Bandura, A. (1977) 'Self efficacy: towards a unifying theory of behavioural change'. *Psychological Review*, **84**, 191–215.

Bandura, A. (1986) *Social Foundations of Thought and Action: A Social-cognitive View*. Engelwood Cliffs, NJ: Prentice-Hall.

Barry, T. (1993) 'Empowerment: the US experience'. *Empowerment in Organisations*, **1**(1), 24–8.

Collins, D. (1999) 'Born to fail? Empowerment, ambiguity and set overlap'. *Personnel Review*, **28**(3), 192–207.

Conger, J. A. (1989) 'Leadership: the art of empowering others'. *Academy of Management Executive*, February, 17–24.

Conger, J. A. and Kanungo, R. B. (1988) 'The empowerment process: integrating theory and practice'. *Academy of Management Review*, **13**, 471–82.

Cunningham, I. and Hyman, J. (1999) 'The poverty of empowerment? A critical case study'. *Personnel Review*, **28**(3), 169–91.

Hochschild, A. R. (1983) *The Managed Heart: Commercialization of Human Feeling*. Berkeley, CA: University of California Press.

Holden, L. (1999) 'The perception gaps in employee empowerment: a comparative study of banks in Sweden and Britain'. *Personnel Review*, **28**(3), 222–41.

Johnson, P. R. (1993) 'Empowerment in the global economy'. *Empowerment in Organisations*, **1**(1), 13–18.

Johnson, R. and Redmond, D. (1998) *The Art of Empowerment: The Profit and Pain of Employee Involvement*. London: Pitman Publishing.

Lashley, C. (1995) 'Towards and understanding of employee empowerment in hospitality services'. *International Journal of Contemporary Hospitality Management*, **7**(1), 27–32.

Lashley, C. (1996) 'Research issues in employee empowerment in hospitality operations'. *International Journal of Hospitality Management*, **15**(4), 333–46.

Lashley, C. (1997) *Empowering Service Excellence: Beyond the Quick Fix*. London: Cassell.

Lawler, E. E. (1973) *Motivation in Work Organisations*. Monterey, CA: Brooks/Cole.

Lawler, E. E. (1986) *High Involvement Management* New York: Jossey Bass.

Lockwood, A. (1996) 'Empowerment: the key to service quality: an operations perspective'. *Conference Papers: Fifth Annual Hospitality Research Conference*. Nottingham: Nottingham Trent University.

McClelland, D. C. (1975) *Power: The Inner Experience*. New York: Irvington Press.

Marchington, M., Goodman, J., Wilkinson, A. and Ackers, P. (1992) *New Developments in Employee Involvement*. Department of Employment, Research Series No 2. Sheffield: HMSO.

Maslow, A. H. (1954) *Motivation and Personality*. New York: Harper.

Poole, M. (1986) *Towards a New Industrial Democracy: Workers Participation in Industry*. London: Routledge.

Poole, M. (1989) *The Origins of Economic Democracy*. London: Routledge.

Potterfield, T. A. (1999) *The Business of Employee Empowerment: Democracy and Ideology in the Workplace'*. Westport, CA: Quorum Books.

Sparrowe, R. T. (1994) 'Empowerment in the hospitality industry: an exploration of antecedents and outcomes'. *Hospitality Research Journal*, **17**(3), 83–98.

Thomas, K. W. and Velthouse, B. A. (1990) 'Cognitive elements of empowerment: an interpretive model of intrinsic task motivation'. *Academy of Management Review*, **15**, 666–81.

van Oudtshoorn, M. and Thomas, L. (1993) 'A management synopsis of empowerment'. *Empowerment in Organisations*, 1(1), 4–12.

16

Managing Diversity in Hospitality Organizations

Connie Mok

ABSTRACT

The globalization of businesses has created a demand for employees who understand their multicultural customers while dealing with a diverse workforce. It is estimated that by the year 2000 multinational corporations will control approximately half of the world's assets (Dulek *et al.*, 1991). In the twenty-first century, organizations will continue to face the diversity challenge inherent in their employee and customer populations. Today's workforce does not look or act like the workforce of the past, nor does it hold the same values, have the same experiences or pursue the same needs and wants. The workforce has changed significantly in terms of age, gender, culture, education, disabilities and values. As a result, interest and concern in managing workforce diversity has grown steadily over the past decade. The objectives of this chapter are to examine the theoretical concepts of workforce diversity, to consider the implications of diversity for hospitality and tourism organizations and to report the different approaches used by international hospitality organizations to manage diversity (best practices), which is supported by a case study.

INTRODUCTION

Rick Jones has been managing hotel chains for years, yet only recently has he begun managing people from different ethnic origins and older workers. He is a fair person, but has problems relating to some of his employees. Recently, some staff complained to his boss about his management style. He doesn't know what this means. He is torn between requests for transfers, hours and time off, different work assignments, and his company policies which he tries to uphold.

This is a common scenario in organizations today. We may see a mismatch between what a company offers and what people want. Managers have to do their best to represent the organization, even when they know that the organization is out of step with the needs of its employees. Although they have some control over what the organization does, they are often constrained by outdated policies and management systems. There is no doubt that managers are faced with constant challenges, but as the workforce becomes more diverse, the 'management' challenge is more pressing than ever.

The globalization of businesses has created a demand for employees who understand their multicultural customers while dealing with a diverse workforce. It is estimated that by the year 2000, multinational corporations will control approximately half of the world's assets (Dulek *et al.*, 1991). A vast majority of the companies that we identify as American companies such as McDonald's, Wendy's, Holiday Inns and others may saturate the American market but may no longer be domestic companies. Holiday Inns, for example, entered the European market in 1968 and the Asian market in 1973. Globalization of the hotel industry has continued since that time and has greatly increased over the last ten years. Whether multinational enterprises (MNEs) are driven by resource, market or efficiency objectives, an inevitable consequence of having operations in multiple countries is greater workforce diversity.

In the twenty-first century, organizations will continue to face the diversity challenge inherent in their employee and customer populations. Today's workforce doesn't look or act like the workforce of the past, nor does it hold the same values, have the same experiences or pursue the same needs and wants. The workforce has changed significantly in terms of age, gender, culture, education, disabilities and values.

For instance, in the United States the three largest minority groups, African American, Hispanics, and Asian Americans/Pacific Islanders, make up over 26 per cent of the population. This figure will grow to 36 per cent by 2020 and to 47 per cent by 2050, according to the recent census projections (Nykiel, 1998). Since the Hudson Institute's Workforce 2000 report (Johnson and Packer, 1987), it is widely accepted that women, people of colour, and immigrants now constitute the majority of new workforce entrants and will continue to represent an increasingly larger portion of the workforce in America. These demographic trends, coupled with the ageing of the population and the passage of the American Disabilities Act, will produce a dramatically more diverse workforce and present new opportunities and challenges for American managers (McKendall, 1994; Cox and Blake, 1991). As a result, interest and concern in managing workforce diversity has grown steadily over the past decade, which can be witnessed by the amount of published information on the topic. In 1994 alone, 23 articles on diversity were published in three leading hospitality journals (Woods and Sciarini, 1995).

The purpose of this chapter is to consider the implications of diversity for hospitality and tourism organizations and to examine the different approaches to manage diversity effectively. More specifically, the objectives of the chapter are:

- to define diversity and its theoretical underpinnings;
- to examine the organizational implications of diversity;
- to discuss the different approaches used by international hospitality organizations to manage diversity; and
- to examine the best practices for diversity management which are then supported by an international case study.

DIVERSITY: A THEORETICAL PERSPECTIVE

The literature tends to define diversity as the differences among people (Cox 1993; Cross *et al.*, 1994). Generally, 'diversity' refers to gender and race differences among people. But in regard to an organization's workforce, the term encompasses other important differences, or dimensions, as well. According to Reece and Brandt (1996), there are primary and secondary dimensions of diversity, in other words, characteristics that describe people. The primary dimensions are those core elements about each individual that do not change, such as age, gender, race, physical traits and sexual orientation. Together they form an individual's self-image and the filters through which she or he views the rest of the world. These inborn elements do not stand alone; they are interdependent. Each exerts an important influence throughout life. The greater the number of primary differences between people, the more difficult it is to establish trust and mutual respect. Culture clash – conflicts that occur between groups of people with different core identities – can have a negative effect on human relations in an organization. There are few organizations that are immune to the problems that result from the interaction between the sexes and among the races and the generations. When primary dimensions are added to secondary dimensions of diversity, effective human relations become even more difficult (Mok and Noriega, 1999).

The secondary dimensions of diversity are those elements that can be changed or at least modified. They include a person's communication style, education, relationship/ marital status, parental status, religious beliefs, work experience and income. These factors all add an additional layer of complexity to the way people see themselves and others and in some instances, can exert a powerful impact on core identities. A recent vocational-technical school graduate may have far different expectations from a four-year-college graduate. Even though specific situations might intensify the impact of particular secondary dimensions, they do not diminish the primary impact of core dimensions. Instead, they add depth to the individual. This interaction between primary and secondary dimensions shapes a person's values, priorities and perceptions throughout life (Reece and Brandt, 1996). For the purpose of this chapter, diversity is defined as those primary and secondary dimensions as described in Figure 16.1 which make people uniquely different (*ibid.*).

It is these secondary dimensions that educators and managers will have to prepare the workforce to deal with in the global marketplace. In the 1980s, Shames (1986) and Tanke (1988) emphasized the importance of staffing the hospitality and tourism industry with multilingual and multicultural employees who possess a combination of foreign-language abilities and cultural awareness. The idea that multilingual employees will be able to satisfy all of the needs of customers is not sustainable. Additionally, with the complexity of multicultural backgrounds, cultural awareness alone will not account for other aspects of the secondary dimensions of diversity. It is the adjustments and understanding of these secondary dimensions that present an ongoing problem. McKendall (1994) discussed a programme that was developed to deal with issues of diversity, but she stated that she also chose to deal with the primary dimensions of diversity. She found that during discussions, the issues of age and generational diversity produced an interaction, but relatively neutral reaction. It is the differences of the secondary dimension that will stimulate interest.

The primary and secondary dimensions illustrate why diversity training is not another form of dealing with affirmative action. The 1964 Civil Rights Act established affirmative action and the cases brought forth have dealt mainly with the primary

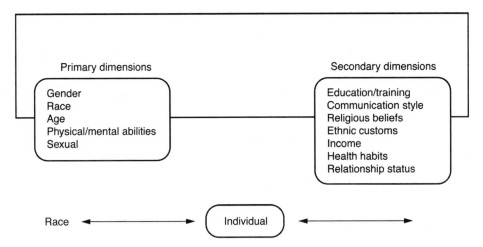

Figure 16.1 Dimensions of diversity

Source: Reece, L. B. and Brandt, R. (1996) *Effective Human Relations in Organization*. Boston: Houghton Mifflin, 411–38.

dimensions of diversity, as these core elements were seen as permanent factors. Diversity training is a means of establishing respect and developing sensitivity for all of the differences among employees and customers. Reducing cultural myopia and ethnocentrism in employees, so they may interact more favorably with employees and customers, is essential in developing a diverse workforce. For companies to be competitive in the global marketplace, organizations will have to orient themselves toward these secondary issues.

Pannell Kerr Forster (PKF) Consulting, an international hospitality consulting firm headquartered in San Francisco, completed a survey of human resource issues in the United States hotel industry in 1996. Based on a survey of 535 hotels across the US, the study concentrated on such issues as diversity in the workforce, employee recruitment and retention, and performance-reward systems. The purpose of the survey was to provide the industry with a snapshot of its workforce. Diversified workforce immigration is an issue that not only makes political headlines, but presents a distinct challenge to business owners and operators (www.hotel-online.com/Neo/Trends/PKF/Special/Diverse_Workforce.html). It was found that the average hotel has 5.2 nationalities represented in its workforce. With more than 50 per cent of the surveyed hotels having four or more nationalities in the workforce, balancing the variety of customs, holidays and value systems of multiple nationalities is quite a challenge for supervisors and managers. Diversity also means a multilingual workforce. The majority of hotel employees speak English as their first language; however, 23 per cent of the employees surveyed speak English as their second language. The results of this survey show that embracing diversity in the workforce is not a choice but a necessity.

MANAGING DIVERSITY FOR COMPETITIVE ADVANTAGE

Workforce diversity can be a source of strength for hospitality organizations if the organization manages that diversity effectively (Christensen-Hughes, 1992). Research shows that the more varied the group, the more diverse their ideas, attitudes and approaches, the better the decision-making capacity, and the more solid and reliable the results (Lebo, 1996; Morrison, 1992; Nykiel, 2000). Various studies have reported benefits from managing diversity (Morrison, 1992; Cox and Blake, 1991; Jafari and Way, 1995).

Cox and Blake (1991) identified six diversity factors where sound management can create a competitive advantage as noted below.

1. Cost. Research findings show that workforce diversity has a negative effect on labor turnover, absenteeism, and job satisfaction. Nevertheless, several studies reported that sound diversity management efforts have reduced absenteeism and turnover costs (Youngblood and Chambers-Cook, 1984; Kim and Campagna, 1981; Darmon, 1990). Companies that handle diversity well will thus create cost advantages over those who do not.
2. Resource Acquisition. With increasing representation of minority groups in the workforce, companies must compete to hire and retain workers from these groups. Some companies are identified as the 'best companies' for women and ethnic minorities. These companies are likely to win the competition for the best personnel.
3. Marketing. Intercontinental and cross-border tourism traffic continues to grow along with the global economy. Our customers are becoming as diverse as the workforce. Enhancing the quality of our product and service offerings begins with the link to diversity. Members of a given cultural group are in a better position to understand the needs and preferences of customers from their own group. A culturally diverse workforce represents a possible advantage in competing in the global marketplace if cultural diversity is managed well.
4. Creativity. Research results show that workforce heterogeneity promotes creativity and innovation. Mixed sexes and personalities seem to have freed groups from the restraints of the solutions given in the problem. The most innovative companies purposely establish heterogeneous teams to create a marketplace of ideas.
5. Problem Solving. Studies also show that a culturally diverse workforce creates a competitive advantage by making decisions of higher quality. Diverse work groups provide a larger number of alternatives, higher level of critical analysis, and lower probability of groupthink.
6. System Fexibility. Research found a significant relationship between gender and tolerance for ambiguity. Tolerance for ambiguity in turn, was found to be related to cognitive complexity and ability to excel in performing ambiguous tasks. Bilinguals have higher levels of divergent thinking and of cognitive flexibility. Organizational openness to diverse cultural viewpoints is a critical first step to overcoming resistance to change.

APPROACHES TO DIVERSITY MANAGEMENT

The Investors' Diversified Services (IDS) of the American Express Financial Corporation conducted a study to identify best diversity management practices among 32 benchmark companies, including fast-food and services companies. The study was an attempt to benchmark a specific work process for themselves and other companies. IDS, in designing a diversity enhancement effort, wanted to benefit from the experience of other organizations to avoid 'reinventing the wheel' (IDS, 1997). IDS reported detailed information gathered from their benchmark partners, but four success factors for enhancing diversity kept resurfacing from various organizations during their study processes. They named these factors 'key best practices':

- Building knowledge and skill training for enhancing diversity.
- Providing information and resources to assist in the process.
- Possessing top-down/bottom-up leadership influence for support.
- Establishing incentives and accountability to support initiatives.

IDS also identified five 'prescriptions' for the successful enhancement of diversity within an organization:

- Accepting diversity as a management and strategic planning opportunity.
- Assessing diversity-related needs and concerns and developing action plans with support to address and resolve them.
- Providing diversity awareness, training and education to support desired goals and objectives.
- Being willing to revamp policies, systems and practices as needed to enhance diversity.
- Providing for and assuring necessary reinforcement and accountability in diversity areas.

As IDS identified the strengths of their benchmark partners, they aligned their findings with their own diversity business strategy, which groups such strengths into four categories they call 'LEAD': Leadership, Environment, Acquisition, Delivery. Each of these is outlined below.

Leadership

Among the benchmark partners, a top-down commitment to put diversity in the forefront of corporate posture is loud and clear. The senior managers' personal commitment to diversity is regularly and forcefully communicated to all the staff in the company. All senior management personnel are required to go through diversity training and the monitoring and control is decentralized. In fact, diversity training is mandatory for all employees, and each business unit goes through training as a group. One of the most important components of the training is to create long-term diversity goals for the units.

Environment

An environment to promote and foster diversity is created in benchmark partner companies. Some of the practices for creating such an environment include:

- Management bonus pay is tied to diversity improvement criteria.
- A newsletter reporting management practices for conducting business in the global age is published and circulated. This provides an excellent communication vehicle

and keeps the opportunity of diversity in front of all employees.

- A question-and-answer brochure on diversity was published and distributed. This helps employees understand the inclusive nature of a broad definition of diversity, communicates the extent of company commitment to diversity; provides examples of how to handle selected situations; and answers questions typically asked.
- Guiding principles for diversity are provided to management and employees. This is a simple communication that provides a rationale for supporting diversity.
- Sales brochures are printed in a second language to assist representatives in the sales process.
- A one-day awareness programme about the value of human diversity is provided to all employees.
- Diversity is on the agenda of every quarterly sales meeting. This keeps diversity in front and illustrates to employees that it should be considered a business issue like any other business issue.
- A diversity department was established, consisting of complaint management, EEO/Affirmative Action compliance programmes, and diversity administration and development.
- Business units prepare an 'organizational audit' each year that includes several indicators including financial performance, diversity measures and other people management indicators.
- In any diversity activity, the white maleism issue was addressed immediately. White males should not feel left out.

Acquisition

Various conscious efforts to facilitate minority recruitment are exerted. Companies establish relationships with colleges to support minority recruitment and a specific budget is allocated for this purpose. Such efforts range from organizing retreats between faculty members and employees to help raise awareness of diversity issues, to offering internship programmes that match people with interests for six months.

Delivery

To facilitate the successful implementation of diversity policies, benchmark partner companies used various forms of incentives, rewards for executives, retention methods and awards. For example, an award system was developed for diversity management. This award acts as an incentive and recognition for employees who promote diversity initiatives at a local level. The award is considered to be very prestigious within the company, and keeps the diversity issue in front of the employees. Management-level bonus criteria include diversity efforts. Managers must show expertise or growth in all areas to get 100 per cent of the bonus. The evaluation doesn't focus only on numbers, but also on environment, attitude, turnover etc. Expectations are set up front, so there are no surprises at review time. Succession planning is used to identify management subordinates who show talent for moving to a higher level position in company. Succession planning is also used to monitor the progression of minorities and women into greater levels of responsibilities.

MARRIOTT INTERNATIONAL INC.

An Overview

The Marriott International Inc. can be considered to have the broadest portfolio of hospitality brands in the world. It operates a diversified portfolio of lodging brands – from luxury to economy, and from extended stay to resort timesharing. Marriott is also recognized as a symbol of quality and consistency in senior living and distribution services. Marriott International has over 1900 operating units in the United States and 58 other countries and territories. Marriott Lodging operates and franchises hotels under the Marriott, Ritz-Carlton, Renaissance, Residence Inn, Courtyard, Fairfield Inn, Spring Hill Suites, Ramada International and Towne Place Suites brand names; develops and operates vacation ownership (timeshare) resorts under the Marriott, Ritz-Carlton and Horizon brands; operates executive apartments and conference centres; and provides furnished corporate housing through its ExecuStay by Marriott division. Other Marriott businesses include Brighton Gardens Assisted Living, Maple Ridge Assisted Living Community, Village Oaks Assisted Living, Marriott Distribution Services and The Marketplace Marriott. The company is headquartered in Washington, D.C., and has approximately 143,000 employees. In the fiscal year 1999, Marriott International reported total sales of US$8.7 billion.

Today's Marriott International is the product of a metamorphosis, which began more than fifteen years ago. The evolution of Marriott from a broadly diversified service company in the early 1980s to a worldwide hospitality leader of the late 1990s can be illustrated by looking at five major trends which define the organization:

- segmentation of the hotel business;
- the globalization of Marriott Lodging;
- meeting the changing needs of our guests;
- extending Marriott hospitality to the seniors' market; and
- turning support functions into business opportunities.

Marriott International opened their first international hotel in 1969 in Acapulco, Mexico, but twenty years later, when it reached the 500-hotel milestone, only fifteen of its properties were located outside the United States. During the past ten years, Marriott International has transformed itself from a predominantly US hotel chain to a truly global lodging organization. They recently opened their 250th international property, and now have nearly 67,500 hotel rooms and timesharing villas outside the United States.

In November 1999, it was announced that Marriott International planned to accelerate its worldwide presence by adding 1000 hotels and 175,000 new rooms across its global portfolio of brands by 2003. They expect to manage and franchise a hotel in every gateway city in the world and in 70 countries within the next five years, bringing their system-wide total to 2600 hotels and 480,000 rooms by 2003.

'One of the Best Companies to Work for': A Chronology

In August 1997, Marriott International hosted a day-long career fair at the Chicago

Marriott-Downtown. The company was looking to fill 400 job openings at Marriott properties within the Chicago metropolitan area. These openings included entry- and management-level employment opportunities in areas such as sales, dietary planning, administration and maintenance. Marriott officials hoped that the Chicago Career Fair would be especially effective in attracting a more culturally and ethnically diverse group of applicants than had been previously attracted through the hospitality industry's standard personnel recruitment initiatives. The Vice-President for diversity relations at the Washington, D.C.-based Marriott International stated:

> Our Chicago Career Fair is a key component of Marriott's efforts to ensure that we retain a diverse workforce. In addition to recruitment efforts, here and around the country, Marriott Lodging established, more than five years ago, a Customer Diversity Council comprised of representatives from our customer base. The group provides counsel and feedback to assist our ongoing diversity initiatives.

In July 1998, Marriott International was ranked fifth in *Fortune* magazine's survey of the 50 Best Companies for Asian, Blacks and Hispanics. Marriott responded to the survey results saying, 'Marriott International continues to focus on diversity as a strategic imperative. We have a policy of opportunity deeply embedded in our corporate culture, and Marriott's top management is fully committed to our company's broad diversity initiatives.' At the typical 'best' company, minorities account for 11.7 per cent of the board, 7.6 per cent of corporate officers, 13.9 per cent of officials and managers, 7.2 per cent of the 25 highest-paid employees, 24.9 per cent of the total workforce, and 23.8 per cent of new hires. Charity donations to programmes that primarily benefit minorities average 35.3 per cent and 4.4 per cent of purchasing is done with minority-owned suppliers (www.hotel-online.com/Neo/News/1998_July_14/p.14n.900439094.html).

In September 1998, Marriott International opened the Marriott Employment Center (MEC) in downtown Washington, D.C. The Center expects to fill up to 5000 positions annually throughout the district. Working with local community groups, the MEC recruits, screens and places employees in new and vacant positions in the 127 Marriott International and related businesses in the area. First introduced as a pilot in the Boston area in 1997 (and then in Phoenix in January 1998), the Washington, D.C. Center will serve as the prototype for new Centers planned for Baltimore, Dallas, Orlando, Detroit and Philadelphia. Marriott International believes MECs will help fuel business growth, employment and career opportunities by matching potential associates with available positions more effectively and efficiently.

In September 1999, Marriott International had, for the ninth time, been named one of the '100 Best Companies for Working Mothers', according to the September issue of *Working Mother* magazine. In fact, Marriott is the only hospitality company to be recognized by *Working Mother*. The publication spotlights outstanding workplaces for women and tracks family-friendly workplace trends. *Working Mother* especially recognized Marriott's first-ever Woman's Leadership Conference, the establishment of a Leadership Development Initiative, including a specific focus on women and minority development, and the company's launch of several new projects to promote flexibility in the workplace. Marriott's Work-Life Initiatives began in 1990 to help Marriott employees pursue careers while balancing the demands of their personal lives. The programmes include financial support through a family care spending account, childcare discounts, education and training for employees, an on-site child development centre, referral services for child-, elder- and family-care issues, and assistance for the company's low-income employees. One of Marriott's most innovative Work-Life programmes is the Marriott Associate Resource Line, which provides confidential counselling through a one-stop resource that can address a wide range of personal issues. The nationwide toll-free Associate Resource Line, staffed by social workers, is available in more than 150 languages to all Marriott employees.

In October 1999, Marriott International was selected to receive the 1999 Corporate Leadership Award from the Terri Lynne Lokoff Child Care Foundation. The Foundation honors Marriott for its innovative programmes on behalf of quality childcare and the needs of working parents. Marriott established an on-site childcare centre at its Washington, D.C. corporate headquarters in 1993. The company also established a childcare centre in Atlanta for lower-income families as a way to reinforce its commitment to the community, and will shortly open another in Washington, D.C. In addition to flexible work schedules and family care leave, Marriott offers the following innovative programmes:

- resource and referral service for childcare solutions at all of its lodging properties;
- associate resource line for all employee families;
- childcare Discount Programme that offers a 10 per cent discount at 4000 centres across the US;
- baby club, offering childcare products to employees at below-wholesale prices;
- family care spending account programme, which give employees tax-free credit on US$5000 for childcare, parenting and family education video programmes;
- management training on work/family issues; and
- Marriott Family Services Fund, which provides grants to local non-profits that are effective in helping employee families find support with such issues as childcare, elder care, housing and transportation.

Also in October 1999, Marriott International was named 'best' in the lodging industry for delivering excellence to guests, employees and investors, according to a survey called, American Lodging Excellence: The Key to Best Practices in the U.S. Lodging Industry. The study was funded by American Express in partnership with the American Hotel Foundation. One of Marriott's best awards include Overall Best-Practice Individual Champion in Corporate Management: J.W. Marriott, Jr who was recognized for his care for the guests, employees and owner, development and franchisee relationships. He was also commended for his ability to challenge and encourage his employees to always improve the level of service and guests, stating that 'success is never final'.

In December 1999, Marriott International was named as one of the '100 Best Companies to Work for in America' by *Fortune* according to the 10 January issue of the magazine. Marriott was named to the *Fortune* list for the third year in a row. The list was compiled through a poll of more than 33,400 randomly selected employees at hundreds of companies nationwide. Marriott International's Executive Vice President, Human Resources responded, saying, 'We are proud of our associates' ongoing commitment to service excellence. In addition, we are pleased that we can make a difference in the quality of their worklife.'

In March 2000, Marriott International was selected for inclusion in *Hispanic* magazine's new list: the '2000 Hispanic Corporate 100'. *Hispanic* cited the company's efforts to provide opportunities for Hispanics and contributions toward the advancement of the Hispanic community in the areas of recruitment, scholarships and minority vendor programmes. Marriott's Senior Vice-President, Staffing and Development, noted that, 'Marriott International's top leadership is committed to minority community outreach as an integral part of the company's business strategy. This is reflected by our support of such organizations as the National Council of La Raza, the United States Hispanic Chamber of Commerce, and the Hispanic College Fund.'

In March 2000, Sodexho Marriott Services, North America's largest provider of outsourced food and facilities management, donated $20,000 to the Multicultural Foodservice Hospitality Association (MFHA). MFHA is a non-profit organization committed to being a resource on multicultural diversity issues for the restaurant, food-service and hospitality industries. Sodexho Marriott Services' sponsorship demonstrates their commitment to multicultural diversity. Through this kind of support, Marriott is able to better leverage the economic benefits of diversity in the food-service and hospitality industries, helping to recruit and retain talented workers with diverse backgrounds.

DISCUSSION AND CONCLUSIONS

The above case study describes the mission and management philosophy of Marriott International, Inc. and provides a sample of the company's events and human resource management practices in chronological order. The purpose of the case study is to illustrate some of the diversity management practices that Marriott adopted, which make it one of the best companies to work for in the eyes of the employees and business community. It shows that a company that embraces and practices diversity management effectively could achieve excellence not only in service quality but also in worklife quality for its employees. Having knowledge of Marriott International's innovative initiatives to promote diversity among its workforce, it is useful to take at look at how they contrast with the traditional human resource management practices.

Companies that emphasize efficiency and mass production characterize the traditional model for running a business. The traditional model considers diversity to be a condition that should be avoided because it creates uncertainty, and interferes with smooth, predictable, and low-cost operations. The traditional model minimizes diversity among employees in a number of ways: recruiting practices emphasize finding candidates from sources that have proven to be 'reliable' in the past; selection processes emphasize filling positions with candidates who are similar to those who have succeeded in the past and screen out entry-level applicants and promotion candidates who appear to not 'fit' the organization's style; socialization and training programmes intended to produce uniform ways of thinking and behaving; attendance policies to standardize and regulate the scheduling of work; and, by relying on a centralized, bureaucratic approach to managing the workforce, the traditional model intentionally limits the discretionary latitude given to supervisors and managers for handling the special needs of individual employees. human resources management practices such as these evolved over time because they fit the needs of many organizations (Jackson, 1992; Johnson and Packer, 1987). As mentioned earlier in this chapter, quite a number of scientific studies document the fact that some types of diversity can enhance creative problem-solving. Many managers realize that creative problem-solving and flexibility are required of any organization that must continually adapt to a changing environment. For this reason, executives intentionally design some types of diversity into their top management teams. In organizations that value creativity and flexibility over bureaucratic efficiency, it seems reasonable to expect that initiatives aimed at supporting workforce diversity may meet relatively less resistance.

If a flexible management concept is appealing, why is it that more organizations have not adopted it? The reason is that change is never easy and it must contend with existing barriers. Jackson (1992) suggested that there are four simple principles that should guide change processes related to working through diversity:

1. develop a comprehensive understanding of the issue of diversity;
2. stay close to the customers throughout all phases of the process;
3. be prepared to deal with the possible problems that may arise as new initiatives are introduced; and
4. institutionalize the organizational learning that occurs.

Although these principles could easily apply to any organization, the most effective approach is likely to differ from one organization to the next. Those companies wishing to improve an organization's effectiveness must be willing to learn as they go.

It is evident from the amount of literature concerning diversity that the move toward a global market-place and the need to maintain a competitive strategy dictates that employees must be able to conduct business in the increasingly diverse market-place. For a significant foundation to be laid, the process should initially take place in the academic environment. However, both academics and industry must be responsible for this education as feedback is needed from industry to determine if the education is successful. Since the need for diversity training and changes in organizational policies must come from the top, educational programmes in the hospitality field supply an ideal forum for implementing the concerns for this education.

Diversity is a complex and topical issue with many facets, yet relatively little is known about the most effective ways to work through diversity in hospitality organizations. The concern shown for diversity awareness and management calls for an industry-wide action plan for training personnel to appreciate and effectively manage diversity. As hospitality and tourism educators or industry practitioners, it is time to seriously consider how we can contribute to this industry-wide agenda.

SELF-ASSESSMENT QUESTIONS

1. What are the major diversity challenges that face hospitality organizations today?
2. What are the primary and secondary dimensions of diversity and how are they different?
3. Why is effective diversity management important to today's hospitality organizations?
4. What are the six diversity factors where sound management can create a competitive advantage?
5. Summarize the various approaches to diversity management.
6. Identify the key diversity practices of Marriott International, Inc. that make it one of the best lodging companies to work for.

REFERENCES

Christensen-Hughes, J. (1992) 'Cultural diversity: the lesson of Toronto's hotels'. *The Cornell H.R.A. Quarterly*, **33**(2), 78–87.

Cox, T. H. (1993) *Cultural Diversity in Organizations: Theory, Research and Practices*. San Francisco, CA: Berrett-Koehler Publishers.

Cox, T. H. and Blake, S. (1991) 'Managing cultural diversity: implications for organizational competitiveness'. *Academy of Management Executive*, **5**(3), 45–56.

Cross, E. Y., Datz, J. H., Miller, F. and Seashore, E. W. (1994) *The Promise of Diversity*. Burr Ridge, IL: Irwin.

Darmon, R. (1990) 'Identifying sources of turnover costs'. *Journal of Marketing*, **54**, 46–56.

Dulek, R. E., Fielden, J. S. and Hill, J. S. (1991) 'International communication: An executive primer'. *Business Horizons*, **10**, 20–5.

Investors' Diversified Services (IDS) (1997) *Diversity: Report to Benchmark Partners*. Minneapolis, MN: American Express Financial Advisors.

Jackson, S. E. (1992) *Diversity in the Workplace: Human Resources Initiatives*. New York: The Guilford Press.

Jafari, J. and Way, W. (1995) 'Multicultural strategies in tourism'. *Cornell H.R.A. Quarterly*, December, 72–9.

Johnson, W. and Packer, A. (1987) *Workforce 2000: Work and Workers for the 21st Century*. Indianapolis, IN: Hudson Institute.

Kim, J. S. and Campagna, A. F. (1981) 'Effects of flexitime on employee attendance and performance: a field experiment'. *Academy of Management Journal*, December, 729–41.

Lebo, F. (1996) *Mastering the Diversity Challenge*. Delray Beach, FL: St Lucie Press.

McKendall, M. (1994) 'A course in "work-force diversity": strategies and issues'. *Journal of Management Education*, **18**(4), 407–23.

Mok, C. and Noriega, P. (1999) 'Towards a cross-cultural diversity perspective in hospitality curriculum development'. *Journal of Hospitality and Tourism Education*, **11**(1), 30–4.

Morrison, A. (1992) *The New Leaders: Guidelines on Leadership Diversity in America*. San Francisco, CA: Jossey-Bass.

Nykiel, R. A. (1998) 'Managing in the multicultural millennium'. *The Consortium Journal*, **2**(1), 81–8.

Nykiel, R. A. (2000) 'The perception and realities of diversity in the 21st century'. *The Consortium Journal*, **4**(1), 73–7.

Reece, L. B. and Brandt, R. (1996) *Effective Human Relations in Organizations*. Boston: Houghton Mifflin, pp. 411–38.

Shames, G. (1986) 'Training for the multicultural workplace'. *Cornell H.R.A. Quarterly*, February, 25–31.

Tanke, M. L. (1988) 'Course design for multicultural management'. *Cornell H.R.A. Quarterly*, August, 67–8.

Woods, R. H. and Sciarini, M. P. (1995) 'Diversity programs in chain restaurants'. *Cornell H.R.A. Quarterly*, 18–23, June.

www.hotel-online.com/Neo/Trends/PKF/Special/Diverse Workforce.htm

www.hotel-online.com/Neo/News/1998_July_14/p.14n.900439094.html

Youngblood, S. A. and Chambers-Cook, K. (1984) 'Child care assistance can improve employee attitudes and behavior'. *Personnel Administrator*, February, 93–5.

17

Hospitality and Emotional Labour in an International Context

Shirley Chappel

ABSTRACT

A major feature of the hospitality workplace is the encounter between the server and the served. In these encounters hospitality employees perform emotional labour. Through the performance of emotional labour, hospitality employees seek to convey a desirable image designed to please the customers. Employees must manage their feelings to achieve the desirable image. This product of emotional labour has an exchange value. Customers buy it, businesses sell it and employees earn wages for producing it. In international hospitality settings, the host–guest encounter brings together people of different cultures with different perspectives on service provision and the public display of emotion. Differences in cultural identity have the potential for causing misunderstanding in such encounters. The challenge to human resource managers in the international hospitality industry, discussed in this chapter, is to determine the best ways to achieve quality service encounters that take account of cultural identity.

INTRODUCTION

Aims and Objectives

The chapter will:

- define the term 'emotional labour';
- examine the role and importance of emotional labour in hospitality workplace settings;

- discuss the ways in which emotional labour in hospitality settings resembles a dramatic performance;
- explore the likely impact of cultural identity on the performance of emotional labour;
- evaluate the consequences of emotional labour for hospitality employees; and
- determine the ways in which human resource managers can ensure the appropriate performance of emotional labour in international hospitality settings.

Context

The Hospitality Service Encounter

The hospitality service encounter is the meeting between the server and the served. In the hotel dining-room, for example, the waiter and the guest engage in the hospitality service encounter. According to Powers (1992, p. 418), the provision of service 'is made up of transactions that are numerous, diverse, and often private'. They are often beyond the watchful eye of the supervisor. Each server–guest interaction is 'a separate unique event' (*ibid.*). Such interactions take place in 'a particular workplace geography, involving spatial and temporal co-presence of producers and consumers' (Crang 1997, p. 139). Because the producer of the service (the waiter) is in the same space at the same time with the consumer of the service (the guest), the producer cannot afford to make mistakes. As Powers puts it, 'there can be no recall of a defective product' (1992, p. 408). Jan Carlzon (1987, p. 2) describes the interaction between service providers and service recipients as 'moments of truth' and asserts that such moments determine the success or failure of a business enterprise. The challenge for the hospitality industry is to ensure that the 'moments of truth' are a positive experience for the recipients of the service.

Service Quality

Parasuraman (1995, p. 143) defines service quality as 'the degree and direction of discrepancy between customers' service perceptions and expectations'. With fellow researchers Zeithaml and Berry (cited in Parasuraman, p. 145), he proposed that perception of quality is 'posited along a continuum ranging from ideal quality to totally unacceptable quality with some point along the continuum representing satisfactory quality'. The perception of quality is context-specific. According to Mars and Nicod (1984, p. 28): 'In a transport café [the perception of quality] can mean no more than passing the sauce bottle with a smile. In the Savoy it might mean making prodigious efforts to supply a rare delicacy or indulging a customer's particular preference or foible.'

To measure service quality Parasuraman *et al.* (PZB) developed the SERVQUAL model that, after some refinement, consisted of five dimensions of quality as follows:

TANGIBLES	Appearance of physical facilities; equipment; personnel
RELIABILITY	Ability to perform the promised service dependably and accurately
RESPONSIVENESS	Willingness to help customers and provide prompt service

ASSURANCE   Knowledge and courtesy of employees and their ability to
                   inspire trust and confidence; trustworthiness, believability and
                   honesty
EMPATHY   Caring, individualized attention to customers; approachabil-
                   ity and ease of contact; keeping customers informed in
                   language they understand; listening to customers; making the
                   effort to know customers and their needs; recognizing regular
                   customers.
                                   (Adapted from Parasuraman, 1995, pp. 146–7)

In developing the SERVQUAL instrument, PZB conducted focus-group interviews
with customers in retail banking, credit card, stock brokerage, and appliance repair and
maintenance service sectors. They concluded, however, that the results of their research
showed that, 'regardless of the type of service being considered, consumers used similar
criteria to determine service quality' (cited in Lam *et al.*, 1998, p. 30). A decade after
reaching this conclusion, Parasuraman (1995, p. 150) indicated that 'SERVQUAL is
not a panacea for all service-quality measurement problems, nor should it be treated by
companies as the *sole* basis for assessing service quality'. By that time, however,
SERVQUAL's acceptability across the service sectors had been indicated by its use in a
diversity of service industries, including hotels, airlines, restaurants, the club industry
and ski areas (Lam *et al.*, 1998, p. 31). SERVQUAL's applicability to the hospitality
industry is obvious from an examination of the descriptors for the five dimensions of
the SERVQUAL model.

The SERVQUAL model demonstrates the importance of both tangible and
intangible services in the achievement of service quality. The waiter must not only be
technically competent in the performance of tangible service skills such as serving the
wine but must also perform the skills in an emotionally appropriate manner. In the
SERVQUAL descriptors of empathy, the emotional dimension is captured in words
such as 'caring', approachability' and 'ease of contact'.

The Cultural Dimension

In recent years scholars have given considerable attention to the important role of
culture in human affairs. Social psychologist Geert Hofstede (1991, p. 5), describes
culture as 'the collective programming of the mind which distinguishes the members of
one group or category of people from another'. The programming involves the
establishment within the person of 'patterns of thinking, feeling and potential acting'
that Hofstede calls 'the software of the mind' (*ibid.*, p. 4). Besides belonging to cultural
groups people are also unique personalities. Uniqueness does not, however, diminish
the importance of culture. According to Singer (1987, p. 53), 'uniqueness does know
bounds'. Culture sets the bounds for the groups with which individuals identify. In
international hospitality settings the server and the served bring to the service encounter
their own cultural identities that may affect their attitudes to service provision and the
public display of emotion.

EMOTIONAL LABOUR

Since the publication of Arlie Hochschild's seminal work *The Managed Heart: Commercialization of Human Feeling* in 1983, researchers have given some attention to emotional labour in the hospitality industry. Hochschild (1983, p. 7) defines emotional labour as 'the management of feeling to create a publicly observable facial and bodily display; emotional labour is sold for a wage and therefore has exchange value'. According to Hochschild (p. 7), the performance of emotional labour 'requires one to induce or suppress feeling in order to sustain the outward countenance that produces the proper state of mind in others'. The attentive bartender, for example, listens sympathetically to the unhappy drunk who needs a shoulder to cry on because his wife and children have just deserted him. Privately, the bartender impatiently waits for his shift to end so that he can get away from the maudlin outpourings of his inebriated customer. Until that happens his 'publicly observable facial and bodily display', combined with the appropriate tone of voice must convey sympathy to his unhappy customer. It is part of the job for which he receives his wages.

According to Hochschild, emotional labourers perform their work by means of surface and deep acting. Surface acting involves using facial expressions, gestures and voice tone to convey a socially appropriate image. The bartender mentioned in the previous paragraph is performing surface acting. Surface actors pretend to feel emotions they do not really feel. They may deceive others about the way they really feel but they do not deceive themselves. The waiter's smile is part of the waiter's make-up for the performance. Surface acting is a body-language performance. 'The body, not the soul, is the main tool of the trade' (p. 37). The surface actor may or may not be particularly concerned with the customer's welfare (Ashforth and Humphrey, 1993).

In deep acting, according to Hochschild (1983, p. 35), 'the actor does not try to *seem* happy or sad but rather expresses spontaneously ... a real feeling that has been self-induced'. Deep acting goes well beyond a smile or expression of concern that has merely been 'painted' on to the face. According to Hochschild, it involves inventing stories about a particular situation in order to achieve an appropriate feeling. Colloquially, it may be described as 'psyching' oneself to deal with a particular situation. Hochschild provides the following anecdote from a Delta Airlines flight attendant to explain deep acting. In order to deal with a difficult passenger, the flight attendant tells herself the following story (p. 55): 'I try to remember that if he's drinking too much, he's probably scared of flying. I think to myself "he's like a little child". Really, that's what he is. And when I see him that way, I don't get mad that he's yelling at me. He's like a child yelling at me then.'

In this way the flight attendant suppresses anger and resentment and induces an appropriate feeling that enables her to accept the difficult passenger's behaviour. Because of the 'psychic effort' involved in deep acting, it would seem that this kind of emotional labour implies a high level of concern for customers (Ashforth and Humphrey, 1993). Despite the effort, however, there is no guarantee that the emotional labour performance will satisfy the customers (*ibid.*).

For Hochschild (1983), the performance of emotional labour requires active management of emotions. It is a dramatic performance. Ashforth and Humphrey (1993) point out, however, that Hochschild's description of emotional labour does not allow for the truly spontaneous expression of genuine emotion. They give as an example of effortless emotional labour, a nurse's sympathy for an injured child. In the tourism literature, Manning's (1979) study of tourism in Bermuda suggested that, to black

Bermudians (at least at the time of the study), 'meeting and greeting' of tourists was a spontaneous cultural ritual. Manning warned, however, that the 'depersonalizing effects' (1979, p. 173) of modern tourism might make spontaneous encounters logistically difficult. In modern commercial hospitality the fast-food chains, such as McDonald's, provide examples of the contrived, non-spontaneous forms of emotional labour. In a society where people are constantly in a hurry, efficiency is the watchword. Efficiency, in these circumstances, is 'the best available way to get [customers] from being hungry to being full' (Ritzer, 1996, p. 9). In McDonald's this desired outcome is to be achieved through rules and regulations intended to guarantee that McDonald's' employees work efficiently. Their scripted performance of interaction with customers would appear to allow no chance for the 'spontaneous expression of genuine emotion'. Gabriel (1988, p. 107, cited in Urry 1990, p. 78) found, however, that 'employees [in the fast food industry] maintain a measure of autonomy and put their mark on work that they otherwise would find immensely monotonous'.

THE IMPACT OF EMOTIONAL LABOUR ON EMPLOYEES

Hochschild (1983) is critical of the commercial exploitation of the employee's emotions in the performance of emotional labour. She bases her criticism on her explanation of the importance of feelings to human beings. 'Like the sense of hearing,' Hochschild argues, 'emotion communicates information ... From feeling we discover our own viewpoint on the world' (1983, p. 17). Through their feelings people 'determine their reactions to events' (p. 22). Feelings provide 'a useful set of clues in figuring out what is real' (p. 31). From people's display of feelings, we can infer their viewpoint on a particular matter. Similarly, 'we decide what we ourselves are really like by reflecting on how we feel about ordinary events' (p. 32). Through the manipulation of feelings in the performance of emotional labour we may 'lose access to feeling' and to 'a central means of interpreting the world around us' (p. 188).

According to Hochschild (p. 187), the performance of emotional labour ultimately has damaging psychological effects for its performers and for the quality of service they provide. For those who identify 'too wholeheartedly' with their work, they risk 'burnout' (pp. 187–8) that Hochschild describes as 'emotional numbness' (p. 188). To illustrate the impact of burnout on the provision of service, Hochschild quotes the words of an emotionally numb flight attendant 'interacting' with a passenger (pp. 187–8): 'I wasn't feeling anything. It was like I wasn't really there. The guy was talking. I could hear him. But all I heard was dead words.' Hochschild claims that service providers who do distinguish themselves from the job may escape burnout but may denigrate themselves for their insincerity in the performance of emotional labour (p. 187). Even those workers who accept emotional labour as appropriate in the provision of service nevertheless may become cynical about their role as 'illusion makers' (p. 187).

THE CRITIQUE OF EMOTIONAL LABOUR

Although researchers acknowledge Hochschild's key role in developing the concept of emotional labour, her work has its critics. Stephen Fineman (1993, p. 19) argues that '[t]he negative picture of corporate control over emotions is a seductive one, but somewhat overstated.' According to Fineman (p. 3), emotional labour 'can be fun; an exquisite drama' or 'stressful and alienating'. In a service encounter in the hotel dining-room, the waiter and guest find fun and pleasure in the performance of their respective roles. They know they are playing a game and that the feelings expressed are not quite genuine. In his description of public-relations workers in bars in Mediterranean resorts, Crang (1997, p. 151) captures the idea of emotional labour as fun. These workers are employed to drink, chat and flirt with customers. The division between work and play is blurred. According to Crang (*ibid.*), 'Play is rationalised to a work ethic; but, in the same entanglement, commodified labor is also made playful.' He argues that people engaged in emotional labour may enjoy the opportunity to play many roles 'seeing none as more false or real than any other' (p. 153).

Researchers have identified autonomy as an important component of psychological wellbeing and job satisfaction in the performance of emotional labour. In the following quotation, Hochschild (1983, p. 89) identifies the negative consequences of a lack of autonomy:

> The more often 'tips' about how to see, feel, and seem are issued from above and the more effectively the conditions of the 'stage' are kept out of the hands of the actor, the less she can influence her entrances and exits and the nature of her acting in between. The less influence she has, the more likely it is that one of two things will occur. Either she will overextend herself into the job and burn out, or she will remove herself from the job and feel bad about it.

While acknowledging Hochschild's position on the consequences of a lack of autonomy, Amy Wharton (1996) highlights the role of autonomy in securing a positive relationship between emotional labour, emotional health and job satisfaction. From the results of her 1989 research, she concludes that low job autonomy, combined with other negative factors such as long hours of work, results in emotional exhaustion (1996, p. 101). To illustrate the importance of autonomy, Wharton cites Greta Paules's 1991 study of waitresses in a New Jersey restaurant. According to Paules (1991, p. 162, cited in Wharton, 1996, p. 95), 'Like all social actors, the waitress monitors her projected personality and manipulates her feelings in the course of social interaction, but she does so knowingly and in her own interests. This manipulation of self does not induce self-alienation or emotional disorientation.' According to Paules's study, the waitresses gained satisfaction from their skilful performance of emotional labour and viewed their expression of emotion 'as an assertion of autonomy'. Given the degree of negativity associated with the concept of emotional labour, Wharton (p. 105) suggests a need for research concerning the rewards of emotional labour.

CULTURAL IDENTITY AND EMOTIONAL LABOUR

Identities

In international hospitality settings, cultural and ethnic identities have the potential to influence the encounter between servers and customers. Gudykunst and Kim (1997) discuss a variety of social identities that influence communication with strangers. Three of these identities (cultural, ethnic and role) are relevant to a discussion of the likely impact of culture on emotional labourers and their customers.

In relation to cultural identity, Gudykunst and Kim (p. 18) state that 'boundaries between cultures usually, but not always, coincide with political, or national, boundaries between countries'. Thus, they refer to the culture of the United States, despite the ethnic heterogeneity of the United States. The cultural identity of those inhabitants of the United States who identify strongly with its culture is American. Americans accept the content of the culture of the United States. They accept, for example, the importance of individualism in American culture.

Ethnic identity is based on defining characteristics, such as language, religion, race and ancestral homeland. On the strength of such shared characteristics, members of an ethnic group perceive themselves to be different from the rest of the community and engage in shared activities that reflect their common identity (Yinger, 1994, pp. 3–4, cited in Gudykunst and Kim, 1997, p. 94). Within a nation, some people may identify more strongly with the ethnic group to which they belong rather than with their cultural identity. In line with Confucian values, for example, Chinese Americans may place greater emphasis on family identity than on individual identity.

Role identity is based on 'role expectations' associated with positions people hold (Gudykunst and Kim, 1997, p. 105). In a hospitality setting, for example, there are 'role expectations' associated with the way in which the waiter should do the job. People conform to 'role expectations' when the role is clearly defined and when there is a high level of agreement on the behaviours expected in the role (p. 105). In international hospitality settings the different cultural or ethnic identities of server and served may result in disagreement concerning the appropriate behaviours required in the performance of a role.

Cultural Difference and Role Expectations

Differences in hospitality role expectations stem from cultural differences in identification of appropriate styles of service. Citing Feig and Blair (1975, p. 31), Gudykunst and Kim (1997, p. 105) refer to 'different behavioral expectations across cultures in the *degree of personalness* expected in a role relationship'. To illustrate this point they quote the words of a Kenyan student who noted the absence of *personalness* in the hospitality service he received in the United States. In the words of the Kenyan student, 'Waiters extend courtesy to get a bigger tip or because the manager is around. They are very impersonal; it's just a job to them' (quoted in Gudykunst and Kim, 1997, p. 106). 'In Kenya, waiters and waitresses are expected to see customers as people' (*ibid.*).

In Asia, according to Mattila (2000, p. 264), citing Schmitt and Pann (1994), 'the key ingredient of good service seems to be personal attention or customization and not the efficiency and time savings that appear so highly valued in the West'. Platt *et al.* (1991) indicate that the expectation of personal attention is particularly important to Japanese customers. According to Platt *et al.* (1991, p. 86), 'the time taken to greet Japanese customers courteously when they enter a restaurant and to thank and farewell them when they leave is time well spent'.

The intercultural communications literature draws distinctions between low- and high-context cultures. From these distinctions it is possible to infer culturally different interpretations of role expectations in hospitality service encounters. According to Mattila (p. 264), most western cultures are low-context. They are 'more informal' than high-context cultures and 'allow more equality in interaction by placing less emphasis on hierarchies' than is the case in high-context cultures (Irwin, 1996, p. 41). They favour 'precise, direct, logical, verbal communication' (p. 41) and 'focus their evaluations on task completion and efficient delivery' (Mattila, 2000, p. 265, citing Riddle, 1992). Individuals in low-context cultures are likely to be 'spontaneous', 'emotionally expressive', 'self-promoting', 'egocentric', 'individualistic' (Irwin, 1996, p. 53, citing Chan, 1992, p. 252). Their behaviour is flexible in social situations; there are 'no strictly observed rules' (Irwin, 1996, p. 41, citing Brislin, 1993, p. 22).

Mattila (2000, p. 265) states that most Asian cultures are high-context and differ from low-context cultures in many significant ways. Irwin (1996, p. 53, citing Chan, 1992, p. 252) describes traditional Asian high-context cultures as 'indirect', 'formal', 'emotionally controlled', 'self-effacing' and 'modest'. They have 'rules, norms and guidelines for various types of social encounters' and these rules 'are unambiguous and widely known' (Irwin, 1996, p. 41). They are 'more attuned to non-verbal cues and messages' and 'rely less on verbal communication' (*ibid.*). A waiter's unawareness of such cultural differences and of strategies to deal with them creates the potential for uncertainty and embarrassment in intercultural service encounters.

The smile, as a form of emotional labour, is a commonly used facial display in hospitality service encounters. Yet the smile has different meanings in different cultures because cultures have different display rules. According to Ekman (1972, cited in Gudykunst and Kim, 1997, p. 227), display rules 'tell us when to express emotions and when not to expose them'. Although it is expected of American hospitality employees that they 'smile at customers and act friendly', in Israel customers interpret the smile of the supermarket cashier, for example, 'as a sign of inexperience' (Rafaeli and Sutton, 1989, p. 9). If, ethnocentrically, customers decode the facial display of the server according to their own display rules, there is the possibility of misunderstanding. Globalization of the hospitality and other service industries is likely to provide examples of this. When the first McDonald's fast-food outlet was opened in the early 1990s in Moscow, the employees were required to smile in true McDonald's style. Muscovite customers, unaccustomed to such displays of emotional labour, thought they were being laughed at (Ashforth and Humphrey, 1993).

EMOTIONAL LABOUR IN AN AUSTRALIAN CONTEXT

Hospitality Service in Historical Perspective

'The nature of guest–employee interaction in the contemporary international tourism industry is closely linked to the historical origins of tourism' (Baum, 1997, p. 92). Before the advent of modern tourism, in the nineteenth century, aristocratic grand tourists in Europe found accommodation 'in the great houses of families of the same class and background' (Baum, 1997, p. 93). The 'rich and well-bred' took their servants with them when they frequented the resorts and spas of eighteenth-century England (*ibid.*). In neither case did they depend upon the provision of commercial hospitality. When travel became a middle-class activity in the nineteenth century, the new travellers lacked the contacts and the servants to avail themselves of aristocratic standards of service provision. Therefore, commercial provision of hospitality for travellers expanded. Nevertheless, the traditional idea of social distance between guest and service employee still influenced guest expectations and 'continued to reflect its origins in master/mistress–servant roles' (p. 95). Anglo-Celtic Australians were inheritors of this attitude to social distance between server and served.

This inheritance did not augur well for the appeal of hospitality service as an employment option in Australia, where the egalitarian ideal is a major strand in Australian identity. Although Australian society has never been free of class differences, from colonial times the idea of egalitarianism has influenced Australians' perceptions of themselves. In 1901, Australia's great poet, Henry Lawson, captured the egalitarian ideal when he wrote of men who 'call no biped "lord" or "sir" And touch their hats to no man!' (Lawson, 2000, p. 178 [first published in 1901]).

In the 1960s, Australian social commentator Donald Horne painted a word picture of the egalitarian ideal when he noted that '[t]axi drivers prefer their passengers to sit in the front seat' (1968, p. 20). For the passenger to sit in the back seat gives the impression of a master–servant relationship. In 2000, novelist Martin Armiger allowed his character, William, a *maitre d'* in an Australian bistro, to voice the Australian egalitarian ideal in the following words: 'Look, it's an egalitarian country, supposedly. No-one wants a grovelling waiter.The trick is to say to the customer, in so many words, "I am your equal, but I will serve you." Isn't that what people want?' (Armiger, 2000, p. 41)

Whyte (1946, cited in Guerrier and Adib, 2000, p. 260), in his famous study of human relations in the restaurant industry, drew attention to the link between egalitarian cultures and negative attitudes to service work in hospitality provision. He commented that European waiters, 'accustomed to class differences and low social mobility', created fewer problems than egalitarian American waiters who were 'resentful of social distinctions'. Negativity towards the idea of serving people in commercial hospitality settings has been identified as a male, working-class phenomenon in both Australia and the United States. According to Leidner (1993, cited in Guerrier and Adib, 2000, p. 260), male Americans of the working-class associate 'deferential behavior', 'forced amiability' and 'interactive service jobs' with 'servility' and low-status 'women's work'. David Rowe (1993, p. 263) comes to a similar conclusion concerning male Australian attitudes to the idea of serving people.

In addition to noting negative male Australian attitudes to 'servility' and 'women's work', Rowe (1993, p. 263) also concludes that the hedonistic component of 'Australianness' is not compatible with the demands of employment in hospitality service provision. In his article he refers to the 'lucky country' version of 'Australianness', according to which 'work is represented less as a spiritual commitment than as a temporary expediency to facilitate leisure' (1993, p. 256). He argues that this attitude to work and leisure 'is popularly celebrated as one defining characteristic of egalitarian, sensual Australianness' (p. 257). Such an attitude does not fit well with hospitality service work marked by low wages, inferior working conditions, job insecurity and 'an erosion of leisure time and quality' (p. 263).

Although Rowe's conclusions on the links between 'Australianness' and negative attitudes to hospitality service work were published in the 1990s, by that time there were forces at work that, arguably, improved the image of hospitality as an employment option. Economic restructuring in Australia in the 1970s and 1980s, and rising levels of unemployment, necessitated the search for new sources of income and employment in new kinds of industries. Tourism, including labour-intensive hospitality, was regarded, rightly or wrongly, as the antidote to the ills of rapid economic change.

As the Australian tourism industry began to grow in the 1970s, education and training were considered necessary to ensure a quality product for tourists. Lifestyle changes in Australia that made dining out commonplace added to the pressure on the hospitality industry for quality service. Hotel schools, vocational colleges and universities now provide courses that delineate career paths for hospitality employees.

Within these educational institutions, hospitality lecturers are role models capable of enhancing the image of hospitality as a career choice. There is also the attraction of the glamour of working in five-star hotels and luxury resorts, whether or not this image is false.

Another factor ameliorating the negative image of service work is the decline in the potency of the master–servant relationship in tourism service employment. Baum (1997, 95–6) attributes this situation to the 'relative social and economic equality' between visitors and tourism service employees in the developed world and to the sophistication of the employees acquired through their own experiences as guests during international travel. He does suggest, however, that the 'service ritual' in cruise liners, hotels and restaurants 'may [still] give the appearance of encouraging notions of servility' (1997, 96).

Emotional Labour and Cultural Identity in an Australian Coffee Shop: A Case Study

The focus of the case study is a coffee shop that forms part of a hotel property in a major Australian city. The hotel is a member of an accommodation chain that has hotels, motels, resorts and apartments in over 80 countries around the world. The coffee shop provides food and beverages throughout the day for Australian and international house guests and for staff employed in organizations nearby. The servers in the coffee shop are young Australian males and females from a variety of ethnic backgrounds. Some are tertiary students for whom employment in the hospitality industry is not their major vocational goal. For others, hospitality service work has become their usual occupation and means of gaining income.

Bell and Valentine (1997, p. 126) refer to 'the performative nature of food service work'. For the actors (servers) in the coffee shop, the performance has two components: the technical performance and the emotional performance. Like actors on the stage, the servers must be competent in the performance of the technical skills (for example, preparing a cup of coffee) and must deliver the service in an emotionally appropriate manner. Their stage is the coffee shop with all its properties (for example, tables and chairs). Donning their uniforms (costumes) is the signal that the performance is about to begin.

Different kinds of drama require different kinds of emotional performance although the fundamental technical skills of acting are likely to be similar for each kind. A Greek tragedy, for example, differs in its emotional performance style from a musical comedy. The audience expects to be able to notice the difference. Similarly, in hospitality service delivery the servers must style their performance to suit the requirements of the customers. According to Campbell-Smith's seminal work *The Marketing of the Meal Experience* (1967, cited in Wood, 1995, p. 103), 'when dining out, people are concerned not only with the nature and quality of the food they eat, but with the total environmental experience of dining out'. For example, diners in search of a 'sense of romance' might find it 'in an exclusive and atmospheric bistro' where the servers perform in a manner to suit the mood (p. 105).

Unlike the 'atmospheric bistro', the coffee shop exists primarily to satisfy customers' tangible needs for food and drink. The kinds of customers who frequent the shop are likely to be more interested in prompt and efficient service rather than obvious displays of mood-setting emotional labour. Nevertheless, given the characteristics of the clientele, there are particular kinds of emotional labour relevant to the work of the service providers in the coffee shop. From time to time, for example, they may feel the need to show apparent interest in the stories of tourists excited by a day of sightseeing. In the middle of a busy shift, such a situation may require all their surface acting skills 'to create a publicly observable facial and bodily display' (Hochschild, 1983, p. 7) that indicates that the tourists' stories are receiving their complete attention.

In modern hospitality settings, according to Guerrier and Adib (2000, p. 265), 'the hospitality employee as non-person has been replaced by the hospitality employee as friend'. Arguably, when this kind of friendly relationship is established, spontaneity can replace acting in the encounter between server and served. The establishment of a friendly relationship is a test of the employees' ability to judge whether or not the customer wants the server–served transaction to be friendly or formal. Mars and Nicod (1984, pp. 55–7) describe two kinds of server–customer transactions in hospitality settings. Boundary-open transactions 'foster intimacy' and 'joking relationships' (1984, p. 56). Boundary-closed transactions 'reduce the waiter to obvious subordination' and place the emphasis on 'ritualised formality' (1984, p. 57). With experience, according to Mars and Nicod (1984, p. 59), waiters can determine the kind of transaction the customer is likely to favour.

It is likely that experienced travellers, regardless of cultural origins and preferences, have become accustomed to a standardized set of food-service rituals around the world. In the coffee shop, the first encounter between server and served is facilitated by the performance of these rituals. 'Rituals are there to make difficult passages easier' (Visser, 1991, p. 22). At this point, the employee's communication with the guest exemplifies the preciseness and directness associated with low-context cultures (Irwin, 1996, p. 41). The aim is 'task completion' and 'efficient delivery' (Mattila, 2000, p. 265, citing Riddle, 1992). The employee's performance is relatively formal but not servile.

Beyond the point of the initial transaction, however, the encounter is subject to the decisions made by experienced hospitality workers regarding open and closed boundaries. For short-term house guests, staying only a few nights at the hotel, the hospitality workers may decide to maintain the 'ritualized formality' of the boundary-closed transactions. Such a decision may be influenced by language differences that make communication between servers and guests difficult. It may be that the more formal style of guests from high-context cultures does not invite the informality of servers from low-context cultures. Because of the short stay of the house guests there is no time for the development of greater familiarity that may result in the conversion of boundary-closed to boundary-open transactions.

With many regular customers who work in nearby organizations, however, boundary-open transactions are commonplace. A major feature of these transactions is 'the hospitality employee as friend'. Mars and Nicod (1984, p. 61) have identified certain primary traits of waiters and diners that facilitate boundary-open transactions. Such transactions, for example, are more likely between a waiter and a diner *not* of the same sex. Mars and Nicod argue that men assume that female service providers conform to the expectation 'that waitresses should be more boundary-open than waiters' (1984, p. 62). While there is some evidence to support this assumption in coffee-shop encounters, it is by no means always the case. Whether or not it is so seems to depend, at least to some extent, on the confidence that comes from the female server's length of experience in the hospitality industry. In some instances employees, who have recently joined the service staff of the coffee shop appear to take their cues from experienced employees before engaging in boundary-open transactions with customers.

It cannot be predicted that customers will engage in the same kind of transaction at all times. According to Mars and Nicod (1984, p. 62), 'Customers often oscillate between the two boundary-type extremes; for instance, in relation to the different kinds of company they keep.' Workers from nearby organizations visit the coffee shop for various purposes in addition to eating and drinking. Sometimes it is a place at which to confer with business acquaintances. On such occasions, they are likely to adopt a more formal, less inclusive approach towards the servers. This is no doubt a cue to the hospitality worker that the time is not right for their usual chatting and joking. For the servers also, the level of activity in the coffee shop dictates the time available for boundary-open activities.

Australians pride themselves on their easy-going, friendly egalitarianism. In boundary-open transactions in the coffee shop, hospitality employees are free to display these characteristics of 'Australianness'. Their presentation of self is informal within the limits required by civility, job efficiency and customer cues. Their national culture accepts smiling as an appropriate form of emotional display but the intensity of their emotional expression depends on the personality of the servers and their experience of self-projection.

EMOTIONAL LABOUR, CULTURAL IDENTITY AND HUMAN RESOURCE MANAGEMENT

The literature on emotional labour, cultural identity and intercultural communication identified in this chapter has implications for the practice of human resource management in the international hospitality industry. This section of the chapter summarizes the ways in which the processes of selection, training and maintenance of hospitality staff can, at least, be informed by new insights gained from a study of the emotional and cultural dimensions of front-line hospitality service.

Emotional Labour and human resource Management Perspectives

The role of front-line hospitality employees serving an international clientele involves some measure of emotional labour combined with the need to communicate across cultural boundaries. Given the diversity of the role components of front-line hospitality employment, the criteria for selection include much more than the capacity to perform the required technical skills. If it is accepted that food-service workers in the hospitality industry must be 'performative personalities', then the employer, according to Bell and Valentine (1997, p. 126), must look for attributes such as extroversion and sociability. The successful performance of the employees in the coffee shop suggests, however, that, while employees must be at ease in communicating with strangers, a high level of extroversion is not required in that particular setting.

Training is regarded as an important input into the development of human resources. Training hospitality employees to perform emotional labour, however, raises several questions. For example, should the display rules of McDonald's and Disneyland be the benchmark for emotional labour styles internationally? Or should the authentic emotional style of the host society at a destination prevail? According to Baum (1997, p. 99), 'The local encounter is a central attraction within the vacation experience.' If this is accepted, why should emotional styles around the world become homogenized?

Emotional-labour training also raises questions concerning the alleged damaging psychological consequences of acting insincerely. Hochschild (1983, p. 187) warned of the deleterious psychological effects of emotional labour. However, Mary Kay Ash

(1984, cited in Rafaeli and Sutton, 1989, p. 14) suggests that 'faking it' will have positive attitudinal consequences: 'You've got to fake it until you make it – that is – act enthusiastic and you will become enthusiastic.' It may be the case that emotional-labour training is required only for those occasions when employees' emotional wellbeing is under attack from hostile customers. Learning the script for managing emotions in these difficult moments may prove to be training time well spent. Although critical of the 'fake friendliness of scripted interaction' in fast-food restaurants, Ritzer (1996, pp. 82, 84) acknowledges that scripts do enable employees 'to protect themselves from the insults and indignities that are frequently heaped upon them by the public'.

The importance of Carlzon's idea of 'moments of truth' (1987, p. 2) to a company's competitive advantage challenges managers to find the best ways to ensure the peak performance of their front-line employees.This performance depends not only on the technical competence of the employees but also on their ability to handle the likely stresses and strains of face-to-face encounters with customers in an emotionally appropriate way. While Hochschild's account of the damaging effects of emotional labour may be somewhat overstated (1983, p. 187), it is, nevertheless, necessary for human resources managers to be aware of emotional labour's potential for causing stress and burn-out. It is not enough for front-line employees to be trained in the behavioural performance of their job. For the sake of their wellbeing they should also be aware of ways to manage the emotional demands of their employment. Wharton (1996, p. 95) identified autonomy as a key factor in promoting emotional health and job satisfaction.

Empowerment is a workplace process that makes job autonomy possible. 'Empowerment,' according to Baum (1997, p. 107) 'means enabling and encouraging front-line staff to make decisions that will solve customers' problems or meet their needs, without reference to an interminable management hierarchy.' Baum claims that empowerment 'is at the heart of the guest–employee encounter' (1997, p. 107). Since the immediate attention of staff to customers' problems is likely to remove the cause of customer dissatisfaction, the spin-off effect is less stress for the employees. Successful empowerment depends on clear guidelines for the staff and the knowledge that management trusts them to do the right thing and will support them in the decisions they make. Provided that employees are psychologically suited to accepting this responsibility, empowerment has the potential to increase their self-esteem and job satisfaction.

Culture: Identity, Diversity and Communication

To ensure effective intercultural communication, hospitality workers should be culturally-literate. That is, they must understand, and be sensitive to, other cultures. Sensitive and effective communication across cultural boundaries requires more than mere training in procedures. According to Irwin (1996, p. 22), intercultural communication 'is contextual because it occurs within a setting or situation which has social, cultural and possibly historical characteristics which influence the process'. Preparation for effective intercultural communication, therefore, has a cognitive component and involves culture learning through which the learners gain knowledge of their own and contrasting cultures. Culture learning 'accepts and celebrates cultural diversity' (Irwin, 1996, p. 134) and is, therefore, attitudinal, as well as cognitive, in its purpose. While it 'advocates knowledge, understanding and sensitivity', it does not require the learning of a bewildering array of new behaviours' (Irwin, 1996, p. 134).

Platt *et al.* (1991, p. 102) advised Australian employees in tourism and hospitality: 'Maintain your identity. *Do not* aim to become Japanese in your approach. *Do* aim to understand and provide services necessary to meet the needs of Japanese tourists in Australia.'

Culture learning cannot be acquired in short training sessions. Its acquisition is a lifelong process. While much of the groundwork for culture learning can be established in the education system across the various sectors of education, Irwin argues that 'most learning will take place simultaneously with contact as those involved observe, interact and reflect upon the experience' (1996, p. 134). For this to happen, the appropriate mindset that values intercultural knowledge and understanding must be in place. At the height of the Asian economic miracles, when Australia saw its economic destiny in Asia, governments tried to convince industries, including tourism and hospitality, of the benefits of culture learning. Through financial assistance, governments sought to foster culture learning to create a workforce freed from stereotypes and at ease communicating with Asians. Employers, in turn, were encouraged to implement employment policies that favoured employees with 'Asian skills'.

CONCLUSION

The growing literature on emotional labour approaches the subject from the perspectives of several academic disciplines and vocational areas. This chapter cannot take account of all the complexities of these various approaches. All it can do is raise awareness of the subject and, hopefully, provide the beginnings of a conceptual framework for further research.

Although the chapter has considered aspects of intercultural communication and public emotional displays in hospitality settings, it merely hints at individuals' perceptions of the cultural dimensions of hospitality service. Questionnaire-type surveys may provide some insights into these individual perceptions. In-depth, open-ended conversations with recipients of hospitality service are likely to be a more useful means of ascertaining the importance of the cultural factor. It may well be, however, that in an era of global homogenization, the cultural factor is losing its importance.

SELF-ASSESSMENT QUESTIONS

1. What does 'emotional labour' mean? Why does Arlie Hochschild refer to its performance as 'commercialization of human feeling'?
2. Argue a case for or against the proposition that technical competence is more important than the performance of emotional labour in service encounters in hospitality settings.
3. Provide a critique of Hochschild's argument that emotional labour impacts negatively upon those who perform it.
4. Explain the ways in which cultural identity may influence encounters between guests and employees in hospitality settings.
5. To what extent can management control the service encounter in hospitality settings? In what ways can this be done?
6. What contribution can empowerment of employees make to the successful

performance of emotional labour in hospitality settings?
7. What factors should be taken into account when choosing employees for front-of-house positions in hospitality establishments with an international clientele?
8. Identify suitable content for a training programme for hospitality employees in an establishment with an international clientele.

REFERENCES

Armiger, M. (2000) *The Waiters*. Melbourne: Text Publishing Company.
Ashforth, B. E. and Humphrey, R. H. (1993) 'Emotional labour in service roles: the influence of identity'. *Academy of Management: The Academy of Management Review*, **18**(1), January, 88. Available online at http://global.umi.com/pqdweb.
Baum, T. (1997) 'Making or breaking the tourist experience: the role of human resource management', in C. Ryan (ed.), *The Tourist Experience: A New Introduction*. London and New York: Cassell.
Bell, D. and Valentine, G. (1997) *Consuming Geographies: We Are Where We Eat*. London and New York: Routledge.
Carlzon, J. (1987) *Moments of Truth*. New York: Harper and Row.
Crang, P. (1997) 'Performing the tourist product', in C. Rojek and J. Urry (eds), *Touring Cultures: Transformation of Travel and Theory*. London and New York: Routledge, pp.137–54.
Fineman, S. (1993) 'Organizations as emotional arenas', in S. Fineman (ed.), *Emotion in Organizations*. London: Sage Publications, pp. 9–35.
Gudykunst, W. B. and Kim, Y. Y. (1997) *Communicating with Strangers: An Approach to Intercultural Communication* (3rd edn). Boston, MA: McGraw-Hill.
Guerrier, Y., Adib, A. (2000) 'Working in the hospitality industry', in C. Lashley and A. Morrison (eds), *In Search of Hospitality: Theoretical Perspectives and Debates*. Oxford: Butterworth-Heinemann.
Hochschild, A. (1983) *The Managed Heart: Commercialization of Human Feeling*. Berkeley, CA: University of California Press.
Hofstede, G. (1991) *Cultures and Organisations: Software of the Mind*. London: HarperCollins.
Horne, D. (1968) *The Lucky Country: Australia in the Sixties* (2nd revised edn). Harmondsworth: Penguin.
Irwin, H. (1996) *Communicating with Asia: Understanding People and Customs*. St Leonards, NSW: Allen & Unwin.
Lam, T., Yeung, S., Chan, A. (1998) 'Service quality and determinants of customer expectations: the case of club industry in Hong Kong'. *Asia Pacific Journal of Tourism Research*, **2**(2), 29–36.
Lawson, H. (2000) [1901] 'The Shearers' in *Henry Lawson: Poems*. Introduction and Chronology by Colin Roderick. Sydney: Harper Collins.
Manning, F. E. (1979) 'Tourism and Bermuda's black clubs: a case of cultural revitalization' in Emanuel de Kadt (ed.), *Tourism: Passport to Development?* New York: Oxford University Press, pp. 157–76.
Mars, G. and Nicod, M. (1984) *The World of Waiters*. London: George Allen and Unwin.
Mattila, A. (2000) 'The impact of culture and gender on customer evaluations of service encounters'. *Journal of Hospitality and Tourism Research*, **24**(2), 263–73.
Parasuraman, A. (1995) 'Measuring and monitoring service quality', in W. J. Glynn and J. G. Barnes (eds), *Understanding Services Management*. Chichester: John Wiley and Sons, pp. 143–77.
Platt, A., McGowan, V., Todhunter, M. and Chalmers, N. (1991) *Japanese for the Tourist Industry: Culture and Communication* (2nd edn). Melbourne: Hospitality Press.
Powers, T. (1992) *Introduction to the Hospitality Industry* (2nd edn). New York: John Wiley and Sons.
Rafaeli, A. and Sutton, R. I. (1989) 'The expression of emotion in organizational life', in L. L.

Cummings and Barry M. Staw (eds), *Research in Organizational Behavior: An Annual Series of Analytical Essays and Critical Reviews,* Volume 11. Greenwich, CT: JAI Press Inc., pp. 1–42.

Ritzer, G. (1996) *The McDonaldization of Society: An Investigation into the Changing Character of Contemporary Social Life,* Revised edn, Thousand Oaks, California: Pine Forge Press.

Rowe, D. (1993) 'Leisure, tourism and "Australianness"'. *Media, Culture and Society,* **15**, 253–69.

Singer, M. R. (1987) *Intercultural Communication: A Perceptual Approach.* Englewood Cliffs, NJ: Prentice Hall.

Urry, J. (1990) *The Tourist Gaze: Leisure and Travel in Contemporary Societies.* London: Sage Publications.

Visser, M. (1991) *The Rituals of Dinner.* New York: Penguin.

Wharton, A. S. (1996) 'Service with a smile: understanding the consequences of emotional labour', in C. L. Macdonald and C. Sirianni (eds), *Working in the Service Society.* Philadelphia: Temple University Press, pp. 91–112.

Wood, R. C. (1995) *The Sociology of the Meal.* Edinburgh: Edinburgh University Press.

Index

The index covers subjects and author references in chapters 1–17 but not abstracts or self-assessment questions. Alphabetical order is word-by-word. Page references followed by t refer to tables, f to figures and b to boxes.